Pitt Series in Composition, Literacy, and Culture
. . . .

David Bartholomae and Jean Ferguson Carr, Editors

RHETORICA · XXIII ·

C

Z3

Plate from *Die Tarocchi. Zwei italienische Kupferstichfolgen aus dem XV. Jahrhundert* (Cassirer, 1910: Berlin). Ascribed to the painter Mantegna.

Reclaiming Rhetorica

Women in the Rhetorical Tradition

Andrea A. Lunsford, Editor

University of Pittsburgh Press
Pittsburgh and London

Published by the University of Pittsburgh Press, Pittsburgh, Pa., 15260
Copyright © 1995, University of Pittsburgh Press
All rights reserved
Manufactured in the United States of America
Printed on acid-free paper

Designed by Jane Tenenbaum

Library of Congress Cataloging-in-Publication Data

Reclaiming rhetorica: women in the rhetorical tradition/Andrea A.
    Lunsford, editor.
        p. cm.—(Pitt series in composition, literacy, and culture)
    Includes bibliographical references and index.
        ISBN 0-8229-3872-3.—ISBN 0-8229-5553-9 (pbk.)
        1. Rhetoric—History. 2. Women authors. 3. Women orators.
        I. Lunsford, Andrea A., 1942– .   II. Title: Women in the
    rhetorical tradition.   III. Series: Pittsburgh series in
    composition, literacy, and culture.
    P301.R346   1995
    808'.0082—dc20   95–3298
                                                          CIP

A CIP catalogue record for this book is available from the British Library.

Eurospan, London

With deep affection, this book is dedicated to
Bernice Stone Cohen (1929–1987)
and
Joanne Wagner (1960–1991),
friends sorely missed

Contents

Foreword   *ix*
James J. Murphy

Acknowledgments   *xiii*

1   On Reclaiming Rhetorica   *3*
       Andrea A. Lunsford

2   Aspasia: Rhetoric, Gender, and Colonial Ideology   *9*
       Susan Jarratt and Rory Ong

3   A Lover's Discourse: Diotima, Logos, and Desire   *25*
       C. Jan Swearingen

4   Reexamining *The Book of Margery Kempe*:
       A Rhetoric of Autobiography   *53*
       Cheryl Glenn

5   Christine de Pisan and *The Treasure of the City of*
       Ladies: A Medieval Rhetorician and Her Rhetoric   *73*
       Jenny R. Redfern

6   Mary Astell: Reclaiming Rhetorica in the
       Seventeenth Century   *93*
       Christine Mason Sutherland

7   Daring to Dialogue: Mary Wollstonecraft's Rhetoric
       of Feminist Dialogics   *117*
       Jamie Barlowe

8   Inventing a Feminist Discourse: Rhetoric and
       Resistance in Margaret Fuller's *Woman in the*
       Nineteenth Century   *137*
       Annette Kolodny

9   To Call a Thing by Its True Name: The Rhetoric of
       Ida B. Wells   *167*
       Jacqueline Jones Royster

10   "Intelligent Members or Restless Disturbers":
       Women's Rhetorical Styles, 1880–1920   *185*
       Joanne Wagner

11   Woman Suffrage and the History of Rhetoric at the
      Seven Sisters Colleges, 1865–1919   *203*
      Kathryn M. Conway

12   Sojourner Truth: A Practical Public Discourse   *227*
      Drema R. Lipscomb

13   *The Telling:* Laura (Riding) Jackson's Project for a
      Whole Human Discourse   *247*
      James Oldham

14   Susanne K. Langer: Mother and Midwife at the
      Rebirth of Rhetoric   *265*
      Arabella Lyon

15   A Rhetoric for Audiences: Louise Rosenblatt on
      Reading and Action   *285*
      Annika Hallin

16   Julia Kristeva: Rhetoric and the Woman as Stranger   *305*
      Suzanne Clark

      Afterword   *319*
      Index   *339*
      Notes on Contributors   *351*

Foreword
· · · · · · · · ·

This book is not a history of women rhetoricians, or women orators, or women writers. It is instead a glimmer of possibilities, an array of glances—an enthymeme.

The enthymeme presented by this set of essays holds that everywhere you look you find surprises of womanly rhetorical capacity. But it is left to the reader to wonder what else is left uncovered, since even a doughty band of fifteen writers can uncover only a few facets of what—for many who are familiar only with traditional histories of rhetoric and rhetoricians—may appear a surprising womanly capacity.

Aristotle was the first westerner (as far as we know) to recognize the innate desire of all human beings to take pleasure in their own personal intelligence. It is this discovery that underlies his concept of *peripety*, or "Recognition," in the *Poetics*, and forms the basis for his brilliant observation in the *Rhetoric* that people actually want to reach their own conclusion before a speaker spells it out for them. "Man by nature desires to know," he points out at the beginning of his *Metaphysics*, and he reinforces this notion in the field of persuasion by noting that people long to find logical structures in the universe: they not only want to know but also want to know how things fit together. So, in the *Rhetoric*, he argues for the use of what he calls "enthymemes"—apparently logical structures that guide a hearer/reader down a path of partial knowledge until that listener makes a personal, pleasurable jump to agreement with the speaker.

So it is with this book. The title, *Reclaiming Rhetorica*, is much more than a simple pun on the traditional femininity of Lady Rhetoric. The reader is asked to follow some guides along a path of partial knowledge—to be surprised, perhaps, at capacities from Aspasia to Sojourner Truth—but always with the enthymeme of discovery close at hand.

A modern writer has described life as a long corridor with many doors visible on each side. Success lies in opening the right doors, failure in leaving them closed. As people move past each closed door they do not know whether to open it or go past it. Sometimes, as they move past one of the doors, hearing gaiety and laughter from the other side, they feel sad at what they have missed. But still they do not know whether to open the next door. Only with experience does the courage come to open new doors, to explore the possibilities of what is still ahead.

The reader of this book is shown many doors. The remarkable career of Mary Astell—literally a self-made woman—as she wrote her way to success in the 1690s and early 1700s, is microcosmic in that she overcame virtually every hazard of her day. Orphaned, almost penniless, virtually homeless, subject to religious bias, deprived of education after the age of thirteen, Mary nevertheless went on to become a popular author. The phenomenon of the illiterate woman author—the fifteenth-century Margery Kempe dictating her third-person autobiography to a scribe—opens another kind of door. There are many doors after these.

Some patterns do run through these essays, despite their apparent diversity. In many cases the woman in question has to devise her own voice or, like Olive Schreiner, write under a male pseudonym, in a culture that posits womanly silence as a virtue. Virtually all find that their audiences are surprised at their capacity. Some, like Susanne K. Langer, make important theoretical contributions that go unacknowledged for decades, or, indeed, forever. These are seldom explored patterns of history. History is, after all, a gesture towards the future. The doors to future knowledge about the past need still to be opened. This book opens several such doors onto a past extending back more than two thousand years, but even these glimpses present a strong argument that there is much more to be seen.

This book does not present a sustained argument for a radically "revisionist" history or rhetoric: no one can deny that Cicero, Campbell, and Blair dominated rhetorical thought in their own times, in cultures assumed to be male-oriented. But as Jan Swearingen points out in her essay, knowing Socrates or even multiple "Socrateses" does not preclude our knowing Diotima at the same time. Realizing that the former slave and orator Sojourner Truth was a contemporary of both Henry Clay and Abraham Lincoln—and how much we know about them and how little of her—surely leaves room for some exploration. For example, what did she and Lincoln talk about when they met? Did she actually address the United States Senate?

Russell Conway is said to have delivered his "Acres of Diamonds" speech to American audiences more than a thousand times near the end of the last century. His title comes from the story of a man who wandered the world in search of riches, only to find that there were diamonds in his own back yard. He simply did not know where to look. In this same vein Andrea A. Lunsford and the authors in this collection point to new places to look—the most obvious places, perhaps, where Quintilians and Melanchtons have already been found. Anthony Grafton and Lisa Jardine have done just that in their recent book, *From Humanism to the Humanities*, where they deliberately devote a chapter to the education of Renaissance women humanists such as Isotta Nogarola and Cassandra Fedele to demonstrate what can be found when different historical questions are asked.

Let the reader of this book be warned, then, that these guides to partial knowledge offer a sort of enthymematic Newton's Third Law— that the reader's mind, once set in motion, may well stay in motion.

James J. Murphy
University of California, Davis

Acknowledgments

· · · · · · · · · · · · ·

The authors wish to thank all those who have supported the development and publication of this work. Rensselaer Polytechnic Institute provided crucial help in initiating the project through a Paul Beer Trust Mini-Grant Award, 1987–1988, for the Project on Women Rhetoricians. Ohio State University provided much-needed time for preparing and editing the final manuscript. Patrick McSweeney generously undertook to produce a draft of the index and spent many hours compiling and correcting the final manuscript. Beth Ina worked diligently to convert disparate texts to one coherent computer base. Aneil Rallin coordinated a voluminous correspondence among authors, assembled a final draft, and assisted the editor in innumerable kind and insightful ways. Evelyn Ward of the Cleveland Public Library and Jim Bracken and Linda Krikos of the Ohio State Library came to the rescue with last-minute reference research assistance. Claudia Hunter generously agreed to help in preparing a final draft of Joanne Wagner's essay after Joanne's untimely death. In this regard, we are most grateful to Rensselaer Polytechnic Institute for establishing a scholarship fund in Joanne's memory to which any proceeds for this volume will be contributed. (Readers wishing to join us in contributing to the Joanne Wagner Memorial Fund should contact the Department of Language, Literature and Communication at Rensselaer.)

We are also grateful to James J. Murphy for his ongoing interest in and support of this project and to our publisher, the University of Pittsburgh Press. David Bartholomae and Jean Ferguson Carr, editors of Pittsburgh's Series in Literacy, offered astute and generous response to this volume and also solicited most helpful criticism from two anonymous reviewers. In addition, we have been aided throughout by many others who are acknowledged in the individual essays in this volume.

Most of all, however, the contributors wish to acknowledge the collaborative spirit of this volume and the numerous ways in which we have helped one another—by reading and criticizing each other's essays, by joining in long-distance telephone, E-mail, and snail mail brainstorming sessions, and simply by believing in the importance and power of the work we were doing, individually and as a group. This project has succeeded, as Arabella Lyon points out in the afterword, because of the long-term commitment of its contributors and a growing feminist community demanding attention. For the atmosphere that allowed this project to find a home and for the ongoing support and encouragement offered by each contributor to this volume and by feminist rhetoricians across the country, we give very special—and continuing—thanks.

Reclaiming Rhetorica

1

On Reclaiming Rhetorica

Andrea A. Lunsford

The story of *Reclaiming Rhetorica* is a long one, full of the gaps and silences and erasures that also characterize its subject, the history of women in rhetoric. I entered this story late in 1990, when I received a cryptic request from a university press to review a manuscript they had received. Its title was *Reclaiming Rhetorica*; I did not receive the names of its authors.

Fresh from directing a dissertation on women in the history of rhetoric from classical times to the Renaissance, I read through the manuscript eagerly and soon after wrote to the press, saying, "This volume proves to be the first of its kind" and thus "extremely important." I urged that the authors revise with an eye to more inclusiveness and that the press publish the result as soon as possible. Consequently, I expected to hear that such a volume was forthcoming sometime fairly soon. How surprised I was, then, to receive a letter many months later, from two contributors to the volume saying they had not found a publisher and asking if I would consider joining the project.

I jumped at the chance to work with this exciting material, and I was delighted to find that, indeed, I already knew some of the contributors to the original collection in manuscript. I thus set about augmenting that collection, soliciting additional contributions (on Aspasia, Diotima, Margery Kempe, Mary Astell, Mary Wollstonecraft, Ida B. Wells, and Julia Kristeva) which attempted to reach back to classical and medieval times as well as to add some additional American and contemporary women's voices to the collection. Eventually the new submissions arrived; contributors read one another's essays, the entire volume, and then revised accordingly; and we traded seemingly endless memos and E-mail and

3

fax messages to compose the afterword to this volume. As a result, some two years later we had a new manuscript ready to submit for publication.

As these remarks suggest, I was a latecomer to *Rhetorica*, for the story of this volume actually began in 1986–1987, when Annette Kolodny, then professor of literature in the Department of Languages, Literature, and Communication at Rensselaer Polytechnic Institute, was approached by a group of students who wanted to study the history of women as rhetoricians and theorists of rhetoric. Annette writes:

> The students' approaches were marked by hesitation and frustration: hesitation because they were uncertain as to whether much material really existed; and frustration because none of their courses in rhetoric had introduced them to women or even hinted at women's contributions. . . . Increasingly, I was coming to share my students' frustration at the absence of women in these materials. And, no less important, I was seeing interesting parallels and coincidences between discussions of contemporary rhetorical theory and the ongoing debates over literary critical theories and methods. (Letter to author)

During the 1987–1988 year, Annette taught a two-semester graduate seminar on "Women Rhetoricians," a seminar whose members included the original contributors to this volume. (Only one of those seminarians, Colleen O'Toole, has been unable to participate in this project.) They spent the year doing difficult archival research, sharing the results of that research, defining and refining their views on the positioning of particular women in rhetoric, and drafting essays. Annette describes it this way:

> Perhaps the most exciting outcomes of our year together were these: a powerful bonding based on friendship and mutual respect, which included everyone. And an excited sense that we had uncovered a rich and unexplored field that would sustain us for years to come. I do not recall any one of us ever getting bored with our projects. On the contrary, we felt we were at the beginning of a much larger enterprise. And we knew that the history of women as rhetors and rhetoricians needed to be written.

By the end of their year together, Annette and her students were convinced that they had the core of a potentially important book. When Annette left Rensselaer Polytechnic Institute in the summer of 1988 to become dean of the faculty of humanities at the University of Arizona, however, the process of editing a final manuscript necessarily slowed. Still, the students persisted, Annette remained in contact with them, and gradually the conception of the book outgrew the confines of the original seminar. It was at this point that I was enlisted as a potential editor and contributor. As Annette remembers it, "The students in the seminar knew better than I did how important this book could be. And they were determined to see the project through to completion."

Why were the contributors to this volume so impassioned, so persistent in their pursuit of publication? Although the reasons vary widely, one stands out as paramount: if ever woman's place in the rhetorical tradition were to be reconfigured, if ever a new rhetoric full of such influences were to arise, the work of this volume had to be done.

Of course, many have called for or invoked "new" rhetorics before, most notably George Campbell in his 1776 work, *A Philosophy of Rhetoric*, and Daniel Fogarty in his 1959 volume, *Roots for a New Rhetoric*. In that work, Fogarty identifies what he calls the "old model" of "current-traditional rhetoric," against which he posits his own version of a "new" rhetoric. To illustrate the roots of this new rhetoric, Fogarty turns to the work of I. A. Richards, Kenneth Burke, and Alfred Korzybski, arguing that their views can form the basis of an art and science of communication that provides an "understanding of the basic presuppositions underlying the functions of discourse, makes use of the findings of literature and science, and teaches the individual how to talk, listen and read" (Fogarty 134).

In spite of its contributions, however, Fogarty's "new rhetoric" is limited—as was Campbell's—by both training and tradition to an exclusively masculinist reading of rhetoric, one that in many ways continues to echo Locke's earlier and decidedly not "new" views on the subject:

> 'Tis evident how much Men love to deceive, and be deceived, since Rhetoric, that powerful instrument of Error and Deceit, has its established Professors, is publicly taught, and has always been had in great Reputation. And, I doubt not, but it will always be thought great boldness, if not brutality in me, to have said thus much against it. Eloquence, like the fair sex, has too prevailing beauties in it, to suffer it self ever to be spoken against. And 'tis in vain to find fault with those Arts of Deceiving, wherein Men find pleasure to be deceived. (Locke 106)

The essays in *Reclaiming Rhetorica* attempt to move beyond such limited—and limiting—understandings. In doing so, however, they do not attempt to redefine a "new" rhetoric but rather to interrupt the seamless narrative usually told about the rhetorical tradition and to open up possibilities for multiple rhetorics, rhetorics that would not name and valorize one traditional, competitive, agonistic, and linear mode of rhetorical discourse but would rather incorporate other, often dangerous moves: breaking the silence; naming in personal terms; employing dialogics; recognizing and using the power of conversation; moving centripetally towards connections; and valuing—indeed insisting upon—collaboration. The characteristic tropes for a reclaimed Rhetorica include, therefore, not only definition, division, and synecdoche, but also metonymy, metaphor, and consubstantiality; its characteristic and principal aim is not deception or conquest—as Locke and much of the familiar rhetorical tradition would have it—but understanding, exploration, connection, and conversation. Taken together, the essays in *Reclaiming Rhetorica* suggest that the realm of rhetoric has been almost exclusively male not because women were not practicing rhetoric—the arts of language are after all at the source of human communication—but because the tradition has never recognized the forms, strategies, and goals used by many women as "rhetorical."

The authors of *Reclaiming Rhetorica* hope, then, to add to recent work—particularly in books by Karlyn Kohrs Campbell, Patricia Bizzell and Bruce Herzberg, Miriam Brody, and Sonja Foss, and in articles by scholars such as Catherine Peaden, Nan Johnson, Anne Ruggles Gere, Susan Miller, Karyn Hollis, Sue Ellen Holbrook, and others, who are currently carrying on the archaeological investigations necessary to the success of this project. More particularly, the essays in this volume aim to contribute to that work first of all by *listening*—and listening hard— to and for the voices of women in the history of rhetoric; by becoming, as Cheryl Glenn suggests, the audience who can at last give voice to women lost to us; by examining in close detail their speech and writing; and by acknowledging and exploring the ways in which they have been too often dismissed and silenced.

For the women whose voices animate the pages of *Reclaiming Rhetorica* are a widely diverse group. Some deliberately learned and used the conventions of scholarly rhetoric to make a place for women among the voices of men. Others, self-taught and working within the context of strong religious and political communities, spoke and wrote with deep conviction shaped through conscious rhetorical technique. Still others created comprehensive theories or approaches to language in the tradition of academic scholarship. Some were recognized as prominent rhetoricians in their own time and have since been forgotten, while others made contributions to language that are only now being recognized as vitally rhetorical.

Like the women whose work this volume seeks to reclaim, the contributors to this volume hold widely varying views about their subjects and take widely varying approaches to them. Some, comfortable with more traditional definitions of rhetorical aims and taxonomies, work to illuminate the dark corners of the discipline to which women have often been banished. Others, dismissing not only the traditional male canon but also the rhetorical theorists and practitioners of that tradition, develop new definitions that encompass the set of excellences demonstrated by the women they study. The underlying principle of this volume is not unity, therefore, but diversity and inclusivity; we seek most of all to embody here widely varying and contrasting approaches, methodologies, scholarly styles, and individual voices.

But such diversity should not suggest iconoclasm or disengagement from one another. Rather, a rich and intense collaboration—beginning with the original graduate seminar and expanding to include all contributors—has been indispensable as both the technique and the spirit of the writing of this book. Through group critiques and the reading and rereading of all the essays gathered here, the contributors have developed ideas in a far more communal and supportive environment than is usually possible in the academic setting or in a collection of this kind. While each essay in this book is separate, then, it owes much to the common ground so laboriously marked out in years of conversation and correspondence. If this book holds the echoes of the women it studies, its individual pages also echo the voices of all of its authors who, together, persist in reclaiming Rhetorica—in all her shapes, forms, and voices.

REFERENCES

Bizzell, Patricia, and Bruce Herzberg, eds. *The Rhetorical Tradition: Readings from Classical Times to the Present.* Boston: Bedford, 1990.

Brody, Miriam. *Manly Writing: Gender, Rhetoric, and the Rise of Composition.* Carbondale: Southern Illinois UP, 1993.

Campbell, George. *The Philosophy of Rhetoric.* 1776. Ed. Lloyd Bitzer. Carbondale: Southern Illinois UP, 1963.

Campbell, Karlyn Kohrs. *Man Cannot Speak for Her.* New York: Greenwood, 1989.

Fogarty, Daniel John. *Roots for a New Rhetoric.* 1959. New York: Russell, 1986.

Foss, Karen A., and Sonya K. Foss. *Women Speak: The Eloquence of Women's Lives*. Prospect Heights: Waveland Press, 1991.

Gere, Anne Ruggles. "Kitchen Tables and Rented Rooms: The Extracurriculum of Composition." *College Composition and Communication* 45.1 (1994): 75–92.

Holbrook, Sue Ellen. "Women's Work: The Feminizing of Composition." *Rhetoric Review* 9.2 (1992): 201–29.

Hollis, Karyn. "Liberating Voices: Autobiographical Writing at the Bryn Mawr Summer School for Women Workers, 1921–1938." *College Composition and Communication* 45.1 (1994): 31–60.

———. *Liberating Voices: Writing at the Bryn Mawr Summer School for Women Workers, 1921–1938*. New York: Prentice, Writing and Culture Series, 1995 (forthcoming).

Johnson, Nan. *Rhetorical Performance and the Construction of Culture* (work in progress).

Kolodny, Annette. Letter to author.

Locke, John. *An Essay Concerning Human Understanding*. Vol. 2. New York: Dutton, 1961.

Miller, Susan. "Things Inanimate May Move: A Different History of Writing and Class." *College Composition and Communication* 45.1 (1994): 102–07.

Peaden, Catherine Hobbs. "Jane Addams and the Social Rhetoric of Democracy." *Oratorical Culture in Nineteenth Century America: Transformations in the Theory and Practice of Rhetoric*. Ed. Gregory Clark and S. Michael Halloran. Carbondale: Southern Illinois UP, 1993.

———. , ed. *Nineteenth-Century Women Learn to Write: Past Cultures and Practices of Literacy*. Charlottesville: U of Virginia P (in press).

Rhetoric Society Quarterly 22.1 (1992). Special Issue on "Feminist Rereadings in the History of Rhetoric."

2

Aspasia: Rhetoric, Gender, and Colonial Ideology

Susan Jarratt and Rory Ong

So very difficult a matter is it to trace and find out the truth of anything but history, when, on the one hand, those who afterwards write it find long periods of time obscuring their view, and on the other hand, the contemporary records of any actions and lives, partly through envy and ill will, partly through favor and flattery, pervert and distort truth.

—Plutarch, Pericles

Even from the relatively close distance of only a few centuries beyond the Golden Age of classical Greece, Plutarch approached the task of history writing with a gingerly respect for its complexities.[1] Finding and authenticating sources present one kind of problem, but diving into layers of representation, with their inevitable colorations of "envy and ill will," "favor and flattery," deepens the mystery. As we embark on a much later but related historical enterprise, Plutarch's historiographical hesitations inform our project. The attempt to reconstruct Aspasia as a rhetorician of fifth-century B.C.E. Greece calls to mind the three propositions that the sophist Gorgias, her contemporary, offers in a speculation *On Nature*, with its playful subtitle, *On the Nonexistent*. Did Aspasia exist? If so, can she be known? And then, is that knowledge communicable?[2] Our aim here is to address the first two of these questions through an overview of the classical sources and current commentary, and then to concentrate on the third: the interpretive historiographical tasks involved in an encounter with a woman engaged in classical rhetoric.

A visual representation of Aspasia illustrates the multilayered operation of historiography in another way. The first volume of Mary Ellen

Waithe's courageous *History of Women Philosophers* is adorned with a photograph of a fresco entitled "Aspasia's Salon" from the portal of the main building of the University of Athens (fig. 1). Although Waithe points out the temporal fusion of centuries required in seating the fifth-century rhetorician with fourth-century Plato and third-century Archimedes, she neglects to tell us that the university was built only between 1838 and 1888. A "reading" of this representation of "Aspasia" would have to acknowledge at least the Romantic reinterpretation of Greek antiquity, the designs of the German empire under which nineteenth-century Greece was being reconstructed, and the heritage of the Enlightenment "salon" as a site of intellectual activity within a specific epistemic field and sociocultural moment. Our reconstruction of "Aspasia" will no more accurately recapture the "real" woman than do the figure in the fresco or the character in Plutarch's and Plato's texts, but rather will reflect back to us a set of contemporary concerns. That Aspasia existed is of profound importance for the project of recovering women in the history of rhetoric; that she marks the intersection of discourses on gender and colonialism, production and reproduction, rhetoric and philosophy makes her a rich site for interpretive work.

Aspasia the Rhetorician

Aspasia left no written remains. She is known through a handful of references, the most substantial of which are several paragraphs of narrative in Plutarch's life of Pericles and an oration attributed to her in Plato's dialogue *Menexenus*. Allusions to her by four of Socrates's pupils help to confirm Plutarch's assertion that Aspasia was indeed a real person, a teacher of rhetoric who shared her knowledge and political skill with Pericles, perhaps helping him to compose the funeral oration attributed to him by Thucydides.[3] The few available details of her past outline an intriguing figure. Aspasia came from Miletus, one of several Greek colonies in Ionia, a narrow strip on the coast of Asia Minor. Her origin in Miletus is significant because of the philosophical tradition there and because of its proximity to Persia. Western philosophical speculation was only a century or so old when Aspasia was born, its very earliest contributors having come from Miletus. Although there is no recorded contact between Aspasia and any Milesian philosopher, it is logical to assume that she came in contact with early philosophical thought in some form. In general, Milesian philosophers such as Thales, Anaximenes, and Anaximander sought to explain the natural world through abstrac-

Photograph of fresco over portal of the main building of the University of Athens, Greece. With the kind permission of Professor Michael P. Stathopoulos, Rector of the University of Athens.

tion and physical law rather than divine agency and anthropomorphic mythical figures, a direction of thinking quite compatible with an assumption of early Greek rhetoric, namely, that human deliberation and action are responsible for human destinies and can be shaped by thought and speech.[4] The second point about her Eastern origins is more a matter of reputation: Plutarch reports a rumor that Aspasia emulated Thargelia, a courtesan who seduced Greek men of power and won them over to Persian interests. This rumor should be understood in the context of the long-standing animosity between Hellenes and the inhabitants of the Middle Eastern land mass—Persians in the Archaic and Classical eras, but Trojans in the Dark Ages of Homer's epic. That rumor, which associates a bright and articulate woman with a Persian seductress, bespeaks a gendered xenophobia, linking qualities of deception, excess, passion, and decadence clustering around the "Orient" to a dangerous femininity. The auras of both the oriental (or Ionian) and the feminine hovered around rhetoric in the fourth century, thanks to classical philosophy, through an operation of difference we will pursue in more detail later.

Aspasia appeared in Athens in the mid-440s in association with the great statesman and democrat Pericles. She lived with Pericles in an arrangement that was unusual, perhaps even unique, in Athens at that time. Athenian women who were not slaves (the word *free* simply has no meaning here) were defined in relation to men as wives, concubines, hetaerae, or prostitutes (Cantarella 38–51).[5] Wives brought dowries to increase family wealth and guaranteed an unquestioned line of inheritance; there was no assumption in Greek culture that a wife would be sexually appealing or personally compatible with the man to whom she was bound contractually by her father or uncle. Concubines served as regular sexual companions for married men, and some may even have taken up dwelling with married couples. Hetaerae held a somewhat higher status; they attended symposia—festive dinner and drinking parties—where they engaged in witty conversation, but they were also expected to engage in sexual play. Aspasia fit properly into none of these categories. Before she arrived in Athens, Pericles had been married to a woman from the aristocratic class who bore him two sons. Years later the couple separated, apparently by common agreement. Six or seven years after his divorce, Pericles met Aspasia and brought her into his home as a beloved and constant companion. Diogenes Laertius reports that Pericles's love was so great that he kissed Aspasia every day, morning and evening, when he left for the agora and when he returned. That

such behavior was worth reporting gives evidence of the customary absence of affection between husbands and wives. Aspasia's unconventional status, as well as her influence with Pericles, was often distorted
through the use of labels such as *mistress* and *courtesan*. In Aristophanes's comedy *Acharnians* (425 B.C.E.), for example, the main character, an irritable farmer called Dicaeopolis, attributes the beginning of
the Peloponnesian War to the theft by a Spartan ally of "two of Aspasia'a
hussies" (l. 525). Aspasia bore a child who was later granted status as
an Athenian citizen; this anomalous enfranchisement was ironic, given
that Pericles himself had initiated a law limiting citizenship to individuals
with two Athenian parents, whereas before that time only the father's
citizenship was at issue.

Aspasia's interest for a history of rhetoric lies in her accomplishments
in political arts. Pericles's passion for her was said to have sprung from
her knowledge and skill in politics. She taught the art of rhetoric to many,
including Socrates, and may have invented the so-called Socratic method.
It would be difficult to overestimate how extraordinary such behavior
would have been in Athenian society in the fifth century B.C.E. Although
women in earlier periods of Greek history and in other locations in
Greece had a larger scope of cultural activity if not political power (see
Snyder), one of the ironies of the history of the West lies in the particular
suppression of women that went along with its first democracy:

> There is, of course, nothing unique in the democracy's exclusion of
> women from the political sphere, nor did the subordination of women
> originate with the democracy. Nevertheless, it remains a remarkable
> feature of Greek history that the position of women seems to have de-
> clined as the democracy evolved, and that in non-democratic states—
> notably Sparta and possibly the Cretan cities . . .—they enjoyed a more
> privileged status, especially in their rights of property. (Wood 115)

In Athens during the fifth century B.C.E, aristocratic women's activities, movement, education, marriage, and rights as citizens and property
holders were extremely circumscribed. Women were confined within
the house at all times, except on the occasions of religious festivals. At
the same time, opportunities for political participation by male citizens
had expanded greatly over the last two centuries. Wood offers an analysis
of this development based on the creation of the peasant-citizen through
a series of democratic reforms. When the basis for participation in the
decision-making assemblies and in the courts was shifted from the

aristocratic "houses" to geographical "demes," status differences were radically reduced for men as far as political power was concerned. Certainly, the old families with their wealth could afford to buy the training necessary for leadership in the Assembly, Council, and courts, but voting and selection of most public offices by lot guaranteed a broader distribution of power across different backgrounds, occupations, and economic statuses than ever before.

Determining the place for women under this new political system is, on the one hand, extremely straightforward: they were not considered citizens and thus did not participate in any formal public functions. On the other hand, women's lives in the various economic strata may have been differently affected in complex ways. For the farmers and artisans, it is possible that generally improved status for male heads of households lightened the burden of exploitation for women. But for aristocratic women, Wood and others deduce just the opposite effect. It is possible that

> the privileged political status of the male widened the gap between men and women, and perhaps pressures for the cultural devaluation of women were reinforced as the extension of citizenship carried with it a concomitant ideological impulse to harden the remaining principles of exclusion. (Wood 117–18)

The expanded role of public speaking, along with the development of literacy, created more and more venues for the expression of these "principles of exclusion," weaving them into the very fabric of democratic political theory and practice. The reforms of Ephialtes and Pericles in the middle of the fifth century completed a process of democratization begun by Solon in the early sixth century—a process allowing for, even requiring, Athenian males to develop the ability to listen to, understand, and speak about deliberative and judicial affairs of the city. Given this paradoxical opening up and closing down of discursive fields for men and women, the appearance and persistence of a female teacher of rhetoric in fifth-century Athens is nothing less than astounding.

Information about Aspasia's expertise is slim but engrossing. Plutarch reports that Socrates visited Aspasia alone and with others, and that at times men even brought their wives along on these visits. We can imagine situations such as those Plato often created in his dialogues about the sophists (*Protagoras, Gorgias*)—meetings at the house of a prominent citizen among wise older men and enthusiastic younger followers where intense discussions of ethical, political, and philosophical issues ensued. The youthful Cicero records a dialogue called *Aspasia* by Aeschines, a pupil of Socrates, that contained an exchange between Xenophon and his wife (*De inventione* 1.31). The manner of questioning "recalls" the dialectic of Plato's Socrates: Aspasia takes each interlocutor through a series of analogous questions, leading each to an embarrassed aporia, an admission of dissatisfaction with his or her spouse. Aspasia's role as "midwife" in this fragmentary report and her reputed origination of the "Socratic method" call to mind another figure associated with Pericles, the sophist Protagoras, and raise a question about the relationship between philosophy and rhetoric. Protagoras is also credited with creating a method of questioning taken up by Socrates; presumably it was derived from his practice of generating contradictory propositions (*dissoi logoi*) on any subject. The point here is not to determine who, in fact, originated the questioning process, but rather to associate all these figures with the sophistic practice of rhetoric.[6] Although Plato's representation of Socrates—as the philosopher constantly at odds with the devious rhetoricians—has fixed him in that role within the intellectual tradition , classical materials occasionally open onto a sophistic "Socrates" who shared methods and aims with rhetoricians in the lively intellectual and political atmosphere of the fifth-century polis.

More evidence for Aspasia's method of teaching appears in the opening of Plato's *Menexenus*, itself a complex interpretive puzzle. In this dialogue, Menexenus, a young citizen who has recently finished his education, comes from the Council full of news that that administrative group is in the process of choosing a speaker for the ritual state funeral for men who have died in battle. To be chosen to give this speech was a great honor. Socrates responds with ironically exaggerated praise of rhetoricians for their skill in "steal[ing] away our souls with their embellished words" (par. 235), the humor of which does not escape his interlocutor: "You are always making fun of the rhetoricians, Socrates" (par. 235). When Menexenus asks Socrates whether he himself would be able to respond to such a challenge, the philosopher replies, "That I should be able to speak is no great wonder, Menexenus, considering that I have an excellent mistress in the art of rhetoric—she who has made so many good speakers, and one who was the best among all the Hellenes—Pericles, the son of Xanthippus" (par. 235). Acknowledging that Aspasia was indeed his teacher, Socrates reports that he heard her only the previous day composing a funeral oration, and offers an account of the manner of composition of such orations:

I heard Aspasia composing a funeral oration about these very dead. For she had been told, as you were saying, that the Athenians were going to choose a speaker, and she repeated to me the sort of speech which he should deliver, partly improvising and partly from previous thought, putting together fragments of the funeral oration which Pericles spoke, but which, as I believe, she composed. (par. 236)

Plato's Socrates shows Aspasia engaging in a practice common to both training and performance in classical rhetoric. Speeches were generated out of common materials arranged with some spontaneity for the occasion and purpose at hand. To prepare for performance, small seminar-type groups of students working with an accomplished rhetorician would listen to and memorize speeches composed by their teacher and would practice composing and delivering speeches among themselves. The production of whole monologues would go along with closer work with topoi (topics or commonplaces); for the sophists, such work would have entailed generating arguments on contradictory propositions, or *dissoi logoi*. The composition involved here was collaborative in the sense that the materials of any speech were common elements of current thinking, a collection of shared opinions on topics of public concern. But the rhetor's task was not merely the recycling or dressing up of well-accepted public opinion. The technique of juxtaposing propositions foregrounded the contradictions found in any complex social order; rhetorical training created a critical climate within which to question, analyze, and imagine differences in group thought and action.

Locating Aspasia within the realm of sophistic rhetoric is a crucial interpretive step in answering Gorgias's second question: how can we "know" Aspasia? Commentators differ in their positions on Aspasia as sophist. Waithe, a philosopher, makes little of the rhetorical connection, probably because she identifies the sophists' project narrowly with the goal of confusing their listeners (Waithe 79). She seems more interested in establishing the authenticity of the speech, assuming it to be a competing version of the famous *epitaphios* attributed to Pericles by Thucydides (2.34–46). We do not agree that deciding on the "real" *epitaphios* is the best interpretive question to ask of Plato's text, and indeed prefer Edmund F. Bloedow's intertextual reading of the two speeches. Bloedow locates parallel stylistic and thematic elements in the two (33–34), but finds the serious distortions of historical data in Aspasia's speech more intriguing. The key lies in placing each author, Thucydides and Plato, at a particular historical juncture in Athenian history and within a particular

perspective on Athens's military exploits. Although Thucydides represents Pericles at a pinnacle of military success in the Peloponnesian War
(431 B.C.E.), he himself writes in exile from the nadir of Athenian fortunes—after the defeat by Sparta and the oligarchic coups of the late fifth
century.[7] Thus, Bloedow claims, Thucydides offers an ironic self-portrait
of Athens at an earlier, confident moment. Plato is even farther away,
both historically and ideologically, from the buoyant, democratic, imperialist Athens at her brightest moment. Creating in Aspasia's speech an
outlandishly sugarcoated account of Athens's military blunders up to the
time of the King's Peace in 386, Plato draws with a heavy hand the most
ironic possible picture of the triumphant warrior state generously bury-
ing its dead. This absurdly overdrawn picture of Athens, coming in the
form of a funeral oration authored by Aspasia, "co-architect of sophistic
rhetoric," would constitute for Plato's audience a very negative view of
popular oratory and a sharp attack on its detrimental influence in contemporary political life (Bloedow 47–48). Although he doesn't use the
word "ideology," Bloedow uses a method that brilliantly highlights the
ideological function of the funeral oration as a form of speech through
which the hearts and minds of Athenians were won over or kept loyal
and centered on the value of the city, especially in the affirmation of its
acts of war.

We turn now to the task of establishing some interpretive measures
by which to reconstruct the "Aspasia" Plato creates within this attributed
text.

Plato's "Aspasia"

Here we arrive at a version of Gorgias's third question: How can a knowledge of Aspasia be communicated? To translate this question into the
terms of contemporary rhetorical theory, we could ask what sort of discursive technologies are operative in Plato's representation?[8] We might
begin to address such a question at the place where Bloedow ends his
astute analysis. He asks what Plato signifies in choosing Aspasia as the
author of the funeral oration he constructs, focusing his answer on rhetoric and democracy. We want to extend that analysis by asking what
other kinds of difference are at work in the dialogue. If "Aspasia" represents for Plato a collection of ideas including not only the fifth-century
democracy and rhetoric in general but a sophistic rhetoric practiced almost exclusively by non-Athenians, then "Aspasia" as a proper name—
i.e., as a representation—runs slantwise through multiple strata of dif-

ferences. Plato spent much intellectual energy opposing this cluster; in the *Menexenus* he sounds the themes of rhetoric and democracy through the voice of a non-Athenian woman. While Bloedow focuses on Plato's democratic politics, we seek Aspasia at the intersection of the axes of gender and colonialism. Taking Aspasia not only as a key member of the sophistic movement but also as a woman and a foreigner, we ask how gender and colonialism work as discursive technologies to construct layers of meaning in Plato's text.

Gender in Menexenus

Reading the literary text against the social text, we find Plato giving voice to a woman at a time when women were mostly denied public voice, and fixed most effectively in the role of reproduction. A gendered analysis could take Plato's embodiment of his teacher's female teacher as an expansion of possibilities of real women. How does Plato stand on the woman question? We know from Book 5 of the *Republic* that he would have given women an equal share in education and in physical training in the ideal state, placing some of them in the guardian class with men. But we also know from a closer reading of these utopian plans that, insinuated throughout this offer of equality, are assumptions of inequality, implications that women still would gain their status primarily from association with well-born men, and that they would look ludicrous naked on the playing/battle field. This ambiguity in Plato regarding women—an ambiguity Irigaray has catalogued in "On the index of Plato's Works: Woman" (Speculum 152–59)—colors our reading of "Aspasia" in *Menexenus*.

Rather than seeing this dialogue as a foreshadowing of the progressive stance Plato takes on women in Book 5 of the *Republic*, we find it more aptly fits both Wood's and Page duBois's views that fourth-century philosophy advanced the task of hardening exclusionary categories (duBois, *Sowing*). Even though he attributed the *epitaphios* to a female author, Plato chose a form that typically referred to women only in terms of their single acceptable contribution to Athenian military pursuits: as reproducers of warriors. Plato fixes woman in that role most forcefully through his handling of the issue of autochthony. Autochthonous birth, the birth of men directly from the soil of Athens, is a fantasy of male autonomy (duBois, *Centaurs* 114). The reference to autochthony is standard in funeral orations, but in Aspasia's speech it takes a strangely elaborate form:

> For as a woman proves her motherhood by giving milk to her young
> ones (and she who has no fountain of milk is not a mother), so did this
> our land prove that she was the mother of men, for in those days she
> alone and first of all brought forth wheat and barley for human food,
> which is the best and noblest sustenance for man, whom she regarded
> as her true offspring. And these are truer proofs of motherhood in a
> country than in a woman, for the woman in her conception and genera-
> tion is but the imitation of the earth, and not the earth of the woman.
> (*Menexenus* pars. 237–38)

This passage aligns Aspasia's oration with other *epitaphioi*, all of
which guarantee the inherited excellence (*physis*) of Athenians of the
day through the birth of their ancestors directly from the earth of their
superior polis. Plato reproduces the typical gesture of the funeral orator,
interpellating Athenians as a naturally distinct and superior "race," but
he puts the speech in the mouth of a woman named Aspasia, who herself
bore a child to Pericles.[9] While he mimics the funeral oration's typical
gesture of hailing women as reproducers of warriors, Plato moves
woman out of the central position in matters of conception and generation. Man's autochthonous origin in Athenian citizenship is prior to his
origin in the body of the woman. By putting this displacement in the
mouth of a woman, "Aspasia," who was more than a reproductive instrument of the polis and was in fact a teacher and speaker despite her
gender, Plato makes the subordination of reproduction more powerful.
The manipulation of reproduction in *Menexenus* can be read alongside
Plato's *Phaedrus*, where Socrates appropriates reproduction for the male
philosopher (duBois, *Sowing*). In this key dialogue on rhetoric and pedagogy, Socrates presents the male teacher/philosopher as midwife, thus
metaphorically transferring the power of physical reproduction from
woman to the actions of the philosopher, who gives birth to (or at least
acts as a midwife in the birth of) the *psyche* of the beloved, the student.
In *Menexenus*, the woman speaker distances herself from somatic reproduction through metaphor: she insists on the authenticity and priority of
the male citizen's birth from the soil of Athens—it is the genus while
women's reproduction is merely the species. Thus in both dialogues,
though the discursive technique is different, there is a similar effect of
diminishing woman's power and creativity. In the one case, it is meta-
phorized (*Phaedrus*): birth of body becomes birth of soul. In the other
case (*Menexenus*), it becomes the metaphorical: birth of body is an an-
alogue of the birth of the citizen. In Plato's appropriative gestures, the

gender of the speaker is crucial—the very point. The male philosopher's assertion, "Women's reproductive capacity is merely the physical vehicle for the more important birth of the soul," performs the same function as the female rhetorician saying, "Women's reproduction is only a case of the more important 'birth' from Athenian earth of the citizen." Plato's "Aspasia" is caught in a contradiction: by reputation she exceeds the gendered boundaries of Greek citizenship; but through her, Plato ventriloquizes the very principles of exclusion she challenges.

Colonial Ideology in Menexenus

In *Gorgias*, *Protagoras*, and *The Sophist*, Plato consistently ridicules young Athenian men for allowing themselves to be taught (and therefore beguiled) by foreigners who have no natural knowledge of the virtues of Athens or of its citizens. In the *Menexenus*, Plato's choice to speak through Aspasia, a non-Athenian woman, echoes his ridicule in other dialogues of those naive enough to listen to the words of an outsider. Menexenus's wonderment that Aspasia, who is only a woman, should be able to compose such a speech (par. 249) ironically emphasizes the Platonic disdain for the foreigner/woman/sophist who would presume to have knowledge about the virtues of Atheno-androcentric citizenship. Through Socrates, Plato refers to foreigners as outsiders who, through the persuasion of the funeral oration, become enchanted with the virtuosity and nobility of the Athenians (par. 235). In this way the *epitaphios* persuades the listeners to better themselves: foreigners would admire and dream of becoming like Athenians, and Athenians would become stronger admirers of themselves. But Socrates, at first transfixed by the oration, gradually comes back to his senses—an indication from Plato that any transformation by rhetoric must necessarily be temporary.

Within the frame of the *epitaphios*, the dream of becoming Athenian can never be fulfilled. The important thing for Plato in the *Menexenus* is that the Athenian relationship to Athens begin with the very soil of Attica:

> Their ancestors were not strangers, nor are these their descendants sojourners only, whose fathers have come from another country; but they are the children of the soil, dwelling and living in their own land. And the country which brought them up is not like other countries, a stepmother to her children, but their own true mother. (par. 237)

In other words, being a citizen of Athens could not be achieved by simply becoming entranced by persuasory discourse or by attending state functions: rather, citizenship could come about only by being related to the very Attic earth out of which the ancestors of Athens came. Further, Plato locates the distinction between true Athenian descendance and alien origin in different familial relationships: "true mother" for Athenians and "stepmother" for others. Foreigners had no more than a distant relationship to any country because they were wanderers and travelers who might settle in one area and then another. Athenians, on the other hand, were not wanderers but were situated on the land that had created them.

These differences—mother vs. stepmother, Athenian vs. Foreigner—can be seen as discursive spaces articulated or mapped by the speech: the mother/Athenian space is whole, unitary, and continuous whereas the stepmother/foreigner space is fractured and discontinuous. Nicole Loraux notes the way these mappings in the *epitaphioi* construct a reality that conceals the fact that there were "others" *within* the city, "strangers" labeled metics or slaves (331).[10] In the *Menexenus* these distinctions are blurred "as if they did not exist or, at least, as if the slaves, those outcasts of the city, constituted a presupposition of the oration [that] the Athenians never met with slaves [but] only met one's neighbor!" (Loraux 331). The concealment of "others" constitutes for Loraux the presence of an "ideological attitude" in the *epitaphios*, a blindness to the economic realities of the polis:

> In fact their silence [on the existence of slavery] brings us back to a much more general omission: the oration ignores whatever does not belong to the sphere of war or politics, that is, everything related to the physical subsistence of the city, from the work of the slaves to the commercial role of the metics, from the artisans to the importation of wheat. (Loraux 334)

The discursive opposition Athenian/foreigner masks the multiple power relations involved in production and accepted as a way of life within the Athenian polis. Defining the norm through a polar opposition wipes out differences within each pole, differences that, in this case, expose the relations of production in an imperialist economy.

We might consider extending Loraux's discussion of ideology to Plato's representation of Aspasia's speech specifically in terms of a colonial ideology. For not only does ideology disguise difference in terms of modes of production, it also masks other social and cultural relations of power. Thus the funeral oration conceals what Edward W. Said has called "the possessing of possession . . . that is the power of culture by virtue of its elevated or superior position to authorize, to dominate, to legitimate, denote, interdict, and validate: in short, the power of culture to be an agent of, and perhaps the main agency for, powerful differentiation within its domain and beyond it too" (9). If we think of the Athenian attempt to dominate Hellenic culture, those discursive spaces of "stranger," "sojourner," and "woman"—spaces occupied simultaneously by Plato's "Aspasia"—can be seen as sites generated by, and thus possessed by, the "virtuous and noble" in order to define, privilege, and legitimate their own view of the world.

Aspasia, perhaps the first female orator in the Western tradition, attracted not only the admiration of Pericles and the fascination of Socrates but also the critical attention of a Plato intent on rereading the rhetorical world to which she gave voice. If we cannot recover the lost voice of Aspasia, we can set the echoes of her speech reverberating again for an age with its own concerns about democracy and political participation, production and reproduction, gender and citizenship.

NOTES

1. Plutarch, a Greek who lived during the Golden Age of the Roman Empire (46–120 C.E., produced "lives" of Greek and Roman leaders that established biography as a distinctive—and problematic—historical genre.

2. For an outline of Gorgias's treatise, see Sprague.

3. For a complete list of sources on Aspasia see Hill 367. Pupils of Socrates who refer to Aspasia are Aeschines, Xenophon, Antisthenes, and Plato. The narrative in the text is based on Plutarch's *Pericles* 24, except where another source is indicated.

4. See Kirk, Raven, and Schofield for a fuller discussion of pre-Socratic philosophy.

5. The title of Sara Pomeroy's early study succinctly categorizes, in a slightly different way, the "options" for women in classical Greece: *Goddesses, Whores, Wives, and Slaves.* Women held as slaves were expected to be available for sexual use by their owners without remuneration, while prostitution was practiced by both slave and nonslave women with limited resources. But Ellen Meiskins Wood reminds contemporary readers that class considerations complicate this brutally clear picture of women's limited scope of activity: indeed, "poor women . . . in practice had considerable freedom of movement, to go about their necessary business, perhaps sometimes to labour as artisans and shopkeepers" (116).

6. For more on Protagoras and sophistic rhetoric, see Jarratt.

7. Thucydides's *History* was probably composed in 404 B.C.E.

8. See Scott on the function of gender as an analytic category in history and de Lauretis for a feminist elaboration of Foucault's theory of discourse.

9. See Althusser on "interpellation," the process by which people are "hailed" or "recruited" as subjects within ideologies, sustaining specific social relations.

10. A metic was a free foreigner who took up residence in Athens. Metics could work and own land but paid a special tax and could not participate in the running of the polis.

REFERENCES

Althusser, Louis. *Lenin and Philosophy and Other Essays*. London: New Left, 1971.

Aristophanes. *The Acharnians*. In *Aristophanes I*. Trans. Benjamin Bickley Rogers. Cambridge: Harvard UP, 1950.

Bloedow, Edmund F. "Aspasia and the 'Mystery' of the Menexenus." *Wiener Studien*. Zeitschrift für Klassische Philologie und Patristic. Neu Folge. 9 (1975): 34–48.

Cantarella, Eva. *Pandora's Daughters: The Role and Status of Women in Greek and Roman Antiquity*. Trans. Maureen B. Fant. Baltimore: Johns Hopkins UP, 1987.

De Lauretis, Teresa. *Technologies of Gender: Essays on Theory Film and Fiction*. Bloomington: Indiana UP, 1987.

DuBois, Page. *Centaurs and Amazons: Women and the Pre-history of the Great Chain of Being*. Ann Arbor: U of Michigan P, 1982.

———. *Sowing the Body: Psychoanalysis and Ancient Representations of Women*. Chicago: U of Chicago P, 1988.

Hill, G. F. *Sources for Greek History Between the Persian and Peloponnesian Wars*. Rev. ed. R. Meiggs and A. Andrewes. Clarendon: Oxford UP, 1951.

Irigaray, Luce. *Speculum of the Other Woman*. Trans. Gillian C. Gill. Ithaca: Cornell UP, 1985.

Jarratt, Susan C. *Rereading the Sophists: Classical Rhetoric Refigured*. Carbondale: Southern Illinois UP, 1991.

Kirk, G. S., J. E. Raven, and M. Schofield. *The Presocratic Philosophers: A Critical History with a Selection of Texts*. 2nd ed. Cambridge: Cambridge UP, 1983.

Loraux, Nicole. *The Invention of Athens: The Funeral Oration in the Classical City*. Trans. Alan Sheridan. Cambridge: Harvard UP, 1986.

Plato. *Menexenus*. Trans. Benjamin Jowett. In *The Dialogues of Plato*. Vol 2. Oxford: Oxford UP, 1892.

Plutarch. *Eight Great Lives. The Dryden Translation*. Rev. Arthur Hugh Clough. Ed. Charles Alexander Robinson Jr. New York: Holt, 1960.

Pomeroy, Sarah B. *Goddesses, Whores, Wives, and Slaves*. New York: Schocken, 1975.

Said, Edward W. *The World, the Text, and the Critic*. Cambridge: Harvard UP, 1983.

Scott, Joan Wallach. *Gender and the Politics of History*. New York: Columbia UP, 1988.

Snyder, Jane McIntosh. *The Woman and the Lyre: Women Writers in Classical Greece and Rome*. Carbondale: Southern Illinois UP, 1989.

Sprague, Rosamond Kent, ed. *The Older Sophists: A Complete Translation by Several Hands of the Fragments in Die Fragmente der Vorsokratiker* (Ed. Diels-Kranz. Weidmann Verlag). Columbia: U of South Carolina P, 1972.

Thucydides. *History of the Peloponnesian War*. Trans. Rex Warner. Middlesex: Penguin, 1954.

Waithe, Mary Ellen, ed. *A History of Women Philosophers*. Vol. 1: *600 B.C.–500 A.D.* Dordrecht: Martinus Nijhoff, 1987.

Wood, Ellen Meiksins. *Peasant-Citizen and Slave: The Foundations of Athenian Democracy*. London: Verso, 1988.

3

A Lover's Discourse:
Diotima, Logos, and Desire

C. Jan Swearingen

Wonder, awe, fear, astonishment
Petrify the eternal myriads
At the first female form now separate
They call'd her Pity, and fled.
—*William Blake,* The First Book of Urizen

Diotima may seem an unlikely candidate for inclusion in any rhetorical tradition. However, her claims to rhetorical presence can be solidly grounded in the public presence of women as teachers, religious celebrants, and orators in classical antiquity. I propose that we examine Plato's representations of Aspasia and Diotima as accomplished speakers and teachers as reflections of these traditions and as extensions of the rebukes directed at women—especially at strong, speaking women—in the literature of the sixth and fifth centuries. The presence of women in public and learned roles in classical antiquity continues to be questioned, dubbed fictional, and charged with wishful thinking. The quickness of such dismissals, I suggest, functions as a different kind of rebuke, for it serves to perpetuate the misogynist belief system that, particularly in Greek antiquity, led to the suppression of women's public presence and of records that represented it as anything but "merely literary" or as jokes (duBois; Waithe). Traces of women's presence and speech are preserved not only in Plato's representations but also in the work of numerous sophists, dramatists, historians, and writers of legal codes. Democritus, for example, asserts that women should not be allowed to practice argument because men detest being ruled by women. In asserting this, he describes a detestable—and not fictional—practice. An edict "On Pleading" from the sixth century A.D. repeats the terms of Democritus's proscription: "It is prohibited to women to plead on behalf of others. And indeed there is reason for the prohibition: lest women mix themselves up in other people's cases, going against the chastity that befits their gender." The origin of this rule is said to be one Carfania, "a most shameless women, who by immodestly bringing cases and bothering the magistrate provided the cause for the edict" (Richlin, "Roman Oratory" 1323). Other examples abound. In a number of anecdotes and illustrations, Aristotle alludes without apparent irony to priestesses and women speakers, among them Cleobulina of Rhodes who, according to his report, was renowned as a public speaker and counselor to her father the king. Diotima, then, merits close study as a figure, as the trace of women teachers, speakers, and religious celebrants. According to Socrates's report, Diotima was called in to avert a plague during the Peloponnesian War and at that time taught him many matters concerning love, discourse, and rhetoric. He likens her speech to a sophist's (208c). On these grounds even a fictional Diotima would seem to warrant a modest note of attention in a project reclaiming women and refiguring representations of women's speech within rhetorical traditions.

A few words on methodology and historicity: I have already described the common practice of dealing with the matter of Diotima's historicity, like that of Aspasia and other women represented in classical literature, by means of one or another erasure. Hence, she is considered merely a literary character, or histories in antiquity are seen to be unreliable and distorted, or there is supposedly no solid material evidence for women in public places, in rhetoric, as teachers, or as leaders. Even the project of writing women into the history of rhetoric has been questioned (see Biesecker). Despite their value in advancing a view of how and where appropriation has taken place, feminist and gender studies have created somewhat reductive victim narratives in their stories of appropriation and in their laments that women figures, if they existed at all, are unrecuperable (e.g., Halperin). These modern erasures, however well intended, have the effect of prolonging the suppression of women's presence and voices that began in Western traditions during the fifth century. For this reason, it is encouraging to see revisionist histories supplementing our received notions of Athens as the paradigm for all of Greece. Even within Athens, as the case of Aspasia so intriguingly suggests, the conventions governing women in public and private spaces, and the divisions between

those spaces, were far from uniform. A number of cautious and responsible scholarly accounts conclude that, in one of the changes in religious
and political forms before and during the rise of the Athenian empire
under Pericles, gender was given a major overhaul in Greek religious
iconography beginning with the Bronze Age (Fornara and Samons).
"Matriarchal influences were relegated to prehistory. Male priests took
over from female ones; the temple at Delphi was originally the temple
of a matriarchal cult of priestesses, who participated in hymns and
chants, but, by the time of the Bronze Age, Delphi was Apollo's; the
Olympian deities replaced the matriarchal ones" (Kintz 29–30; also see
duBois; Fontenrose; Frymer-Kensky; McAlister; Wider; Zeitlin). Recent
scholarship on gender and culture in Greek antiquity has established
that there were substantial differences between Athenian and other ancient Greek communities (Frymer-Kensky 203–12; Kintz; Zeitlin).

To say that classical evidence is literary, fragmentary, or unreliable
is to say nothing very new. It has long been the case that evidence from
Greek antiquity is sporadic, the result of accidental archaeological discoveries, fragmentary papyrological remains, tortuous manuscript trans-
missions, layers of beliefs imported from later centuries into the interpretation of classical materials and texts, and, finally, silence. "We are
not even aware of what it is that we do not yet know. This fact is somewhat intimidating, for it is dangerous to argue from silence, and we are
constantly aware that carefully worked-out conclusions might be invali-
dated" (Frymer-Kensky 4). In the midst of tortured theoretical self-
examinings, can we not venture a small quiet step forward to gaze upon
a few venerable figures? After all,

> part of the scholarly ferment in recent years has been the realization that
> the reader is always present in the reading of texts, and that the present
> is always part of the interpretation of the past. There is no such thing as
> the totally objective recovery of history, for something informs our
> choice of questions to ask and our selection of data that seems significant
> to us. (Frymer-Kensky ix)

If Socrates's Diotima, as written by Plato, is "merely literary," then
what of Socrates, Protagoras, or Gorgias? In each of these cases the
portrait drawn has long been recognized as a representation crafted by
Plato's mighty literary and rhetorical hand to create a certain picture and
to address specific issues. Since there are not just one but many Socrates
characters across the dialogues, does it follow that Socrates is merely

literary, just a fiction? That there is no evidence of any such person? The nineteenth century grappled with the parallel case for and against a historical Jesus. To so quickly respond that "there is no evidence" of Diotima or Aspasia bespeaks a highly selective theoretical correctness (see Poulakos and Jarratt). If we can have multiple Socrateses, Jesuses, and Moseses, may we not be allowed just one Diotima? And while we are at it, may we perhaps reflect upon the attitudes that lead us, first, to so quickly question the historicity of women, but not of men; and second, to so quickly denounce the men of antiquity as uniformly evil appropriators of women? Inasmuch as we guide the theory that guides our interpretations, can we perhaps harness that theory, however momentarily, to suppress our disbelief? Diotima's theory of love, discourse, and birth has much to say about these matters of method and purpose, motive and passion, desire and language.

A venerable accumulation of readings of the *Symposium* has emphasized polarities in the series of speeches, including Diotima's, which examine myriad representations of Love: Love as one of a number of gods, as a social practice, and as part of mythical accounts of human creation. Many interpreters have posited that in the *Symposium* and elsewhere Plato favors the "higher" forms of love and discourse, such as spiritual and philosophical procreation, the engendering of knowledge, and the bringing of ideas into being. Plato's representations of mental, discursive, and conceptual activities are often interpreted to mean that he fosters the domain proper to "lovers of wisdom," in contrast to "mere" physical eroticism and procreation. Such a hierarchy, once distilled, has been criticized as an appropriation and denigration of both bodily and feminine metaphors and activities (e.g., duBois). Drawing on this set of assumptions, critics have depicted Plato as a progenitor of a series of asymmetrical binaries that render emotion, the physical, and the female as the inferior term in a series of dualisms that have been prominent in Western thinking about intellect, gender, thought, and language (e.g., duBois). According to many nineteenth- and twentieth-century interpretations, the *Symposium* joins other Platonic discussions honoring mental *rather than* physical love and procreation. As a philosophy of love, it has been widely interpreted as favoring male-to-male ascetic love over heterosexual physical love as a vehicle for birth; and as valorizing the birth of knowledge of ideas, not of persons, as the proper goals of love, philosophy, and discourse alike (e.g., Halperin). Yet because Plato's exposition is both ambiguous in genre and difficult to pin down to modern, and especially post-Freudian, terms (duBois), his representation of Diotima and of her speech on love and discourse should be especially inviting to historians of rhetoric. Several subtexts in Plato's depiction of Diotima's teachings on love address the nature of the relationship among discourse, desire, and rhetoric. Her speech as well as its representation touch on matters rhetorical in far more detail than has been discerned by many ancient and modern eyes, and, I will emphasize, with far less finality than Plato is commonly given credit for.

In contemporary postmodern theory, women are enjoined to write their bodies—as opposed to their minds? They are invited to escape the imprisonment of their voices, which has been created by masculine appropriators, and by the restriction of truth to prose and philosophy. Dionysian abandon is promoted as a vehicle for liberating the voice through "writing the body." In the theoretical setting provided by this particular application of postmodern theory to feminism, it seems especially fitting to retrieve an ancient woman's teaching on the intricate complementarity of body and mind, desire and language, love and discourse. Diotima's discourse, and her views of discourse, define her place within a rhetorical pantheon that has long included equally fictional characters of Plato's creation, among them Protagoras, Gorgias, Phaedrus, and Callicles. As represented in the *Symposium*, Diotima's teachings define love as a cognate of desire, and as a vehicle for the transmission of qualities from divine to human as well as within and between individuals. Diotima teaches that Love is a spirit (*daimon*); as a being between the divine and the human, it is necessarily discursive, a messenger and mediator traveling between the divine and the human, between dream and waking reality, the ideal and the lived. In the *Symposium*, a series of speeches provide Love, in the guises of Aphrodite and Eros, with many different genealogies; each speech depicts several of the negative and positive powers of Love: to impel lust, to harness desire, and to drive discourse as one among the many forms of human interactions. After a sequence of speeches, Diotima's oration is presented by Socrates, who concludes just before Alcibiades's drunken entrance is heralded by a flute girl—the accompanist for a performing poet.

Diotima's speech on Love, as recounted by Socrates, explores numerous parallels between physiological, intellectual, and spiritual creation and procreation. Her teaching warns against possession in love, and indeed posits its impossibility, whether one is a lover of persons who yearns for physical procreation, or a lover of wisdom who desires the production of knowledge and the acquisition of wisdom. To understand love as the possession of a desired object, she teaches, is to consign oneself to a life of unfulfilled yearning, even though the ordinary experience of love is that "Love is in love with what he lacks and does not possess" (Hamilton 78, 201b). In a Socrates-like cross-questioning Diotima leads Socrates to the conclusion that because Love is lack, it lacks beauty and goodness and therefore cannot be a God. "Very well then, you see that you are one of the people who believe that Love is not a god" (Hamilton 81, 202d).

Chiding Socrates for his well-known flair for sophistical argumentation while showing that she herself is rather good at it, Diotima's discourse with and to Socrates—represented by Plato, we must constantly remember—develops several points. Socrates has wrongly avoided the physical experiences of desire and love and this avoidance has hampered his pursuit of wisdom. Socrates has been far less reluctant to use his dazzling powers of speech to attract lovers—of wisdom—and indeed this is his life's purpose. Insofar as he beguiles young men with the unfamiliar attraction of intangible, hidden truth and wisdom, he must reflect on psyche, logos, and eros. The fact that he eschews physical intercourse with his lovers does not release him from his responsibility to understand the lesser and greater mysteries. Rather, Diotima suggests, he is obligated to extend the insights imparted by the mysteries to discourse and to the love of wisdom. Finally, and in direct contrast to the views on reincarnation and recollection that Plato's interlocutors defend in other dialogues, Diotima teaches that neither persons and their identities nor knowledge as a static whole or as a body can be transmitted, that neither persons nor knowledge are immortal. Thus, the substance of the interactions between individuals during their lifetimes with those they love, through love-inspired discourse, is of paramount importance.

> Each individual piece of knowledge is subject to the same process as we are ourselves. When we use the word recollection we imply that knowledge departs from us; forgetting is the departure of knowledge, and recollection, by implanting a new impression in the place of that which is lost, preserves it, and gives it a spurious appearance of uninterrupted identity. It is in this way that everything mortal is preserved; not by remaining forever the same, which is the prerogative of divinity, but by undergoing a process in which the losses caused by age are repaired by new acquisitions of a similar kind. It is in order to secure immortality that each individual is haunted by this eager desire and love. (*Symposium* 208a–b)

This segment of Diotima's speech contrasts sharply with the ladder of love she describes in her conclusion, an ascent from dependence upon the physical beauty of one beloved to the capacity to seek and be satisfied by the quality of beauty—that is, the capacity to love—and to give birth to beauty in others.

Within Plato's text representing Diotima's speech, and Socrates's judging it spoken like a sophist, there is manifold ambiguity and ample room for alternative readings. Diotima means "god-honoring." Like Socrates and his daimon, and perhaps as the spokeswoman for both, Diotima honors the divine, the immortal, and thereby, presumably, the incorporeal. We might, however, be led to question this interpretation. Diotima repeatedly asserts the half-human, half-divine nature of all daimons, including Love and, presumably, Socrates's mysterious daimon as well. She goes to great lengths to define irreducible interdependencies among human and divine identity, discourse, love, and wisdom. Close attention to the detailed diversity of the god—Love—that Diotima honors and to her notion of immortality, reveals several features that are inconsonant with dualist interpretations of Plato (see Halperin; Nussbaum 20).

The negative import of Socrates's comment that Diotima's speech is "spoken like a sophist" may be taken to be an extension of ribald jokes linking Gorgias, Aspasia, the sophists, and tricky rhetorical seductions (see Jarratt). This context might direct our attention more pointedly to the speech of Alcibiades that follows Diotima's discourse—a palinode in which Alcibiades, after a characteristically drunken, bawdy entrance, praises Socrates's spare speech as possessing an inner gold covered by outer dross. It would seem that Alcibiades implicitly renounces his own famed outer beauties—of both body and speech—for the far more beautiful, alluring, and elusive inner soul that he has glimpsed through conversation with Socrates. Has Socrates at last been successful in leading him up Diotima's ladder of love? More important with regard to Diotima's twofold teaching, should he be so led or is it he who needs to teach Socrates?

Alcibiades's well-known unconsummated love affair with Socrates over many years is one of the comic elements in his speech and in the dialogue as a whole. In his topsy-turvy, praise-by-blame (or is it blame-by-praise?) palinode, Alcibiades depicts Socrates as a mesmerizer and a tease. He reports that for frightening, unfathomable, mysterious reasons any speech, or even any indifferent report of a speech by Socrates, "stirs us to the depths and casts a spell over us, men and women and young lads alike. . . . Whenever I listen to him my heart beats faster than if I were in a religious frenzy. Nothing of this kind ever used to happen to me when I listened to Pericles and other good speakers" (Hamilton 101,

215d–e). Further, Alcibiades claims, Socrates has insulted him and numerous other lovers: "He has pretended to be in love with them, when
in fact he is himself the beloved rather than the lover" (Hamilton 111,
222b). By virtue of his speech—his *logos*, his *rhetorike*—and the veiled
beauties he discloses only through the intangible vehicle of talk, Socrates
is here charged with being a professional beloved, seeking to stimulate
desires that he himself will not and cannot satisfy (see Wender). For this
reason Alcibiades warns Agathon to withdraw his love of Socrates's wisdom before it is too late (222b).

Complicating any understanding of the comedy—and tragedy—contained in the relationship between Socrates and Alcibiades is the ambiguous "spin" of Plato's bawdy rendering of Alcibiades, Diotima's depicted
role as Socrates's teacher of love, and the unstated backdrop of Pericles's
relationship to both Alcibiades and Aspasia. While he was still the ward
of Pericles, Alcibiades met Socrates in Aspasia's salon (see Davis).
Alcibiades had a mistress named Timandra, or "man honoring" (Nussbaum 177)—a name that provides a neat counterpoint to Diotima, "god-
honoring." Within the complex metaphorical algebra of the *Symposium*,
Alcibiades is represented as sustaining his bawdy courtship of Socrates,
asking Socrates once again to love and honor Alcibiades the man rather
than his elusive, invisible daimon lover. Aspasia's name means "welcome" or, less charitably, "gladhander" (Keuls); she is represented in
Plato's *Menexenos* as the teacher of both Socrates and Pericles, with the
suggestion that she composed Pericles's famous oration. Xenophon depicts Socrates saying to Critobulus, "I will refer you to my wife, Aspasia,
who will inform you better than I can myself" (Xenophon I).

Although widely scorned in Athens as a "dog eyed harlot" in her own
time, Aspasia nonetheless enjoyed renown in antiquity as a teacher.
Along with Plutarch's *Lives*, Athenaeus's *Deipnosophistae*, an account of
ancient love affairs, records that Socrates and Aspasia enjoyed a "strong
friendship." Athenaeus says that Socrates's "soul was deep, yet he laboured with lighter pains when he visited the house of Aspasia" (599b).
"Clever Aspasia" is identified not only as Socrates's teacher of rhetoric
but also as his preceptress in his love for Alcibiades. "Restrain thyself,
filling thy soul with the conquering Muse; and with her aid thou shalt
win him; pour her into the ears of his desire. For she is the true beginning of love in both; through her thou shalt master him, by offering to
his ear gifts for the unveiling of his soul." Later, Aspasia comforts the
unsuccessful Socrates: "Why art thou all tears, dear Socrates? Can it be
that the thunderbolt of desire, rankling in thy breast, stirs thee up—the

bolt which crashed from the eyes of the lad invincible, whom I promised to make tame for thee?" (Athenaeus 219b–e). In the *Symposium*, Alcibiades claims to have been smitten by Socrates's discourses in a manner that torments him. Socrates avoids sitting near Alcibiades for fear of his force. "Agathon, do your best to protect me, for I have found my love for this fellow no trifling affair. . . . The fellow flies into a spiteful jealousy which makes him treat me in a monstrous fashion, girding at me and hardly keeping his hands to himself" (213c–d). Socrates's unreciprocated desire for Alcibiades, and Alcibiades's unsatisfied, burning desire for the wisdom Socrates keeps so well hidden; the renowned skill for speaking held by Alcibiades and Pericles, and in a different register by Aspasia, Diotima, and Socrates; the skill for irresistible, siren-like speech attributed by Alcibiades to Socrates; all these linger in suspended animation throughout the *Symposium*, a reminder of how fluid the practice and understanding of speechmaking and rhetoric remained in Plato's time.

On several counts, the direct and indirect depictions of Diotima and Aspasia—the women who taught the men of Athens everything they knew about love and about rhetoric—form a complex puzzle. From one perspective, Diotima's and Aspasia's representation can be seen as implementing an erasure of women's teachings and characters, and of feminine metaphors, through Plato's appropriation (e.g., duBois; Halperin). Furthermore, the representation of Diotima, like the representation of Plato's characters in general, is of ambiguous reliability by modern standards of historical representation. It is more likely that Plato's characterizations were composed as comic—and perhaps also tragic—distortions of a kind that would have amused the listeners and readers of his dialogues. Plato's versions of Diotima and Aspasia are the only surviving remnants of teachings of this kind—by women, on love—in a form that even remotely resembles a full text. However, in support of the view that Plato's depiction preserves Aspasia and her speech as much as it distorts or appropriates them, we should note that in the histories of antiquity there is no recorded suspicion of the speech's or Aspasia's authenticity. Aspasia's speech as rendered in the *Menexenos* was performed yearly in Athens for centuries after her death (Cicero, *De oratore* 13). Her status as both a rhetor and teacher of Socrates and of others—even if this was considered a joke—parallels Diotima's role in the *Symposium*, a resemblance that has led some interpreters to conjecture that they are stand-ins for one another, and that the joke is on Socrates (Fornara and Samons).

Several other themes link Aspasia to Diotima in the representations of antiquity (Athenaeus; Plutarch; Xenophon). Alcibiades was reportedly Aspasia's student along with Socrates. The powers of speech of both Alcibiades and Socrates are given prominent attention in the *Symposium*, an emphasis that should alert us to Diotima's dual roles of speaking "like a sophist" and teaching an art and philosophy of love. Alcibiades was renowned both for his physical beauty and for his powerfully persuasive speeches. Alcibiades's powers of persuasion were remembered as in- strumental in bringing about many alliances—not all of them popular, particularly as the war wore on and its costs mounted. One such alliance among the Athenians, Argives, Eleans, and Mantineans occurred near the time that Alcibiades was charged with defacing herms (household patronymics of the newer democratic gods of the state cult of Olympian religion) and with demonstrating impiety by mocking the mysteries. He is recorded as having persuaded the rival Lacedaemonians not to claim publicly their plenary power, giving them his word that power would be honored, and then "accusing them before the people as men that had no true meaning nor ever spake one and the same thing" (Thucydides 5.3445). In this way he brought about the alliance. When charged with mocking the mysteries in private houses and with defacing the herms, he was sent to a purgation rather than being arrested, since his absence might alienate "the Mantineans and the Argives, who they thought fol- lowed the war by his persuasion" (6.61).

In his palinode in praise of Socrates, Alcibiades makes much of their comradeship during the war, of their mutual valor and heroism, and of the bravery they displayed in action and speech alike. If we consider Diotima's role as the persuasive priestess from Mantinea who averted a plague for Athens, it is intriguing that Alcibiades persuaded the Manti- neans to sustain their league with the Athenians, and to come under Athenian protection militarily and then governmentally. Plato's delicate weaving together of distant and recent history is evident in the timing of the Symposium as well. Around the time of the *Symposium*'s composi- tion, 385–75 B.C. (Nussbaum 169), Mantinea was dispersed into villages (*Symposium* 145 n.1); its status as an independent city-state was at an end. Aristophanes's speech deems such dispersions analogous to pun- ishment for lack of fidelity to one true Love, and contends that desire comes from previous human form as one, as entire, before splitting. "The craving and pursuit of that entirety is called Love. Formerly, we were one; but now for our sins we are all dispersed by God, as the Arcadians were by the Lacedaemonians" (*Symposium* 193a).

Once the persuader of the Mantineans, is Alcibiades now to be persuaded by a Mantinean, a priestess, a teacher of love? Where Socrates
failed, shall Diotima succeed? And what has Socrates learned from her
teaching? Martha Nussbaum proposes that it is wrongheaded to regard
the *Symposium* as a work that "ignores the pre-philosophical understanding of *eros*." Instead, she suggests, it is "all about that understanding and
also about why it must be purged and transcended, why Diotima has to
come once again to save Athens from a plague." Are we, "like Socrates,
ready to be 'persuaded' by the revisionary speech of Diotima"? (Nussbaum 167).

To address that question, and to establish grounds for the substantial
ties between love and discourse, desire and rhetoric, that are developed
in Diotima's speech, I turn to traces of Pythagorean teachings that are
preserved among pre-Socratic fragments, particularly Empedocles's ren-
derings of love and discourse as unifying principles of the psyche and of
the universe. Like the Mantineans, the Pythagoreans were dispersed
during and after the time of the Peloponnesian wars. Pythagorean communities were scattered throughout Magna Graeca ; many of their teachers were forced into hiding (Waithe 1:11, 59–74; Davidson 98–107). At
the center of Pythagorean teaching was the notion of Harmony, a whole
in nature, society, and the psyche that could be brought about by teaching new principles of natural and social union. Many elements in Pythagorean teaching, and parallel themes in Empedocles, can be aligned
without great difficulty with the notions of divine-human complementarity, of ever-changing qualities and elements that are developed in Diotima's teaching, and of the unity of discourse, lovers, and wisdom that is
sustained throughout the *Symposium* and elsewhere in Plato's dialogues
(Waithe 1:69–71; Harrison, *Themis* 249 n.4, 513–14).

I have provided the interlude that follows to illustrate more directly
than any exposition could the mingling of old and new terms drawn upon
in the metaphorical chemistry, or alchemy, of the *Symposium*. Earlier
Greek cosmologies, and the language in which they are expressed, are
adapted in manifold ways in Plato's depictions of discourse, rhetoric,
philosophy, and love.

> She [Aphrodite] it is who is believed to be implanted in mortal limbs
> also; through her they think friendly thoughts and perform harmonious
> actions, calling her Joy and Aphrodite. No mortal man has perceived her
> as she moves in and out among them. But you must listen to the unde-
> ceitful progress of my argument. . . . The elements alone exist, and run-

ning through one another they become different things at different times, and are ever continuously the same. This process is clearly to be seen through the mass or mortal limbs: sometimes through Love all the limbs which the body has as its lot come together into One, in the prime of flourishing life; at another time again, sundered by evil feuds, they wander severally by the breakers of the shore of life.

(Empedocles, fragments 17, 20, in Freeman 1983)

When intimacy is established and the loved one has grown used to being near his friend and touching him in the gymnasium and elsewhere, the current of the stream which Zeus when he was in love with Ganymede called the "stream of longing" sets in full flood towards the lover. Part of it enters into him, but when his heart is full the rest brims over, and as a wind or an echo rebounds from a smooth and solid surface and is carried back to its point of origin, so the stream of beauty returns once more to its source in the beauty of the beloved.   (Plato, *Phaedrus* 255)

Agathon: Here, Socrates, come sit by me, so that by contact with you I may have some benefit from that piece of wisdom that occurred to you there in the porch. Clearly you have made the discovery and got hold of it; for you would not have come away before.

Socrates: How fine it would be, Agathon . . . if wisdom were a sort of thing that could flow out of the one of us who is fuller into him who is emptier, by our mere contact with one another, as water will flow through wool from the fuller cup into the emptier.

(*Symposium* 175c–d)

Socrates: Any speech ought to have its own organic shape, like a living being; it must not be without either head or feet; it must have a middle and extremities so composed as to fit one another and the work as a whole.

The same is true of the art of rhetoric as of the art of medicine. . . . In both cases a nature needs to be analysed, in one the nature of the human body and in the other the nature of the soul.

(Plato, *Phaedrus* 264, 270)

For there do not start two branches from his back; [he has] no feet, no swift knees, no organs of reproduction; he was a Sphere, and in all directions equal to himself.   (Empedocles, fragment 29)

For man-woman was then a unity in form no less than a name, composed of both sexes and sharing equally in male and female. The form of each person was round all over, with back and sides encompassing it every way; two faces perfectly alike on a cylindrical neck. . . . That which partook of both sexes was born of the moon, for the moon partakes of both. They were globular in their shape as in their progress, since they took after their parents.

(*Symposium* 190a–b)

Dike [Justice] is the way of life of each natural thing, of each plant, each animal, each man, the regular course of that great animal the Universe, the way that is made manifest in the Seasons. Dike is manifest in the changes of the rising and setting of constellations, in the waxing and waning of the Moon and in the daily and yearly courses of the Sun. Dike seems sometimes to take on the semblance of the Moon, sometimes of the Sun.   (*Themis* 517, in Harrison 1966)

Beaming Sun and Earth and Heaven and Sea—reconnected in harmony with their own parts: all those [parts] which have been sundered from them and exist in mortal limbs. Similarly all those things which are more suitable for mixture are made like one another and united in affection by Aphrodite.

(Empedocles, fragment 22)

I will go back to the path of song which I formerly laid down, drawing one argument from another, that [path which shows how] when Hate has reached to bottommost abyss of the eddy, and when Love reaches the middle of the whirl, then in it, [the whirl] all these things come together so as to be one—not all at once, but voluntarily uniting, some from one quarter, others from another.

(Empedocles, fragment 35)

Anyone whom Love touches becomes a poet,
"Though a stranger to the Muse before."
(*Symposium* 196d)

[The heart], nourished in the seas of blood which courses in two opposite directions: this is the place where is found for the most part what men call Thought; for the blood round the heart is Thought in mankind.

(Empedocles, fragment 105)

Heat and cold, drought and moisture, when brought together by the orderly Love, and taking on a temperate harmony as they mingle, become bearers of ripe fertility and health to men and animals and plants, and are guilty of no wrong. But when the wanton-spirited Love gains the ascendant in the seasons of the year, great destruction and wrong does he wreak. . . . So further all sacrifices and ceremonies controlled by divination, namely, all means of communion between gods and men, are only concerned with either the preservation or the cure of Love. . . . Love conceived as a single whole, exerts a complete power, but that which is consummated for a good purpose, temperately and justly, both here on earth and in heaven above, wields the mightiest power of all and provides us with a perfect bliss; so that we are able to consort with one another and have friendship also with the gods who are above us.

(*Symposium* 188b–d)

[A female divinity] clothing *the soul* in the unfamiliar tunic of flesh.

(Empedocles, fragment 125)

It is not possible to bring God near within reach of our eyes, nor to grasp him with our hands, by which route the broadest road of Persuasion runs into the human mind.

(Empedocles, fragment 133)

For he is not equipped with a human head on his body, nor from his back do two branches start; [he has] no feet, no weft knees, no hairy genital organs; but he is Mind, holy and ineffable, and only Mind, which darts through the whole universe with its swift thoughts.

(Empedocles, fragment 134)

God does not deal directly with man; it is by means of spirits that all the intercourse and communication of gods with men, both in waking life and in sleep, is carried on. A man who possesses skill in such matters is a spiritual man, whereas a man whose skill is confined to some trade or handicraft is an earthly creature. Spirits are many in number and of many kinds, and one of them is Love.

(*Symposium* 203a)

What earlier practices of mystery religions, chthonic ritual, or Pythagorean teachings are assembled in Diotima's discourse? (see, e.g., Frymer-Kensky vii–xi, 1–6). Is her speech a forbidden revelation, or even mockery, of the mysteries of the kind that Alcibiades was charged with conducting in private homes? What god does Diotima honor? What is its relationship to Socrates's mysterious daimon? Is it simply as a joke that Plato imports a woman as the ascetic Socrates's teacher of love? What distinguished the priest and priestess from the sophist, poet, and skilled speaker in the era spanned by Socrates and Plato? Diotima's appearance in the *Symposium* addresses all of these questions (Halperin; Nussbaum), and suggests new understandings of the range of discourses we approach as rhetoric.

In *Themis*, her study of early Greek religion, Jane Ellen Harrison comments on the shift that occurred in the meaning of the term "honor" after the Olympian gods supplanted the older Themis, Dike, and Demeter cults. "In place of his old function, his *time* [honor] his *geras*, [the Olympian god] demands a new honour, a service done to him, himself as a personality. Instead of being himself a sacrament he demands a sacrifice. This shift of meaning in *time* [honor] from function that must be performed to honour claimed marks the whole degradation of the Olympian" (467). Each speaker in the *Symposium* addresses the question of *which* god of love is to be honored: the higher or the lower, Aphrodite or Eros, Aphrodite the daughter of heaven or Aphrodite *pandemos*, the "common" Aphrodite (180d). In counterpoint to these binaries stands Diotima's integrative view of love as "begetting on a beautiful thing by means of both the body and the soul" (206b). Embodied in Diotima's name and developed in her teaching are compound questions concerning the nature of Love, the extent to which it is a divinity, and how it is to be honored. Many of her points hearken back to pre-Olympian teachings concerning the *phusis* or nature of the soul, of eros, and of logos as forever intertwined and intertwining, of discourse as love, and of lovers of discourse.

Diotima begins with the assertion that Love is a spirit (*daimon*) that moves between divine and human traits and beings, linking them through discourse and desire. Her approach is apt enough, for in several senses Love (*Philotes, Aphrodite, Eros*) was in the process of being reconceptualized in Plato's era: as a god or gods, as a group of social practices, and as an animating force in discourse. The Olympian gods, whether or not the Athenians took them seriously as divinities (Rosenmeyer; Veyne), were supplanting and diversifying qualities embodied in earlier divinities in the Greek religion of the mysteries: Themis, Dike, Gaia, and Demeter. Hera, reduced in the Olympian pantheon to a jealous wife, had earlier been an aspect of Demeter, Earth, Erde (Harrison 491; Wolf 280–83). Dike—an as yet unblinded Justice—guarded the gate leading to the underground path of insight undertaken by initiates into the mysteries; though unnamed, it is "the goddess" Themis, not Apollo, who teaches Parmenides.

Another trace of the earlier religion's conception of love, identity, and gender can be observed in *The Suppliants*. Simultaneously refusing marriage and rejecting patrimony, the Danaids claim "our Great Mother" alone as progenitrix (Aeschylus 141), a self-designation that their father accepts.

In this theological context Plato's emphasis on the accusation that Alcibiades mocked the mysteries and defaced the herms—a running allusion throughout the *Symposium*—may be viewed as more than a story of ribald roughhousing widely used to defame not only Alcibiades but Socrates as well. The herms retained meanings they had in earlier cults, where they represented epiphanic births and resurrections of "the god," usually a son of the Mother depicted emerging from beneath the earth, surrounded by an escort of attendants—the youthful *kouroi* and *kourai*. Both Herakles and Dionysus first appear in this manner and are only in later accounts of their genesis provided with fathers (see Harrison 364–415).

In explaining why we must go back to before the Olympians to understand the vestigial Greek religion drawn on in Plato's dialogues, Jane Ellen Harrison questions the vague notions of "a sense of the supernatural," or the "instinct for mystery," or the apprehension of an "unknown infinite, beyond the visible world" (488). She asserts, "The mystery, the thing greater than man, is potent, not only or chiefly because it is unintelligible and calls for explanation, not because it stimulates a baffled understanding, but because it is *felt* as an obligation. The thing greater than man [*sic*], the 'power not himself that makes righteousness,' is, in the main, not the mystery of the universe to which as yet he is not awake, but the pressure of that unknown, ever incumbent force, herd instinct, the social conscience. The mysterious dominant feature is not Physis, but Themis" (490).

Questioning the late nineteenth-century notion of Dionysian and bacchic rites as ecstatic abandon and even sanctioned violence, Harrison emphasizes the deliberation and control the mysteries exercised over different modes of consciousness and discourse. "To consult an oracle, a veritable, almost physical, *rite de passage* is indispensable" (512). The oracle's head is veiled; men put on women's clothing at puberty and during initiation rites; Socrates dons the veil to hide his head and removes it after his first speech in the *Phaedrus* (243b). Often demeaned in modern times as trivial jokes about effeminacy or transvestism, such veiling had a nontrivial and well-known function in antiquity. Harrison regards Plato's depiction of both education and philosophizing as a "rationalization of the primitive mysticism of initiation, and most of all of that profound and perennial mysticism of the central *rite de passage*, the death and the new birth, social, moral, intellectual." She notes that with no intent to conceal his borrowings, Plato slightly alters a number of terms that would be familiar to everyone from the mysteries as then practiced; Mnemosyne becomes anamnesis, *andreia* the "reborn," becomes *andros*, "manliness"; and so on for *catharsis, eklexis, anankalypsis,* and *meletan apothneskein* (513).

Another record of how the transition from chthonic Demeter cults to Olympian religion was effected resides in the many narratives relocating the old gods in terms of the new. During the spread of the Zeus cult that supplanted the older deities, the city of Aegina, for example, proudly asserted that it worshipped its native "Saviour Themis who sitteth by Zeus, God of Strangers (*Zeus Xenion*)" (519). Themis, the tacit immanence prior to all religious formulations, becomes a consort; she sits on a throne, on high, whereas in her earlier representations she had been an evocation and emanation of deeply embedded beliefs and values.

According to Alcibiades's palinode in the *Symposium*, Socrates's "music" is prose, not poetry. Socrates's teacherly rhetoric, he asserts, implants desire through an *ekstasis* parallel to that inspired by music. *Ekstasis* was the altered state undertaken by initiates under the guidance of Mnemosyne. Eleusinian initiates entered this state led by a guide, a point that Harrison emphasizes again and again by way of dispelling the denigrating portrait of bacchic rites so common in late fifth-century Greek literature, and later resuscitated in the modern Romantic period. Harrison's reading of material and textual evidence of the mysteries allows us to see the extent to which the wild bacchic Dionysian freedoms and excesses so celebrated at the turn of the century are much more a modern, postromantic, and anti-Victorian invention than a historical rediscovery. Nineteenth-century valorizations of Apollonian genius and reason quickly came to be opposed to Dionysian values and thought, culminating in the Dionysian *fin-de-siècle* revival. Although her work appeared in the 1920s, Harrison's appraisal of the then-new Apollonian-Dionysian dichotomy strikingly anticipates recent feminist appraisals of the consequences of reductive binaries, and of an oppositional sensibility more generally.

It is because religion has been regarded as a tissue of false hypotheses that it has commanded ... the animosity of the rational thinker. When the religious man, instead of being in ecstasy and sacramental communion one with the Bacchos, descends to the chill levels of intellectualism and asserts that there is an objective reality external to himself called Bacchos, then comes a parting of the ways. Still wider is the breach if he asserts that this objective reality is one with the mystery of life and also with man's last projection, his ideal of the good. (487)

In the last act of *Faust* we read, "If, Nature, I stood before you a man alone." This poses the question of projection and oppositionalism in a slightly different way; Christa Wolf asks of this ultimate separation, "Was it necessary that man should come to stand 'alone' before Nature—opposite Nature, not in it?" (Wolf 283).

Harrison's analysis of the fragmentation of earlier Greek religion and social beliefs into Olympian religion defines relationships among custom, religion, and art that further illuminate the discussions of poetry, speech, and love in the *Symposium*. Harrison postulates that the earlier religion had

> in it then two elements, social custom [*nomos*], the collective conscience, and the emphasis and representation of that collective conscience. . . . Two factors indissolubly linked: ritual, that is custom, collective action, and myth or theology, the representation of the collective emotion, the collective conscience. And—a point of supreme importance—both are incumbent, binding, and interdependent. Morality is the social conscience made imperative upon our actions, but morality unlike religion save on questions involving conduct, leaves our thoughts free. (486)

Compare Harrison's appraisal to Diotima's comments on Love and society. "Through [Love] are conveyed all divination and priestcraft concerning sacrifice and ritual and incantations, and all soothsaying and sorcery. God with man [*anthropos*] does not mingle: but the spiritual is the means of all society and converse of men with gods and of gods with men, whether waking or asleep. Whoever has skill in these affairs is a spiritual man" (*Symposium* 202d–203a). Harrison glosses, "Art, which is also, like religion, a representation of the social conscience, has no incumbencies. She imposes no obligation on either action or thought. Her goddess is Peitho, not Themis." And it is Peitho, we rhetoricians recall, Aphrodite's daughter according to Sappho, who beguiles mortal hearts with her arts of persuasion. To Harrison's analysis the rhetorical reader might add that, although "art" may have no social incumbencies, and imposes no obligation on religious or ethical grounds, the arts of persuasion and the arts of love have a multitude of affinities, a point that Diotima's speech teases out with delicacy.

Diotima's speech presents the figure of the daimon—Love—among other gods, as an intermediate spirit that moves through discourse between the divine and the human. Harrison's work allows us to observe multiple parallels between Diotima's and slightly earlier understandings of Daimon in Greek religion, because its comparative methodology integrates phenomena seldom considered in relation to one another: magic, mana, tabu, Olympic games, the drama, sacramentalism, carnivals, hero-worship, initiation, ceremonies, and the Platonic doctrine of anamnesis (544). Her assessment allows us to see the transformation of gender being effected through the replacement of the mysteries by the state Olympian cult. The death cult represented by the Olympic games in commemoration of the war dead celebrates blood not as life-giving, but as giving up life, as sacrifice. The symbolic algebra of this sacrifice is strikingly different from that of the cult in which Herakles, for example, must spend time beneath the earth with Omphale, dressed as a woman, in order to reemerge stronger into the world of men (Kintz 116–18; Wolf 269).

Harrison's student Frances Cornford opines that it is not until the late fifth century—the time of Socrates, Protagoras, and Antiphon—that the contrast between the law of Nature (*Phusis*) and human law (*Nomos*) appears, marking one of the earliest explicit recognitions in Greek tradition that social laws are not divine institutions (42; see also Fornara and Samons; Romilly). Reflecting the high premium placed on individuality and intellectual and moral autonomy that developed in late nineteenth-century scholarship (though Harrison did not adhere to it), Cornford asserts as an axiom: "In the last resort, every individual must see and judge for himself what it is good for him to do. The individual, if he is to be a complete man, must become morally autonomous, and take his own life into his own control" (46).

Contesting the view that Dionysus is the ideal mascot for individualist ethics, Harrison emphasizes that Dionysus first emerged as a symbol of collectivity, supplanting the muses and the ineffable Themis. His *thiasos*, or attending congregation, was translated into Greek drama as the chorus. Dionysus became the patron god of the arts, which had formerly been overseen by the muses, and of the wine associated with anything but self-control and moral autonomy. Harrison's reading of these representations emphasizes that, although Dionysus carries with him vestiges of older collective social and cosmological beliefs, his appearance signals the relegation of those practices to vestigial status, similar to Heraclitus's and Artistotle's denunciations of wild orgiastic bacchic women's rites. Dionysus entered Olympus as an other, as the bad boy of the bacchic cults supplanting the muses as god of poetry, which was now being firmly distinguished from both serious thought and everyday discourse—that is, from the prose rhetoric of the demos. Poetry, then, is the discourse counterpart to the lesser kinds of love that are the subject of the *Symposium* and exemplified by Alcibiades and the flute girl. Martha Nussbaum directly links Dionysus's entry into the Athenian city-state to Alcibiades: "This tough old democrat who fought at Marathon, not the refined comrade of allegedly anti-democratic intellectuals, proves . . . that he is the poet that the soul of Dionysus, god of tragic and comic poetry, desires. He will be brought back from the dead, and, together, tragedy, comedy, and Alcibiades will save Athens from the death of her freedom; also . . . from Socrates" (Nussbaum 170).

What is Diotima's relationship to Dionysus and his cult? Of what cult is she the priestess? She is "god-honoring"; he, the "god of Nyssa"—Nyssa, the legendary field in which Persephone was abducted, or, in earlier versions of the same myth, a field where Dionysus as divine son was escorted from beneath the earth (Burkert 1–21, 44; Harrison 315, 420). Socrates tells us that in his youth, Diotima was called from Mantinea to perform oracles, which for ten years kept the plague out of Athens (*Symposium* 201d). He identifies her as a "teacher of love (201d)." Yet she says to Socrates at the end of their initial dialectic, "So you see . . . you are a person who does not consider Love to be a God" (202d) and reminds Socrates that because he has not yet undergone the mysteries he is not qualified to teach. He refused to accept the earlier or "lesser" mysteries which introduced initiates into the ways of physical sexuality. This, the running joke goes, he has always declined (210ff). If to get to the higher mysteries one must pass through the lower, Socrates is doomed to failure.

The allusions to the mysteries provided in Diotima's speech have been interpreted as appropriations or transformations of earlier ritual traditions (duBois; Harrison) and seen primarily as asceticizing physical love, as affirming the ladder of ascent out of "brute" physical desire, passion, and heterosexual reproduction, transcending them (Halperin). I suggest that if the first and second portions of Diotima's speech are held in dialectical suspension, if they are taken to inform each other, her teaching may also be seen as doubling the narrative of ritual death, descent beneath the earth, and rebirth employed in the mysteries; of philosophizing that narrative so that it serves as a metaphor for both discourse and love. Love and discourse are seen as mutually intersubjective, as consubstantial; Diotima's ladder takes Socrates toward and not away from participation, substance, and the production of discourse as a medium of love, birth, and life. Within the sequence of the dialogue as a whole, the Dionysus who lurks behind the mysteries, and who in the late fifth and early fourth centuries was beginning to be widely rebuked as bacchic, is made manifest in Alcibiades, who appears drunk just after Diotima's speech (see Rosen 296–97; Nussbaum 170). The negative aspects of the Dionysian bacchic rites—Alcibiades's renowned beauty, rhetorical powers, and drunken nights, including his reputed participation in the smashing of the herms and the paradox of his drunken encomium of Socrates's teaching—all of these converge, as if to insult and perhaps even condemn Diotima's lovely and decorous teaching for being altogether too much spoken like a sophist (208) of the methodical, didactic sort, of Socrates's sort.

The placement of Diotima's speech puts it in competition with Alcibiades's discourse, both as teaching and as crafted speech. Diotima's Love is a middle state or condition and a "spirit" moving between, mediating, communicating between the divine and the human. Positing that there can be no direct human knowledge of divine love, wisdom, or beauty, Diotima defines eros—desire—as evidence of that knowledge and simultaneously as the vehicle for its communication. Inasmuch as they desire beauty and goodness, human beings should become progenitors of these qualities. In that way alone they can become the beloved of heaven (212a). Those human beings especially gifted at discourse—including none other than Socrates—are characterized as being in a middle state as well: "It is by means of spirits that all the intercourse between gods and men ... is carried on. A man who possesses skill in such matters is a spiritual man, whereas a man whose skill is confined to some trade or handicraft is an earthly creature" (203a). The passion stirred by discourse and by speakers, a related and frequent topic throughout the *Symposium*, is recapitulated in Alcibiades's tale of Socrates's astounding self-control in erotic as well as other matters, and in the praise of Socrates's speech, which is dull and homely on the surface, but, for those who listen, bears witness to the fact that a god (*daimon*) is speaking.

Madness, love, and desire permeate these distinctions, and are taken up by Diotima in her teaching on love and in her implicit rebuke of Socrates's (lover's) discourse. Diotima's speech asks: is it Love as unifying force or love as possessive desire that impels Socrates's itinerant discussions with young men and with his daimon? What god of love drives his soul toward beauty and knowledge? We are asked to consider such questions within a larger discussion in the dialogue, which scrutinizes poetic versus prose discourse, apparent versus true knowledge in rhetorical and other discourse, and surface, or apparent, beauty and goodness versus intangible beauty and goodness. Alcibiades makes a drunken appearance after Diotima's speech and then proceeds to deliver a palinode rich in praise for Socrates's thought and deceptively homely discourse. His appearance—a virtual satyr play—calls into question the literalness of Diotima's/Socrates's/Plato's allegories of ascent.

If Plato is fundamentally an ascetic idealist, he nevertheless gives the other side its due. Diotima the priestess from Mantinea enjoins Socrates to give up his treasures in heaven, his daimon lover, and to beget excellence through his talent for interlocution, an interlocution unafraid of love. If at the end of Diotima's speech, as rendered by Socrates, as rendered by Plato, we are left in a state of transcendent contemplativeness or contemplative transcendence, the beatific vision is nonetheless short-lived, brought to earth by the flute girl's song announcing Alcibiades's entrance. Diotima's lofty teaching seems reviled by Alcibiades's bawdy appearance (*Symposium* 212d–e). Diotima's ladder of ascent is knocked rudely to earth by Alcibiades's entrance—a sly reference again, perhaps, to his infamous mockery of the mysteries, and a reprise of the earlier discussions of music, poetry, love, and desire. In the portraiture of the *Symposium* Socrates and Alcibiades excel at the arts of rhetoric, and at literary and philosophical discourse as well. After Alcibiades praises the allure of Socrates's rough exterior—his prose speech—Socrates concludes the dialogue with a persistent contention that a single writer can excel at both comic and tragic poetry. Is his concluding assertion a palinode to Plato's art—a self-definition?

Considered as drama, poetry, and dialectic rather than as a competition where one view of love emerges the winner, the *Symposium* represents alternative beliefs concerning love, discourse, and procreation. The rhetoric of Plato's fiction employs the surface beauty of poetry—myth, dramatic dialogue, story, allegory—as a means for depicting how even a superficial beauty like Alicibiades was weaned by Socrates, through the arts of love and wisdom combined, to prefer the bare surfaces of the "prose" discourse that promises the unveiling of hidden truth. But what have these aspects of Plato's poetics and dramaturgics to do with Diotima and with rhetoric? Diotima chides Socrates for his abstemious or austere prose, his plain speech that promises—as a flirtation—a glimpse of hidden truth and beauty.

Diotima's discourse in the *Symposium* remains a cipher. It may be interpreted as a preservation, as an appropriation, or as a distortion of earlier Greek religion and of the discourse of women within that religion. It stands as evidence that women were remembered as teachers, and as speaking sophists. Such remembrances provide an instructive counterpoint to the attempt to denigrate the sophists for being like women (see Jarratt). Plato's representations of Diotima and Aspasia help illuminate the meaning of this double-edged sword. Diotima is indeed a teacher who speaks "like one of our best sophists" (208c): she develops views and positions in a speech; she questions traditional views; and she dissents from those who have preceded her in the dialogue. She is like a sophist in other ways as well. Her emphasis on nonpossessive love and on sustaining and practicing the visible and physical vehicles of human intercourse serve as a corrective to many readings of Plato's thought that characterize it as hyperidealist and anti-body: readings which paradoxically, and dialectically, are supported by the last half of her speech. She chides Socrates with his own tricks. Or is the joke perhaps that she, or Aspasia, was reputed to have taught him the tricks in an *ad feminam* debunking of all sophists, including Socrates? (Jarratt and Ong, this volume; Jarratt 1991). Socrates remains awake and sober at the end of the *Symposium*, still discussing literary genres. Is this a way of rejecting Diotima's teaching in order to engage in the physical realm of love, or in sleep? Or is it a fulfillment of her enjoinder to bring to birth by whatever means virtue, beauty, and truth? As in all of Plato's dialogues, the conclusion is teasingly inconclusive.

In commenting on the religion whose terms and traces linger in Diotima's teaching, Jane Ellen Harrison repeatedly urges that, if we are to look at the intellectual complexities that religion embodies and sustains, we must view it as something other than a tissue of lies. Ritual and belief, she proposes, should be examined as acts of social choice and volition and not simply as reflexes shaped by blind faith. Harrison's ghost is sighted in Woolf's *A Room of One's Own*, where "Fernham" represents Newnham, Harrison's college at Cambridge. "And then on the terrace, as if popping out to breathe the air, to glance at the garden, came a bent figure, formidable yet humble, with her great forehead and her shabby dress—could it be the famous scholar, could it be J—— H—— herself?" (17). Contested in her own time, and repudiated along with other "Cambridge ritualists" by later generations of classical scholars, Harrison is experiencing a deserved revival. She converses comfortably with current thought concerning discourse, religion, and, to borrow Kristeva's title, desire in language (Caffrey; Kintz 118–19). Compare, for example, Harrison's notion of social collectivity and Diotima's teaching on Love as a discursive daimon to an ethics based in language that Kristeva calls " 'herethics', based not on death but on undeath, or love, itself based on the inevitable intersubjectivity of discourse" (Kintz 118). What if feeling, desire, trust, love, and pity are viewed not as mute beasts but as the very animating essence of discourse, and of discourse as the essence of truth (see Kinneavy)? This is the sophist Diotima's insight into discourse, love, and intersubjectivity. In stark contrast, much Western thought since Plato has emphasized the individual over the collective, the separated autonomous agent and speaker over the common voice, the rebel without a clue.

Virginia Woolf characterizes the irreducibly collective consciousness that is given voice in art in her assertion that "masterpieces are not single and solitary births; they are the outcome of many years of thinking in common, of thinking by the body of a people, so that the experience of the mass is behind the single voice" (69). Using a similar paradigm, she enjoins her listeners to write in order to resurrect Shakespeare's sister, Woolf's fictional (or is it?) representation of all the women who died mute in the theater of a common culture that permitted only male voices to speak in and for—or against—the group. "She lives; for great poets do not die; they are continuing presences; they need only the opportunity to walk among us in the flesh. . . . For my belief is that if we live another century or so—I am talking of the common life which is the real life and not of the little separate lives which we live as individuals—. . . then the opportunity will come and the dead poet who was Shakespeare's sister will put on the body which she has so often laid down" (Woolf 118). Ruth Benedict articulated similar challenges to Western notions of individualism, to received views of the natural and proper relationship between individual and society, and to Durkheim's (and later Maslow's) notion of the autonomous or "self-actualizing" individual (Benedict 1–56). Like Harrison and Woolf, Benedict remained resolutely interested in the social construction of individualism, and in the concept of the individual as a social construct.

The lines of thinking and inquiry shared by Harrison, Benedict, and Woolf in the 1920s have been revived in the recent emphasis given to collective and collaborative thinking and writing, to women's ways of knowing, and to the diversity of voices that come to the clearinghouses of the classroom and the political arena. As was true in Plato's time, and expressing views first voiced (in writing) by him, our discussions of gender and culture and canon linger on the notion that dialogue and discourse, rhetoric and intersubjectivity, desire and language, are and yet are not the same for the one and the many. New modes evolve and emerge; some are imposed, others suppressed. The fictional and nonfictional Jane Ellen Harrison, glimpsed by the fictional and nonfictional Virginia Woolf now joins her in returning to save Athens—not from the plague as Diotima did, but from the fictionalization of women like Diotima—and to call for her return. Let us summon many Diotimas, joined perhaps by Shakespeare's sister and a Black Athena or two, to chasten the cults of heroic violence, to sustain and reclaim the common life within which any meaning and identity is formed, embodied by the discourses that have been emboldened by love.

NOTE

Early readings by Lisa Ede and Cheryl Glenn were helpful in initial revisions. For all remaining circuitousness I assume full responsibility. At many points my readings of Diotima have been informed by Martha Nussbaum's reading of the *Symposium* and *Phaedrus* in *The Fragility of Goodness*. My discussions of early Greek religion lean heavily on Jane Ellen Harrison's *Themis* and have been checked against Walter Burkert's *Ancient Mystery Cults*. I thank Pamlyn Casto for pointing out the Athenaeus passages, and credit her substantial dissertation research on reports of Aspasia in antiquity as an important source in my discussion of Aspasia. Marjorie Curry Woods referred me to the passage from Xenophon.

REFERENCES

Aeschylus. *Suppliants*. Trans. Janet Lembke. New York: Oxford UP, 1975.

Athenaeus. *Deipnosophistae*. Trans. Charles Burton Gulik. Cambridge: Harvard UP, 1960.

Benedict, Ruth. *Patterns of Culture*. Boston: Houghton Mifflin, 1989.

Biesecker, Barbara. "Coming to Terms with Recent Attempts to Write Women into the History of Rhetoric." *Philosophy and Rhetoric* 25 (1992): 140–61.

Burkert, Walter. *Ancient Mystery Cults*. Cambridge: Harvard UP, 1987.

Bynum, Caroline Walker, Stevan Harrell, and Paula Richman, eds. *Gender and Religion: On the Complexity of Symbols*. Boston: Beacon, 1986.

Caffrey, Margaret M. *Ruth Benedict, Stranger in This Land*. Austin: U of Texas P, 1989.

Cornford, Francis MacDonald. *Before and After Socrates*. 1932. New York, Cambridge UP, 1962.

Dancy, R. M. "On A History of Women Philosophers, Vol. 1" (Review). *Hypatia* 4.1 (spring 1989), 160–70.

Davidson, Thomas. *The Education of the Greek People.* New York: D. Appleton, 1907.

Davis, Elizabeth Gould. *The First Sex.* New York: G.P. Putnam's Sons, 1971.

DuBois, Page. *Sowing the Body: Psychoanalysis and Ancient Literary Representations of Women.* Chicago: U of Chicago P, 1988.

Fontenrose, Joseph. *The Delphic Oracle, Its Responses and Operations.* Berkeley: U of California P, 1978.

Fornara, Charles W., and Loren J. Samons. *Athens from Cleisthenes to Pericles.* Berkeley: U of California P, 1991.

Freeman, Kathleen, trans. *Ancilla to the Pre-Socratic Philosophers.* Cambridge: Harvard UP, 1983.

Frymer-Kensky, Tikva. *In the Wake of the Goddesses: Women, Culture, and the Biblical Transformation of Pagan Myth.* New York: Free Press, 1992.

Halperin, David M. "Why Is Diotima a Woman?" *Before Sexuality: the Construction of Erotic Experience in the Ancient World.* Ed. David M. Halperin, John Winkler, and Froma Zeitlin. Princeton: Princeton UP, 1990.

Hamilton, Walter, trans. *The Symposium.* By Plato. Baltimore: Penguin, 1959.

Harrison, Jane Ellen. *Epilegomena to the Study of Greek Religion* [1921] and *Themis, a Study of the Social Origins of Greek Religion* [2d edition, 1927]. New Hyde Park: University Books, 1966.

Jarratt, Susan C. *Rereading the Sophists: Classical Rhetoric Refigured.* Carbondale: Southern Illinois UP, 1991.

Keuls, Eva. *The Reign of the Phallus: Sexual Politics in Ancient Greece.* New York: Harper, 1985.

Kinneavy, James. *Greek Rhetorical Origins of Christian Faith.* New York: Oxford UP, 1987.

Kintz, Linda. *The Subject's Tragedy. Political Poetics, Feminist Theory, and Drama.* Ann Arbor: U of Michigan P, 1992.

Maranhão, Tullio. *Socratic Dialogue and Therapeutic Discourse.* Madison: U of Wisconsin P, 1988.

McAlister, Linda Lopez. "Some Remarks on Exploring the History of Women in Philosophy." *Hypatia* 4.1 (spring 1989).

Nussbaum, Martha. *The Fragility of Goodness.* New York: Cambridge UP, 1986.

Plato. *Lysis, Symposium, Gorgias.* Trans. W. R. M. Lamb. Cambridge: Harvard/ Loeb, 1983.

———. *Phaedrus and the Seventh and Eighth Letters.* Trans. Walter Hamilton. Harmondsworth, Eng.: Penguin, 1973.

———. *The Symposium.* Trans. Walter Hamilton. Baltimore: Penguin, 1959.

Poulakos, John, and Susan C. Jarratt. "Forum." *Rhetoric Society Quarterly* 22.2 (1992): 66–70.

Richlin, Amy, ed. *Pornography and Representation in Greece and Rome.* New York: Oxford UP, 1991.

———. "Roman Oratory, Pornography, and the Silencing of Anita Hill." *Southern California Law Review* 65 (1992): 1321.

Romilly, Jacqueline de. *The Great Sophists in Periclean Athens.* Trans. Janet Lloyd. Oxford: Clarendon, 1992.

Rosen, Stanley. *Plato's Symposium.* 2d Edition. New Haven: Yale UP, 1987.

Rosenmeyer, Thomas G. "Gorgias, Aeschylus, and Apate." *American Journal of Philology* 76.3 (1955): 225–60.

Santas, Gerasimos X. *Plato and Freud: Two Theories of Love.* New York: Basil, 1988.

Stokes, Michael C. *Plato's Socratic Conversations: Drama and Dialectic in Three Dialogues.* London: Adllone, 1987.

Thucydides, *The Peloponnesian Wars.* Trans. Thomas Hobbes. Chicago: U of Chicago P, 1989.

Veyne, Paul. *Did the Greeks Believe in Their Myths?* Trans. Paula Wissing. Chicago: U of Chicago P, 1988.

Waithe, Mary Ellen, ed. *A History of Women Philosophers.* Vol. 1: *600 b.c.–500 a.d.* Boston: Martinus, 1987.

———. "On Not Teaching the History of Philosophy." *Hypatia* 4.1 (spring 1989): 132–38.

Wender, Dorothea. "Plato: Misogynist, Phaedophile, and Feminist." *Women in the Ancient World: The Arethusa Papers.* Ed. John Perdatto and J. P. Sullivan. Albany: State U of New York P, 1984.

Wider, Kathleen. "Women Philosophers in The Ancient Greek World: Donning the Mantle." *Hypatia* 1.1 (spring 1986): 3–20.

Wolf, Christa. *Cassandra.* Trans. Jean Van Huerck. New York: Farrar, 1984.

Woolf, Virginia. *A Room of One's Own.* New York: Harcourt, 1957.

Xenophon, *Oeconomicus.* Trans. Sarah B. Pomeroy. New York: Oxford UP, 1994.

Zeitlin, Froma I. "Cultic Models of the Female: Rites of Dionysus and Demeter." *Arethusa* 15 (1982): 63–81.

4
. . . .

Reexamining
The Book of Margery Kempe:
A Rhetoric of Autobiography

Cheryl Glenn

Chaucer's Wife of Bath tells us,

> Experience though noon auctoritee
> Were in this world is right ynough for me
> To speke of wo that is in mariage.

Because she was not a churchman, she had no authority to speak of marriage or of womanhood; because she was not a flesh-and-blood woman, she could tap only fictional experience. Powerful and compelling though they may be, the Wife of Bath and her tale reflect the interest of a man, Chaucer the artist. Neither Wife nor tale is the creation of a woman, and the Wife herself wishes "By God, [that] wommen hadde writen stories" (693).

Nearly fifty years later (1432–1436), a woman wrote a story of marriage and womanhood and religion. Margery Brunham Kempe (1373– ca. 1439) of Lynn, a cosmopolitan English town then called King's Lynn, created her self and her life story with her spiritual autobiography, *The Book of Margery Kempe*. Daughter of a prominent family, wife of a less prestigious burgess, and mother of fourteen children, Margery left her relatively comfortable life to answer God's call to weep (her "gift of tears") and to pray for the souls of her fellow Christians—not in a cell or convent, but throughout England, Europe, and the Holy Land. In old age, she dictated to scribes (to one in about 1431 and to the other in

53

1436) an autobiography that recounted the trials and triumphs of her pilgrimage in the world and of the spirit.

In *Writing a Woman's Life*, Carolyn Heilbrun tells us that "power is the ability to take one's place in whatever discourse is essential to action and the right to have one's part matter" (18). In this essay, I will argue that despite her lack of formal training, Margery Kempe was a skillful and powerful rhetorician, locating herself within the particular discourse of Franciscan affective piety.[1] Within that discourse, she self-consciously created and owned the story of her life, authored her *self*, recorded her spiritual development, and, most important, validated her life and her visions to her authorial audience (the hypothetical audience for whom she designed her text).

Margery did just what the great Cistercian and Franciscan writers had directed the devout to do: she loved Jesus in his humanity, attended the Virgin, and participated with all her emotions in the joy and grief of the Christian story. Her story, then, her autobiography, needed only to be transcribed by an amanuensis. As David Aers tells us in "The Making of Margery Kempe": "She dictated what she considered the most significant experiences of her life in a work from which she hoped readers would derive 'gret solas and comfort,' witnessing the divine mercy and revelation she felt her life exemplified" (73).

A mystic[2] who communicates with God and who demonstrates typical late-medieval longing for the Passion—women mystics rallied around an all-important figure of Jesus the lover, the spouse, the teacher, the mother, but women mystics were especially attached to Jesus the sufferer—the lively and gregarious Margery opens her *Book* with the scene of her first visions, the life-threatening experience of her first childbed, the afterlife-threatening dealings with her confessor, and the appearance of Jesus:

> When this creature was twenty years of age, . . . she was married to a worshipful burgess (of Lynne) and was with child within a short time, as nature would. And after she had conceived, she was belaboured with great accesses till the child was born and then, what with the labour she had in childing, and the sickness going before, she despaired of her life, weening she might not live. And then she sent for her ghostly father, for she had a thing on her conscience which she had never shewn before that time in all her life. . . .
>
> And when she came to the point for to say that thing which she had so long concealed, her confessor was a little too hasty and began sharply to reprove her, before she had fully said her intent, and so she would no

more say for aught he might do. Anon, for the dread she had of damnation on the one side, and his sharp reproving of her on the other side, this creature went out of her mind and was wondrously vexed and laboured with spirits for half a year, eight weeks and odd days.

And in this time she saw, as she thought, devils opening their mouths all inflamed with burning waves of fire. . . . Also the devils cried upon her with great threatenings, and bade her that she should forsake Christendom, her faith, and deny her God. . . . And so she did. . . .

And when she had long been laboured in these and many other temptations, . . . Our Merciful Lord Jesus Christ, ever to be trusted, worshipped be His Name, never forsaking His servant in time of need, appeared to His creature who had forsaken Him, in the likeness of a man, most seemly, most beauteous and most amiable that ever might be seen with man's eye, clad in a mantle of purple silk, sitting upon her bedside, looking upon her with so blessed a face that she was strengthened in all her spirit, and said to her these words:—

"Daughter, why hast thou forsaken Me, and I forsook never thee?" . . . And anon this creature became calmed in her wits and reason, as well as ever she was before, . . . [and she] knew her friends and her household and all others that came to see how Our Lord Jesus Christ had wrought His grace in her. (Butler-Bowdon 1–3)

Her *Book* would lie neglected (but preserved) until 1934, when Hope Emily Allen identified and helped Sanford Brown Meech edit the unique manuscript, long the possession of the Butler-Bowdon estate (which modernized her text). And since the 1940 publication of Margery's *Book* by the Early English Text Society, this historical pilgrim has often been compared to Chaucer's Wife of Bath, her literary antecedent. It is true that both mobile, bourgeois women "hadde passed many a straunge strem" (*GenProl* 464); both travel without their spouses; both are outspoken, opinionated, and strong willed; and both speak frankly about their lives.

Margery Kempe, however, speaks to us on her own, not through a character created by Chaucer. She is the first woman to compose her life story in English, and that story is the earliest extant autobiography in English.[3] Her female literary contemporaries were mostly erudite women, writing in Latin or French under the aegis of religious orders. Her male contemporaries (Chaucer, the Gawain poet, the mystery playwrights, Malory) immediately found the support of a public audience. But Margery gave voice to a largely silent and unsung force, the voice of the uneducated woman. In what is often a moving narration, she reveals herself to be a woman who could neither read nor write, dependent upon amanuenses to record her story. In fact, the manuscript begins with the priest's incipit, recounting his tribulations in attempting to revise the previous priest's transcription of Margery's text:

> Then there was a priest for which this creature had great affection, and so she . . . brought him the [first transcription of the] book to read. The book was so "evil" written that he could discriminate little of it, for it was neither good English nor German, nor were the letters shaped nor formed as other letters were. Therefore, the priest truly believed that no man would ever read it, except by special blessing. . . . [But eventually] he read every word to this creature, she sometimes helping where there was any difficulty. (Meech and Allen 4–5; all modernizations from this edition are my own)

Naturally, any document from the Middle Ages is of historical interest, but *The Book of Margery Kempe* strikes interest above and beyond its place in that early vernacular prose and evangelical literature. Had it originally found a broad contemporary audience, the *Book* would have contributed to the widespread resumption of English as a written medium in the fifteenth century[4] and might have played some small part in the drama of the English Reformation. But for us now, the book merits our attention not only because it may be the earliest extant, large-scale narrative written in English prose (verse was, of course, another matter) but also because it introduces artistic and rhetorical techniques unprecedented in its genre. Margery Kempe's self-disclosing, candid, direct view of contemporary life gives her text a verisimilitude rarely found in devotional or soul-saving literature. No English writer up to that time had committed to writing such an intimate, revealing, and human account of life and thoughts. In *The English Mystical Tradition*, David Knowles writes that Margery "would seem to be an early, if not the first, example in English prose literature of the skilful use of dramatically appropriate dialogue based on the substantial memory of what had taken place" (144). Perhaps only a woman (untrained in and unconscious of academic rhetorical and literary practices) would assert her *self* in this way. Perhaps only a woman would have and could have "written" this earliest extant English autobiography.

Like any autobiographer, Margery was convinced that her life was special, her life story valuable to readers distant in time and space. In service of that significance, then, she had to shape the raw material of her inner and outer experience—spiritual, emotional, intellectual, and interpersonal—into a memorable narrative. And memorable it is, though it is neither predictably coherent nor conventionally chronological.

In the introduction to the modernized Butler-Bowdon edition of 1944, R. W. Chambers writes that *The Book of Margery Kempe* "may disappoint or even shock the reader" and warns us that we "must come to her not expecting too much" (xviii). He was the first of many scholars to discount her spirituality and consider her *Book* an anecdotal curiosity. One deterrent to taking her narrative seriously may have been that she begins her holy revelations postpartum, inviting many scholars to assume she was in the midst of a full-out postpartum depression. Such "hysteria" serves to remind scholars that childbirth had its origin in God's curse against Eve (Knowles 146; Chambers xv–xxvi; Meech and Allen liv, lxv; Stone 35). And scholars continue to view Margery's spirituality as hysterical. For instance, in the 1982 "Margery Kempe in Jerusalem: *Hysterica Compassio* in the Late Middle Ages," Hope Phyllis Weissman, who takes Margery seriously, nonetheless tells us that "to diagnose Margery's case as 'hysteria' need not be to trivialize her significance or reduce her *Book*'s value as cultural testimony" (202). Indeed, the *Book* provides valuable testimony to religious, cultural, commercial, and literary practices.

Like many of Margery's contemporaries, then, her future scholarly audience has often judged her and her book to be incoherent, exaggerated piety, disregarding her circumstances, motivation, and intention. But Margery's mysticism derives its impact from experience of feeling; she offers testimony, not logical proof. Her visions are in accord with the tenor of her personal faith: Jesus had singled her out among women to suffer, to preach (saving souls and improving morals), to receive his steadfast love, and to be saved.

The absence of chronology in Margery's narrative seems to render it logically incoherent, a problem that not even her second scribe could rectify, as explained in this disclaimer:

> This book is not written in order, every thing after the other as it is usually done, but like the matter came to the creature in mind when it should be written, for it was so long before it was written that she had forgotten the time and the order that things happened. And therefore she wrote nothing except what she knew for sure. (Meech and Allen 4–5)

Instead of being linear, *The Book of Margery Kempe* is cyclical and associational, but it is still a record of her spiritual development, the stages exemplified by sickness, conversion, travel, evangelism, persecution, and divine intervention. By associating her own development with incidents in Christ's life, Margery blurs the distinction between her theology and her autobiography. Her narrative is loosely organized—is akin to the homily in structure but to the sermon in theme—yet she effectively marshals the information within each true-to-life, self-contained vignette, like the best of fiction writers. She mingles homely, even commonplace events with rather self-satisfied descriptions of her great devotion, her intimacy with Jesus, and the gradual routing of those who oppose or mock her (opposition, mocking, and routing are practices consistent not only with Jesus' life but with saints' lives as well).

After Jesus's initial appearance to her, which restored her health, Margery returns to her vain, proud, and superficially religious ways. Only after two business failures is she humbled enough to turn wholly to God. The circumstances of her conversion serve as a morality tale for what Peter Rabinowitz would call her "authorial audience,"[5] for her visions led eventually to self-understanding, and to a move from fearful sinner to favorite child of God:

> When this creature had thus graciously come again to her mind, she thought that she was bound to God and that she would be His servant. Nevertheless, she would not leave her pride or her pompous array. . . . Yet she knew full well that men said of her full much villainy. . . . She had full great envy of her neighbours. . . . All her desire was to be worshipped by the people. She would not take heed of any chastisement, nor be content with the goods that God had sent her, as her husband was, but ever desired more. . . .
>
> Then for pure covetousness, and to maintain her pride, she began to brew, and was one of the greatest brewers . . . for three years or four, till she lost much money. . . . Then this creature thought how God had punished her aforetime—and she could not take heed—and now again, by the loss of her goods. Then she left and brewed no more. . . .
>
> Yet she left not the world altogether, for she now bethought herself a new housewifery. She had a horse-mill. . . . [But the hired man simply could not make either of his horses pull, so he left her service.] Anon, it was noised about the town . . . that neither man nor beast would serve the said creature. . . .
>
> Then this creature, seeing all these adversities coming on every side, thought they were the scourges of Our Lord that would chastise her for her sin. Then she asked God's mercy, and forsook her pride, her covetousness, and the desire that she had for the worship of the world, and

did great bodily penance, and began to enter the way of everlasting life as shall be told hereafter. (3–5)

"This creature," as Margery consistently styles herself,[6] projects a sense of radical dependency on God for her ongoing creation, a projection grounded in the topos of humility. Yet this devout/arrogant, humble/forceful, feverish/submissive complex Christian actually creates her self, a complicated and sometimes contradictory—"real"—self. Hence, female spirituality, selfhood, and authorship converge in her work, in a sequential narrative form that sanctions her words and actions. It is this convergence, the projected ethos that subsumes her vernacular evangelical prose, that marks Margery's contribution to rhetorical theory.

In Wayne Booth's term, Margery's "implied author," her implied version of herself, shapes the narration and selects the events to be used to present a carefully wrought ethos.[7] From the outset, the ethos Margery introduces is her only means of self-preservation, both within the written text and within the text of her life. Margery-the-actual-(flesh-and-blood)-author creates Margery-the-implied-author (a persona that dictates to the scribe), who creates Margery-the-character (this "creature"). Hence, Margery Kempe is preserved.

The historical Margery, the actual composer of the text, employs what has come to be known in theoretical circles as "dialogism," a conversation among conflicting intentions, values, claims, opinions—a conversation among her selves. Margery Kempe creates a heteroglossic self,[8] stratified by the voices of the implied author, the third-person narrator, and the character—three Margerys in all. Thus, *The Book of Margery Kempe*, presented as nonfiction, implements highly sophisticated fictional techniques: an implied author, a narrator, and the author-as-character.

What is most impressive—amazing, in fact—about this medieval fictionalized nonfiction is the double effect. Margery's use of "instabilities" and "tensions"[9] among the situations and voices in her *Book* leads to two results. First, the implied author evokes a sympathetic response in the authorial audience (those whom the author wants to read and understand her text)[10] for the historical Margery, who longs for confirmation of her mystic status. Second, the narrator (who was created by the implied author) reveals neither sympathy nor admiration for Margery-the-character, "this creature." Hence, the response to Margery by the narrative audience (readers who agree to believe the narrator and text as real) duplicates that of the characters in the story: both her narrative audience and the characters within her story (the narrative audience) find Margery's single-minded moralizing and constant interference annoying, if not harassing. Such a negative response seems perfectly reasonable given the narrative line. And the implied author, the Margery who dictates her memoirs, ultimately engineers both responses, positive and negative, to a version of her self.

The following scene between Margery and her husband exemplifies the implied author's rhetorical technique; the scene strikes a sympathetic chord in the authorial audience and dissonance in the narrative and immediate audiences. This scene also typifies the narrator's purposeful use of gossipy anecdotes and fresh dialogue, a striking effect strengthened by her natural and homely figurative language. Margery spends many years of her marriage trying to dissuade her husband from their sexual relationship, and her account of her ultimate success is engaging and homespun:

> It befell on a Friday on Midsummer Eve in right hot weather, as this creature was coming from York-ward carrying a bottle with beer in her hand, and her husband a cake in his bosom, that he asked his wife this question:—
>
> "Margery, if there came a man with a sword, who would strike off my head, unless I should commune naturally with you as I have done before, tell me on your conscience—for ye say ye will not lie—whether ye would suffer my head to be smitten off, or whether ye would suffer me to meddle with you again, as I did at one time?"
>
> "Alas, sir," said she, "why raise this matter, when we have been chaste these eight weeks?"
>
> "For I will know the truth of your heart."
>
> And then she said with great sorrow:—"Forsooth, I would rather see you being slain, than that we should turn again to our uncleanness."
>
> And he replied:—"Ye are no good wife." (Butler-Bowdon 16)

The implied author commands Margery-the-character's native tongue for use in her own self-definition and self-defense. Although the implied author is doing the commanding, ensuring that the narrator give Margery-the-character a believable "voice," the narrator is telling the story and the character is doing her own speaking. Yet all this commanding belongs to the flesh-and-blood author, the historical Margery, the artist. The rhetorical style (including tone and voice) is perfectly matched to the implied author's aim: to impress upon her readers (the authorial and narrative audiences) her chastity, a form of spiritual expression that offers psychic freedom. After all, Margery-the-character's witness to God's love (her contrition and compassion) earned her spiritual graces designed to recover and publicly validate her virginal purity, the most valuable of all God's gifts. The implied author is taking full advantage of the opportunity to justify "this creature's" behavior, re-making, re-membering, and re-creating her life to her readers, her authorial audience.[11]

Yet this created Margery seems to have no good sense of immediate audience (the other characters within her story), for her accounts are replete with her offensive behavior at home and abroad. Not having taken a vow of silence, Margery-the-character reproves even the highest church officials for what she considers moral lapses (want of moral courage or shirking responsibility).[12] She also preaches to people wherever she finds them. Her absolute certainty of her own moral and spiritual superiority, her dizzying intimacy with Jesus, her inconceivable apprenticeship as a saint, characteristics that fuse into a formidable and flamboyant self-glorification, annoy her immediate and narrative audiences. In fact, her fellow Christians taunt, harass, molest, and abandon her; she is an especially easy target for their derision for traveling without the protection of her husband.

Her incessant religious harangues, her moralizing, and her sobbing fits infuriate nearly everyone she meets, especially those on pilgrimage:

> They were most displeased because she wept so much and spoke always of the love and goodness of Our Lord, as much at the table as in other places. And therefore shamefully they reproved her, and severely chid her, and said they would not put up with her as her husband did when she was at home and in England.
>
> And she answered meekly to them:—"Our Lord, Almighty God, is as great a Lord here as in England, and as good cause have I to love Him here as there, blessed may He be."
>
> At these words, her fellowship was angrier than before, and their wrath and unkindness to this creature was a matter of great grief, for they were help right good men and she desired greatly their love, if she might have it to the pleasure of God.
>
> And then she said to one of them specially:—"Ye cause me much shame and great grievance."
>
> He answered her anon:—"I pray God that the devil's death may overcome thee soon and quickly," and many more cruel words he said to her than she could repeat. . . . They did her much shame and much reproof. . . . They cut her gown so short that it came but little beneath her

knee, and made her put on a white canvas, in the manner of a sacken apron, so that she should be held a fool and the people should not make much of her or hold her in repute. They made her sit at the table's end, below all the others, so that she ill durst speak a word.

And, notwithstanding all their malice, she was held in more worship than they were, wherever they went. (Butler-Bowdon 51–52)

In her witness to God's love, Margery-the-character's retrospective narrative answers her critics and explains apparent mistakes and incon-sistencies, but in no way does her account, especially of her degrading attire, mitigate the response of the other characters.

R. W. Chambers's observation can be seen to illustrate Margery's rhetorical purposefulness as she creates herself as a character:

Things might have been easier for Margery, if she had been a recluse [an anchorite or nun]. At large in the world, people found her a nuisance. In a cell, where people could come and speak to her when they wished, and depart when they liked, Margery would have fitted better into me-dieval life. But that she should wander about, rehearsing tales of scrip-ture, was felt to be irregular. (xix)

For instance, when her visions transport her to the scene of Jesus's interment,[13] Margery treats the mournful Blessed Mother as though she were just another Christian to be helped, giving Mary unsolicited care and advice:

Then the creature thought, when Our Lady was come home and was laid down on a bed, that she made for Our Lady a good caudle [a warm, medicinal beverage], and brought it her to comfort her, and then Our Lady said unto her:—

"Take it away, daughter. Give me no food, but mine own Child." The creature answered:—

"Ah! Blessed Lady, ye must needs comfort yourself and cease of your sorrowing." (Butler-Bowdon 178)

But such behavior—appreciated or not—establishes Margery-the-character's ethos; she wants to present herself and be recognized as a religious woman, one singled out above all other humans, to be saved at once (without the pains of Purgatory). J. H. Leuba explains her attitude:

Certain aspects of the behavior of the great mystics, especially their profession of humility and obedience and their apparent readiness to suffer
anything, however offensive, has led to an altogether wrong interpretation of their character. They have been assimilated with the humble and
purposeless. This is a misunderstanding; they are, on the contrary, determined not only to be worthwhile but also to be recognized as such;
they will not tolerate the "inferiority complex." Their light shall not shine
under a bushel. They show the firmest purpose and accept no influence
that does not lead where they want to go. (120–21)

Far from being an incoherent hysteric, Margery-the-implied-author
is, instead, a careful artist, fashioning a character who behaves consistently within a well-established social and spiritual context.

In addition to her good works and witnessing, Margery-the-character
is also intensely concerned with her weeping fits and her clothes (an
interest that makes the sacken apron episode even more humiliating).
All these concerns emerge as a feature of female authorial consciousness. The implied author determines what best reflects Margery-the-
character's ethos[14] in terms of her successful evangelizing. In the Holy
Land, Margery receives her "gift of tears"—a gift of the spirit that is not
always comfortable or convenient. Margery copiously manifests her gift
of tears every day for ten years and at less frequent intervals over an
additional fifteen, whenever reminded of Jesus or the Passion. The implied author skillfully creates a devout weeping spell in such a way that
the authorial audience sympathizes with Margery, delights in her eccen-
tricity, all the while understanding why Margery-the-character vexes the
characters within the immediate audience:

On the Purification Day, or otherwise Candlemas Day, when the said
creature beheld the people with their candles in church, her mind was
ravished into beholding Our Lady offering her Blissful Son to the
priest. . . . She was then so comforted by the contemplation in her soul,
that she . . . might full evil bear up her own candle to the priest, . . . but
went wavering on each side like a drunken woman, weeping and sobbing
so sore, that scarcely could she stand on her feet, for the fervour of love
and devotion that God put into her soul through high contemplation.

And sometimes she could not stand, but fell down among the people
and cried full loud, so that many men wondered and marvelled what ailed
her; for the fervour of the spirit was so great that the body failed, and
might not endure it. (Butler-Bowdon 181–82)

Margery's "gift of tears" was a physical token of her special sanctity, akin to Saint Francis's gift of the stigmata. Thus, Franciscan ethos and pathos color her dramatic piety, her love of God, in an unqualified, unconditional, and fearless manner.

Although Margery-the-flesh-and-blood-author, Margery-the-implied-author, and Margery-the-character all wanted to live chastely with her husband, Margery was, indeed, a married woman. Her decision to dress as the bride of Christ, completely in white wool, and to wear a gold ring engraved *Iesu est amor meus* was an effrontery to the townspeople, her immediate audience. White clothes could indicate either chaste living or salvation without time in Purgatory,[15] and Margery wore them for both reasons. The townspeople, however, were offended by her attire, and instead of accepting her sainthood, they often accused her of being a hypocrite. In Lambeth, for instance, a townswoman came forward to curse Margery: "I would bring a faggot to burn thee with. It is a pity thou art alive" (Butler-Bowdon 28). Since Margery had a newborn son and a living husband, her behavior was considered anomalous, if not scandalous.

Several passages underscore Margery's recurring concern for her attire as a reflection of her spiritual status. In the following passage, she has just been abandoned by her irritated fellow pilgrims, who refuse to travel with this overbearing evangelist; providentially, Jesus appears to the frightened Margery with advice:

> "Dread thee not, daughter, for I will provide for thee right well, and bring thee in safety to Rome and home again into England without any villainy to thy body, if thou wilt be clad in white clothes, and wear them as I said to thee whilst thou were in England."
>
> Then this creature, being in great grief and distress, answered Him in her mind:—"If Thou be the spirit of God that speaketh in my soul, and I may prove Thee for a true spirit with the counsel of the Church, I shall obey Thy will; and if Thou bringest me to Rome in safety, I shall wear white clothes, though all the world should wonder at me, for Thy love." (Butler-Bowdon 64)

Although the authorial audience can be amused or even impressed by Margery's willingness to bargain with Jesus with regard to her costume, rarely does her narrative support her spiritual confidence, her self-proclaimed holiness, or her costumes, nor does her immediate audience appreciate them. In the opening chapters, the young, proud, attention-seeking Margery dresses in the gayest new fashion for the sole purpose of outshining the other merchants' wives.

And she knows full well that men said of her much villainy, for she wore gold pipes on her head, and her hoods, with the tippets, were slashed. Her cloaks were also slashed and laid with divers colours between the slashes, so that they should be the more staring to men's sight, and herself the more worshipped. (Butler-Bowdon 3)

Throughout her life, Margery-the-character offends many people with her choice of dress, a physical expression of her ethos: before her conversion, she is garishly stylish; after her conversion, she wears the powerfully symbolic white; and finally, when her white attire becomes too controversial, she resorts to the safer black. When a German priest commands her to wear black, she feels "that she pleased God with her obedience" (Butler-Bowdon 73). Margery-the-character's costume changes thus reflect her spiritual condition.

The immediate audience's reaction to Margery-the-character is most often perplexity and exasperation, depending on her behavior (leaving her husband and children for pilgrimage, insisting the pilgrimage conversation be limited to her pontification). Occasionally, this audience appreciates her "good works," her nursing and serving the poor and the sick, or her counseling the bereaved and insane. At the same time, the authorial audience, in response to the author's artistic design and intentions, consistently delights in the antics of Margery presented by the narrator and told by the implied author, and applauds her decisions. The authorial audience fully understands the negative reactions of the characters in the text, yet remains sympathetic to Margery-the-implied-author. This rhetorical technique of using a double ethos, one for the implied author and another for the character, is a major contribution to rhetorical theory—Margery Kempe's unique contribution.

Margery Kempe is one of the most important Englishwomen to participate in the medieval rhetorical tradition, although the rhetorical (male) tradition necessarily inscribes her *out*. She is not so much practicing rhetoric in its traditional sense as inscribing it in a *different* way. Although never before recognized by rhetorical scholars for their contributions to rhetoric, Margery's fifteenth-century writings have rightfully enjoyed special attention from scholars of other stripes who have been attracted to her ability to elaborate with considerable sophistication her theological convictions and practices. Margery Kempe represents a unique strain in the most important literary activity by women in the Middle Ages: the flowering of religious writing into the writing and dictation of mystical treatises. Our medieval literary foremothers, such as

Julian of Norwich, Hildegard von Bingen, and Margery, participated in the Continental mystic tradition, beginning with after-illness visions. This tradition of dramatic piety was able to provide women a socially accept-able and respected medium of religious expression and personal asser-tion, especially if they were attached to religious orders and thus edu-cated in the intellectual tradition. Julian and Hildegard are regarded as valid mystics because they belong to this world of confined, virginal, and intellectual religious experience. A bourgeois laywoman, wife, and mother like Margery simply could not meet the traditional requirements of mysticism.

Mystics in any period, however, are vulnerable to charges of heresy and disobedience, because their direct communication with God by-passes the services and sacraments of the Church. Margery was espe-cially vulnerable, not only because she was an outspoken woman and layperson without formal education, but also because she lived at a time of serious disruption in the Church at home and on the Continent. As Despres tells us:

> Her spiritual independence in seeking the difficult balance between the active and contemplative lives . . . baffled her contemporaries and caused many to question her orthodoxy. . . . Both men and women remarked with hostility on the impropriety of Margery's wandering, as well as the presumptuousness of her teaching. A frustrated intolerance surfaced most frequently in the attitudes of her tormentors. Unable to "define" Margery's behavior by placing her in those roles appropriate for either religious women or laywomen, her contemporaries felt threatened by her. (87)

But we must understand that Margery's teaching, her blending of personal and scriptural history, was Franciscan in spirit and orthodox in its origins, and that her visions gave her a *public* language and a visible office in the world, despite her position as a woman.

The works of the female mystics[16] spoke to religious communities and struck a chord in the developing popular piety, a piety seeking emo-tional and rational stimulation. Moreover, these works were accessible to the populace: works such as Margery's were generally written in the vernacular, and these writings were akin to the sermon, the central dra-matic participatory event in Christian corporate life. The themes, struc-ture, and didactic purpose of sermons would have been readily familiar to Margery, for the Church was her primary source of lifelong teaching and comfort, a basic constituent of her worldly as well as "ghostly" (i.e., spiritual) life, and an essential framework for her calling. But most important, the Church provided Margery with the language and with the opportunity to use it.

The fragmented nature of her autobiography may, indeed, demonstrate her ambiguous role as an effective Christian and layperson—especially in a society where her gender deprived her of the authority to teach or preach. But this fragmented story anticipates the conclusion of recent scholars: women's autobiographies tend to be less linear, unified, and chronological than men's autobiographies.[17] Women's autobiographies are often novelistic, women's novels autobiographical. And because of the continual crossing of self and other, the continual conversation among the voices, women's writings often blur the line between public and private—just as Margery's writing does. Margery's autobiography, her rhetoric, inscribes feminine conversation rather than masculine dialectic.

Although presented as nonfiction, Margery's account implements highly sophisticated fictional techniques, in addition to dialogism. Hers is the timeless, quintessential woman's story of irreducible and irreconcilable gendered-language limitations. Yet, in other ways, her story is a morality tale about asserting those language differences and seeking appropriate—though nontraditional and, hence, "feminine"—forms of fulfillment. Psychologist Carol Gilligan tells us that women often speak "in a different voice," one concerned with creating and sustaining human connections (167–68). The conversational quality of Margery's discourse depends on such connections: her discourse relies on others to come into existence, whether those *others* are scribes or those to whom she testifies.

Margery Kempe insisted on being recognized—and heard. Although she lacked the necessary language skills for writing her own story and had no guarantee that her story would ever reach an audience, this religious mystic was, nonetheless, determined to tell that story. She used her "inner voice" for knowing and then turned to so-called correct or public voices for composing and speaking. And in Margery's case, as in the case of so many other women, the same mind can live in several voices.

This first English autobiographer provides us with a powerful example of successful double-voiced discourse, articulating her private, disenfranchised experience through the public discourse of religion. It is an inherently interesting text that is also a resounding response to religious instruction. Yet most remarkable of all is Margery Kempe's ability to introduce and balance a double ethos: she faithfully presents the annoying Margery character, but at the same time, she writes the life of the implied author with a disarming and utterly convincing sincerity. *The Book of Margery Kempe* not only redefines the rhetorical tradition to include such female works but also constitutes an innovative example of purposeful and persuasive feminine inscription.

NOTES

1. In "Franciscan Spirituality: Vision and the Authority of the Scripture," Denise Louise Despres writes, "The Franciscans encouraged the laity to meditate freely on the Gospels and to use their imaginations. They instructed penitents to mesh individual history with the sacred history of the Scripture, for only by experiencing life with Christ could the sinful fully understand the sympathy Christ had for the human condition, and the nature of the supreme sacrifice he willingly chose with love" (3).

Franciscan affective piety, then, emphasized fellowship with Jesus and individual participation, the distinctive elements being penitence, participation, and responsibility for the welfare of one's own soul. Despite twentieth-century suspicion with regard to Margery's spirituality, she was practicing within an established and respected fifteenth-century tradition of affective piety.

2. Mysticism is, among other things, an intellectual tradition that seeks to demonstrate the mind's kinship with spiritual realities; therefore the mystic's path did not exist separate and apart from the rest of life in the Middle Ages. In "Medieval Women Visionaries: Seven Stages to Power," Elizabeth Petroff writes that the medieval woman mystic

> was representative of a sizeable group of medieval women [e.g., St. Brigid of Sweden (d. 1373), St. Catherine of Siena (d. 1380), St. Katherine of Sweden (d. 1391), Bl. Dorothea of Prussia (d. 1394), St. Frances of Rome (d. 1440)] with religious vocations, for whom their fantasies—their visions—were the signal to others that they were women of power. Visions were the necessary credentials for a medieval woman whose abilities and strengths demanded that she take an active role in the larger world. . . . Her power was used to improve the human condition and to encourage others in their paths of selfhood and union with the divine. (n.p., quoted in Lagorio 162)

Mysticism was not separate from medieval society and culture, but rather functioned effectively within them.

3. The first woman to write about herself (though she did not write her own life story) seems to have been anchoress and mystic Julian of Norwich (1343–1415), who also dictated to a scribe her *Revelations to Divine Love*, sometimes referred to as her *Book of Showings*. Dame Julian was a spectacular exception to the truth that Englishwomen in general did not write books.

4. According to Paul Szarmach, the writings of the women mystics play their part in the late medieval process commonly called "the triumph of the vernacular," the growing use of the vernacular as a medium not only to "translate" the ideas of thinkers and scholars for the people but also to compose original works (14). Dame Julian and Margery were both from the Norfolk area, a region that seems to have led the way in the civic revival of English, having abandoned the official use of Latin and French.

5. In "Truth in Fiction: A Reexamination of Audiences," Rabinowitz deftly categorizes three kinds of audiences: (1) the *actual audience* or flesh-and-blood people who read the text; (2) the *authorial audience* or the hypothetical audience for whom the author designs the text; and (3) the *narrative audience* or the person each flesh-and-blood reader must pretend to be in order to believe the text is real and to respond appropriately to the narrator. The author has no guaranteed control over the *actual audience*.

6. Margery's consistent reference to herself as "this creature" is probably in deference to her Creator—a fairly common medieval usage. However, "this creature" also serves to remind us that the illiterate Margery didn't actually write the book herself, that she was in constant collaboration with her scribes: she told her story to men who then wrote about her. By conflating autobiography with biography, she moves easily from author to character.

7. In *The Rhetoric of Fiction*, Booth explains the "implied author" in these terms (this was before he adopted nonsexist language):

> As he writes, [the author] creates not only an ideal, impersonal "man in general," but an implied version of "himself" that is different than the implied authors we meet in other men's works. To some . . . it has seemed, indeed, that they were discovering or creating themselves as they wrote. . . . [And] it is clear that the picture the reader gets of this presence is one of the author's more important effects. . . . Our reactions to his various commitments, secret or overt, will help determine our response to the work. . . .
>
> The "implied author" chooses, consciously or unconsciously, what we read; we infer him as an ideal, literary, created version of the real man; he is the sum of his own choices. (71, 74–75)

8. The *heteroglossic self* is Bahktin's term for one who has incorporated another's speech in another language. Heteroglossia serves to express authorial intentions but in a refracted way, usually through an author's character.

9. In *Reading People, Reading Plots*, James Phelan explains the dynamics of narrative progression in terms of "instabilities" and "tensions," terms with Burkean resonances. Kenneth Burke tells us that form in literature is "an arousing and fulfillment of desires" (124) and that form is " 'correct' in so far as it gratifies the needs it creates" (138). Phelan builds on that notion, explaining that narrative movement is shaped by "instabilities between characters (which are) created by situations, and complicated and resolved through actions" and by "tensions" among values, beliefs, opinions, knowledge, and expectations within the discourse itself (15). Phelan uses "instabilities" to designate unstable relations within the story and "tensions" to designate those in discourse. The *Book of Margery Kempe* manifests both.

10. The authorial audience is, of course, made up of flesh-and-blood readers, the actual audience; however, not every reader will want to be able to join the author's hypothetical audience.

11. In his introduction to the Butler-Bowdon edition, R. W. Chambers tells us that the novelty of Margery's book lies in the fact that we are not dealing with the revelations of a recluse, but rather with the life of a religious enthusiast remaining in the world. Thus, the interest of her book is twofold—Margery herself, and her relations to her contemporaries (xix).

12. It is important to note that although these same Church officials may have questioned her behavior, none of them refuted her doctrine or denied her persistent petitions. She was eventually granted clerical permission to live apart from her husband, wear white clothes, go on pilgrimage, and receive weekly communion; in other words, to live the life God commanded and that she wanted for herself.

13. Franciscan participatory meditation requires the penitent to envision or re-create scriptural events. These consciously embellished scenes, then, are a source of solace and affirmation.

14. And always in the balance is the relationship of the implied author's ethos to the ethos of Margery-the-character.

15. As Margery "lay in contemplation for weeping," Jesus came to her and said: "I have promised thee that thou shouldst have no other Purgatory than the slander and speech of the world" (Butler-Bowden 41).

16. Julian's *Revelations of Divine Love* and Hildegard's *Know the Ways* and *Book of Divine Works* were some of the best-known works of this kind.

17. Consider the autobiographical works of Adrienne Rich, Mary McCarthy, Maxine Hong Kingston, and Carolyn Heilbrun.

REFERENCES

Aers, David. "The Making of Margery Kempe: Individual and Community." *Community, Gender, and Individual Identity: English Writing 1360–1430*. London: Routledge, 1988. 73–116.

Bakhtin, M. M. *The Dialogic Imagination*. Ed. Michael Holquist. Trans. Caryl Emerson and Michael Holquist. Austin: U of Texas P, 1981.

Booth, Wayne C. *The Rhetoric of Fiction*. 2d ed. Chicago: U of Chicago P, 1961.

Burke, Kenneth. *Counter-Statement*. Berkeley: U of California P, 1931.

Butler-Bowdon, W., ed. *The Book of Margery Kempe*. New York: Devin-Adair, 1944.

Chambers, R. W. Introduction. In Butler-Bowdon, xv–xxiii.

Chaucer, Geoffrey. *Canterbury Tales: The Complete Poetry and Prose of Geoffrey Chaucer*. Ed. John H. Fisher. New York: Holt, 1977.

Despres, Denise Louise. "Franciscan Spirituality: Vision and the Authority of Scripture." Diss. Indiana U, 1985.

Gilligan, Carol. *In a Different Voice*. Cambridge: Harvard UP, 1982.

Heilbrun, Carolyn G. *Writing a Woman's Life*. New York: Norton, 1988.

Knowles, David. *The English Mystical Tradition*. London: Burns, 1961.

Lagorio, Valerie M. "The Medieval Continental Women Mystics: An Introduction." In Szarmach, 161–93.

Leuba, J. H. *The Psychology of Religious Mysticism*. London: Kegan Paul, 1925.

Meech, Sanford Brown, and Hope Emily Allen, eds. *The Book of Margery Kempe*. Early English Text Society, 212. London: Oxford UP, 1940.

Petroff, Elizabeth. "Medieval Women Visionaries: Seven Stages to Power." *Frontiers* 3 (1978): 34–45.

Phelan, James. *Reading People, Reading Plots*. Chicago: U of Chicago P, 1989.

Rabinowitz, Peter. "Truth in Fiction: A Reexamination of Audiences." *Critical Inquiry* 4 (1977): 121–41.

Stone, Robert Karl. *Middle English Prose Style*. The Hague: Mouton, 1970.

Szarmach, Paul, ed. *An Introduction to the Medieval Mystics of Europe*. Albany: State U of New York P, 1984.

Weissman, Hope Phyllis. "Margery Kempe in Jerusalem: *Hysterica Compassio* in the Late Middle Ages." *Acts of Interpretation: The Text in its Contexts, 700–1600: Essays on Medieval and Renaissance Literature*. Ed. Mary J. Carruthers and Elizabeth D. Kirk. Norman, OK: Pilgrim, 1982. 201–17.

5

Christine de Pisan and *The Treasure of the City of Ladies*: A Medieval Rhetorician and Her Rhetoric

Jenny R. Redfern

May all the feminine college and their devout community be apprised of the sermons and lessons of wisdom. First of all to the queens, princesses and great ladies, and then on down the social scale we will chant our doctrine to the other ladies and maidens and all classes of women, so that the syllabus of our school may be valued.
—*Prologue to* The Treasure of The City of Ladies *(1405)*

Almost five hundred years ago, Christine de Pisan addressed the "community" of women in medieval society on matters of honor and persuasive discourse. Her stated objective was to instruct them in the means of achieving virtue. Her lessons and vignettes, she believed, would demonstrate the humility, diligence, and moral rectitude of which all women were capable. Duly educated, Christine's "feminine college" would become worthy residents of the glorious City of Ladies, her allegorical refuge for women whose good lives refuted stereotypes of weakness and immorality (*Book*). The vehicle for her address is *The Treasure of the City of Ladies* (hereafter referred to as *The Treasure*), a syllabus that derived its power from her own experience. Christine's life was a model for the strategy and mother-wit that women needed to navigate the perils of a society often hostile to their gender.

A rhetoric for women and a literary artifact of early fifteenth-century France, *The Treasure* reflects both the late medieval and early Renaissance characteristics of that transitional period. For example, in the first portion of *The Treasure*, Christine draws on Augustine and various other saints for advice on how the noble lady may achieve a love of God; this strategy echoes the style and concern of medieval scholastics. Yet she also refers to Seneca's advice to speak kindly to one's subjects, an indication that she and her audience were reawakening to classical humanist ideas (*Treasure* 48–49). On one level, *The Treasure* belongs to the genre of didactic works, which advised the medieval woman on her obligations as daughter and wife. On another, however, it encourages the development of individual women's minds. It thus breaks with medieval scholasticism by promoting the Renaissance acquisition of secular knowledge as well as divine grace and also by promoting such activity for women.

The Treasure of the City of Ladies merits inspection by anyone looking for evidence of women's lost rhetoric. Within carefully ordered chapters, Christine instructs the "feminine college" in the lessons they must follow to achieve both the good life and the good afterlife. She speaks through the allegorical figures of God's daughters—Reason, Rectitude, and Justice—who represent the Three Virtues most important to women's success. Through the secular examples of these Virtues, Christine directs all women to discover meaning and achieve worthy acts in their lives. Invested with the Virtues' divine authority, Christine continues the work she began in *The Book of the City of Ladies*, in which she and the Virtues constructed an imaginary city from the biographies of virtuous women. Her objective was to counteract the slander of the female sex so prominent in texts of the time. *The Treasure* prepares women of the age for residence in this sanctuary. By legitimizing women's words, Christine's advice affirms women's worthiness in an androcentric world. Although she neither calls herself a rhetorician nor calls *The Treasure* a rhetoric, her instruction has the potential to empower women's speech acts in both public and private matters. Her most important lesson is that women's success depends on their ability to manage and mediate by speaking and writing effectively.

I

Christine de Pisan's prolific poetry and prose, forty-one known pieces written over a career of at least thirty years (1399–1429), earned her fame as Europe's first professional woman writer. During her lifetime, Christine achieved such credibility as an author that royalty commissioned her prose and intellectual contemporaries copied her manuscripts into their libraries. After her death (ca. 1430) and during the bloom of the Renaissance, many authors acknowledged her intellectual influence and borrowed from her work (Yenal). Her writings remained popular, and eighteen manuscript editions of *The Book of the Three Virtues,* or *The Treasure of the City of Ladies,* still exist (Willard, "Three Virtues").[1] Portuguese and Dutch editions of *The Treasure* date from the fifteenth century, and French copies were still being printed in 1536. Its precursor, *The Book of the City of Ladies,* was translated into English in 1520 and published in English by H. Pepwell in 1521 (Willard, "Three Virtues").

On the whole, Christine's work struck a responsive chord in a culture beginning to rediscover the value of classical philosophy and humanistic ideals. Her outspoken defense of women, however, was an anomaly in its time. Although it fascinates modern feminists, Christine was not an advocate of change in the social and gender hierarchies. Rather, Christine's vindication of womanhood derived from her personal struggle to avoid the penury of widowhood. Her activism resulted from her literary self-education, part of her effort to prepare for a legitimate trade. In that pursuit, her encounters with popular misogynist texts—Ovid's *Art of Love,* Jean de Meun's *Romance of the Rose,* and particularly Matheolus's *Lamentations*—drove her first to despair of both womankind and her own femininity:

> All philosophers and poets and . . . orators . . . concur in one conclusion: that the behavior of women is inclined to and full of every vice. . . . I could hardly find a book on morals where, even before I had read it in its entirety, I did not find . . . certain sections attacking women, no matter who the author was. . . . And I finally decided that God formed a vile creature when He made woman. . . . Great unhappiness and sadness welled up in my heart, for I detested myself and the entire feminine sex, as though we were monstrosities in nature. (*Book* 4–5)

As long as she accepted the "authorities'" perverted sense of the feminine, she was unable to help herself.

Soon, though, her "great love of investigating the truth through long and continual study" impelled her to speak out about "those outrageous villains who have assailed [women] with various weapons" (*Book* 10). Her readings of ancient history and her commonsense grasp of women's worth informed her arguments; in fact, Christine had earlier entered the debate on courtly love as a female rhetor on behalf of women (Ward). Some popular works (such as Boccaccio's *De claris mulieribus*) sketched the lives of both mythical and historical heroines, and her family's association with the French nobility had acquainted her with several strong female figures. These resources gave her the materials with which to publicly refute woman-hating stories. As a result of her enculturation, Christine did not argue for equality with men, but rather for increased respect for the image of womanhood and for individual women within the existing social order.

As she explains in part of *The Vision of Christine* (1405), the profession of public didact and rhetor did not occur naturally to this woman, who had been taught to be only an obedient wife and mother. Born in Venice in 1364, Christine was the daughter of Tommaso di Benvenuto da Pizzano (Thomas de Pisan), a physician, professor of astrology, and Councillor of the Republic of Venice. Her mother, whose own name is never mentioned, was the daughter of Tommaso Mondini of Forli, and married Pizzano after he had studied with her father at the University of Bologna. Not long after Christine's birth, Thomas de Pisan accepted an appointment to the court of Charles V of France, as the king's astrologer, alchemist, and physician, disciplines commonly allied during the Middle Ages.

Christine benefited from her father's extensive education and intellectual connections. Although she would later complain in *The Changes of Fortune* (1400–1403) that her education was limited by custom, the autobiographical passages in *The Vision of Christine* indicate that she enjoyed leisurely reading and wished she had more time to read and write. Indeed, literacy had become more common in the Middle Ages than is generally recognized (Stock). Letters and autobiographies from as early as the eleventh century document that wives carried on extensive correspondence with Crusader husbands, while tradeswomen kept records of both business and private matters (Beard 248–54). Christine lived among the intellectual elite, and the open atmosphere of Charles V's court acquainted her with the rediscovered classics and humanism of the early Renaissance. She would fulfill her intellectual curiosity and claim her authority as a writer, however, only after she had been widowed as a young woman.

When she was fifteen, Christine's parents married her to Etienne du Castel, a royal secretary to the court. At that time court clerks and secretaries were exposed to the forefront of knowledge, educated in rhetoric and philosophy, exposed to the newest ideas, and entrusted with state and diplomatic correspondence. Christine was already literate in French and Italian, and it is likely that she learned Latin and some skills in copying texts during her husband's tenure. Later, these abilities, augmented by the new intellectual climate, would literally save her from poverty.

Christine's marriage turned out to be affectionate and secure. With both her husband and her father well employed in the King's service, her family faced a prosperous future. Soon after the de Pisan-du Castel alliance, however, Charles V died and with the change in monarchy de Pisan's and du Castel's positions and salaries were reduced. Within a few years, both men died, leaving Christine as a grieving twenty-five-year-old woman, with three children, a niece, and her mother to support. She had no means of income and faced complicated lawsuits to recover salary due her husband.

In the autobiographical portion of her ballad *The Changes of Fortune* (1400–1403), Christine regarded this period as the turning point in her life, saying that her happiness and good fortune ended with her husband's death. In retrospect, she warned other widows of the unfair treatment awaiting them as socially disadvantaged women. Her *Vision of Christine* (1405) reveals that she, who had been "nurtured on the finer things of life," was completely unprepared to work to support her household (Petroff 338). She turned to a scholarly life of study and writing, partly because no other means of livelihood seemed open to her, partly because studying the classics consoled her grief, and partly because she had always wanted to be a scholar like her father and husband, but had not had the opportunity. As she explained it, "I had been naturally since birth inclined to study, [but] family affairs common to married folk took me away from such pursuits, and also the frequent bearing and care of children" (Petroff 338). Christine's connections to the French court probably gave her access to the royal library, to which Charles V had added vernacular translations of classical Greek and Latin texts on rhetoric and philosophy. Her self-education thus included history, science, and poetry from Greek and Roman authors as well as from contemporaries such as Dante and Boccaccio.

By 1393, five years after her husband's death, Christine was writing love ballads, which caught the attention of wealthy patrons. She was encouraged to write more and sell her work:

I made [the French nobility] a present of my new volumes; . . . they saw willingly and accepted with great pleasure. And the more I held to my unaccustomed image of a woman of letters, the more esteem came and with it, dignity, so that, within a short time, my said books were discussed and circulated in various parts and countries.(Petroff 339)

By the end of the century, she was a popular author. By 1405, she had written "fifteen principal volumes, not counting other small ditties, which together fill about fifty quires of large format" (*Treasure* 19).

II

Christine's growth as a rhetorician may have begun with the realization that her gender would cause her authority as a writer of serious prose to be called into question. Certainly she struggled to develop a style and ethos that would support a strong female perspective. Christine broke with the tradition of presenting learned texts in Latin, a language that for hundreds of years had been taught solely to men and that only unusually privileged women could read (Ong 113). Although her often prolix syntax mimics the multiple subordinate clauses of clerical Latin, most of her work is in the vernacular of the French court (Curnow 254).

Moveover, her lengthy allegorical poem, *Road of Long Study* (1402–1403), shows her stylistic debt to Dante. In his *Inferno*, Dante had credited his "long study" of Virgil for his decision to use the vernacular (*Book* xliii). Christine followed this lead, combining periodic Latinate syntax with French words and neologisms. By selecting the stylistic features she admired most from both classical and early Renaissance humanist authors, she created a unique vehicle for her lessons in morality and persuasion.

By the time Christine began to work on *The Book of the City of Ladies* and *The Treasure*, her self-perception and projected ethos had changed. Looking back on her early bereavement as the beginning of a new life, Christine asserted that at first she succeeded only because allegorical Fortune turned her into a man at the time of her loss, so that she would have the strength to fend for herself:

Then my mistress (Fortune) came toward me,
Who takes joy from many.
And touched me all over my body.

I felt changed all over.
My limbs were much stronger than before,
Which felt strange,
And the crying had stopped.
I felt most astonished.

And my appearance was changed and strengthened,
And my voice become deeper,
And my body, harder and more agile.
But the ring that Hymen had given me
Fell from my finger,

Which troubled me, as indeed it should
For I loved it dearly.

Now I will prove that
I became a real man.

                    (Le livre, in Bornstein 12–13)

Such a visionary narrative represented the deliberate creation of a self that could cope with unanticipated crises, something that the real Christine had not been taught to do (Petroff 22). Her imagined transformation is both sexual and emotional, suggesting the uncommon strength required of her for survival. Viewed in retrospect, this imputed gender transformation was a major step toward developing her authority as a teacher and rhetorician.

Christine's portrayal of herself with stereotypical masculine traits also had a cultural, and somewhat prophetic, grounding. In the early fifth century, for example, Martianus Cappella's *Book of Rhetoric,* contained within *The Marriage of Mercury and Philology,* personified rhetoric as a powerful woman, carrying weapons and clothed in armor, "the very image of Jupiter, able herself to hurl his thunderbolts" (in Miller, Prosser, and Benson 3). This image of Rhetorica as a strong, armed woman was a familiar motif in medieval illustrations (Vickers 11).[2] In contrast, conventional medieval attitudes about women usually attributed the expected feminine qualities of tenderness, mercy, and compassion only to the Virgin Mary. Contemporary women were considered weak and less resilient than men, a characterization that Christine de Pisan used to an extent in her own early love ballads. By comparison, writers who praised a woman's strength usually credited her with some male qualities while ignoring the stereotyped feminine traits of frailty, lack of resolve, and inconsistency (Shahar 169). When she claimed that Fortune had made her a man, Christine used such characterizations to her advantage. Her "change" allowed her to move toward a womanliness that would be acceptable to both female and male audiences. Then, when she felt comfortable enough to claim that women could speak authoritatively for their own gender, she gave allegorical woman-figures the same strengths as men. In each case, Christine claimed a privileged vantage point in her analysis of women's roles in their own society.

Christine's skillful use of persuasion and style derived both from her study of the classical philosophers, rhetoricians, and poets, and from her familiarity with medieval rules for eloquence. In her own writing, she occasionally referred to rhetoricians and to rhetorical eloquence as a goal of the accomplished speaker and writer. Sometimes these references allowed her to present herself as a legitimate participant in literary discourse. At other times, she mentioned rhetoric in artful apologias, denying her own eloquence while preparing to verbally demolish her opponent. In 1401, for example, de Pisan responds to Jean de Montreuil, who had written her a treatise defending the misogynist sentiments expressed in *The Romance of the Rose*. She begins by referring to her correspondent as an "expert in rhetoric" as compared to herself, "a woman ignorant of subtle understanding and agile sentiment" (Petroff 340). She goes on to thank him for his "small treatise composed in fine rhetoric and convincing arguments," a distinction that suggests she saw rhetoric as ornamentation and as separate from persuasive argument (Petroff 341). She continues her apologia, belittling her own style as not having a pleasing arrangement and ornamentation, the marks of good rhetoric:

> And however much I do not possess great knowledge nor am I schooled in the use of subtle styles of language (from which I might know how to arrange words pleasingly and in polished style and order to make my ideas shine forth), I will not allow to be said in any way whatsoever a vulgar opinion of my understanding, merely because I do not know how to express it in ornate well-ordered words. (Petroff 345)

Obviously, the elaborate apologia is itself an example of the rhetorical strategy she claims not to possess. By writing against the grain of her meaning, Christine uses the rhetorical figure of antiphrasis, a term she defines later through the voice of the Virtue Reason in the opening chapter of *The Book of The City of Ladies* (7).

Christine demonstrated that she was an accomplished rhetorician, and was determined to capture her audience's attention and exercise the art of persuasion she had taught herself. In both *The Book of the City of Ladies* and *The Treasure*, her presentation of three allegorical women is similar to Boethius's rhetorical use of Lady Philosophy in his *Consolation*. The three Virtues allow Christine to display her facility with reasoned argument and her familiarity with both the classics and scriptural teachings. Through Reason, she displays her knowledge of Plato, Aristotle, and Augustine and her facility with logical persuasion (*Book* 7). Through Rectitude, Christine exhorts honorable women "to say and uphold the truth" (*Book* 12). When she wants to rebut a common proverb that women should not speak or preach in public, Christine is reassured by Reason that "God endowed women with the faculty of speech" in complete good faith, so that even the news of Christ's resurrection could be carried by a woman (*Book* 28). When she wants to demonstrate the bias against women in classical literature, she cites Virgil as "more praiseworthy" than Ovid or Cato, who attack the character of all women (*Book* 24–25). In *The Treasure*, she refers to Seneca (49), and to Solomon's proverb on the persistent effect of good rhetoric, quoting "Proverbs in the twenty-fifth chapter: 'By long forebearing is a prince persuaded, and a soft tongue breaketh the bone' " (*Treasure* 51).

More important than Christine's familiarity with classic lessons on rhetoric, however, is her use of the allegorical Virtues to establish an authoritative feminine ethos. Her synthesis of experience and study had brought her to the conclusion that common stereotypes would not permit perception of women as credible sources of philosophy or social commentary. Her arguments on behalf of women might be discredited because of her sex. She had already risked such dismissal with her open attack on a popular ballad, *The Romance of the Rose*. Christine was the only woman who publicly and formally argued against the immorality popularized by *The Romance*. Her fame grew as she energetically defended women's integrity, which she believed was maligned by this allegory of courtly love. *The Romance*, begun around 1230 by Guillaume de Lorris and finished by Jean de Meun around 1280, had great appeal in the Middle Ages. Its theme was the seduction of a lady—represented as a jealously guarded prize rose—by her lover. The poem defends three principles of courtly love much admired in medieval literature, even if they were not practical forces in people's lives: that love is a wonderful kind of suffering; that the lover's virtue increases through his devotion to the woman; and that love cannot exist between husband and wife because of the forceful nature of the marriage contract. Theologians and intellectuals debated *The Romance*'s promotion of questionable attitudes on love, morals, and women. In 1401, Christine argued that the allegory subverted public morality, extolled carnal acts, and incited licentious conduct, all the while purveying false notions of the true feminine character (Kelly 12).

She was supported by Jean Gerson, the chancellor of the University of Paris, against her main adversaries, Jean de Montreuil and the brothers Gontier and Pierre Col.[3] Although *The Romance* remained popular, the public nature of the dispute yielded positive results for her career as a writer. First, it motivated her to refute other abusive, male-dominated literary treatments of women. Second, it established Christine's reputation as a female intellectual, a well-educated, outspoken woman who could argue effectively and defend her positions. And finally, it pointed to her character and credibility as a rhetor, important progress in the development of her ethos.

Participation in the debate developed Christine's self-confidence as an authoritative rhetor, to the point that she could argue with aplomb from a woman's perspective. Thus, she drew on Lady Reason as the source of logical argument in both of her influential treatises, *The City* and *The Treasure*. In *The City*, her description of Lady Reason reveals the persona of a woman who commands respect:

> The famous lady spoke these words to me, in whose presence I do not know which one of my senses was more overwhelmed: my hearing from having listened to such worthy words or my sight from having seen her radiant beauty, her attire, her reverent comportment, and her most honored countenance. . . . She had so fierce a visage that whoever, no matter how daring, looked in her eyes would be afraid to commit a crime, for it seemed that she threatened criminals unceasingly. (8)

Here Christine was ready to rebut the "outrageous villains," and she no longer needed to rely on adopted male strength to do so. Instead, her feminine alter egos, the Ladies Reason, Rectitude, and Justice, would carry the arguments for their own gender.

These Ladies first appear to Christine as champions of womanly virtue. They lift her from despair over the misogyny of her times and set her to work on behalf of all women. As previously mentioned, Christine's rhetorical motivation for *The Book of the City of Ladies* and *The Treasure of the City of Ladies* derived in part from a chance reading of *The Lamentations of Matheolus* (ca. 1300). In his *Lamentations*, Matheolus describes in unsavory detail the wrongs that he believes women are guilty of perpetrating on men. In *The City*, Christine remembers that she had no desire to finish reading the harangue, but its subject matter continued to haunt her: here was yet another author who could write nothing but wicked and slanderous things about the general character and virtue of women. Was it possible that woman had been created as a creature of less worth than man?

In response to Christine's despair, three crowned women appear before her and announce themselves as God's daughters. This constitutes the first chapter of *The City* (6–14). Their holy parentage and calm reasonableness present a feminine ethos of unquestionable authority. Through their voices, Christine can present what she sees as theological confirmation of women's virtue as well as affirmation of her own literary authority. Together, she and the Virtues create a forum to speak on issues of consequence to all women.

In *The City*'s catalog of biographies, Christine affirms women's worth and selfhood within the rhetorical framework of the Three Virtues' answers to her questions. The epideictic effect of praising notable women imitates other medieval treatises written for women's edification, such as Boccaccio's *De claris mulieribus* (1355–1359) and Jean Le Fevre de Ressons's 1371 *Livre de Leesce* (Curnow 126–27). Christine's text differs from these in that its movement between question and answer is presented from a completely female perspective. Only female voices, examples, and opinions provide evidence. Logical progression from one example to the next permits Christine to establish truths about women that contradict the negative stereotypes, or "stones," which she has identified in literature and popular myth. Each didactic story also represents a building block. The Virtues direct Christine's construction of a walled city of words into which they will invite all honorable women, to protect them from unjust verbal attack. Every stone she digs up and discards undermines another slander against women; every block of granite that she places on the walls reconstructs a story of virtuous feminine behavior.

In *The Treasure*, Christine de Pisan turns her attention from the persuasiveness of *The City*'s role models to the persuasive effect of women's speech and action in contemporary life. In each chapter of *The Treasure*, Christine's advice reflects her concern about the inseparability of women's private and public lives. The medieval lifestyle of family-centered politics and commerce took precedence over notions of personal and family privacy. Particularly for women of the nobility and the upper social strata, the actions and speech of private life were never far removed from public discourse and intercourse. Castles and manors were both homes and public meeting places. The "princesses, empresses, queens, duchesses, and high-born ladies" to whom Christine dedicated Book 1 of *The Treasure* were constantly in the public eye. Their marriages, childbirths, and deaths were as interwoven with politics as were their fathers' and husbands' declarations of war and peace (Beard 240–41). Given this reality, *The Treasure*'s lessons in self-discipline and chastity were indeed prudent rather than priggish, as a modern audience might think. A princess's governance of her own behavior had more than personal consequences. If she did not defend her chastity before marriage and her honor afterward, her family could suffer politically, socially, and financially.

Christine de Pisan's dedication of *The Treasure* to Marguerite of Burgundy, then, evidences precisely such a concern for a young woman's vulnerable sexuality and potential influence. In 1404, the child's marriage to the Dauphin, Louis of Guyenne, was a political coup arranged by her father, John the Fearless (Willard, "Feminine" 99). It is not clear whether the father commissioned *The Treasure* to guide his daughter through the moral and political perils of the French court or whether Christine wrote it to educate Marguerite in particular and socially active women in general. Either way, the book's preoccupation with chastity and honor, spotless behavior and reasoned speech, reflects very real concern for women forced to live their private lives in public.

The Treasure's lecturing of women on such matters is not an extraordinary feature of the text, since other authors, including Boccaccio and the author of *Le Livre*, had also written treatises on the proper moral education of women. Instead, the most noteworthy feature of *The Treasure*'s rhetoric is its authoritative female voice. The first nine chapters of Book 1 of *The Treasure* acknowledge the Church's power by speaking through daughters of a male deity, but these Virtues are informed by women's experience in medieval life and theology. When they warn the unnamed princess of the consequences of sloth, pride, avarice, and anger, they address her as "a simple little woman who has no strength, power or authority unless it is conferred on [her] by someone else" (43). This is not said as an insult, but rather as a protofeminist warning for the princess to understand the social infrastructure of her own life before attempting to influence it.

The Three Virtues—Reason, Rectitude, and Justice—focus the Platonic concern for the otherworldly in the first nine chapters in Book 1 of *The Treasure*. The princess is admonished to avoid the deadly sins, in part because it is a reasonable, right, and just way to live in the here and now, but especially because a woman's first concern must be to "account to God, for her life in comparison to the life everlasting is only a short time" (47). This preparation for the path to heaven was probably a genuine reflection of Christine's training and faith, and a reflection of the fact that medieval life could be brutally short. Threatened by war, plague, and septic childbirth, even a noblewoman had to be prepared to face death at any time.

The Virtues divide *The Treasure* into three major sections of advice, according with Christine's perceptions of three major divisions in the social hierarchy. Book 1 is addressed to princesses and other women of the nobility; Book 2 advises the women who serve those in Book 1; and Book 3 addresses every other sort of woman—wives of merchants, artisans, and laborers; widows, who are advised to remain single if they wish to regain control over their lives; young and old women; servants; virgins; prostitutes; peasants; and the poorest beggar. Book 1 is the longest of the three, not only because Christine believes that noblewomen have the most complex positions and responsibilities, but also because much of the same advice will apply to women in the other books (145).

In Book 1, Christine's directions for accomplishing good works in the active life include models of effective speech with which the good woman can achieve humility and charity, which are steps to the pious life:

> The princess will . . . speak softly . . . greeting everyone with lowered eyes. She will greet people in words so humane and so sweet that they may be agreeable both to God and to the world; . . . charity . . . is not to be understood as helping another person only with money from your purse, but also with help and comfort by your speech and advice wherever the need arises. (47)

Her directions for sweet reasonableness may seem excessive to modern audiences, but they were subtle exercises in achieving control over potentially volatile social situations. Once Christine has "sufficiently described the teachings that the love and fear of God" give her noble audience in Book 1, her rhetoric turns to practical matters (55). She instructs all women in the means of determining the best course of action in the medieval mix of private and political life. At this point the worldly subordinates the eternal, and Reason, Rectitude, and Justice surrender the podium to a more earthly apparition, Worldly Prudence. Here Christine anthropomorphizes other virtues to teach feminine morality, and has Worldly Prudence introduce Sobriety and Chastity, the restraints a woman must exercise to achieve honor. Prudence, Sobriety, and Chastity form a solemn triumvirate, complementing the other trio of virtues. Christine's choice of earnest, temperate representatives is characteristic of a rhetoric anchored in logos and ethos, rationality and good character. Certainly appeals to her audience's feelings, an element of pathos, would also have been persuasive. But she was mindful that her detractors, ever ready to accuse women of unreliable emotionalism, could turn that mode of argument against her.

A review of Christine's rhetorical lessons shows that while she maintained and advised an ethos of calm reasonableness for all audiences, she also balanced deliberative rhetoric, the art of decision making, with the epideictic, the art of praising and blaming (Aristotle 32).[4] When making the argument that women must recognize and promote their own value, she credits women with the vital skill of peacemaking, a skill she believes men lack due to their hotheadedness. She persistently repeats that noblewomen should strive to achieve and maintain peace within marriage. Also, they need skills in forensic rhetoric for those times when they would speak on behalf of their absent husbands:

> And so this lady will be . . . an advocate and mediator between the prince her husband (or her child if she is a widow) and her people. . . . The good princess will never refuse to speak to [her husband's plaintiffs], nor will she make a great show of keeping them waiting. . . . She will reply wisely and suitably with the help of the good advice of [her advisors]; she will excuse her husband and speak well of him. (49)

The same skill in discourse would allow a wife to mediate between her husband and subjects: "She will speak to her husband well and wisely, calling in other wise persons if necessary, and will very humbly petition him on behalf of the people. She will show the reasons, which she will understand thoroughly" (80).

These passages exemplify the overlap of private and public concerns that characterized medieval life. Christine knew from experience that domestic and civil tranquillity were joint enterprises.

She also recognized that women had always carried the burden of war's devastation, and she implied that rhetoric would be a better means of settling differences:

> She will urge the people, her husband and his council to consider this matter carefully before undertaking [war], in view of the evil which could result from it. . . . It would be much better to think of some more suitable way to reach agreement. . . . In connection with this, Solomon says in proverbs in the twenty-fifth chapter: "By long forbearing is a prince persuaded, and a soft tongue breaketh the bone." (51)

This is a powerful argument for persuasion by means of rhetoric rather than direct force. Writ small, it appears in Christine's advice to the new widow that she "will refrain from using hot and hasty words to anyone, but she will protect her rights; she will state her case or have it stated courteously to everyone." Again, in Book 3, when she advises the "wise lady or housewife" that if her husband is "bad or quarrelsome, she ought to appease him as much as she can by soothing words." Men are not directly the objects of Christine's advice, but they are told that "some of them need it if they would be well instructed. . . . There are many men who are so churlish and so ignorant that they do not know how to see or recognize goodness and common sense" (80). Her instruction shows little patience for men who fail to recognize the value of their wives' competence and eloquence.

Several times in *The Treasure*, Christine relies on rhetorical questions to show women the truth of a given situation and to lead them through lessons on morality. Early in Book 1, she assumes an unusual vernacular voice by using the persona of Christ to speak "home truths" to the princess, helping her negotiate the path to the well-lived life:

> Oh poor woman, do you want to sink into such damnation and lose by your folly the grace that God promises you if you try to deserve it by only a little effort? . . . Which [path] will you take? (42)

Of course the answer is supposed to be self-evident—no woman of honor would deliberately risk eternal damnation. In another instance, Christine's instruction has the practical quality of an inner conversation, a whispering conscience:

> And what things therefore are more suitable to perfect one's honor? In truth they are good manners and behavior. And what is the use of these good manners and behavior? They perfect the noble person and cause her to be well regarded. (55)

It is conceivable that such short dialogues were intended to be repeated and memorized by very young women such as Marguerite of Burgundy.

Once Christine has established that skill in discourse should be part of every woman's moral repertoire, she directs women to concern themselves more with speaking the truth than with persuasive eloquence. Sobriety begins by setting the parameters:

> Sobriety will so correct, chastise and control the mouth and the speech
> of the wise lady, whom she will keep principally from talking too much
> (which is a most unseemly thing in a noble lady, or in any women of
> quality), that she will hate with all her heart the vice of lying. She will
> love truth. . . . This virtue of truth is more becoming in the mouth of a
> prince and of a princess than in that of other people because it is right
> that everyone should believe them. Sobriety will prevent her from saying
> any word, especially in a place where it could be passed on and reported,
> that she has not well examined. Prudence and Sobriety will teach the
> lady to have controlled speech and sensible eloquence, neither too sol-
> emn nor too frivolous. (57)

This instruction privileges the ethical practice of speech over personal
assertiveness. If her words are not to place her in jeopardy, then a noblewoman's speech must be as spotless as her reputation. Christine proceeds with examples of occasions for prudent speech, each with its element of rhetorical strategy: "No dispute will be conducted [at the dinner
table]. . . . She will speak to [dinner guests] in a thoughtful manner, with
a pleasant expression; to the elderly people in a more serious manner,
to the young people in a different and merrier one" (61).

In general, the strategy is to speak the truth yet bend to the occasion,
rather than resist openly when no advantage can be gained. The possibility of compromise and peace always should be kept open. This advice
pertains to intimate relations, too:

> She will be overjoyed to see [her husband], and when she is with him
> she will try hard to say everything that ought to please him, and she will
> keep a happy expression on her face. . . . She will speak well of [her in-
> laws] and praise them. She will not allow herself to be drawn into ar-
> guments. (62–65)

These passages would surely help a teenager such as Marguerite negotiate life with her in-laws, particularly when she is bound to them by
political arrangements more than by genuine affection.

The possibility that Christine de Pisan might have written *The Treasure* as a guide for a young princess bride in maintaining her honor in
morally perilous surroundings is supported by the content and tone of
chapters 23 through 26, which close Book 1. These sections are directed
to women who must serve as chaperons to young noblewomen. Here
Christine demonstrates that, even in roles subordinate to men's, women
could increase their strength and influence by attending carefully to the

cause, appearance, and consequence of each interactive behavior, especially when speaking and writing. She expresses as much concern for the chaperon's sense of duty as for the young woman's honor, because the chaperon is held responsible for the other woman's speech and conduct. This scenario reveals the complex relationships between women as well as between women and men, and suggests that the community of women had much to gain by supporting one another in difficult situations. For example, if the chaperon notices that a knight, squire, or "certain" type of man persists in making overtures to her young charge, the older woman should draw him aside discreetly and say: "Without making you a very long sermon about this or going on at too great a length, I tell you quite briefly and once and for all, that so long as I am living and in her company, this young lady . . . will do no wrong" (91).

If the young lady in question behaves with "bad judgment" and continues a flirtation, Prudence advises the chaperon to leave her service with a carefully worded resignation, so that the lady's tainted reputation will not rub off on the chaperon. If she has left the young lady's service but still cares about both reputations, the chaperon may express her concern in a carefully worded letter, which should be delivered to its subject by a priest.

This insertion of an act of literacy into a text that otherwise deals with orality is carefully planned. By committing herself to writing, the chaperon establishes distance between herself, the knower, and the lady's act of dishonor, the known, thereby increasing her objectivity in the situation, and relieving her of responsibility for the affair (Ong 114). On the one hand, the cautionary letter that Christine dictates through Prudence is a deeply felt expression of concern for another woman's religious, moral, and physical well-being. On the other hand, it is offered as a pragmatic method for a servant to extract herself from potentially damaging circumstances.

Christine offers her analysis of the rhetorical significance of sending such a message by letter. She predicts specifically that the chaperon "will be compelled by great love to write to [her mistress] and recapitulate the warnings that she used to give her in case she might be able to benefit her after all, because what is written down is sometimes better remembered and penetrates the heart more than what is said orally" (*Treasure* 99).

Christine must truly have believed in the persuasive value of such a written plea, since she had previously included the same lengthy missive in her romantic poem *The Duke of True Lovers* (1401–1405). The letter resembles a condensation of *The Treasure*'s advice, admonishing the married princess to "surpass all other ladies in good prudence" and to forsake "empty pleasure" (*Treasure* 99–100). As a written record of discourse, its length and the relative permanence of its medium suggest that it would be the record of note if the chaperon's motive and objectivity were to be questioned. If intimate advice can have consequences equal to those of a public declamation, then both require documentation. In Christine's time, what began as the ancient Greek tradition of oral persuasion on public issues had been transformed to sets of rules for, among other purposes, the conduct of private correspondence. Indeed, this letter proceeds in the textbook fashion of the *ars dictaminis*, with an ornate salutation and securing of good will, followed by sections of narration, petition, and conclusion: a complete piece of formulaic rhetoric (Murphy 3–4).

The chaperon's last warning to her former charge reminds the girl of the potential for consequences in a public figure's private behavior: "Thus the lady cannot blink, say a word, laugh or make a sign to anyone without everything being noticed and remembered by many people and then reported in various places" (*Treasure* 106).

Thus, Christine's authority, amplified through Prudence and the familiar persona of the chaperon, instructs women to attend to all discourse, whether casual, deliberate, oral, visual, or written.

Books 2 and 3 of *The Treasure* contain more examples of practical applications of rhetoric to common needs: widows must be able to defend their legal rights in court; an upper-class woman must know the right things to say so that lower-class visitors will feel comfortable in her home; all women must be able to keep secrets for one another; housewives must manage with calm speech both quarrelsome servants and husbands; wives of merchants must know how to conduct business in their husbands' absence; and both the very old and very young women must find the right words to bridge the generations. *The Treasure*'s historical context and pedagogical intent allowed Christine de Pisan to develop a woman's guide to the use of rhetoric and to defend women's intrinsic worth. She presented her female audience with models of successful rhetoric and with herself as the model rhetor (Willard, "Feminine" 113).[5]

Christine de Pisan wanted women to gain eloquence, but she also wanted them to gain skill with the persuasive discourse that could shape private and public affairs. As she concludes *The Treasure*, Christine expresses confidence that her directions will affect women's lives: "This work will not remain useless and forgotten. It will endure in many copies all over the world without falling into disuse, and many valiant ladies and women of authority will see and hear it now and in time to come" (180).

Christine directed women to speak and write for the good of society, and to affirm the best of themselves and their accomplishments in the world. The very fact that manuscripts of *The Treasure* are still being studied helps to keep alive the tradition of women as rhetors and rhetoricians.

NOTES

Jenny R. Redfern thanks husband Bob and son Jerry for their emotional support, and especially thanks daughter Joanna for her companionship and understanding during the two years when a dead French author competed for her mother's attention. Cheers, Jenny.

1. MS 1528 is preserved in the Boston Public Library, a 1405 copy from the Paris atelier where the "Christine Master" worked.

2. The plate is from *Die Tarocchi: Zwei italienische Kupferstichfolgen aus dem XV Jahrhundert* (Berlin: Cassirer, 1910). It may have been created by the painter Mantegna. The image of a strong, beautiful, armed woman can be compared to the image of the Queen of Wands in the tarot deck.

3. In a letter to Jean de Montreuil, provost of Lille, Christine writes: "As I am indeed a woman, I can bear better witness to the truth than those who have no experience of the state, but only speak through supposition or in general terms" (Willard, "Franco" 333–36).

4. Christine certainly passes judgment on behavior that might jeopardize a woman's virtue (see *Treasure* 112 and 154, for example), but she does not suggest that women may participate in the judicial rhetoric of ecclesiastical or civil courts.

5. The Renaissance idea that texts could advise in the development of the model citizen or the perfect prince are also reflected in other works by Christine, such as *Epitre d'Othea*, *Livre du corps de policie*, and *Faits et bonnes meurs de Charles V.*

REFERENCES

Aristotle. *Rhetoric*. 335–322 B.C.E. Trans. W. Rhys Roberts. In *The Rhetoric and Poetics of Aristotle*. New York: Modern Library, 1984.

Beard, Mary. *Woman as Force in History*. New York: Macmillan, 1946.

Boccaccio. *De claris mulieribus*. 1355–1359. Ed. and trans. Guido Buarino. New Brunswick: Rutgers UP, 1963.

Bornstein, Diane, ed. *Ideals for Women in the Words of Christine de Pisan*. Detroit: Published for Michigan Consortium for Medieval and Early Modern Studies, Distributed by Fifteenth-Century Symposium, 1974.

Capella, Martianus. "The Book of Rhetoric." *De nuptiis Philologiae et Mercurii, V*, (410–429) Trans. Joseph M. Miller. In J. M. Miller, M. H. Prosser, and T.

W. Benson, eds., *Readings in Medieval Rhetoric*. Bloomington: Indiana UP, 1973.

Curnow, M. C. *The "Livre de la cite des dames" of Christine de Pisan: A Critical Edition*. Nashville: Diss. Vanderbilt U, 1975.

De Pisan, Christine. *The Book of the City of Ladies*. 1401. Trans. Earl Jeffrey Edwards. New York: Persea, 1982.

———. *Lavision-Christine*. 1405. Trans. Nadia Margolis. In Elizabeth Petroff, *Medieval Women's Visionary Literature*. New York: Oxford UP, 1986. 513–56.

———. *Le livre de la mutacion de fortune*. 1400–1403. Ed. Suzanne Solente. Paris: SATF, 1959. Trans. D. Bornstein. "Self-Consciousness and Self Concepts in the Work of Christine de Pisan." In *Ideals for Women in the Writings of Christine de Pisan*. Ed. D. Bornstein. Albany: State U of New York P, 1974.

———. *The Treasure of the City of Ladies: or, The Book of the Three Virtues*. Trans. Sarah Lawson. Harmondsworth: Penguin, 1985.

Kelly, Joan. "Early Feminist Theory and the Querelle des Femmes, 1400–1789." *Signs* 8.1 (1982).

Ong, Walter J. *Orality and Literacy: The Technologizing of the Word*. New York: Methuen, 1982.

Petroff, Elizabeth Alvilda. *The Visionary Tradition in Medieval Women's Writings: Dialogue and Autobiography*. New York: Oxford UP, 1986.

Shahar, Shulamith. *The Fourth Estate*. Trans. Chaya Galai. New York: Methuen, 1983.

Stock, Brian. *Listening for the Text*. Baltimore: Johns Hopkins UP, 1990.

Vickers, Brian, ed. *Rhetoric Revalued*. Binghamton: State U of New York P, 1982.

Ward, Charles Frederick. *The Epistles on the Romance of the Rose and Other Documents in the Debate: A Dissertation*. Chicago: The U of Chicago P, 1911.

Willard, Charity Cannon. "A Fifteenth-Century View of Women's Role in Medieval Society." *Ideals for Women in the Works of Christine de Pisan*. Ed. Diane Bornstein. Detroit: Published for Michigan Consortium for Medieval and Early Modern Studies, Distributed by Fifteenth-Century Symposium, 1981. 91–116.

———. "The 'Three Virtues' of Christine de Pisan." *Journal of the History of Ideas* 27.3 (1966): 433–44.

Wilson, Katarina M., ed. *Medieval Women Writers*. Athens: U of Georgia P, 1984.

Yenal, Edith. *Christine de Pisan: A Bibliography of Writings by Her and About Her*. Metuchen: Scarecrow, 1982.

6

Mary Astell: Reclaiming Rhetorica in the Seventeenth Century

Christine Mason Sutherland

Mary Astell has been celebrated as one of the earliest English feminists. Certainly in her own day she was well known and highly regarded. Yet, like many other women who made their mark upon their own times, she was almost completely forgotten after her death. George Ballard, it is true, published a short account of her life in *Memoirs of Several Ladies of Great Britain Who Have Been Celebrated for Their Writings or Skill in the Learned Languages, Arts and Sciences* (1752), but thereafter little was written about her until this century, when first Florence Smith and then, much later, Ruth Perry brought her to the attention of feminist scholars.

In recent years, and especially since the publication of Ruth Perry's biography of her (1986), the importance of Mary Astell to the development of the struggle for women's education has been increasingly recognized; but from a rhetorician's point of view, the most interesting aspect of her work is her mastery of the art of eloquence, and her bold invasion of the masculine stronghold of traditional rhetoric. Both as a practitioner and as a defender of the ability of women to participate in rhetorical activities, Mary Astell may be said to have "reclaimed Rhetorica" in her own day. I begin this paper with a brief survey of Astell's life and works; this is necessary because she is still not as well known as she ought to be. I then argue her claim to be recognized as contributing to the rhetorical tradition.

Mary Astell was born in 1666 in Newcastle. The Astells were gentry: minor gentry, perhaps, but they were armigerous. Although a cousin of Mary Astell's owned an estate, the family based its fortunes not in the land but in the professions. Astell's ancestors were lawyers and preachers, even soldiers. Originally the family came to prominence as a result of military success in the Hundred Years War (Perry 29).

Astell's father was an official in the coal industry. If this suggests the contamination of trade, later so deplored by the English middle classes, we must bear in mind that the coal industry in Newcastle at this time was dignified by its association with an ancient medieval trade guild, the Hostmen, who were, to quote Ruth Perry, "the official hosts of feudal Newcastle" (29). The Astells were in no way representative of new money, often considered at the time to be "vulgar." In their own way, they were part of a privileged class, with rights and traditions going far back into English history. Certainly they prided themselves on belonging to the gentry. Mary Astell's father and grandfather were firm supporters of the Stuarts, conservative in their political and religious affiliation, Anglicans in the tradition of Laud, and unafraid of the sympathy the later Stuart kings showed toward Roman Catholics.

Mary Astell, then, was brought up as a gentlewoman. She had one brother, Peter, whose education was assumed by their uncle, Ralph Astell, an Anglican priest at the church of St. Nicholas nearby. In spite of his alcoholic tendencies, Ralph Astell seems to have been an admirable man. It may have been from him that Astell derived her unusual degree of piety. Certainly she received much of her education from him, for Ralph Astell educated her along with her brother. Unfortunately, Ralph Astell died when Mary was only thirteen, and her formal education was cut short at this point. During his few years as her teacher, her uncle seems to have taught her not only to read and write but also, more unusually, to value the life of the mind and take an interest in the political, religious, and intellectual issues of the day.

Mary Astell's early years were probably happy. Her parents, though not particularly rich, were reasonably well-to-do, and she grew up with the advantage of a comfortable home. All this changed within a relatively short time. First, her father died. It then became apparent that his financial position was insecure. Newer interests were challenging the supremacy of the Hostmen, and Peter Astell did not leave his family well provided for. Any money that there was had to be set aside for the education of young Peter, Mary's brother. There was nothing left over to provide an adequate dowry for her. Soon after the death of her father, her formal education came to an end with the death of her uncle. She continued to live with her mother and her aunt—two other Mary Astells—until their deaths. But as time went by, and the financial position of the Astells did not improve, it became more and more apparent that the world had no place for young Mary. A young girl of her class was, of course, expected to marry—provided she had a dowry. Mary Astell had none. Some few dowerless girls might make a good marriage if they were exceptionally attractive; the evidence suggests that Mary Astell was not, though admittedly the only extant account of her appearance is derived from someone who did not know her when she was young. It comes from the granddaughter of her friend Lady Mary Wortley Montagu. Lady Mary did not meet Astell until Astell herself was in middle age. She found her "rather ill-favoured and forbidding, and as far from 'fair and elegant' as any old schoolmaster of her time" (Perry 23). This description might, of course, refer rather to her typical manner and expression than to her features; nonetheless, it seems that even in girlhood Astell would not have been pretty enough to attract a husband in her dowerless condition, certainly not one from her own class. She might possibly have married beneath her, though it is clear that such a course would have been repugnant to her; and it is unlikely that any man below her own class would have wished to marry so dauntingly intelligent a woman as Mary Astell.

If she could not marry, what could she do? Had she not been a gentlewoman, she might have found some kind of menial work, however disagreeable; but her class precluded any such solution to her problem. Had she been a man, she could have turned her intelligence and her learning to good account. These, combined with her piety, would have made a career in the Church a real possibility. But this solution was not open to her because of her sex. It is true that during the Interregnum there had been numerous women preachers, but they had certainly not been Anglicans, and they had been firmly repressed by the Restoration government.

It is not surprising that for some time after the death of her mother, Mary Astell was in a state of extreme depression: the world seemed to have no use for her. The only advantages she had—her extraordinary intelligence and her capacity for strenuous intellectual activity—were ones that her society would not let her use.

Nevertheless, she decided to try. In 1688, she moved to London to seek her fortune in the emerging world of letters of the late seventeenth century. Predictably, she had no success. She appears to have counted on help from distant relations and friends of the family, but if they helped her at all, their assistance had dried up by the end of her first year. In desperation, she approached William Sancroft, archbishop of Canterbury, who was known for his generosity. She compares herself to the steward in the gospel: "Worke I cannot, and to beg I am ashamed" (Perry 66). It is characteristic of Astell's wit that she compares herself with the *unjust* steward: no doubt Sancroft appreciated the joke. Certainly he helped her. As an expression of gratitude, she sent him some of her own poems, stitched into a book. She describes it as "but of Goats' hair and Badger skins" (Perry 401) but explains that it is all that she has to give— another little theological joke, for it was of goats' hair and badgers' skins that the Holy Tabernacle of the Israelites was partly made.

Eventually, with the help of Sancroft, Mary Astell established herself: she was introduced to a bookseller, Rich Wilkin, who greatly admired her work and strenuously promoted it. She also found friends among the intellectual women of London—friends who were able not only to appreciate and encourage her but also to help her financially. Like many another writer, she found a patron, Lady Elizabeth Hastings. Among her other friends were Lady Catherine Jones, with whom she lived for some time, and Lady Mary Wortley Montagu.

From the early 1690s until 1709, Mary Astell published a number of books and pamphlets, and became celebrated as a woman of eloquence and learning. She published no new works after 1709, though she revised some of her early works. Most of her time seems to have been spent promoting the education of girls—a cause very close to her heart. She was involved in the foundation of a charity school for girls in Chelsea, where she lived. For the last twenty years of her life, Mary Astell lived more privately. But it was a life of great usefulness and piety, and it seems she was happy among her circle of friends. Nevertheless, death, when it came, was not unwelcome to her. She contracted breast cancer, and the tumor eventually had to be removed—too late, as it turned out. She died less than two months later. She faced her end with great courage— even with eagerness. She had her coffin brought into her bedroom, and for the last two days refused food, drink, and company. She died on May 9, 1731.

What kind of person was Mary Astell? The answer must be: a very unusual person. There can be little doubt that she was in many ways a formidable personality, a woman who could, and did, daunt her acquaintances with her wit and honesty. But beneath this forthright manner, there was a deep concern for her friends, and a real commitment to what she saw as their prosperity. She did not hesitate to scold them when she thought it necessary, but she did so because she loved them. Her forthrightness and honesty were tempered by her good humor and her dry, understated wit. Above all, she was a pious woman. Her love for God was deep and genuine. Her life was founded upon it. Almost immediately after her death, Mary Astell was forgotten, except by her circle of friends. She had, of course, lived a private life for the last twenty years, and the novelty of her earlier works had worn off. Fortunately, when George Ballard was collecting materials for his book, some of her friends and acquaintances were still alive. But his fellow researchers had never heard of her, so quickly had she been forgotten.

Mary Astell's output was not large: six books, two pamphlets, and a record of her correspondence with John Norris of Bemerton on the subject of the love of God. I give here a list of her works in chronological order:

1694: *A Serious Proposal to the Ladies for the Advancement of Their True and Greatest Interest.* By a Lover of her Sex.

1695: *Letters Concerning the Love of God, Between the Author of the Proposal to the Ladies and Mr. John Norris.*

1697: *A Serious Proposal to the Ladies Part II Wherein A Method Is Offer'd for the Improvement of their Minds.*

1700: *Some Reflections Upon Marriage, Occasion'd by the Duke and Duchess of Mazarine's Case; Which Is Also Consider'd.*

1704: *Moderation Truly Stated: Or, A Review of a Late Pamphlet Entitul'd Moderation a Vertue. With a Prefatory Discourse to Dr. D'Avenant, Concerning His Late Essays of Peace and War.*

1704: *A Fair Way with the Dissenters and Their Patrons. Not Writ by Mr. L——y, or Any Other Furious Jacobite Whether Clergyman or Layman; But by a Very Moderate Person and Dutiful Subject to the Queen.*

1704: *An Impartial Enquiry into the Causes of Rebellion and Civil War in this Kingdom: In an Examination of Dr. Kennett's Sermon Jan. 31, 1703/4. And Vindication of the Royal Martyr.*

1705: *The Christian Religion. As Profess'd by a Daughter of the Church of England.*

1709: *Bart'lemy Fair: Or, An Enquiry after Wit: In Which Due Respect is Had to a Letter Concerning Enthusiasm. To my Lord * * * By Mr. Wotton.*

It would be possible to claim a place for Mary Astell in the history of rhetoric solely on the grounds of her magnificent practice of it. In her own day, she was renowned for her eloquence: John Evelyn refers to her writing as "sublime" (Perry 99); Lady Schomberg wishes that she had "but the least part of Mrs. Astell's eloquence" (487); John Norris speaks of her "moving Strains of the most natural and powerful Oratory" (79); John Dunton refers to her as "sublime" (487). As the passage from Norris indicates, those who had been trained in the rhetorical tradition— that is, the men—could recognize in her achievement an illustration of the principles with which they were familiar. A rhetorician studying her works cannot fail to be impressed by their fidelity to rhetorical principles. I propose to look at three of the more accessible of her works to demonstrate her mastery of the art of rhetoric.

A Serious Proposal to the Ladies (1694), her first book, was an immediate success, and it made her reputation. Further editions of the book appeared in 1695, 1696, 1697, and 1701. So rapidly did the fame of the book spread that when, in the year after its publication, she and John Norris published a volume of their correspondence, she was identified as the author of the *Proposal* (*Letters Concerning the Love of God, Between the Author of the Proposal to the Ladies and Mr. John Norris*).

The book is the fruit of her bitter experience when she first came to London, and of all her years of desperation when she was destitute, redundant, without work, without money, without friends. When with the help of Archbishop Sancroft Mary Astell emerged from this desolate time and began to find not only the means of subsistence but also an outlet for her gifts, she was determined, if she could, to do something for other women in the desperate position she had herself known. It was not only women in urgent need of employment with whom she was concerned: even more serious than the economic plight of some women was the moral and spiritual destitution of many more, particularly among the rich. As Astell began to move in relatively high society, she was deeply shocked by the superficiality of the lives of most women. Morally, they were as impoverished as she, until recently, had been materially. *A Serious Proposal* records her distress: she is horrified by the waste—of time, of intelligence, of talents given by God. Something had to be done. Her proposal is addressed to the ladies, but she has half an eye on the men too, and many of her arguments seem directed at them as much as at the women.

The proposal is to establish what she calls a "Protestant Nunnery" where women who could not, would not, or at least did not marry could take refuge in a life of holiness and service. Those who continued celibate could thus spend their lives usefully and happily, educating children and doing good among the poor. Life in a religious community would provide them with much-needed companionship, and help them in the attainment of the most important goal in this life—preparation for the life to come. Those who eventually did marry would have spent their time of waiting profitably, and would be prepared by their education for the nurture of their own children. Such an institution could do nothing but good, from every point of view.

But Mary Astell's proposal for a Protestant nunnery for women was not new. During the earlier part of the seventeenth century, this solution to the problem of unmarried women had been not only recommended but actually tried by Anglicans of her own—that is, the Laudian—persuasion. In the 1630s, Nicholas Ferrar had formed such a community of women for his mother, sisters, and nieces at Little Gidding in Huntingdonshire. It had lasted thirty years. A similar community was organized by Lady Lettice, Viscountess of Falkland, at Great Tew, and another by Mary and Anne Kemys at Naish in Glamorganshire (Smith 64–70). Such communities always aroused suspicion in the authorities for political reasons: they were suspected of being in sympathy with the Roman Catholics. The attempt of the Spanish in 1588 to conquer England and reimpose the authority of the pope had not been forgotten. Nor had the Gunpowder Plot of 1605. For these and other reasons, the communities had not survived; but the idea was not new.

If her proposal to establish a community for women was not a new idea, why was it so well received? I believe we can attribute its success directly to its eloquence. Although it appears to be spontaneous, it is in fact a most carefully crafted work, as a little study of it will show. Her care and skill are apparent in her selection of arguments, her arrangement of them, and her style: to use rhetorical terminology, in her *inventio*, *dispositio*, and *elocutio*. In selecting her arguments, she is careful to take into consideration what will most probably appeal to the various interests represented among her readers: obviously she has made a study of her audience. She explicitly addresses the *ladies*. That is, she considers herself to be speaking to women of the upper classes. Such ladies at the time Astell was writing were notorious for their preoccupation with their appearance. She therefore begins by declaring that her only design is "to improve your Charms and heighten your Value." Her aim is "to fix that Beauty, to make it lasting and permanent, which Nature with all the helps of Art cannot secure" (4). Astell is sure that a trained mind and an understanding heart are far more attractive than any mere physical attributes, and since the ladies in her audience are above all concerned with attracting favorable attention, she appeals to them on those grounds. But the frivolous ladies in high society are not the only ones who will read the proposal, even though it is to them that it is specifically addressed: Astell is astute enough to be aware that if her proposal is to receive support, it must interest the men too. They, after all, control most of the money. Her appeal must obviously be as wide as possible. She therefore takes into account not only ladies in high society but also prudent parents, pointing out that the cost of sending their unmarried daughters to such an institution is much lower than the dowry that would be required to find them acceptable husbands. On the other hand, for those whose daughters are so richly endowed as to attract inconvenient and unscrupulous suitors, she recommends the girls' temporary retirement to her academy, where they can be kept out of harm's way. For the intelligentsia, she uses cogent arguments based upon her understanding of faculty psychology : the soul, she says, "always Wills according as she understands, so that if she understands amiss, she Wills amiss" (64). Finally, to the public-spirited and the socially concerned, she shows the advantages of training competent teachers to promote the manners and morals of the upcoming generation. If the women marry, they will have been excellently prepared for their responsibilities as mothers; if they do not, they may function as salaried teachers and thus contribute usefully to the community as well as providing for themselves.

If Astell shows great skill in the selection of her arguments, she shows just as much in her arrangement of them. She does not actually make her proposal until about one-third of the way through. (We might compare this to Swift's similar postponement of his recommendation in *A Modest Proposal*.) The first fifty pages are devoted to preparing the ground—to outlining the problems and whetting her readers' appetites for a solution. She then makes her proposal with great clarity and brevity: it is "to erect a Monastery . . . or Religious Retirement, and such as shall have a double aspect, being not only a Retreat from the World for those who desire that advantage, but likewise an Institution and previous discipline to fit us to do the greatest good in it" (48). The ladies are to meditate, to attend worship services, to study, and to perform works of mercy. She elaborates to some degree, setting forth the requirements for tutors. On the whole, however, she gives very little detailed description of the curriculum or the timetable; she merely outlines the general principles, leaving the details to be worked out later by those chiefly concerned. The rest of the *Proposal* consists of a further analysis of the benefits to be derived from the institution (*confirmatio*) and answers to some of the objections that might be raised (*refutatio*, in its proper place according to the canons of traditional rhetoric). It is, in fact, a standard proposal, but one so smoothly put together that its effectiveness as persuasion is almost inevitable.

Added to the artistry of her selection of arguments and her arrangement of them is the eloquence of her style. In this work, we are most particularly aware of her speaking voice—the accents of persuasion. It is above all the rhythmic balance of her sentences that underlines the persuasiveness of her arguments. The reasonableness that she advocates is echoed in the measured balance of her clauses, the considered structure of her sentences, which suggest control without sacrificing liveliness. Hers is the voice of reason. By its very sound, it engenders trust. It is the Moderate style—not dull or sparse, but not richly decorated either, and making little use of startling metaphors or emotional exclamations. Its passions are well under the control of reason—and this too is persuasive.

Such was the success of *A Serious Proposal* that for a while it appeared that the institution it recommended might be endowed. Some great lady, possibly Lady Elizabeth Hastings but more probably Princess Anne, seriously considered contributing ten thousand pounds to its foundation. Ultimately, she was persuaded by Bishop Burnet to change her mind: he, like others in authority before him, was suspicious of anything that sounded so "Popish" (Perry 134). However, for some time, it looked as if the proposal might succeed.

It was possibly with a view to encouraging Princess Anne to proceed with her plans for endowment that Mary Astell dedicated Part 2 of *A Serious Proposal* (1697) to her. In the introduction to Part 2, Astell expresses her disappointment that, so far, no one had acted upon her suggestion. She says that she would be happier "to find her Project condemn'd as foolish and impertinent, than to find it receiv'd with some Approbation, and yet no body endeavouring to put it in Practice" (3). What can it be that hinders them? Is it "singularity"? "Are you afraid of being out of the ordinary way and therefore admir'd and gaz'd at?" (5). Or is it that the project seems too strenuous? "Is it the difficulty of attaining the Bravery of the Mind, the Labour and the Cost that keeps you from making a purchase of it?" (7). More probably, she decides, simple ignorance of study habits has discouraged women from attempting the life of the mind. They are afraid to embark upon something they so little understand. Their parents and guardians have "taught them perhaps to repeat their catechism and a few good sentences, to read a chapter and say their prayers, tho perhaps with as little understanding as a Parrot" (16). And for the parents, that was enough. What they chiefly lack is method. Admitting that in Part 1 she gave only a general outline, she offers now, in Part 2, to go into detail. She sees the instruction she is about to give as only a temporary measure, till the seminary can be erected. She hopes both to provide interim instruction and to whet her readers' appetites for more.

Apart from the introduction, which is a splendid example of the use of the exordium to establish ethos, particularly goodwill, Part 2 is not a work of persuasion but of instruction: Astell is supplying a method. In most respects, then, Part 2 is very different from Part 1. It is much longer: Part 1 has just under 150 pages, Part 2 nearly 300. Its arrangement is more formal: it is divided into four chapters. Chapter 1 deals with the relationship between knowledge and virtue (something she referred to only briefly in Part 1). Chapter 2 discusses the preliminaries—the avoidance of sloth, selfishness, and pride, and the elimination of prejudices arising from authority, education, and custom. Chapter 3, by far the longest, gives directions for the improvement of the understanding; and Chapter 4 for the regulation of the will and the "government of the Passions."

Astell's eloquence is as apparent in Part 2 as in Part 1. Once again, she shows her skill in understanding and accommodating her audience. As an example of this rhetorical wisdom, we may consider the title of the first chapter: "Of the Mutual Relation Between Ignorance and Vice, and Knowledge and Purity." She is careful to begin her work with something that is sure to appeal to anyone serious-minded enough to take up her book. Most responsible people, both men and women, were far more concerned to promote women's morality than to encourage their education. And as Kathleen Jamieson has demonstrated, there was in the minds of the people of the time a direct, if to us illogical, connection between facility in speech and impurity of life (Jamieson 70). The chaste woman was thought to be identical to the silent woman: indeed, silence was said to be a woman's rhetoric (Maclean 54). As a writer herself, and as a promoter of other women's writing, Mary Astell shows herself well aware of the possible prejudices of her audience. She must refute their conviction that verbal facility leads to adultery. In fact, she does more: she reverses the argument, demonstrating that the training of the mind (which necessarily includes training in the arts of discourse) actually promotes morality. It does so by developing the understanding, which, according to seventeenth-century faculty psychology, should control the passions and direct the will. It therefore follows that, unless women have no rational souls, everything should be done to develop that rationality which alone can promote moral behavior.

As in Part 1, Astell's word choice and sentence structure serve her purpose. In Part 2, as we have noted, her primary purpose is to clarify, to teach, rather than to persuade her audience to adopt a particular course of action. In this work, it is above all the pace of the style that contributes to the work's force and clarity—this, and the superb control of the syntax. Here we particularly notice how she demonstrates relationships between ideas by the use of long sentences that hold those ideas in suspension. Doing so allows her to keep them in balance and to avoid overstatement. We sense that we are in the hands of an excellent navigator. She keeps the ship of her argument on course by constant adjustments, qualifications, and compensations. Here is one example:

> God does nothing in vain, he gives no power or Faculty which he has not allotted to some proportionate use, if therefore he has given to Mankind a Rational Mind, every individual Understanding ought to be employ'd in somewhat worthy of it. The Meanest Person shou'd think as Justly, tho' not as Capaciously, as the greatest Philosopher. And if the Understanding be made for the contemplation of Truth, and I know not what else it can be made for, either there are many Understandings who are never able to attain what they were design'd for, which is contrary to the Supposition that GOD made nothing in Vain, or else the very meanest must be put in the way of attaining it. (123)

If Part 1 of *A Serious Proposal* demonstrates Astell's powers of persuasion and Part 2 those of argumentation and explication, *Some Reflections Upon Marriage* reveals her skill in satire. In this work, Astell, though herself unmarried, speaks for the women of her time who were oppressed by a tyranny worse, because less escapable, than any political tyranny. She brings to bear upon her argument many of the current issues of her day, especially including contemporary discussions of the philosophy of government and of human nature. She successfully turns the opposition's own weapons against them, showing the logical implications of the arguments they use.

The occasion for this work was the death of the notorious Duchess of Mazarin, who had been a neighbor of Astell's in Chelsea. Married while still a young teenager to the fanatical, indeed insane, Duke of Meilleraye and Mayenne, and thereupon taking the name of her uncle the famous cardinal, the duchess had endured psychological and physical

agonies before eventually escaping to England. There, living at the court
of her friend Charles II, she had led a life typical of the decadence of the
courtiers of the Restoration. What made her unusual was not her sexual
immorality but her defiance of her husband and her escape from him.
The story was old in 1700, when Astell wrote her book, but the scandal
had been aired again when the duchess died in 1699. Astell immediately
saw how she could take advantage of current interest in the affair to
make a defense of and a plea for the abused women of her day. She sees
the scandalous history of the duchess as one more demonstration of the
absolute necessity of giving women a proper education. Devout Anglican
that she is, she does not ask for improved divorce laws; but she does
plead for a more sympathetic understanding of the married woman's
plight and a recognition that marriage, far from being a necessary condition for a woman's happiness, is more likely than not a means of de-
stroying it.

In this work Astell demonstrates with particular clarity the rhetorical
astuteness of her argumentation. She takes advantage of the recent political situation—the Glorious Revolution of 1688, when James II was
forced to abdicate—and the current interest in the rights of man, to plead
the cause of women. Married women, she believes, are no better than
slaves, though, she comments bitterly, they are "for the most part Wise
enough to Love their Chains, and to discern how very becomingly they
set" (Preface 23). Astell explicitly compares the condition of married
women to that of "a poor People, who groan under Tyranny, unless they
are Strong enough to break the Yoke, to Depose and abdicate" (27). In
public matters, her readers were all for the liberty of the citizen. Not so
in private matters: "Whatever may be said against a passive obedience
in another case, I suppose there's no Man but likes it very well in this;
how much soever Arbitrary Power may be disliked on a Throne, not
Milton himself wou'd cry up Liberty to poor Female Slaves, or plead for
the Lawfulness of Resisting a Private Tyranny" (27). Drawing again upon
the language of politics, she continues: "He who would say the People
were made for the Prince who is set over them would be thought to be
out of his Senses as well as his Politics" (47).

Astell does not advocate revolt; instead, she recommends extreme
caution. A woman should be educated to understand the risks involved
in marriage, and to choose her "sovereign" rationally. At a time when all
a woman's money became her husband's upon her marriage, she had to
be particularly on her guard against the fortune hunter, lest she later be
obliged to "make court to him for a little sorry alimony out of her own

estate" (14). But a woman should equally beware of suitors who fall in love with her wit or beauty: "He who doats on a Face, he who makes Money his Idol, he who is charm'd with vain and empty Wit, gives no such Evidence, either of Wisdom or Goodness, that a Woman of any tolerable Sense wou'd care to venture her self to his Conduct" (31).

Some Reflections Upon Marriage not only demonstrates Astell's skill in argumentation, but also provides some of the best examples of her mastery of style. In her discussion of the dangers of courtship, she reverses the triumphant metaphors of conquest so often used in love poetry, taking the position of the pursued rather than the pursuer. Hers are metaphors not of conquest but of capture, and they are sinister, representing marriage as at best only a reluctant capitulation: "It were endless to reckon up the divers stratagems Men use to catch their Prey, their different ways of insinuating which vary with the Circumstances and the Ladies Temper. But how unfairly, how basely soever they proceed, when the Prey is once caught it passes for lawful Prize" (70). Astell's command of the satirical style embraces everything from straight invective to sarcasm to the most subtle and understated irony, from the coarse to the delicate. Surprisingly, she can at times approach the scatological, as when she refers to the tyrants' "Impiety and Immorality which dare . . . to devour Souls . . . leaving a stench behind them" (Preface 25). As an example of sheer invective, it is hard to match the following: A proud and peevish man has "Learning and Sense enough to make him a Fop in Perfection; for a Man can never be a complete Coxcomb, unless he has a considerable share of these to value himself upon" (28). Occasionally we find a little touch of sarcasm, as when she refers to "his great Wisdom so conspicuous on all occasions" (43), or to the "manly, mannerly" jests that men make not only against women but also against religion (50). But best of all are those passages of understated irony where, for example, she refers to men's "courage . . . in breaking through all the Tyes Sacred and Civil" in order to achieve success in the "great Actions and considerable Business of this World" (87); or where she praises them for their achievements: "All famous Arts have their Original from Men, even from the Invention of Guns to the Mystery of good Eating, and to shew that nothing is beneath their Care, any more than above their Reach, they have brought Gaming to an Art and Science, and a more Profitable and Honourable one too, than any that us'd to be call'd Liberal" (88).

Mary Astell, then, has some claim to be considered as belonging to the rhetorical tradition by virtue of her eloquence. In her selection of arguments, in her arrangement of them, in the stylistic choices she makes, she unerringly accommodates her audience and carries her point. Whether she was herself taught to write by her uncle, whether she taught herself by reading such books as *L'art de penser* and *L'art de parler*, or whether she simply internalized models of good writing, we do not know. Possibly there was a combination of all three.

But Mary Astell's right to be accorded a place in the history of rhetoric does not depend only upon her successful practice of it. Perhaps even more important than her eloquence is her insistence upon the ability and the right of women to participate in a rhetorical tradition from which they had hitherto normally been excluded by their ignorance of classical culture, particularly the Latin language. According to Father Walter Ong, Latin was "a sex-linked language written and spoken only by males, learned outside the home in a tribal setting which was in effect a male puberty rite setting, complete with physical punishment and other kinds of deliberately imposed hardships" (Ong 113). As long as rhetoric was based upon a working knowledge of Latin, which enabled a thorough grounding in classical history, philosophy, and literature, women were effectively excluded from it.

When Descartes not only called into question the usefulness of the whole apparatus of ancient and medieval learning but also used the vernacular as the language of scholarship, he unwittingly began a process that would enable women to participate in the intellectual life of their times. It was Poulain de la Barre who first saw the implications of this scholarly revolution for women (Perry 71). Mary Astell was undoubtedly familiar with his work, which was influential in England during the 1690s. As far as rhetoric is concerned, she was also influenced by the Port Royalists, and by the Oratorian Bernard Lamy, whose works she quotes in Part 2 of *A Serious Proposal*. Encouraged by these and other French thinkers, Astell follows up on the implications of these new ideas for women. "And since Truth is so near at hand, since we are not oblig'd to tumble over many Authors, to hunt after every celebrated Genius, but may have it for enquiring after in our own Breasts, are we not inexcusable if we don't obtain it?" (*Serious Proposal* Part 2, 122). Later in the same passage she specifically denies the importance of the learned languages in developing the powers of reasoning: "All have not leisure to Learn Languages and pore on Books, nor Opportunity to Converse with the Learned; but all may *Think*, may use their own Faculties rightly, and consult the Master who is within them" (124).

It is this principle of the naturalness of human reason and human speech that informs Mary Astell's rhetorical theory. Basing herself on the ideas of the scholars of Port Royal and the Oratory (themselves Cartesians), she is nonetheless original in the ways she applies her ideas to women. It is not enough to follow Descartes and the French rhetoricians in asserting that the ability to think and to write is natural; if she is to claim a place for women in logic and rhetoric, she must show that they are natural *to women*. At the time, this was by no means obvious to everybody. Astell argues this point in two ways. She asserts that women, as human beings, are of course endowed with reason; and she shows in detail how they can become fully competent as writers by using the knowledge they already have.

Astell's most sustained defense of women's rationality comes in the lengthy preface she added to the third edition of *Some Reflections Upon Marriage* (1706). An attack had been made upon this work, originally published in 1700, on the grounds of women's natural inferiority. This attack Astell refutes at length in the new preface. Much of her argument consists of the well-worn traditional citations by famous women, a standard defense that had been used for centuries. But some of it is more unusual. Her choice of the analogy of pig-keeping, for example, not only clarifies the point she is making but also adds some subtle innuendo: she claims that Woman was made primarily to serve God, not Man. "The Service she at any time becomes oblig'd to pay to a Man, is only a Business by the Bye. Just as it may be any Man's Business and Duty to keep Hogs; he was not made for this, but if he hires himself out to such an Employment, he ought conscientiously to perform it" (Preface 5). Still on the theme of domestic animals, she argues tellingly and bitterly that if indeed women have no powers of reason, they should, like these creatures, be kept restrained. It is neither fair nor wise to demand reasonable moral behavior from those who have no natural capacity for it (Preface 23). But she quickly dismisses this as nonsense. Associating reason with the power of speech, she points out that men have always complained that women speak too much rather than too little. It follows that one cannot seriously question the fact that they are endowed with reason. If their reasoning powers are in any way inferior to men's, that is because of a lack of exercise. The remedy is to provide the exercise and thus strengthen the faculty.

It is the exercise of the power of reason and of speech that Astell attempts to promote in Part 2 of *A Serious Proposal*. Although she never mentions Petrus Ramus, she is obviously working within a tradition in-

fluenced by him: She takes it for granted that thinking (including rhetorical *inventio*) belongs to logic rather than to rhetoric. Much of the
sixty pages she devotes to a discussion of the method of thinking is
heavily indebted, directly or indirectly, to Descartes. The Port Royalists
who wrote *L'art de penser*, Antoine Arnauld and Pierre Nicole, were
strongly influenced by Descartes. It is therefore not always easy to tell
where Astell is influenced directly by Descartes, and where she is receiving his ideas mediated through Arnauld and Nicole. In her passage on
logic, Astell quotes directly from Descartes's *Principes de la philosophie*:

> That (to use the Words of a Celebrated Author) may be said to be "Clear
> which is present and Manifest to an attentive Mind; so as we say we see
> Objects Clearly, when being present to our Eyes they sufficiently Act on
> 'em, and our Eyes are dispos'd to regard 'em. And that Distinct, which
> is so Clear, Particular, and Different from all other things, that it contains
> not any thing in it self which appears not manifestly to him who considers
> it as he ought." (135)

A little later on, she gives six rules for clear thinking, which are
obviously derived in part from the four rules put forward by Descartes
in Discourse 2 of *Discourse on Method* (41). Here she acknowledges that
she is drawing on the work of others, though she does not specify which.
The rules are as follows:

1. We should in the first place Acquaint our selves thoroughly with
   the State of the Question, have a Distinct Notion of our Subject,
   whatever it be, and of the Termes we make use of, knowing precisely what it is we drive at: that so we may in the second
2. Cut off all needless Ideas and whatever has not a necessary Con-
   nexion to the matter under Consideration.
3. To conduct our Thought by Order, beginning with the most Simple and Easie Objects, and ascending as by Degrees to the Knowledge of the more Compos'd.
4. Not to leave any part of our Subject unexamin'd. . . . To this rule
   belongs that of Dividing the Subject of our Meditations into as
   many Parts as we can, and as shall be requisite to Understand it
   perfectly.
5. We must Always keep our Subject Directly in our Eye, and Closely
   pursue it through our Progress.

    6. To judge no further than we Perceive, and not to take any thing for Truth which we do not evidently know to be so. (143–49)

Like Arnauld and Nicole, Bernard Lamy, author of *L'art de parler*, was strongly influenced by Descartes. Here too, it is not easy to tell which ideas Astell derives immediately from Descartes and which from Descartes through Lamy. Her advice on the importance of attention is obviously Cartesian; according to Thomas M. Carr in *Descartes and the Resilience of Rhetoric*, attention is central to the Cartesian program (41). For Descartes, an important attention-getting device is admiration (in its seventeenth-century sense of wonder). The following passage in Astell is, then, obviously influenced by him: "Now attention is usually fixt by Admiration, which is excited by somewhat uncommon either in the Thought or way of Expression" (*Serious Proposal* Part 2, 194). Again, the importance she places upon clarity, exactness, and method in her advice on rhetoric is obviously to be attributed to the direct or indirect influence of Descartes: "Scarce anything conduces more to Clearness, the great Beauty of Writing, than Exactness of Method" (179). Strongest of all, however, is the Cartesian idea of the naturalness of thought and expression.

    The question of the sources of Astell's rhetorical theory is complicated, and I have discussed it in more detail elsewhere ("Outside the Rhetorical Tradition"). What is most interesting about her theory is how she applies it directly to the situation of the women she addresses. She even challenges the rhetorical tradition itself, as I shall show later.

    In Astell's view, women are fully competent to engage in rhetorical activity, with one exception: public speaking. She gives no reason for thus excluding women from such an important part of rhetoric—she merely assumes that it is inappropriate for them. But apart from this exception, she believes that women can and should participate fully. Traditionally, if women wrote at all, they usually confined themselves to producing handbooks of devotion or composing elegant letters to their friends. They also wrote fiction, plays, and poems—Aphra Behn is a case in point. But in Astell's time some few women were beginning to join in political and philosophical debate; she did so herself, as did her opponent Damaris Masham. Astell strongly defended women's ability thus to engage in intellectual discussion at the highest level. Guided to the same degree by the natural light of reason, women were fully competent to join men in the pamphleteering that was such a feature of the day.

Astell begins her discussion of rhetoric by asserting once again the naturalness of intellectual activity, whether in thinking or writing: "As Nature teaches us logic, so does it instruct us in Rhetoric much better than Rules of Art, which if they are good ones are nothing else but those Judicious Observations which Men of Sense have drawn from Nature, and which all who reflect on the Operations of their own Minds will find out 'emselves. The common Precepts of Rhetoric may teach us how to reduce Ingenious ways of speaking to a certain Rule, but they do not teach us how to Invent them, this is Nature's work and she does it best" (175).

She then goes into detail, covering in turn each of the parts of rhetoric except invention—which she has already discussed in her passage on logic—and memory. Again and again she shows that women have nothing to fear, that they already know all they need to know, and that all they have to do is recognize that they know it and put it into practice: "The Method of Thinking has been already shewn, and the same is to be observed in Writing, which if it be what it ought, is nothing else but the communicating to others the result of our frequent and deep Meditations, in such a manner as we judge most effectual to convince them of those Truths which we believe, Always remembering that the most natural Order is ever the best" (180).

As with arrangement, so with style: the guiding principle is to follow Nature:

> In short, as Thinking conformably to the Nature of Things is True Knowledge, so th'expressing our Thoughts in such a way, as most readily, and with the greatest Clearness and Life, excites in others the very same idea that was in us, is the best Eloquence. For if our Idea be conformable to the Nature of the thing it represents, and its Relations duly stated, this is the most effectual Way both to Inform and Persuade. . . . If therefore we thoroughly understand our Subject and are Zealously affected with it, we shall neither want suitable words to explain, nor persuasive Methods to recommend it. (188)

In matters of grammar and spelling the same principle holds. Spelling is not the mystery to women that it is commonly proclaimed to be. The trouble is that women have been told that correct spelling is both difficult and unladylike: "As to spelling, which they're said to be defective in, if they don't believe as they're usually told, that its fit for 'em to be so, and that to write exactly is too Pedantic, they may soon correct that fault, by

Pronouncing their words aright and Spelling 'em accordingly." True, phonetic spelling will not always answer, because of "an Imperfection in our Language," but "in this case a little Observation or recourse to Books will assist us; and if at any time we happen to mistake by Spelling as we Pronounce, the fault will be very Venial, and Custom rather to blame than we" (193). Astell obviously thinks the fuss made about women's spelling is disproportionate. The same goes for grammar. Once again, Astell denies that women are as deficient in it as they are reputed to be— and comments that they are not the only transgressors. A little extra care will solve this problem: women should avoid hastiness and take the trouble to proofread. The only guide they need is their natural good sense of language: "Those who speak true grammar, unless they're very careless cannot write false, since they need only peruse what they've writ and consider whether they wou'd express themselves thus in Conversation" (194).

Astell not only answers men's objections, and women's fears, that writing according to a masculine standard is beyond them; she also asserts that in some ways women are not men's equals but their superiors in rhetoric. They have certain *natural* advantages. She declines to give any advice about delivery (which she calls "Pronunciation") on the grounds that it is unnecessary: women will not engage in public speaking, and "Nature does for the most part furnish 'em with such a Musical Tone, Perswasive Air and Winning Address as renders their Discourse sufficiently agreeable in Private Conversation" (192). The art of conversation—which she believes comes naturally to women—is extremely important in Astell's theory of rhetoric. Not only is it a sure guide in matters of correctness, but it is also essential in the formation of a good writing style: "I have made no distinction in what has been said between Speaking and Writing, because tho they are talents which do not always meet, yet there is no material difference between 'em. They Write best perhaps who do't with the gentile and easy air of Conversation; and they Talk best who mingle Solidity of Thought with th'agreeableness of a ready Wit" (192). This is, as we know, the position of Quintilian and Cicero. There is no direct evidence that Astell was familiar with the work of either, but their ideas had of course passed into the rhetorical tradition. There is no suggestion that Astell considers the art of conversation at all inferior to the art of public speaking. It is not second-best eloquence, something with which women may comfort themselves for being denied the glories of the public platform. Not only in her theory but also in her experience, conversation was of the first importance: it was the foundation of those friendships with other women that provided the basic satisfactions of her life.

Another advantage possessed by women, according to Astell, is a good ethos. Like Augustine, Astell considers ethos of the highest importance. The lack of it will surely undermine the best-informed discourse. It is, she says, "to little purpose to Think well and speak well, unless we live well" (201). The advantage that women enjoy in this respect is implied in the rather sour comment she makes in discussing the teaching of children: The education of the young, "at least the foundation of it, on which in a great measure the success of all depends, shou'd be laid by the Mother, for Fathers find other Business, they will not be confin'd to such laborious work, they have not such opportunities for observing a Child's Temper, nor are the greatest part of 'em like to do much good, since Precepts contradicted by Example seldom prove effectual" (210).

The high value that Astell thus places upon moral considerations is typical of her rhetorical theory throughout. If Nature is one sure guide for women attempting to learn the arts of discourse, Christian morality is the other. "The way to be good Orators is to be good Christians" (189), she tells her audience of women—useful advice, for whatever the deficiencies of their education, they are unlikely to be entirely ignorant about morality. All they have to do is apply Christian principles to the practice of communication. Again, she is making the point that they *already know* how to proceed. They have nothing to fear.

Like the Cartesian principle of the sufficiency of natural gifts to develop and direct the arts of discourse, this belief in the efficacy of Christian precepts to produce good writing is derived from Astell's French sources. But she goes beyond her sources in extending such principles to include the discourse of women. She challenges women's exclusion from the rhetorical tradition, and thus contributes to that tradition.

But Astell's contribution to rhetoric does not end here, for she attempts, on behalf of women, not only to join the rhetorical tradition but also to question it. Throughout the history of rhetoric there has been a recurrent tendency to think of it in terms of a metaphor of warfare: the opposition (and in practice, this frequently means the *audience*) is the enemy, who is to be vanquished. No doubt the very strong forensic element in classical rhetoric, particularly in Roman times, contributed largely to this tendency; but it did not end with the Romans. It is this tradition of confrontation that Astell finds repugnant; it is this she disallows in women's practice of the arts of discourse:

To be able to hold an argument Right or Wrong may pass with some perhaps for the Character of a Good Disputant, which yet I think it is not, but must by no means be allow'd to be that of a Rational Person. . . . For indeed Truth not Victory is what we should contend for in all Disputes, it being more glorious to be Overcome by her than to Triumph under the Banner of Error. And therefore we pervert Reason when we make it the Instrument of an Endless Contention. (*Serious Proposal* Part 2, 162)

Connections with Modern Feminism

It is in her strong objection to the patriarchal tendency to reduce all discussions to a win/lose conflict that Mary Astell is at her most feminine. Recent research has shown that feminine epistemology is often distinguished from masculine by a distaste for confrontation, and by a concern for the protection of both sides against needless humiliation:

> In general, few of the women we interviewed . . . found argument . . . a congenial form of conversation among friends. The classic dormitory bull session with students assailing their opponents' logic and attacking their evidence, seems to occur rarely among women. . . . Women find it hard to see doubting as a game; they tend to take it personally. Teachers and fathers and boyfriends assure them that arguments are not between *persons* but between *positions*, but the women continue to fear that someone may get hurt. (Belenky 105)

This quality of caring, identified by Nel Noddings as typical of women's approach to ethics, is seen by Belenky and her colleagues as informing their ways of knowing generally: "We posit two contrasting epistemological orientations: a separate epistemology, based upon impersonal procedures for establishing truth, and a connected epistemology in which truth emerges through care" (102).

The principle of caring is observable throughout Astell's discussion of rhetoric. It is, in fact, one of its most important distinguishing features. In particular, it helps to differentiate Astell's particular contribution from that of her most important source, Bernard Lamy. Her use of Christian morality as a guide to the practice of rhetoric is especially well suited to her audience of women, but it is not original. Most of the Christian principles she identifies as helpful guides to rhetorical practice had already been suggested by Lamy. But there is often a great difference in tone and emphasis between Astell and Lamy, and more often than not it has to do with the principle of caring. For example, in his discussion of good-will in ethos, Lamy allows that it may be genuine, yet seems far from convinced that it usually is: "One may put on the face of an Honest man, only to delude those who have a reverence for the least appearance of truth; yet it follows not but we may profess love to our Auditors, and insinuate into their affections, when our love is sincere, and we have no design but the interest and propagation of truth" (359). Astell's version of the same point transforms it: "By being True Christians we have Really that Love for others which all who desire to perswade must pretend to" (*Serious Proposal* Part 2, 190). Similarly, both Lamy and Astell recommend the avoidance of pride, but their reasons for such a recommendation are different, and demonstrate somewhat different moral priorities. Lamy's counsel is based upon his own experience as the humiliated loser in verbal warfare. "Many times our obstinacy and aversion to the truth, is caused only by the fierceness and arrogance wherewith an Orator would force from our own mouths an acknowledgement of our Ignorance" (354). Astell's concern, on the other hand, is with others rather than with herself; whereas he looks inward, she looks outward in compassion: "I believe we shall find, there's nothing more improper than Pride and Positiveness, nor any thing more prevalent than an innocent compliance with weakness: Such as pretends not to dictate to their Ignorance, but only to explain and illustrate what lay hid or might have been known before if they had consider'd it, and supposes that their Minds being employ'd about some other things was the reason why they did not discern it as well as we" (185). In another passage, she takes up Lamy's point again, and specifically warns against taking a confrontational position: "And since many would yield to the Clear Light of Truth were't not for the shame of being overcome, we shou'd Convince but not Triumph, and rather Conceal our Conquest than Publish it. We doubly oblige our Neighbours when we reduce them into the Right Way, and keep it from being taken notice of that they were once in the Wrong" (186).

It might be objected that in attributing so much importance to the genuine concern of the speaker for the audience, the writer for the readers, Astell is merely following Augustine. Indeed, I have argued elsewhere that Augustine's fundamental rhetorical principle is love (Sutherland, "Love as Rhetorical Principle" 139–55). Certainly Astell's French sources in Port Royal and the Oratory were strongly Augustinian, though as we have seen, Lamy appears to be less interested in this particular aspect of the relationship between morals and rhetoric than Astell herself. But without denying that she may indeed have been influenced, directly or indirectly, by the rhetoric of Augustine, I think his conception of what love of the audience means differs in practice from hers. When Augustine speaks of the benefit of the audience, what he has in mind is their reception of the gospel. This is the great good which the Christian orator must bear in mind at all times. It is this that must inform his rhetorical practice from beginning to end. Astell's precept is more lowly. Of course she thinks it is important that people be good Christians—she says so repeatedly. But what she specifically recommends is tenderness towards the feelings of the audience. However misguided her opponents may be, she wants to spare them the pain of humiliation. I do not recall that Augustine's principle of love reaches down quite so far.

There are solid grounds, then, for claiming Mary Astell as a contributor to the rhetorical tradition: as a practitioner of rhetoric, she exemplifies the art of writing at its best; and as a theorist, she introduces the feminine element into what had hitherto been a masculine preserve. Both in her accommodation of Cartesian principles of naturalness to women's thinking and writing, and in her insistence upon genuine caring as a necessary element in effective persuasion, Astell makes her mark upon rhetorical history. It is time for us all to read what she has inscribed there.

REFERENCES

Arnauld, Antoine. *The Art of Thinking.* 1662. Trans. James Dickoff. Repr. New York: Bobbs-Merrill, 1964.

Astell, Mary. *A Serious Proposal to the Ladies for the Advancement of Their True and Greatest Interest by a Lover of Her Sex.* London, 1694.

———. *A Serious Proposal to the Ladies Part II Wherein a Method's Offer'd for the Improvement of Their Minds.* London, 1697.

———. *Some Reflections Upon Marriage, Occasion'd by the Duke and Duchess of Mazarine's Case, Which is Also Consider'd.* London, 1700.

Ballard, George. *Memoirs of Several Ladies of Great Britain Who Have Been Celebrated For Their Writings or Skill in the Learned Languages.* Oxford, 1752.

Belenky, Mary Field, Blythe McVicker Clinchy, Nancy Rule Goldberger, and Jill Mattuck Tarule. *Women's Ways of Knowing: The Development of Self, Voice, and Mind.* New York: Basic, 1986.

Carr, Thomas M. Jr. *Descartes and the Resilience of Rhetoric.* Carbondale: Southern Illinois UP, 1990.

Descartes, Rene. *Discourse on Method and the Meditations.* Trans. F. E. Sutcliffe. London: Penguin, 1968.

———. *Principes de la philosophie.* Trans. Rodger Miller and Reese P. Miller. Boston: D. Reidel, 1983.

Jamieson, Kathleen Hall. *Eloquence in an Electronic Age: The Transformation of Political Speechmaking*. New York: Oxford UP, 1988.

Lamy, Bernard. *The Art of Speaking*. 1676. Repr. in *The Rhetorics of Thomas Hobbes and Bernard Lamy*. Ed. John T. Harwood. Carbondale: Southern Illinois UP, 1986. 167–377.

MacLean, Ian. *The Renaissance Nation of Women*. Cambridge: Cambridge UP, 1980.

Noddings, Nel. *Caring: A Feminine Approach to Ethics and Moral Education*. Berkeley: U of California P, 1984.

Ong, Walter J. *Orality and Literacy: The Technologizing of the Word*. London: Methuen, 1982.

Perry, Ruth. *The Celebrated Mary Astell: An Early English Feminist*. Chicago: U of Chicago P, 1986.

Smith, Florence. *Mary Astell*. 1916. Repr. New York: AMS, 1966.

Sutherland, Christine Mason. "Love as Rhetorical Principle: The Relationship Between Content and Style in the Rhetoric of St. Augustine." *Grace, Politics and Desire*. Ed. Hugo A. Meynell. Calgary: U of Calgary P, 1990. 139–54.

———. "Outside the Rhetorical Tradition: Mary Astell's Advice to Women in Seventeenth Century England." *Rhetorica* 9.2 (spring 1991): 147–63.

7

Daring to Dialogue: Mary Wollstonecraft's Rhetoric of Feminist Dialogics

Jamie Barlowe

Of the many remarkable aspects of Mary Wollstonecraft (1759–1797)—best known for her feminist manifesto, *A Vindication of the Rights of Woman* (1792)—perhaps the most remarkable was her steadfast belief in her *right* to participate in dialogues with the philosophers, politicians, educators, historians, and artists of her day as an informed, capable, rational thinker. Such public dialogues were not generally considered to be a woman's province, but Wollstonecraft neither questioned nor apologized for her own intellectual self-assurance. Whether she was challenging eighteenth-century cultural norms—as in her novels *Mary* and *Maria*—or responding to men such as Burke, Rousseau, Paine, and Talleyrand—as in her two *Vindications*—or writing letters to Gilbert Imlay or William Godwin, she consistently and persuasively argued for the rights of women. Thus, though her use of genres varied and though she grew increasingly radical, she never altered her goals of exposing the irrationality of the arguments used to debase and exclude women and of examining the pernicious, unquestioned assumptions on which those arguments rested.

Some critics have faulted Wollstonecraft for not explicitly engaging in dialogues with other contemporary women, particularly French-women, such as Olympia de Gouges and Etta Palm d'Aelders, who spoke out in the opening stages of the French Revolution. Instead, these critics note that she talked with men; some even go so far as to say that she appears not to "like women" (see Lorch; Butler and Todd; and for an opposing view, Brody). Yet by talking to men, Wollstonecraft became a representative dialogist—a rhetor, standing for other women of her time, especially those who had no understanding of their oppressed conditions. We can, in fact, applaud her bold assumption that she could and should talk to men, especially since men's notions not only shaped the thinking of her time but the policy as well. For Mary Wollstonecraft was engaged in a theoretical dialogue as a means to the practical ends of changing conditions and laws.

Wollstonecraft set out to persuade men that the natural extension of their logical positions would lead them to include rather than exclude women, that they were irrational in their thinking about women, that they had relativized virtue by trivializing and marginalizing women, that they violated "natural" laws, and that they created and shaped cultural conditions that ultimately victimized themselves as well as women. Moreover, she urged upper- and middle-class women to resist tyranny, first, by recognizing the wretchedness of cultivating the graces and perpetuating childish dependencies, and then by refusing to be complicit in that oppression. Their resistance—and consequent action—could alter the oppressive conditions of poor women as well as their own conditions. In fact, she refused to patronize women for their failures to recognize their own complicity, addressing them as "rational creatures" and thus implying their potential dignity and ability (*Vindication of Woman* 81).

My analysis of Wollstonecraft rests on the assumption that as modern readers we are in dialogue with her work as we try to understand her dialogics, her positions and methods, and the consequences of all her work. As I see it, such an analysis necessarily generates an argument for considering her private letters, not as the context of her public writings, but as equally valuable and valid texts in themselves, which also reveal her particular rhetorical strategies, her passionate commitment to a feminist ideology, her formidable intuitive and analytical skills, and her personal struggles.

Too often, critics have argued that Wollstonecraft's personal life betrayed her feminist positions and that her letters to Gilbert Imlay violated her intellectual integrity. In view of such thinking, we can understand why such critics want to create separate categories, viewing her personal life as mired in the oppression of female emotions and desire and her public writing as increasingly radical. For example, Jennifer Lorch says that "to reach an accurate assessment of Mary Wollstonecraft's relevance to the late twentieth century is to disentangle her political writings, her career, and her private life" (109). Mary Poovey argues that Wollstonecraft never incorporates into her personal life her own intellectual challenges, thus "falling hostage . . . to the very categories she was trying to escape," and that the "difficulties Mary Wollstonecraft encountered again and again in her private life and her literary works all center on the issue of feeling" (48).

Rather than trapping our examination of Wollstonecraft's writings in the binary oppositions of reason/emotion and public/private that her culture depended on to separate men and women (and denigrate and isolate women), we can refuse such oppositions by examining both her private letters and published works as they reveal her consistent resistance to those limiting categories. In doing so, I will not be renarrativizing her life; instead, to the ends I have articulated, I will examine some representative pieces of Mary Wollstonecraft's work as they fall into categories of genre: political writing; novels; and letters, discussing them in terms of the dialogues they imply and the rhetorical strategies they employ as a way to achieve their feminist aims of effecting changes in belief and understanding—in the hope of real social changes.

I

Although few readers of *A Vindication of the Rights of Men* (1790) or of *A Vindication of The Rights of Woman* (1792) fail to see the immensity of their public force, many scholars criticize these pieces in terms of methodology; often the criticism takes the form of lamentations about what Wollstonecraft did not do rather than considerations of what she did do and how she chose to do it, given her larger purposes. Like many readers, I will look at *A Vindication of the Rights of Woman* as an extension of the argument developed in the first *Vindication*, even while analyzing it in terms of its own feminist ends and its dialogic and rhetorical means. In addition to refuting Burke's dramatic and emotional response to Dr. Price's sermon "Discourse on the Love of Our Country," Wollstonecraft's *Vindication of the Rights of Men* supports the idea of the inherent, natural rights of all human beings. This is in opposition to Burke's insistence on the perpetuation of a class system, the very existence of which, he claimed, constituted its justification. Belief in natural rights, he scoffed, was the province of philosophers and metaphysicians; for him, a natural right was the right to maintain the social and political position into which one was born:

The pretended rights of these theorists are all extremes; and in proportion as they are metaphysically true, they are morally and politically false.
The rights of men are in a sort of *middle*, incapable of definition, but not
impossible to be discerned. . . . This sort of people are so taken up with
their theories about the rights of man, that they have totally forgot his
nature. . . . We [the English] are not the converts of Rousseau; we are
not the disciples of Voltaire; Helvetius has made no progress amongst
us. Atheists are not our preachers; madmen are not our lawgivers. . . .
In England . . . [we] fear God; we look up with awe to kings; with affection
to parliaments; with duty to magistrates; with reverence to priests; and
with respect to nobility. Why? Because when such ideas are brought
before our minds, it is *natural* to be so affected; because all other feelings
are false and spurious, and tend to corrupt our minds, to vitiate our
primary morals. . . . Society is indeed a contract. . . . Each contract of
each particular state is but a clause in the great primaeval contract of
eternal society, linking the lower with the higher natures, connecting the
visible and invisible world, according to a fixed compact sanctioned by
the inviolable oath which holds all physical and all moral natures, each
in their appointed place. This law is not subject to the will of those, who
by an obligation above them, and infinitely superior, are bound to submit
their will to that law. (1271–87)

In *A Vindication of the Rights of Woman*, Wollstonecraft extends her
argument about natural rights to women, this time taking on such thinkers as Rousseau—who, compared to Burke, seemed liberal and enlightened, but who refused to see women as rational beings, thus violating
his own philosophic and political positions. She views Burke as holding
fully irrational beliefs, and also considers Rousseau irrational—in part
because he uses the *consequences* of women's treatment—their irrational
behavior—as evidence for their *incapacity* for rationality, just as Burke
used the behavior of men as evidence for their incapacity for rational
behavior. Women act in irrational ways, she argues, because they have
been deprived of the knowledge and skills which would allow them to
behave rationally. Even so-called educated women have been taught in a

false system of education; the minds of women are enfeebled by false
refinement . . . the books of instruction, written by men of genius, have
had the same tendency as more frivolous productions . . . they are treated
as a kind of subordinate being, and not as part of the human species,
when improvable reason is allowed to be the dignified distinction which
raises men above the brute creation, and puts a natural scepter in a feeble
hand. (79–80)

She dedicates this *Vindication* to Talleyrand, hoping, as Miriam Brody tells us, "to influence legislation before the French Assembly on women's education" (18):

> Pardon my frankness, but . . . I call upon you . . . now to weigh what I have advanced respecting the rights of woman and national education; and I call with the firm tone of humanity, for my arguments, sir, are dictated by a disinterested spirit—I plead for my sex, not for myself. Independence I have long considered the grand blessing of life, the basis of every virtue; and independence I will ever secure by contracting my wants. It is then an affection for the whole human race that makes my pen dart rapidly along to support what I believe to be the cause of virtue; and the same motive leads me earnestly to wish to see woman placed in a station in which she would advance, instead of retarding, the progress of those glorious principles that give a substance to morality. My opinion, indeed, respecting the rights and duties of woman seems to flow so naturally from these same principles, that I think it scarcely possible but that some of the enlarged minds who formed your admirable constitution will coincide with me. (85)

In other words, Wollstonecraft takes the men on where they are: if they believe in morality as a consequence of rationality, which is natural to human beings, and if they believe that education is one of the ways to cultivate virtue through rationality, then women, as human creatures, will "stop the progress of knowledge and virtue" if they "be not prepared by education to become the companion of man" (86). That education— what she calls the "perfect education"—is

> an exercise of the understanding as is best calculated to strengthen the body and form the heart. Or, in other words, to enable the individual to attain such habits of virtue as will render it independent. In fact, it is a farce to call any being virtuous whose virtues do not result from the exercise of its own reason. This was Rousseau's opinion respecting men; I extend it to women; . . . I may be accused of arrogance; still I must declare what I firmly believe, that all the writers who have written on the subject of female education and manners, from Rousseau to Dr. Gregory, have contributed to render women more artificial, weak characters, than they would otherwise have been; and consequently more useless members of society. (103–04)

Wollstonecraft's purposes and her confident expression of them have radical potentialities. Of course, she refrains from stating the implications of her argument—full independence of women—because otherwise her argument would have been so threatening as to be disregarded. Instead, she argues that if men desire certain societal ends, then one of the means to reach those ends is to educate women to help achieve—rather than thwart—them. Since she believes in full independence in her own life— having already proposed the unconventional arrangement of living with a married couple, the Fuselis; having already decided against marriage for herself; and having chosen writing as a way to achieve financial independence—she knows the implications and potentialities of her argument. What she cares about—more than possible future consequences—is getting men of power to listen to her argument and then getting changes instituted.

Thus, her goals seem radically feminist: on the local, immediate level, she seeks to change the educational system and thus perhaps women's self-estimation, in order to gain the respect of men; on the vaster level, she seeks women's independence. She does not, I'll admit, dialogue— except implicitly—with women, nor does she ever write the projected Part 2 of the *Vindication*, which would have included discussions of "women's legal and political rights." Neither does she specifically discuss "the individual woman's self-realization" (Butler and Todd 15). While such omissions may be "frustrating" from a twentieth-century feminist point of view, her arguments—and her life—do not close out such possibilities. As Margaret Fuller was to do half a century later in America, Wollstonecraft publicly demanded a recontextualization of women inside the generally received notions of human beings and their souls, as both a moral action and a means to social morality.

The remainder of the long *Vindication*, divided into sections, serves as supporting arguments and evidence for her positions, her statements of problems, and her proposals of solutions, always anticipating and accounting for objections. She remains in the dialogic mode throughout the piece, addressing this audience of so-called enlightened men, assuming their desire to live up to the terms of their own philosophical and political systems and assuming their intelligence and morality. She pushes them gently at times and shoves them around rhetorically at others. She also assumes her own ability to reason, to argue, and to persuade. She ends the *Vindication* with these words, using irony as one of her persuasive tools:

> Let woman share the rights, and she will emulate the virtues of man [the "enlightened" men she is directly addressing]; for she must grow more

perfect when emancipated or justify the authority that chains such a weak being to her duty. If the latter, it will be expedient to open a fresh trade with Russia for whips: a present which a father should always make to his son-in-law on his wedding day, that a husband may keep his whole family in order by the same means; and without any violation of justice reign, wielding this scepter, sole master of his house, because he is the only thing in it who has reason:—the divine, indefeasible earthly sovereignty breathed into man by the Master of the universe. Allowing this position, women have not any inherent rights to claim; and, by the same rule, their duties vanish, for rights and duties are inseparable. Be just then, O ye men of understanding; and mark not more severely what women do amiss than the vicious tricks of the horse or the ass for whom ye provide provender—and allow her the privileges of ignorance, to whom ye deny the rights of reason, or ye will be worse than Egyptian task-masters, expecting virtue where Nature has not given understanding. (319)

II

Wollstonecraft's advertisement for her first novel, *Mary* (1788), describes the book as "an artless tale, without episodes," but one in which "the mind of a woman, who has thinking powers is displayed" (5). In a letter she calls it "a tale, to illustrate an opinion of mine, that a genius will educate itself" (4), following Rousseau. In this rather short but intense third-person narrative, no dialogue breaks the relentless account of an empathetic, energetic female of genius whose external circumstances help shape her sensibility, changing her from a naive, vulnerable, unsettled young girl to a woman who "struggled for resignation" (73). Faced with continual painful events in her life—often a loved one's death—Mary does not so much overcome the events as internalize them to become ever more attuned to the pain of others, often to her own discomfort. Through reading and writing, she works to include reason into her own deliberations; reason, in fact, curbs the passions, which, unshaped and unstrengthened, lead to full immersion in sentimentality, sensuality, idleness, and self-indulgence—in other words, to becoming someone like Mary's mother, Eliza. In fact, just in case the reader might misunderstand the initial direction of this novel, the narrator ironizes the portrait of Eliza's life:

When she could not any longer indulge the caprices of fancy one way, she tried another. The Platonic Marriage, Eliza Warwick and some other

interesting tales were perused with eagerness. Nothing could be more
natural than the development of the passions, nor more striking than the
views of the human heart.

What delicate struggles! and uncommonly pretty turns of thought! . . .
Fatal image!—. . . What a *heart-rending* accident. . . . Alas! Alas! If my
readers would excuse the sportiveness of fancy, and give me credit for
genius, I would go on and tell them such tales as would force the sweet
tears of sensibility to flow in copious showers down beautiful cheeks, to
the discomposure of rouge, etc. etc. Nay, I would make it so interesting,
that the fair peruser should beg the hair-dresser to settle the curls himself, and not interrupt her. [Eliza] had besides another resource, two
most beautiful dogs, who shared her bed. . . . These she watched with
the most assiduous care. (8)

But Mary, the daughter, is "neglected in every respect, and left to
the operations of her own mind." Mary, too, is filled with passions, although hers take the form of "sublime ideas . . . always connected with
devotional sentiments; extemporary effusions of gratitude, and rhapso-
dies of praise would often burst from her" (11). More important, as un-
formed and uninformed as Mary's passions are as a young girl, their
consequence is not idle self-indulgence, but action. She helps others:
"Her benevolence, indeed, knew no bounds; the distress of others carried her out of herself; and she rested not till she had relieved or comforted them. The warmth of her compassion often made her so diligent,
that many things occurred to her, which might have escaped a less interested observer" (16). The movement from passion/emotion through
reason to action, in fact, becomes Mary's primary mode of operation.
Reason, engendered through reading and writing and discussion, does
not mitigate or overpower the emotions, but informs them so that, combined, they can lead to action—not merely to theories or more abstract
thinking—but to real human actions. These actions often take the form
of resisting the culture's strictures, undoing, in fact, its inevitable destruc-
tive consequences by intruding into the lives of its victims, nurturing
them emotionally and supporting them financially. Moreover, Mary's rational thinking allows her respite from her own grief and the power to
persuade men that she should be trusted to make decisions and act in
terms of them, for example, when she persuades her husband (a man
she neither knows nor loves) that she should take her friend Ann, who
is dying, to Portugal or southern France and care for her there.

In other words, Mary, given the cultural codes and rules, feels she
has no choice but to seek his approval for her trip, and given human

frailty and providential decisions, knows she cannot change the course of her friend's illness. If such uncontrollable circumstances could be seen as forming the circumference of Mary's external world, then, even in this context, she finds the means of active resistance—of action itself. Meena Alexander has suggested that Mary's resistance takes the form of writing, which allows her to "discover an authentic self, capable of both action and expression" (41). Perhaps we are to see that in other, less limiting circumstances, a thinking/feeling woman like Mary would be liberated, fully independent, and free to develop her genius, as Rousseau envisions for men.

Although this early novel is often categorized as merely sentimental, I see it instead as the initial working out of Wollstonecraft's feminist project of envisioning a life of independence for women and envisioning and re-envisioning a society that will allow it. In fact, the last lines of *Mary*, which strongly rearticulate one of the lessons of this text, also prepare us for Wollstonecraft's last work, another novel, the unfinished *Wrongs of Woman: or, Maria* (1798): "[Mary's] delicate state of health did not promise long life. In moments of solitary sadness, a gleam of joy would dart across her mind—She thought she was hastening to that world where there is neither marrying, nor giving in marriage" (73). Thus, while I would agree with such feminist critics as Alexander and Lorch that Wollstonecraft's last novel, *Maria*, is more radical in form and content than her first, *Mary* (see Poovey; Ferguson; and Butler and Todd for other views), the groundwork for that radicalism has already been laid in *Mary*. In fact, the groundwork covers much more than Wollstonecraft's attitudes about marriage; a variety of social ills, from property rights to impressment and women's spheres of action are also reexamined. In *Maria* the female protagonist is locked inside a prison, effecting change both inside and outside the walls as well as in the minds and hearts of others. Like Mary, she persuades others, through language informed by reason and passion, to help her or at least to agree with her methods. Maria, however, resists the strictures of her own life in ways Mary would not have considered. Mary's resistance—though certainly not passive—is never great enough to generate punishment (all her "punishment" or pain is a result of illness and death), but Maria's resistance is more consequential. Leaving her marriage, in fact, results in her imprisonment and the kidnapping of her child.

Even critics such as Poovey, who consider *Maria* a failure in both its form and political aim, find Wollstonecraft's characterization of Jemima innovative and feminist. As Poovey says,

Jemima's story—which is a radical, indeed feminist, story—has the potential to call into question both the organizational principles of bourgeois society and the sentimentalism that perpetuates romantic idealism. For the anarchy implicit in Jemima's brief assertion of female sexuality combines with the stark realism of the narrative to explode the assumptions that tie female sexuality to romance and thus to the institutions men traditionally control. (104)

Poovey faults Wollstonecraft, however, for not fully developing Jemima's character and her political potential, and she feels that Maria—as well as the narrator—is crippled by "sentimental idealism" (105). Yet others consider, as I do, the inclusion of issues of class and gender to be politically radical and potentially subversive. Poovey also argues that Wollstonecraft's novel fails in "reconciling her intended 'purpose' with the genre, which here shapes the 'structure' of the work." According to her sketchy preface, Wollstonecraft had a political purpose, yet her choice of genre, which allowed for the dramatization of "finer sensations [which] were deeply implicated in the values—indeed, the very organization—of bourgeois society," caused her severe problems (96).

Instead, Wollstonecraft reshaped the genre of sentimentalism to fit her political, feminist purposes. If her characters demonstrate "finer sensations," it is always with the goal of solving their immediate problems at the level of story, which reflect the larger political ends of Wollstonecraft. Her characters, in other words, work in the service of Wollstonecraft's political themes. Examining both her novels in light of their feminist aims, we can see that her rhetorical strategies often demanded subversion of typical expectations of genre and that her continual dialogic mode puts the reader in a specific relationship to Wollstonecraft's characters—and to Wollstonecraft as author—who request attention, acknowledgement, and action.

III

Finally, I want to consider as part of her feminist aims, rhetorical strategies, and dialogic method Mary Wollstonecraft's letters to Gilbert Imlay (the man with whom she lived during the early years of the 1790s and with whom she had a daughter, Fanny), although, as I indicated in my introduction, even feminist critics have generally categorized these letters as personal and thus separate from her public writings. In part, that separation is a consequence of a kind of embarrassment. The fact that the woman touted as writing the first feminist manifesto could twice attempt suicide after Gilbert Imlay's rejection of her is a source of ideological discomfort. For example, Jennifer Lorch argues that Wollstonecraft mythologized Imlay and the beginnings of their relationship, believing in capacities he did not have and then refusing to acknowledge her mistake: "She clung to the notion that she could improve her Gilbert." Lorch sees Wollstonecraft as violating what she had earlier written in *Thoughts on the Education of Daughters* (1789), namely, that one should root out passion that is unapproved by reason; Lorch also deplores what she sees as Wollstonecraft's emotional and financial dependence on Imlay (45–47).

Although viewing Wollstonecraft generally as one who "proclaimed the new feminist viewpoint" and in whose works "may be found a chronicle of an epoch," Moira Ferguson and Janet Todd consistently undermine Wollstonecraft as they interpret her letters to Imlay, primarily through their tone and their use of charged, negative words:

> Wollstonecraft's love letters prove her to be a woman very much swayed by emotions . . . a woman . . . unafraid to express [her feelings] extravagantly, unabashed by lavish sentiments. . . . As Imlay withdrew his affection, she shifted into a . . . more frenzied emotional gear. At first when his affections waned she burst with fury and resentment . . . [showing an] absence of control to the point of suicide. . . . She reproves Imlay for her sufferings, discomfits him with stories of her fatigue and disorders, while petulantly (and paradoxically) reminding him that she does not complain. In an apparent attempt to reforge their emotional links, she attempts to arouse a sense of guilt in him as she chides him about the health and general disposition of their daughter. (13–15, 91–93)

Up against these letters, Ferguson and Todd put the published *Letters Written During a Short Residence in Sweden, Norway, and Denmark* (1796), praising them for their "control and power" (103). Yet they "fancy" that her pleading in *An Historical and Moral View of the French Revolution* (1794) is an "imposition of rationalism onto the chaos of indulged emotion" in which there is a "parallel to her efforts at rationally controlling her frantic infatuation with the retreating Imlay" (82). They go on to say that the "ultimate optimism of *The French Revolution*, so qualified even in its closing chapters, is more darkly undercut when the book is placed in the context of Wollstonecraft's life. Perhaps it is fortunate in being the only one of her later works that does not insist on this context" (88). Their argument about her personal life—at times explicit and at others implicit—is that it always imposes on her writing, usually in negative ways. The personal life, then—including her letters to Imlay—is a context into which they place her texts.

Equally appreciative of *Letters in Sweden*, Mary Poovey argues that they "enable [Wollstonecraft] to objectify her tumultuous emotions in a form that does not demand an integrated, fully formed persona . . . as the mirror of a maturing self and self-consciousness; . . . the *Letters* details the narrator's passage from an initial state of poised expectation through a period of energetic exploration, observation, and self-discovery, to a gradual decline into melancholy and anger" (91–92). Thus, her experiences with Imlay, as related in her personal letters to him, provide a context (positive rather than negative, as in Ferguson and Todd) for the published, polished, controlled *Letters in Sweden* (see also Alexander; Brody; Butler and Todd).

I want to look at Wollstonecraft's letters to Imlay, not as a context for her public writings—either positive or negative—or as a fully separate category, but as another equally important genre in which she expresses her fundamental right to argue her case. In that light, they are rhetorically interesting, ideologically sound, and dialogically motivated. Just as she believes she should argue for her ideas about the education and rights of women in her other writings, Mary Wollstonecraft is arguing for her personal rights in these letters to Imlay. To see them in such a light may require that we shift away from the long-held perspective that they are not feminist in aim or method.

What we know now—and what she did not know for certain when writing these letters—is that her passionate and reasoned arguments to him would not touch him emotionally or move him to action. The fact that she believed in him—and in her power to move him—continued to motivate her until she fully recognized that she had failed. She could not know that she would fail, yet we judge her as though she should have known. Interestingly, however, we do not judge her negatively for failing to institute radical social changes as a consequence of her *Thoughts on the Education of Daughters*, the two *Vindications*, or the two novels. We applaud and analyze her efforts, her ideas, and her voice in those public writings, even though when she died, her society had not incorporated any of her ideas into their political, educational, or economic system. Similarly, Gilbert Imlay refused to change or to incorporate her arguments into his life, to examine his ethical inadequacies, or to live up to the terms of their earlier relationship; yet we seem to be more embarrassed by Wollstonecraft's rhetorical failures than by his ethical ones.

The alternative to her letters might have been silence or passivity, reactions eschewed for obvious reasons by Wollstonecraft and by today's feminists. Some might suggest that, even if she decided to maintain a dialogue with him, she should have argued less passionately or suppressed her anger, pain, and despair. At the very least, some say, she should have not harangued him for his failures. Yet, had she adopted these means to her end of persuading Imlay, she would have been false to herself. She would also have violated her sense, at that time, of her best methods of persuasion. In all her previous public writings, she argued strongly, even *haranguing*, about the ills of her culture, the failure of men to live up to their own professed notions of rationality, and of women to take themselves seriously. Yet since she also knew that women were victims and thus hardly responsible for their weaknesses and failures, she directed most of her arguments to men with ideational, political, and economic power. If, as we saw in her political writings and novels, the system were to change, then women themselves would change. As a consequence, men would change, too, and life would improve for all. In her letters to Imlay, she directs her personal argument (seeing herself as a victim of his irresponsibility and insensibility) to a man with emotional, if not ideational or economic, power. If he would only listen, understand, and take action, both their lives would be better.

It seems unlikely that Imlay would have been surprised by her intensity and commitment to her beliefs, not the least of which was her desire to convince him to stay with her and give up his pursuit of commercial interests. Yet critics consistently condemn Wollstonecraft's desire and understand Imlay's wish to escape her intensity and any commitment to her perspective. She took herself—and him—so seriously, however, that it never occurred to her that her love for him was silly, misdirected, or wrong, nor did she realize—at least for a while—that he would find justification for his rejection of her and of her expectations of him.

Her early letters to Imlay, I would argue, rest on the same assumptions as her letters to her publisher, Johnson, or later to her husband, William Godwin: mutual respect and shared understanding, which ostensibly reflected their relationship to that point. Whether her assumptions fully reflect his sense of the relationship, we have no idea. Given Wollstonecraft's intelligence and intuition, however, we can infer with some assurance that they shared something emotionally powerful, whether or not his emotional commitment was primarily physical. For example, in letters dated from June 1793 to [December 30], 1793, she tells him:

> I obey an emotion of my heart, which made me think of wishing thee, my love, good-night! before I go to rest. . . . Cherish me with that digni-fied tenderness, which I have only found in you. (Letter 2)

> You have often called me dear girl. (Letter 3)

> I have just received your letter, and feel as if I could not go to bed tran-quilly without saying a few words in reply—merely to tell you, that my mind is serene, and my heart affectionate. . . . I am going to rest very happy, and you have made me so.—This is the kindest good-night I can utter. (Letter 5)

> My best love, your letter to-night was particularly grateful to my heart. . . . There was so much considerate tenderness in your epistle tonight, that, if it has not made you dearer to me, it has made me forcibly feel how very dear you are to me, by charming away half my cares. (Letter 8)

Yet she is also sensible of differences between them and of the prob-lems caused by his absence, and she is *always* arguing her points and beliefs:

> The way to my senses is through my heart; but, forgive me! I think there is sometimes a shorter cut to yours. With ninety-nine men out of a hun-dred, a very sufficient dash of folly is necessary to render a woman *pi-quante*, a soft word for desirable; and, beyond these casual ebullitions of sympathy, few look for enjoyment by fostering a passion in their hearts. One reason, in short, why I wish my whole sex to become wise, is, that the foolish ones may not, by their pretty folly rob those whose sensibility keeps down their vanity, of the few roses that afford them some solace in the thorny road of life. I do not know how I fell into these reflections, excepting one thought produced it—that these continual separations were necessary to warm your affection. Of late, we are always separating. Crack!—crack!—and away you go.—This joke wears the sallow cast of thought; for, though I began to write cheerfully, some melancholy tears have found their way into my eyes. (Letter 4)

His repeated absences demonstrate to her the problems caused by separation; she describes the "fancies" she conjures up when alone, and her fears, yet does so in a way that makes her descriptions seem more like rhetorical strategies than admissions of weakness:

> I will never, if I am not entirely cured of quarrelling, begin to encourage "quick-coming fancies," when we are separated. Yesterday . . . I could not open your letter for some time; and, though it was not half as severe as I merited, it threw me into such a fit of trembling, as seriously alarmed me. . . . This morning I am better; will you not be glad to hear it? You perceive that sorrow has almost made a child of me, and that I want to be soothed to peace. One thing you mistake in my character, and imagine that to be coldness which is just the contrary. For, when I am hurt by the person most dear to me, I must let out a whole torrent of emotions, in which tenderness would be uppermost, or stifle them altogether; and it appears to me almost a duty to stifle them, when I imagine that I am treated with coldness. (Letter 12)

> What is the reason that my spirits are not as manageable as yours? Yet, now I think of it, I will not allow that your temper is even, though I have promised myself, in order to obtain my own forgiveness, that I will not ruffle it for a long, long time—I am afraid to say never. (Letter 17)

She continues to argue that he should live with her and their daughter, Fanny, and give up commerce. In December 1794, she says, "How I hate this crooked business! This intercourse with the world, which obliges one to see the worst side of human nature!" (Letter 30). Moreover, she repeats her threats to leave with their child if he continues his absences. She is worried about her own financial situation, of course:

> I am determined to try to earn some money here myself, in order to convince you that, if you choose to run about the world to get a fortune, it is for yourself—for the little girl and I will live without your assistance, unless you are with us. I may be termed proud—Be it so—but I will never abandon certain principles of action. The common run of men have such an ignoble way of thinking, that, if they debauch their hearts, and prostitute their persons, following perhaps a gust of inebriation, they suppose the wife, slave rather, whom they maintain, has no right to complain, and ought to receive the sultan, whenever he deigns to return. . . . You know my opinion of men in general; you know that I think them systematic tyrants, and that it is the rarest thing in the world, to meet with a man with sufficient delicacy of feeling to govern desire. . . . You will call this an ill-humored letter, when, in fact, it is the strongest proof of affection I can give, to dread to lose you. . . . You have always known

my opinion—I have ever declared, that two people, who mean to live together, ought not to be long separated.—If certain things are more necessary to you than me—search for them—Say but one word, and you shall never hear of me more.—If not, for God's sake, let us struggle with poverty—with any evil, but these continual inquietudes of business, which I have been told were to last but a few months, though every day the end appears more distant. (Letter 31)

Yet he continues to make her believe, according to her letters, that he will return and that he also returns her affections, even if the moments of affection are punctuated by their quarrels. She describes the difficulties she faces in order to prod him to action, not merely to "complain," as she has been accused of doing by those who want to place her in a context that she so desperately wanted to escape: that of expectations for women. Nor does she want him to act out of guilt, but rather out of a shared affection. In fact, she consistently refuses his offers of financial assistance after it is clear his passion has cooled.

Even as late as June 1795—after her first suicide attempt and her subsequent trip to Scandinavia—she argues her case, based on her belief in him and in herself: "Well! you will ask, what is the result of all this reasoning? Why I cannot help thinking that it is possible for you, having great strength of mind, to return to nature, and regain a sanity of constitution, and purity of feelings—which would open your heart to me.— I would fain rest there" (Letter 44). We can infer that he begins to accuse her of failures to show him respect, yet she considers her most profound signals of respect to be manifested in her unlimited confidence in his capacity to live up to expectations.

She finally begins, however, to admit to herself the magnitude of his rejection, and her despair grows; yet she never stops trying to persuade him to listen to her reason and to honor his various commitments to her, not cultural commitments of marriage or finances, but those of the heart, affection for her and Fanny. When she is hurt—which is quite often— she tells him so openly and honestly, speaking out, as she had always done, refusing to be silenced by his actions or by the world that had oppressed her:

I have been hurt by indirect enquiries, which appear to me not to be dictated by any tenderness to me.—You ask "If I am well or tranquil?"— They who think me so, must want a heart to estimate my feelings by.— I chose then to be the organ of my own sentiments. I must tell you, that

> I am very much mortified by your continually offering me pecuniary assistance. (Letter 73)

> I do not perfectly understand you.—If, by the offer of your friendship, you still only mean pecuniary support—I must again reject it. . . . I have been treated ungenerously—if I understand what is generosity.—You seem to me only to have been anxious to shake me off—regardless whether you dashed me to atoms by the fall.—In truth I have been rudely handled. (Letter 75)

These two sections of letters were written after she discovered he was living in London with a mistress. She is angry, yes, and actively argues against him. She is planning another attempt at suicide, yet she continues to answer each of his letters, believing in her own rhetorical and dialogic power and in the possibilities of language to make changes in her terrible situation. Even her very last letter to him maintains her position of intellectual integrity and justification for her love of him, no longer because he deserves it, but because it is *her* feeling to have, not his to discard:

> I now solemnly assure you, that this is an eternal farewell.—Yet I flinch not from the duties which tie me to life. That there is "sophistry" on one side or other, is certain; but now it matters not on which. On my part it has not been a question of words. Yet your understanding or mine must be strangely warped—for what you term "delicacy," appears to me to be exactly the contrary. I have no criterion for morality, and have thought in vain, if the sensations which lead you to follow an ancle or step, be the sacred foundation of principle and affection. Mine has been of a different nature, or it would not have stood the brunt of your sarcasms. The sentiment in me is still sacred. If there be any part of me that will survive the sense of my misfortunes, it is the purity of my affections. The impetuosity of your senses, may have led you to term mere animal desire, the source of principles; and it may give zest to some years to come.— Whether you will always think so, I shall never know. It is strange that, in spite of all you do, something like conviction forces me to believe, that you are not what you appear to be. I part with you in peace. (Letter 78)

IV

To conclude this essay, I wish to examine a few of the important implications for us as academics of considering Mary Wollstonecraft's writing. The first concerns the targeted audiences of feminist academics, whether their work be that of reclaiming lost (or suppressed) texts by women; providing a hearing for hitherto unheard female voices; recontextualizing the work of women who have been undervalued, ignored, misunderstood, or vilified by the culture; criticizing the texts that depict women; or theorizing about texts, authors, readers, and language from feminist perspectives (the work of this collection of essays). Too often, we address our work primarily—sometimes exclusively—to other women, assuming perhaps that we are working only to educate one another. Although that is a significant part of our task—sharing our research and challenging one another—part of our task, too, is to follow Wollstonecraft's lead and, as often as possible, publicly address ourselves directly to the source of problems—institutionalized power that, intentionally or indirectly, allows oppressive practices to continue: in hiring, committee assignments, and course loads; through texts selected from publishers as well as for class syllabi; and through decisions about administrative positions, women's studies departments and programs, and tenure and promotion—just to name a few potentially problematic areas. No matter how much we would like to believe the contrary, that kind of work is never completed. Even if certain fundamental goals have been achieved at certain institutions by certain women, there is no evidence that there is general change, especially at small universities and colleges, both public and private.

Sexism is so deeply ingrained in our culture—including academic life—that our best efforts have so far merely begun the work of examining its extent and the means by which it is perpetuated. And if we see the immense amount of work to be done in academe, the work in the general community is even more daunting. The sexism of many of our students and colleagues should be confronted more directly. We should feel compelled, once again, to bring up sexism and its consequences in department and university meetings, at conferences, and in our classrooms. In the spirit of Gerald Graff's idea of "teaching the conflicts" and in the spirit of Wollstonecraft's belief in the rhetoric of feminist dialogue, we can generate discussions that guarantee even more public airings of the issues of sexism in texts, in decisions, in power, and in life, especially at places where these discussions are limited or discouraged—and there are many such places. Frank and open dialogues should be especially encouraged at institutions where there are (often unacknowledged) punitive consequences for being a feminist. "The New Rhetorics," explored and explained in this collection through the contributions of women, encourage us to break silences, to dialogue, to connect, and to collaborate.

Moreover, we may want to rethink any decisions we might make to teach unproblematically texts that perpetuate exclusionary ideas because we feel uncomfortable about our own prospects for tenure and promotion or about students' opinions. Two hundred years ago Mary Wollstonecraft felt compelled to speak out against such men as Burke and Rousseau—doing work that was well known (if not well loved) at the same time. Yet how many classes in eighteenth-century thought (in literature, history, rhetoric, and philosophy) teach the texts of these men and never once consider the value of putting them in dialogue with Wollstonecraft's two *Vindications*? Indeed, how often is there even a general awareness of her texts? In places where Wollstonecraft is part of the work of the classroom, she is often included in the "women's issues" section of the syllabus or in some other kind of isolating category, without the students also reading the works of the men to whom she responds; or she is read only in classes taught by women. In other words, adding her to classes dealing with women's issues or to classes taught only by women is *not enough*. We should work to get her and other women who made significant contributions to intellectual history and to the history of rhetoric more generally accepted and included.

For us to teach the male tradition without putting their work in dialogue with their historical, cultural, linguistic, and ideological contexts and with female thinkers and rhetors is to participate in the perpetuation of beliefs that are oppressive. Students, especially ours in the 1990s, do not automatically challenge such beliefs, for unquestioning adherence to some notion of duty or code of behavior is continually valorized in our culture, whether by socialization learned in school, religious education, or participation in war. However, I also find the decision not to teach the texts of the past problematic. Instead, putting ideas in dialogue with oppositional voices, especially when we can discover contemporaneous ones, allows our students to see, as Mary Wollstonecraft so clearly understood, that reading and writing—as a way of gaining the knowledge and skills to speak with vision and confidence—and then publicly articulating one's concerns can effect change, even if those changes do not fully emerge, as in Wollstonecraft's case, until two centuries later in classrooms in America. Perhaps our students, especially our women students, will understand, too, that the committed—and yes, sometimes passionate—expression of one's ideas and beliefs can make a difference at the personal level, as well as in the public domain.

REFERENCES

Alexander, Meena. *Women in Romanticism: Mary Wollstonecraft, Dorothy Words-worth, and Mary Shelley.* Savage, MD: Barnes and Noble, 1989.

Applewhite, Harriet Branson, Mary Durham Johnson, and Darlene Gay Levy. *Women in Revolutionary Paris, 1789–1795.* Urbana: U of Illinois P, 1979.

Brody, Miriam. Introduction. *Vindication of the Rights of Woman.* By Mary Woll-stonecraft. New York: Penguin, 1985.

Burke, Edmund. *Reflections on the Revolution in France.* In *Eighteenth Century English Literature.* Ed. Tillotson, Fussell, and Waingrow. New York: Harcourt, 1969.

Butler, Marilyn, and Janet Todd. General introduction. *The Works of Mary Woll-stonecraft.* 7 vols. Washington Square: New York UP, 1989.

Ferguson, Moira, and Janet Todd. *Mary Wollstonecraft.* Boston: Twayne, 1984.

Lorch, Jennifer. *Mary Wollstonecraft: The Making of a Radical Feminist.* New York: Berg (St. Martin's), 1990.

Poovey, Mary. *The Proper Lady and the Woman Writer: Ideology as Style in the Works of Mary Wollstonecraft, Mary Shelley, and Jane Austen.* Chicago: U of Chicago P, 1984.

Price, Richard. *A Discourse on the Love of our Country at the Meeting House in the Old Jewry for the Society of Commemorating the Revolution in Great Britain.* London: Cadell, 1790.

Rousseau, Jean-Jacques. *Emile.* Trans. Barbara Foxley. New York: Dutton, 1974.

Wardle, Ralph M. *Godwin and Mary: Letters of William Godwin and Mary Woll-stonecraft.* Lincoln: U of Nebraska P, 1966.

Wollstonecraft, Mary. *Collected Letters of Mary Wollstonecraft.* Ed. Ralph M. Wardle. Ithaca: Cornell UP, 1979.

———. *The Cave of Fancy.* In vol. 1 of *The Works of Mary Wollstonecraft.* Ed. Marilyn Butler and Janet Todd. 7 vols. Washington Square: New York UP, 1989.

———. *An Historical and Moral View of the Origin and Progress of the French Revolution.* In vol. 6 of *The Works of Mary Wollstonecraft.*

———. *Letters to Gilbert Imlay.* In vol. 6 of *The Works of Mary Wollstonecraft.*

———. *Letters to Joseph Johnson.* In vol. 6 of *The Works of Mary Wollstonecraft.*

———. *Letters Written During a Short Residence in Sweden, Norway and Denmark.* In vol. 6 of *The Works of Mary Wollstonecraft.*

———. *Maria, or The Wrongs of Woman.* In vol. 1 of *The Works of Mary Woll-stonecraft.*

———. *Mary.* In vol. 1 of *The Works of Mary Wollstonecraft.*

———. *Thoughts on the Education of Daughters.* In vol. 4 of *The Works of Mary Wollstonecraft.*

———. *A Vindication of the Rights of Men.* In vol. 5 of *The Works of Mary Woll-stonecraft.*

———. *A Vindication of the Rights of Woman.* In vol. 5 of *The Works of Mary Wollstonecraft.*

8
. . . .

Inventing a Feminist Discourse: Rhetoric and Resistance in Margaret Fuller's *Woman in the Nineteenth Century*

Annette Kolodny

When Margaret Fuller's *Woman in the Nineteenth Century* first appeared in the bookstores in the winter of 1845, few readers were prepared to accept her uncompromising proposition that "inward and outward freedom for woman as for man shall be acknowledged as a right, not yielded as a concession" (Fuller, *Woman*, facsimile edition 26; unless otherwise noted, citations from *Woman* are to this edition). Elaborating arguments she had first encountered in Mary Wollstonecraft's *Vindication of the Rights of Woman* (1792), Fuller insisted that because "not one man, in the million, . . . not in the hundred million, can rise above the belief that woman was made for man," woman would have to "lay aside all thought, such as she habitually cherished, of being taught and led by men" (25, 107).[1] Incorporating the platform logic of women's rights and antislavery activists like Angelina Grimké and Abigail Kelley Foster (both are explicitly mentioned in *Woman* 98), Fuller tersely observed that "those who think the physical circumstances of woman would make a part in the affairs of national government unsuitable, are by no means those who think it impossible for the negresses to endure field work, even during

---

pregnancy, or the sempstresses to go through their killing labors" (24). And, risking the charge of employing "language . . . offensive to delicacy,"[2] Fuller wrote graphically about women's sexual bondage in marriage, condemned male sexual license, and insisted upon society's moral obligations even to the "degraded" prostitute, comparing the prostitute's economic exchange of her body with "the dower of a worldly marriage" (133, 132).

To read Fuller today is to be impressed anew with the sheer revolutionary daring of her attempt both to question existing gender hierarchies and to disrupt accepted sexual practices. Unfortunately, the potential impact of her arguments was long ago obscured by critics' reluctance seriously to analyze the even greater daring of her rhetorical strategies. As a result, when the second wave of feminist theorists in the United States began to call for a pluralistic discourse that was both collaborative and noncoercive, they showed no awareness that Fuller had earlier responded to that same challenge. In an article published in 1979, for example, Sally Miller Gearhart expressed her fear that in the "attempt to change others," "any intent to persuade is an act of violence," and she called for "the womanization of rhetoric" as an antidote ("Womanization of Rhetoric" 195). Three years later, in 1982, Jean Bethke Elshtain wondered "what sort of language, public and private, do feminists propose that women speak?" And she asked, "What models for emancipatory speech are available?" ("Feminist Discourse" 605, 606). By the end of the 1980s, Elshtain's questions still had not been answered, prompting Marianne Hirsch and Evelyn Fox Keller to observe that "feminists in the late 1980s have become exceedingly accomplished at articulating theoretical positions on the basis of disagreement and opposition. . . . But with this mastery of disputation, has come a corresponding difficulty in treating other positions with sympathy and respect. The task of clearing space for multiple agendas representing conflicting interests," concluded Hirsch and Keller in 1990, "therefore poses a major challenge" (370). That none of these scholars—and not a single author included in the Hirsch and Keller collection, *Conflicts in Feminism*—looked to Fuller as a potential source for (at least some) solutions, demonstrates how damaging the continuing critical response to Fuller's experimental method has been for feminism.

To be sure, most of the early reactions to *Woman in the Nineteenth Century* were predictable. The Boston-based social reformer, Orestes Augustus Brownson, opened his review by naming Fuller "the chieftainess" of the Transcendentalist "sect," thereby confirming his growing disaffection from the religious radicalism of the New England Transcendentalists and revealing, also, his continuing jealousy over the fact that Fuller had been chosen—instead of him—to edit their journal, the *Dial* (Brownson, "Miss Fuller and Reformers" 19; see also Capper 1:333–34). Brownson's main objections, however, were theological. Writing in his own *Brownson's Quarterly Review* for April 1845, Brownson explained: "She says man is not the head of the woman. We, on the authority of the Holy Ghost, say he is" (Brownson 22). Brownson's view was echoed by the book critic for the Charleston, South Carolina, *Southern Quarterly Review*, who flatly rejected Fuller's claim of woman's "perfect equality with man," declaring "this cannot be" (M., "Condition of Woman" 148). An unsigned series of articles that ran weekly throughout March 1845 in New York City's *Broadway Journal* challenged "the radical error of Miss Fuller's reasoning" as "directly opposed to the law of nature, of experience and revelation." "The restraints which Miss Fuller complains of as hindering women," this reviewer continued, "are the restraints which Nature has imposed." Charles F. Briggs, the ambitious young editor responsible for the series, then damned the entire book by characterizing it as "not sufficiently plain and direct," its materials only "loosely arranged" (Briggs 9, 12, 11, 13).

Even those less hostile to Fuller's views could not accord her work unalloyed praise. In a generally laudatory notice for the same *Broadway Journal*, Fuller's friend and a well-established feminist writer, Lydia Maria Child, tacitly agreed with her colleague Briggs by observing that while Fuller's style was often "vigorous and significant," the book as a whole "is sometimes rough in construction, and its meaning is not always sufficiently clear" ("Woman in the 19th Century" 7). Similarly, the reviewer for the *Christian Examiner* complained that "the book lacks method sadly." For him, it read more like "a collection of clever sayings and bright intimations, than a logical treatise" (Huntington 26).

But it was Brownson who offered the most influential rationale for dismissing *Woman in the Nineteenth Century*. Complaining that "we do not know what is its design," Brownson joined other reviewers in emphasizing discomfort with the book's organization. Unlike the others, however, Brownson exploited Fuller's local reputation as an eloquent conversationalist in order to justify his view of the text's structural flaws. "The book before us ... is no book, but a long talk," Brownson maintained. "It has neither beginning, middle, nor end, and may be read backwards as well as forwards, and from the centre outwards each way, without affecting the continuity of the thought or the succession of ideas.

We see no reason why it should stop where it does, or why the lady might not keep on talking in the same strain till doomsday, unless prevented by want of breath." Although Brownson found it necessary to devote seven full pages to refuting Fuller's arguments, his opening remarks had already effectively characterized the book for his own and subsequent generations: "As talk, it is very well, and proves that the lady has great talkative powers, and that, in this respect at least, she is a genuine woman" (19).

Brownson's accusation that she had produced nothing more than written proof of unrestrained female volubility was (as he knew) one to which Fuller was acutely sensitive. Her most recent biographer, Charles Capper, reminds us that, only weeks after accepting the editorship of the *Dial* in 1840, Fuller confided to her private journal a recurrent concern regarding, in Capper's words, "the gap between her conversational talents and her writing abilities" (1:339). After noting that her uncommon education had given her "an undue advantage in conversation with men"—who were often surprised by such learning in a woman—Fuller expressed her abiding anxiety that "then these gentlemen are surprized that I write no better because I talk so well." "But," as she herself acknowledged, "I have served a long apprenticeship to the one, none to the other" (quoted in Capper 1:339).

Because Fuller corresponded with a wide circle and freely shared her journals with several of her closest friends—including Transcendentalism's intellectual leader, the disaffected Unitarian minister Ralph Waldo Emerson—her doubts about her writing were well known. In fact, Emerson himself contributed to the view of Fuller as a better speaker than writer when he composed his memoir of Fuller after her death in 1850. "In her writing she was prone to spin her sentences without a sure guidance, and beyond the sympathy of her reader," Emerson recalled. "But in discourse, she was quick, conscious of power, in perfect tune with her company" (Emerson, Channing, and Clark 1:337).

Twentieth-century appraisals have tended to follow either Brownson or Emerson, or both. Vernon L. Parrington set the tone in 1927 when, following Brownson—who had stated that Fuller "has little artistic skill" (19)—he portrayed Fuller as "in no sense an artist, scarcely a competent craftsman" (2:418). In 1982 David M. Robinson again raised the question of Fuller's ability to control her text's "design" when he acknowledged that while she "did in fact achieve a good many high moments stylistically," she was nonetheless "often guilty of digression and obscurity" (84). Just two years later, in his reading of *Woman in the Nineteenth*

Century, William J. Scheick gave yet another nod toward Brownson when he noted that "*Woman* shares with other Transcendental works an acknowledgement of its oral heritage" (293).

Not even the renewed interest in Fuller that accompanied the second wave of feminist activism in the United States in the late 1960s succeeded in challenging the dominant view of *Woman in the Nineteenth Century* as devoid of system, method, or "design."[3] With the exception of Marie Urbanski's 1980 study, which read the text "within the sermon framework," relatively few scholars troubled themselves to examine *Woman in the Nineteenth Century* (in Urbanski's words) "as a literary work from the standpoint of form, tone, and use of rhetorical devices" (128). Instead, as Robinson has observed, even into the 1980s, Fuller scholarship remained "heavily biographical, reflecting the general sense that Fuller's life and example far outweigh her work in importance" (83). Largely unchallenged in the current decade, this trend has permitted authoritative editions of *Woman in the Nineteenth Century* to go out of print, leaving us only the posthumous 1855 edition, ineptly cut and repunctuated by her brother, Arthur B. Fuller.[4]

The problem with this cumulative critical consensus is that it commits us to believing that the only woman invited as an intellectual equal into the Transcendental Club of Emerson, Frederic Henry Hedge, George Ripley, Bronson Alcott, and the other reform-minded and Harvard-trained intellectuals of the day—the woman urged by these same men to take up the editorship of the *Dial*—was somehow incompetent. We are asked to believe that a person generally reputed to have been among the best read and the best educated of her generation—responsible for first translating and introducing Goethe and Schiller to American audiences—could not control "the succession of ideas." That the critic and journalist who won praise from her contemporary and fellow New York journalist, Edgar Allan Poe, for a "style [which] . . . is one of the very best with which I am acquainted," could not write clearly (37). That the child who delighted in the descriptions of congressional debates in her father's letters from Washington, the woman who would "ready myself to sleep" by poring over the debates transcribed in the *Congressional Record* (letter from Fuller to Caroline Sturgis, March 4, 1839, in Hudspeth 2:59) could not design an argument. That an individual trained in both classical and contemporary rhetoric, who had taken the initiative to form a rhetoric class for senior girls at the Greene Street School in Providence, Rhode Island, could not compose a "logical treatise." And, further, this consensus asks us to accept Fuller's anxieties about her writing skills as authoritative critical judgments when, in truth, every woman author of the period—British and American—larded her letters, journals, and published book prefaces with apologies for her ineptitude with the pen. Fuller was hardly the only woman of her era to complain that in "fulfilling all my duties" to family and society she had lost the precious time required for concentrated writing "and a literary existence" (letter to Ralph Waldo Emerson, March 1, 1838, in Hudspeth 1:327).

Rather than repeat critical judgments that have served to suppress the truly radical nature of Fuller's text, and rather than accept a consensus so loaded with implausible conjectures, it is time to probe Fuller's rhetorical intentions and measure her book against them. For, if we take seriously Fuller's injunction to her female readers that they set aside the habit "of being taught and led by men," then we understand that Fuller wanted not only to put forward a radical critique of all "arbitrary barriers" to women's free development (*Woman* 107, 158). As a woman speaking for women, she also needed to put forward a treatise that would not simply replicate the strategies that might have been employed by any of her well-intentioned male contemporaries. After all, as she stated repeatedly in *Woman in the Nineteenth Century*, the time had come for women to give over merely following male models and, instead, find "out what is fit for themselves" (51).

In the arena of public oratory, Fuller knew that a few brave women were already beginning to explore just such possibilities. From her own observations and from the reports she had read about the powerful female antislavery lecturers of her day, Fuller concluded that women such as Angelina Grimké and Abigail Kelley Foster, "women who speak in public, if they have a moral power . . . invariably subdue the prejudices of their hearers" (*Woman* 98). A letter from one of her many (male) correspondents, quoted approvingly in *Woman in the Nineteenth Century*, suggests that Fuller also agreed that the female antislavery speakers were better able to reach their audiences than were their male peers. As her correspondent phrased it, the women brought "the subject more into home relations" than did the men because the men, by contrast, "speak through, and mostly from intellect, . . . which creates [combat] and is combative" (99). It was precisely that "combativeness" that Fuller sought to avoid, even as she attempted—through what her contemporaries called "the affluence of her illustrations" (Dall 261) —to bring her subject "more into home relations." The result was the text that Brownson would aptly characterize—albeit for all the wrong reasons—as "a long talk."

II

Scholars have repeatedly recognized a connection between Fuller's teaching at the Greene Street School, her subsequent formalized "conversations" for adult women in the Boston area, and the development of her original essay, "The Great Lawsuit: Man versus Men. Woman versus Women," which appeared in the July 1843 issue of the *Dial* and was then expanded into *Woman in the Nineteenth Century*. Most studies see Fuller's eighteen months at the Greene Street School as an interlude during which "she practiced on the schoolgirls of Providence a progressive style of teaching that she would later apply to the prominent women of Boston" (Fergenson 131). Other studies suggest that, both during the Greene Street period and throughout the Boston conversations, Fuller "was developing her own formative attitudes" towards women's issues, which would then find expression in her essay and book (Albert 43). Even more important, in my view, is the considerable evidence that, beginning with her decision to use Richard Whately's *Elements of Rhetoric*[5] in a course for the senior girls at Greene Street and continuing with her readings in Plato's dialogues to prepare herself for her first Boston conversation series, Fuller was consciously trying to fashion a set of rhetorical strategies appropriate to the emerging feminist consciousness of her era.

Fuller had never anticipated a career in teaching. Through her early twenties, she had continued to read widely among the European Romantics, preparing to become a professional writer, and publishing three early pieces of literary criticism in the June, August, and December 1835 issues of the liberal Unitarian journal, *Western Messenger* (see Capper 1:146–50). But with the unexpected death of her father in the autumn of 1835, the twenty-five-year-old Fuller found herself suddenly responsible for her own support as well as that of her widowed mother and her six younger siblings. During the winter of 1836–1837, she taught briefly in Bronson Alcott's Temple School in Boston, but then left—both because the work kept her from her own reading and writing and, more important, because local disapproval of some of Alcott's experimental teaching methods was causing the school to fail, and Alcott could no longer pay her salary. When Hiram Fuller (no relation to Margaret) offered her a position at his newly established Greene Street School in Providence, Rhode Island, Fuller could not refuse. Hiram Fuller was offering the munificent annual salary of $1,000 and the promise of a teaching schedule light enough to permit her to continue with her own intellectual pursuits.

By the time she took up her duties, however, her schedule proved heavier than anticipated and, in July 1837, Fuller wrote her brother, Arthur, that she was responsible for lessons "in composition, elocution, history, three classes in Latin, . . . two classes in Natural philosophy, and one in Ethics" (Hudspeth 1:289–90). She would later add a class in French and a class in English literature for the senior girls; for this same group, she also took it upon herself to develop a course in rhetoric. Consistent with conventional nineteenth-century gender role expectations, the boys at Greene Street were being trained both in rhetoric and in elocution and, twice monthly, they were expected to speak—or declaim—before the rest of the school. While Fuller had no intention of training her senior girls for this kind of public declamation, she did want to employ the study of rhetoric to overcome the restraints of feminine modesty and provide each student practical tools with which to clearly communicate "what was in her mind" (Johnson 135).

In a letter dated December 20, 1837, a nineteen-year-old from rural Massachusetts, newly enrolled in the Greene Street School, reported to her parents that "[Miss Fuller] formed a class in rhetoric to-day, which I have joined, and which with her, I think will be made very useful and interesting. We are to recite once a week in Whately's Rhetoric." But the weekly recitations in this class were not to replicate the rote memorization that characterized the boys' training. Instead, they were to involve a sharing of ideas through "pleasant conversation" (quoted in Johnson 136). Fuller was trying to develop in her charges both intellectual discipline and independence of mind:

> One of the girls asked her if she should get the lesson by heart. "No," said she, "I never wish a lesson learned by heart, as that phrase is commonly understood. . . . I wish you to get your lessons by mind." She said she wished no one to remain in the class unless she was willing to give her mind and soul to the study, unless she was willing to communicate what was in her mind, . . . that we should let no false modesty restrain us. (quoted in Johnson 135)

Fuller intended the students' exchanges to be "social and pleasant," but as this young correspondent well understood, there was no question that she and the others would be "exerting ourselves" (quoted in Johnson 135).

A month later, writing to her parents on January 18, 1838, this same student again highlighted the conversational nature of the rhetoric class:

I am studying Whately's Rhetoric, which I like very much because we have such pleasant conversation. The lessons are long and hard, and require a good deal of study. In connection with that study, we write definitions of words, which, though difficult, is very useful. The first we wrote were definitions of Logic, Rhetoric, and Philosophy, as these words were suggested by the conversation. (quoted in Johnson 136)

Whately's goal for the "School-boy" for whom his text was intended—like Fuller's goal for each of her senior girls—was to qualify him for "uttering his own sentiments" in a natural manner (Whately 257). In order to develop facility in the rhetorical strategies he was recommending, Whately suggested that students become accustomed to "rational conversation" (222). Clearly, Fuller had taken this to heart, utilizing conversation as a method for generating calls for definition and accuracy in the group's shared pursuit of the meaning of words and ideas. In good Whatelian fashion, in other words, Fuller was insisting upon clarity and lucidity in expression and, at the same time, teaching her charges to inquire together into topics of mutual interest.

Although as a student at Miss Prescott's School in 1824, Fuller had been assigned a different, widely read text—Hugh Blair's *Lectures on Rhetoric and Belles Lettres* (London, 1783)—when it came to her own class, she preferred Whately. First published in England in 1828 and then issued in a Boston edition in 1832, Whately's *Elements of Rhetoric* originally had been composed as a manual for divinity students while Whately (who was later to become archbishop of Dublin) served as the principal of St. Alban's Hall in Oxford. As an introductory manual, it was "designed principally for the instruction of [the] unpracticed" (Whately iv)—which is clearly what attracted Fuller.

Unlike his influential predecessor Blair—who defined rhetoric as a science concerned both with rules for composition and with rules for the critical appraisal of literature—Whately omitted literary considerations altogether and treated rhetoric not as a science but, rather, as a set of procedures for "Argumentative Composition, generally, and exclusively" (5). Burdened neither by theories of human understanding nor by analyses of what constitutes truth in argument, Whately's *Elements of Rhetoric*, as he announced in his introduction, was an "instrumental" text (4). It concentrated on the systematic application of specific rules and procedures for developing and organizing an argument. As long as the central function of logic was not ignored, moreover, Whately expected his "rules" to be applied neither rigidly nor inflexibly. "Instead," as Ray E.

McKerrow has pointed out, Whately's rules functioned more as guides which "may be abandoned whenever greater advantage results from a different approach" (McKerrow 146).

Having been educated by her father in the classical rhetorical tradition and having resisted the assignment of Blair at Miss Prescott's school because she preferred "Cicero's oratory" (Capper 1:75), Fuller should have found Whately relatively elementary. And yet, in January 1838, Fuller wrote to a friend that she was not only reading and teaching Whately's *Rhetoric* but also "thinking it over with great profit to myself" (Hudspeth 1:322–23). It was part of a larger pattern of activity that marked Fuller's eighteen months in Providence.

On August 9, 1837, just two months after her arrival, Fuller defied gender proprieties by attending the otherwise all-male state Whig caucus—not because she had any interest in the issues, but because she wanted to hear the two main speakers, State Representative John Whipple and Rhode Island's most popular orator, Congressman Tristam Burges, former Brown University professor of oratory. As a woman, she had difficulty gaining entrance; and news of her attendance later horrified Hiram Fuller, Greene Street's circumspect principal. Disturbed by neither, Fuller recorded in her journal acute observations of the speakers' style, "manner," and oratorical devices (see Capper 1:213). For the same purpose, she took every opportunity for brief visits to Boston and Cambridge, attending a variety of lectures, including some by her friend Emerson. And in the spring of 1838 she herself participated in a series of debates at Providence's Coliseum Club on the subject of the "progress of Society" (see Capper 1:242–43). The rhetoric class for senior girls and her study of Whately were thus part of an increased engagement in the practical application of rhetorical principles and in what Capper has called "her by now well-ingrained fascination with public oratory" (1:213).

Despite the generous salary, the pleasures she experienced in teaching were not enough to sustain Fuller. The heavier schedule had taken its toll on her health, and she repeatedly complained to correspondents of insufficient time and energy for work on her translation of Johann Peter Eckermann's *Conversations with Goethe in the Last Years of his Life* (see Capper 1:253). She also missed the more sophisticated intellectual activity of Boston and Cambridge. Accordingly, in December 1838, after three terms at the Greene Street School, Fuller resigned her position and rejoined her family in their current home in Jamaica Plain, a suburb of Boston. "I do not wish to teach again at all," she wrote a friend. And yet, in that same December 1838 letter, she confided that she was "not without my dreams and hopes as to the education of women" (Hudspeth 1:354).

Fuller's encounters with the poorly prepared senior girls at Greene Street had reinforced her sense of the inadequate educational opportunities for women. At the same time, the practical strategies she had gleaned from Whately, combined with her continuing fascination with all forms of public discourse, now prompted her to consider some means by which "to systematize thought and give a precision in which our sex are so deficient." Her plan, as she described it in an August 1839 letter to Sophia Ripley, was to organize a series of weekly meetings for "well-educated and thinking women" which would forge intellectual community ("supplying a point of union" in Fuller's words) and, as well, "answer the great questions. What were we born to do? How shall we do it?" Alluding to the pedagogy she had employed in the rhetoric class for senior girls, Fuller declared her "confidence" in her project because "in former instances I have been able to make it easy and even pleasant to twenty five out of thirty to bear their part, to question, to define, to state and examine their opinions." As she had at Greene Street, Fuller would ask her conversation participants to throw off "the garb of modesty" in order to "openly state their impressions and consent to learn by blundering" (Hudspeth 2:86–89).

"Of course," as Capper emphasizes, "these were not 'conversations' in the ordinary sense. The ideal of a conversation as a critical intellectual method derived from Plato," whose Socratic dialogues Fuller had been recently rereading, and from the "great Romantic talkers" like Mme de Stael, Coleridge, and Goethe. Closer to home, Fuller had witnessed Bronson Alcott's efforts to utilize conversational dialogues as a teaching tool at his Temple School (later adapting some of his techniques for her Greene Street classes). And, more recently, as Fuller was aware, "Alcott . . . had launched a series of moderately successful traveling conversations in various towns in eastern Massachusetts" (Capper 1:296). The conversation thus became for Fuller both a mode of feminist activism and a modest source of income.

Beginning in November 1839 and continuing through May 1844, each fall and spring Fuller conducted a series of conversations on different subjects, ranging widely from mythology to philosophy and the arts. Elizabeth Palmer Peabody's Boston bookstore was sometimes the site; at other times George and Sophia Ripley offered their front parlor. For a fee of ten dollars (later raised to twenty) for each three-month series,

Boston-area women found a forum for the investigation and exchange of ideas. Although few series enrolled more than twenty-five, the participants changed often enough that, by 1844, Fuller had counted in her conversations most of Boston's female writers and activists, as well as the wives and daughters of the area's most prominent men. Some participants came from as far away as Providence and New York.

With one exception, no detailed record remains of these conversations.[6] That exception is young Caroline Healey Dall's transcription of ten conversations that she attended, beginning in March 1841, on "The Mythology of the Greeks and Its Expression in Art"—the only series to which Fuller admitted men. Because the men included well-known personages such as Emerson, who tended to dominate discussion, the Dall transcription cannot stand as an accurate index of Fuller's strategies when only women were present. For, with the first conversation on March 1, a pattern emerged that gave way only occasionally in subsequent meetings: The ten males take up far more of the verbal space than do the twelve women present. The results were frequent digressions into areas of interest to only one or another of the men. After the second week's meeting, in a typical observation, Dall recorded that "Emerson pursued his own train of thought. He seemed to forget that we had come together to pursue Margaret's" (Healey 46).

If Dall's chronicle portrays Fuller as often arch in her attempts to restrain a loquacious male, sometimes irritated, occasionally impatient, and even capable of sharp retort, her chronicle also suggests features of Fuller's behavior that may have surfaced more prominently when only women were present. To elicit greater participation from everyone in the group, Fuller understated her own expertise on a subject. To maintain focus and continuity, she habitually recapitulated the main ideas of a discussion at the end of the evening's conversation and again at the beginning of the next. Fuller's ready wit and sense of humor are also apparent. And, perhaps most important to Fuller, she never found herself "haranguing too much"—an early fear that she had expressed in her August 1839 letter to Sophia Ripley (Hudspeth 2:88). Instead, despite the men's tangents and interruptions, Dall's transcription shows us a Fuller determined to enact the role she had first proposed for herself in these conversations: "truly a teacher and a guide" (Hudspeth 2:97). As Fuller had explained at the first meeting of the initial series, she was not there "to teach anything," but "to call . . . out the thought of others" (quoted in Capper 1:296).

The magnetic intensity of Fuller's personal presence, upon which so many of her contemporaries commented, no doubt contributed substantially to the success of the Boston conversations. Additionally, her easy familiarity with literature and philosophy in several languages, along with her reading and teaching in formal rhetoric, now came together to enable her to awaken the enthusiasms of the conversation participants. From the platform orators she admired, she had learned something of the "manner" of public presentation and even an occasional strategy of argumentation. From Whately she had imbibed the importance of "the skilful arrangement" of thought (28). And from Plato, especially in his early dialogues, she had taken the courage to raise questions for which there might not be sure answers. "I have been reading Plato all the week," she informed Emerson as one series began, "hop[ing] to be tuned up thereby" (Hudspeth 2:104). Her vast education supplied the ground upon which she would "open a subject" and offer "as good a general statement as I know how to make." But her study of rhetoric had supplied her with the practical tools for "select[ing] a branch of the subject and lead[ing] others to give their thoughts upon it" (Hudspeth 2:88).

Those same strengths came together once more, as Fuller prepared her first formal "Argumentative Composition." Her long apprenticeship in initiating what Whately had called "rational conversation" prompted her to try a bold experiment, however. Instead of relegating the conversation to an exclusively oral exercise, Fuller would simulate its components in a written treatise. In so doing, she chose her rhetorical devices carefully, emulating the female antislavery lecturers by bringing her "subject more into home relations" and by eschewing "combativeness."

III

While Fuller had first encountered the dialogue as a pedagogical device at Alcott's Temple School, it was not until she began using Whately's text at Greene Street that she found the means to convert dialogue into a full-fledged conversation aimed at probing received wisdom and arriving at collective reassessments. And while Fuller's letters indicate that she consulted Plato throughout the years of the Boston conversations, characteristic Whatelian recommendations—such as understating one's own command of a subject, recapitulating complex arguments, and the judicious use of humor—are clearly evident in Dall's account of the spring 1841 conversation series. Not surprisingly, echoes of Whately's phrasings can also be detected in both the *Dial* essay and in *Woman in the Nineteenth Century*, suggesting that as Fuller attempted her first "Argumentative Composition," Whately continued as an influence.[7] *Elements of Rhetoric* was not simply the rhetoric manual Fuller knew most intimately, however. In addition, as Fuller was aware (and Whately readily acknowledged), it was a highly derivative work, offering a compressed compendium of rhetorical practices from Aristotle, Cicero, and Quintilian through George Campbell's *Philosophy of Rhetoric* (London and Edinburgh, 1776) and Blair's *Lectures on Rhetoric and Belles Lettres*, with copious quotations from and references to each. As a result, reading Fuller's text against Whately's allows us easily to measure what Fuller was prepared to accept—and, no less important, what she felt bound to reject—from the entire rhetorical tradition then available to her.

More to the point, Whately's "System of Rules" (15) was specifically designed for Fuller's present purpose. Her goal, after all, as she began the *Dial* essay, was to prompt readers to their own independent discovery of a "truth" to which Fuller was herself already deeply committed. And for Whately, as for most eighteenth- and nineteenth-century rhetoricians, "the process of conveying truth to others" constituted the very heart of "the Rhetorical process" (23). The divinity students for whom Whately's text was originally intended, we recall, were being instructed in the practical strategies for leading their prospective parishioners to the revealed truths of Christianity.

Fuller, of course, had a different truth to convey. Defining men and women as "the two halves of one thought," in the preface to *Woman in the Nineteenth Century*, she then explained: "I believe that the development of the one cannot be effected without that of the other. My highest wish is that this truth should be distinctly and rationally apprehended, and the conditions of life and freedom recognized as the same for the daughters and the sons" (vi). In urging readers toward their own rational apprehension of this truth, Fuller sought to replicate the rhetorical situation in which she was experiencing her greatest success: the weekly meetings in which women "have time, patience, mutual reverence and fearlessness eno' to get at one another's thoughts" (Hudspeth 2:118).

In order to mimic the polyphony of conversation, Fuller's treatise on women's rights introduces a variety of voices—her own, the autobiographical Miranda's, her anonymous correspondent's, and even the wholly fictive "irritated trader" determined to maintain authority over his wife (18–19). The spontaneity of conversation is captured in Fuller's direct addresses, as when she suddenly changes course by informing the reader that she has already "brought forward" enough on a subject to satisfy her point (49). To suggest the give and take of contested positions, Fuller offers a panoply of conflicting views of women by including lengthy selections from a variety of authors—a speech by John Quincy Adams (128–30), a poem by the young Transcendentalist William Ellery Channing (177–79), and a passage from the French essayist Suzanne Necker (147), among others—even when she does not wholly agree with the point of view expressed. Even more important, following a loose historical chronology, she catalogues "signs of the times" (26), a survey of mythological as well as historical events and personages, each variously interpreted as evidence of the obstacles to women's advancement and as harbingers of what might yet be achieved. And in order to invite her reader to actively participate in the ongoing epistemic inquiry, Fuller enunciates the commitment not to enroll "ourselves at once on either side" but, rather, to "look upon the subject from the best point of view" (20). Her model, she reassures her readers, is the eminent Unitarian minister, the late Dr. William Ellery Channing, who, in Fuller's estimation, "always furnished a platform on which opposing parties could stand, and look at one another under the influence of his mildness and enlightened candor" (101).

With these last two statements, Fuller signaled that she was intent on conducting what Whately termed "a process of Investigation." By and large, her arguments would appeal to those who had not yet formed a hardened opinion, "but are merely desirous of ascertaining what is the truth in respect of the case before them." Fuller was thus enacting what Whately called "Instruction"—a word with which she felt especially comfortable—but a species of instruction that at once preserved Fuller's preferred role as a facilitator and a guide, even as it acknowledged that she had a particular "truth" to convey. The rhetor was "conducting a process of Investigation" relative to readers only, explained Whately, "though not to himself" (24–25).

Whately's "process of Investigation" was also wholly consistent with Fuller's characteristically Romantic notion of "truth" as a process of unfolding revelation, a notion that had been reinforced by her experience with the conversation series. Through the conversations, she had refined the art of carrying on a critical inquiry by means of shared discussion, and she had taught other women to actively participate in the dialectical testing of ideas. In effect, the conversations represented the conceptual model for her treatise's rhetorical design. But, as he had in the past, Whately would provide a source for formal strategies and lead her to "the skilful arrangement of them" (28).

All editions of Whately's *Elements of Rhetoric* are organized into four parts: 1. "Of the Address to the Understanding, with a View to Produce Conviction (Including Instruction)"; 2. "Of the Address to the Will, or Persuasion"; 3. "Of Style"; and 4. "Of Elocution, or Delivery." Because it deals exclusively with oral presentation, Part 4 includes a number of items adapted by Fuller for both the Greene Street School and the Boston conversations; but its imprint is not detected in either "The Great Lawsuit" or *Woman in the Nineteenth Century.* For reasons to be explored shortly, Part 2 had only limited influence as well. Much of Parts 1 and 3, by contrast, help us to understand why Fuller constructed her treatise as she did.

From Part 1 of Whately, Fuller took the kinds of arguments most appropriate to "conducting a process of Investigation," and she followed his advice as to their "various use and order" (70). Her central syllogism, for example, derives from Whately's tactics for shifting the burden of proof to one's opponent when responding to the "Presumption in favour of every existing institution" (Whately 76). In the face of "a Presumption against every Change," advises Whately, the rebuttal is " 'true, but . . . every Restriction is in itself an evil; and therefore there is a Presumption in favor of its removal' " (80). In "The Great Lawsuit" and in *Woman in the Nineteenth Century,* Fuller acknowledges at the outset that popular opinion is against her, "society at large not [being] prepared for the demands" she is about to make (18). Following Whately, her response is to weave into her discourse a syllogism that appeals to patriotic motives and, at the same time, shifts the burden of proof by challenging imposed restrictions: Because the United States has been founded on the belief that "all men are born free and equal," Fuller predicts that it "is surely destined to elucidate a great moral law" for all humanity (15). But slavery and restrictions on women run counter to this founding proposition. Therefore, concludes Fuller, for the nation to attain its destined greatness, it must free slaves and remove all restrictions on women. As Whately had taught her, she now put the opposition on the defensive.

In the second chapter of Part 1, entitled "Of Arguments," Whately catalogues the kinds of strategies that would prove most conducive to "conducting a process of Investigation." He recommends the use of testimony and the cross-examination of adversaries, recommendations that Fuller follows in her introduction of Miranda's first-person narrative and in her own dialogue with "the irritated trader" intent on maintaining his white male privileges. Whately recommends the argument from analogy, to which Fuller repeatedly resorts in her insistence on the parallels between the status of white women and that of slaves. And he urges the efficacy of drawing a conclusion from a single instance and then inferring from that a conclusion "respecting the whole Class" (53). Fuller obviously found this an appealing device, using it regularly. She offers the vignette of the father who would not educate his daughter, for example, to illustrate an instance of the male who does not always act in women's best interest. Fuller then draws from this the general rule undergirding her entire thesis: Because men see only their own needs and "do not look at both sides, ... women must leave off asking them and being influenced by them" (108). In recommending this argument from example, moreover, Whately allows for the "real or invented" (67), as long as the "case [had] ... intrinsic probability" (65). Fuller, of course, includes both, incorporating her knowledge of Greek and Roman mythology, stories from German folk ballads, and the real-life biography of the Polish heroine Emily Plater.

Finally, Whately stresses the value of combining different kinds of arguments, each "singly perhaps of little weight," into the "progressive approach" (49). This gives Fuller license to include the many different kinds of arguments that might mark any spirited conversation, confident that together, they would "produce jointly, and by their coincidence, a degree of probability far exceeding the sum of their several forces, taken separately." The key to success here, continues Whately, is the order in which the different arguments are "considered, and ... their progressive tendency to establish a certain conclusion" (49).

How to achieve that order is the focus of the third chapter of Part 1. Here again Whately draws a distinction between "convey[ing] instruction to those who are ready to receive it" and "compel[ling] the assent, or silenc[ing] the objections, of an opponent" (70). Since Fuller's object is the former, she follows Whately's view that the argument from cause to effect would give the greatest "satisfaction to a candid mind" (70), and she takes seriously his hint that arguments "from Cause to Effect ... have usually the precedence" in the organization of a treatise because they help to prepare "the way for the reception of other arguments" (83–84). In fact, Fuller devotes the first twenty-five pages of the printed book (almost one-sixth of the text) to laying the groundwork for her first major cause-to-effect proposition: Because men can only think of women as "made for man" (25), and because men are bound by habit and convention in this regard, they can never adequately speak for woman or act in her best interests. Not until near the end of the book does she introduce, as a kind of corollary, the more controversial cause-to-effect argument regarding the male's historical abuse of his privileges over the female. The consequence of this unhappy history, Fuller asserts, is that the male now finds himself "a temporal master" rather than a "spiritual sire," "a king without a queen . . . his habits and his will corrupted by the past" (156). Of course, Fuller is here following Whately's view that a "Conclusion . . . likely to . . . offend the prejudices of the hearers" be kept "out of sight, as much as possible . . . till the principles from which it is to be deduced shall have been clearly established" (89).

In short, Fuller adopts most of the advice offered by Whately in Part 1. In the *Dial* essay, the "refutation of Objections" is placed as Whately recommends, "nearer the beginning than the end" (92); and this remains so in the essay's expansion. Fuller works to "avoid an appearance of abruptness" by carefully laying out her basic premises before "enter[ing] on the main argument" (Whately 112). And her conclusion—in both the essay and the book—is the recapitulation called for by Whately.

Similarly, Whately's Part 3, "Of Style," also reads as a kind of rhetorical road map of Fuller's text. From the first chapter on perspicuity, or clarity in language usage, she seems to have adopted Whately's advice on the relative proportion of Saxon and Latinate words. And, even more important, she embraces his view that "the same sentiment and argument" could be offered "in many different forms of expression" in order to expand "the sense to be conveyed" and thereby detain "the mind upon it" (Whately 171). In fact, Fuller circles around the same points and sentiments throughout her book, each time attempting a different analogy or illustration that would arrest attention and, like the women antislavery orators, bring the "subject more into home relations."

From the second chapter of Part 3, "Of Energy," Fuller incorporates advice that she hopes will "stimulate attention, . . . excite the Imagination, and . . . arouse the Feelings" (Whately 183–84). For example, her direct comments to the reader are often framed as questions: "You ask, what use will she make of liberty, when she has so long been sustained and restrained?" (158). Here Fuller follows Whately's observation that a direct interrogative "calls the hearer's attention more forcibly to some important point, by a personal appeal to each individual" (241). To avoid what Whately characterizes as "a tedious dragging effect," Fuller generally constructs her "complex sentences of any considerable length" along Whately's model, with the longer clauses preceding and the shorter phrases concluding the sentence (Whately 233). Her habitual penchant for Latinate syntax is somewhat tempered thereby.

The type and structure of individual sentences, however, is not the only focus of Whately's Part 3. Patterns of organization have an impact in stimulating attention and thus are also a component of "style." Especially important to Fuller as she expanded her essay into the book is Whately's stress on "the energetic effect of Conciseness" (212), a stylistic effect for which she was not widely known. Because she had been criticized by some for "not making my meaning sufficiently clear" in the essay, she now "tried to illustrate it in various ways," expanding the text by almost a third in that effort. Conscious of the possibility that the additional material might strike some readers as only "much repetition" (154), Fuller eagerly follows Whately's advice for creating at least "the effect of brevity" (216). Whately instructs the rhetor "first to expand the sense, sufficiently to be clearly understood, and then to contract it into the most compendious and striking form" (215). This "addition of a compressed and pithy expression of the sentiment"—even after expansion and repetition—Whately promises, "will produce the effect of brevity" (216). In *Woman in the Nineteenth Century,* Fuller explains the form of her new closing peroration by paraphrasing Whately's justification for "the insertion of such an abridged repetition" (Whately 216). And she acknowledges that the authority for this rhetorical strategy is a manual written for future ministers:

> In the earlier tract, I was told, I did not make my meaning sufficiently clear. In this I have consequently tried to illustrate it in various ways, and may have been guilty of much repetition. Yet, as I am anxious to leave no room for doubt, I shall venture to retrace, once more, the scope of my design in points, as was done in old-fashioned sermons. (154)

What follows is a brief compendium of pithy closing statements, including the bold pronouncement for which, at the time, Fuller was most ridiculed: "But if you ask me what offices they may fill; I reply—any. I do not care what case you put; let them be sea-captains, if you will" (159).[8]

Unquestionably the most influential section for Fuller comes in the second chapter of Part 3, where Whately endorses the "Suggestive style" (221). Functioning by means of "slight hints" and "notices of the principles" rather than the particulars (Whately 222), the suggestive style coincides with the advertised intention of the *Dial* to discuss "principles" rather than advocate particular "measures" (see Capper 1:348). Of greater significance for Fuller, however, it also closely approximates the use of conversation as a collaborative device to prompt instruction. It "shall put the hearer's mind into the same train of thought as the speaker's," explains Whately, "and suggest to him more than is actually expressed" (221).

Whately himself makes the comparison explicit when he recommends "rational conversation" as "a very useful exercise" for developing this particular stylistic technique. After all, Whately goes on, "in conversation, a man naturally tries first one and then another mode of conveying his thoughts" (222). Child and others may have judged the effect "rough in construction," but in fact this is Fuller's method. Moving from one type of argument to another, surveying history and mythology for analogies and examples, introducing the authority of Miranda's personal testimony in one place, the authority of the Declaration of Independence in another, Fuller is determined to try out as many means as possible for conveying her ideas. "When I meet people I can adapt myself to them," Fuller had written to a fellow member of the Transcendental Club, William Henry Channing, in 1840, "but when I write, it is into another world" (Hudspeth 2:125). The suggestive style is thus her solution, because it gives her permission to adapt herself to an imagined variety of readers much as she had always adapted herself to different partners in conversation.

Although Whately refrains from "lay[ing] down precise rules for the Suggestive kind of writing I am speaking of" (222), the image he chooses to represent that style resonates in Fuller's closing declaration. According to Whately, the suggestive style might best be compared "to a good map, which marks distinctly the great outlines, setting down the principal rivers, towns, mountains, etc., leaving the imagination to supply the villages, hillocks, and streamlets" (221n). By the time she completed her book, Fuller was confident that she had "now . . . designated in outline, if not in fulness, the stream which is ever flowing from the heights of my thought" (154). Her text does sketch the central questions and "the great outlines." And, as Fuller herself explains, her purpose had never been to "deal with 'atrocious instances' " nor to "demand . . . partial redress in some one matter, but [to] go to the root of the whole. If principles could be established," she was sure, "particulars would adjust themselves aright" (22).

If Fuller's adherence to the suggestive style was risky in its rejection of both explicit program and the drama of "atrocious instances," her boldest gamble was her decision to dispense with almost everything in Whately's Part 2, "Of the Address to the Will, or Persuasion." To be sure, she did not reject it all. Having taught Part 2 at Greene Street,[9] she appreciated the impact of an occasionally "gentle and conciliatory manner" (Whately 151), and she did her best to dwell on areas of mutual agreement in order not to alienate reluctant readers. She was also well aware of the value of "attentively studying and meditating on the history of some extraordinary Personage,—by contemplating and dwelling on his actions and sufferings,—his virtues and his wisdom,—and by calling on the Imagination to present a vivid picture" (Whately 124). As she had done for her pupils at Greene Street, Fuller offers the "extraordinary" lives of exemplary women, from Polish patriot Countess Emily Plater to Cassandra, "the inspired child," emblem of the intuitively gifted woman whom none yet understand (93).

That said, Fuller does not embrace the strategies that Whately claims would call out "passion, sentiment, or emotion" for the purpose of persuasion (125). She does not expend any effort at establishing her own good character, a tactic which, according to Whately, can often "persuade more powerfully than . . . the strongest Arguments" (128). She does not affect the suppression of her own strong feelings on the subject but, instead, declares at the outset that "the subject makes me feel too much" (22). She does not paint in lurid detail the oppressions of women and then call upon her readers "to consider how they would feel were such and such an injury done to themselves" (Whately 140). She never openly ridicules her opponents. She does not deliberately organize her material so as to lead her reader from the calm "to the impassioned" (Whately 142). And she never exhorts her readers "to adopt the conduct recommended" (Whately 131). In short, Fuller does not follow Whately in what he terms "the design laid against [the reader's] feelings" (136). This is where Fuller resisted being "taught and led by men" (107).

In Whately's rhetoric, persuasion is "the art of influencing the Will," and to accomplish that, "two things are requisite": The rhetor's arguments must make "the proposed Object . . . appear desirable," and "the Means suggested should be proved . . . conducive to the attainment of that object" (Whately 117). Fuller attempts only a version of the first, advocating full equality for women as the central condition for the improvement of humankind in general and the fulfillment of national destiny in particular. But, preferring principles to particulars, she details no program or "means" to achieve her ends, and there is no specific "conduct recommended."

Even so, Fuller's unwillingness to propose specific remedies does not entirely account for her decision to reject strategies for "influencing the Will." Rather, her decision was due to Whately's insistence that persuasion could never rest on logical argument but, instead, depended on "Exhortation, i.e. the excitement of men" (Whately 118). To be effective, in other words, persuasion plays not just to the emotions or the feelings, but to the passions. On this point, Whately is unequivocal: "There can be no Persuasion without an address to the Passions" (119). In delineating the strategies for persuasion, however, Whately's imagery suddenly turns suggestively sexual and, at the same time, swerves toward the very combativeness that Fuller had worked so hard to avoid. Clearly, persuasion entails a quality of relationship between rhetor and audience unlike that in any other section of Whately's manual.[10]

Techniques for obliquely arousing an audience, for example, are introduced through the following "homely illustration": "A moderate charge of powder will have more effect in splitting a rock, if we begin by deep boring, and introducing the charge into the very heart of it, than ten times the quantity, exploded on the surface" (Whately 132n). In a lengthy note emphasizing the importance of arrangement, Whately recommends that the "statements and arguments should first be clearly and calmly laid down and developed" and then succeeded by "the impassioned appeal." "The former of these two parts may be compared to the back of a sabre," Whately elaborates, "the latter to its edge. The former should be firm and weighty; the latter keen" (142n). The violence latent in that comparison is then made explicit at the end of the paragraph where Whately describes a properly arranged appeal to the emotions as "an excellent sword" whose "blows would take effect" (Whately 142n). Above all else, however, persuasion functions through an organizational structure that purposefully "raise[d] the feelings gradually to the highest pitch" or, as Whately clarifies, "what Rhetoricians call the Climax" (138).

Given Fuller's belief in man and woman as "two halves of one thought," and given the rhetorical goals articulated throughout her treatise, she had no choice but to reject the tactics of persuasion. Having identified the containment of male sexual aggression as necessary to full equality between the sexes, Fuller would not play upon "the excitement of men" in constructing her arguments. Having condemned the "love of petty power" that derived from women's enforced "ignorance and foolish vanity" (50), Fuller could hardly employ that same power to argue for the rights of women. In her view, after all, the covertly sexual manipulations of persuasion were identical to those she had named as the only available "arms of the servile: cunning, blandishment, and unreasonable emotion" (157). Furthermore, unlike the "Address to the Understanding" in Part 1, persuasion undermines the collaborative conversation that

Fuller had pursued since Greene Street, and it altogether annihilates even the illusion of an unfolding epistemic inquiry. As Whately defines it (and he was hardly alone in this), persuasion emerges as a species of coercion meant to compel the audience members' "resigning themselves" to the feelings evoked (142n). And persuasion accomplishes this end by overriding the audience's independent will. Indeed, that is its purpose: "When the metal is heated, it may easily be moulded into the desired form" (Whately 143).

But molding an audience into some predetermined form had never been Fuller's purpose. Instead, in inventing a discourse appropriate to feminism, Fuller rejects alike the authoritarianism of coercion and the manipulative strategies of the disempowered, endeavoring instead to create a collaborative process of assertion and response in which multiple voices could—and did—find a place. She requires of her readers, in Stanley E. Fish's words, "a searching and rigorous scrutiny of everything they believe and live by" in regard to gender arrangements (1). But she also requires a wholly *voluntary* attentiveness to these matters, in return for which she neither demands a specific remedy nor imposes any single course of action. As she makes plain in her preface, Fuller asks of her male readers no less than "a noble and earnest attention," and she solicits from her female readers the independence of mind "to search their own experience and intuitions" in order to identify the problem and invent its solutions (vi).

Certainly, in conveying her "truth," Fuller's purpose is to initiate a new consensus. But in contrast to the liberal individualism of Emerson's "self-reliance" (Emerson 147–68), Fuller is attempting to forge an ongoing collective search for a social philosophy of *female* "self-dependence . . . and fulness of being" (84). The consensus that Fuller seeks, in other words, is to emerge from the dialectical conversation that her text has set in motion but purposefully not brought to "climax" (or closure). Little wonder that Brownson saw "no reason why it should stop where it does." But then this is precisely Fuller's aim. "And so the stream flows on," predicts Fuller, "thought urging action, and action leading to the evolution of still better thought" (158).

IV

By rejecting persuasion as a tactic for feminist discourse, in effect, Fuller dispensed with those organizing principles that had come to be associated with most public advocacy in her day. As a result, despite the chronological arrangement of her "signs of the times," and despite Fuller's demonstrated command of formal logic and her employment of both inductive and deductive modes of reasoning, she opened herself to the charge that she was aimlessly amassing miscellaneous evidence, merely "collect[ing] . . . clever sayings and bright intimations." In other words, because Fuller did not *order* her treatise in the conventional manner, critics like Brownson—and others after him—simply dismissed the whole as the by-product of stereotypically uncontrolled female talkativeness transferred to the printed page.

Her refusal to build to a conclusive "climax" and thereby bring her treatise to definitive closure served Fuller's purpose in two ways, however. First, without damage to either the structure or intent of her thesis, Fuller was able simply to add to the *Dial* essay in order to turn it into *Woman in the Nineteenth Century*. As Urbanski has pointed out, while Fuller "occasionally . . . changed a few words to clarify or modify the meaning of a sentence" and made some other minor alterations (130), she left the original essay essentially intact and appended to it the bulk of her new material. With contemporary references and "more trenchant social criticism," Urbanski notes, these additions contained some of "the most daring subject matter in the book" (130). Here were frank discussions of sexual matters, including male sexual appetite and the rehabilitation of prostitutes, as well as Fuller's famous remark about allowing women to be sea captains. While her informing arguments remained the same, the new examples added "energy" to what Whately had called the *suggestive style* by giving readers contemporary—rather than historical or metaphorical—references to ponder.

Second, the lack of closure opened the way for still further recastings. From another letter that Fuller sent to William Henry Channing in November 1844, we know this was her intention. In the midst of expanding the *Dial* essay into *Woman in the Nineteenth Century*—and finding it "spinning out beneath my hand" (Hudspeth 3:241)—Fuller told Channing that she was now bent on revising the book draft before sending it on for his reading and advice. Certain that the manuscript would "be much better" after these revisions, Fuller not only confirmed the considered crafting that was going into her work but also indicated that she saw no necessary end to this process. "I should hope to be able to make it constantly better while I live," Fuller told Channing, and she expressed her expectation for "subsequent editions" (Hudspeth 3:242).

But the few years that remained to Fuller afforded no time for any new editions, and she never even witnessed the practical impact of her work on the organized women's rights movement. With a platform deeply indebted to the ideas promulgated in *Woman in the Nineteenth Century,* the first women's rights convention in the United States convened in Seneca Falls, New York, in July 1848—while Fuller was covering the political upheavals in Italy for Horace Greeley's *New York Tribune.* By the time the first national convention opened in Worcester, Massachusetts, in October 1850, she was already dead. Returning from Italy in May, Fuller had drowned in a shipwreck off Fire Island.

Although Fuller's death at this crucial juncture was a profound loss to the women's movement, her conversational strategies proved revolutionary and enduring. With many of her former students arranging similar activities of their own, women's conversation groups proliferated. Elizabeth Cady Stanton, a founder of the Seneca Falls Convention, had attended a Fuller series in Boston one winter and later initiated a series in upstate New York—as Stanton put it, in conscious "imitation of Margaret Fuller's Conversationals" (quoted in Urbanski 160). Without question, "conversationals" functioned for the first wave of United States feminists in much the same way that the consciousness-raising groups of the late 1960s and early 1970s functioned for the second wave: as a galvanizing force, as Fuller had phrased it, "supplying a point of union." "In calling forth the opinions of her sex," wrote the editors of the *History of Woman Suffrage* in the 1880s, "Miss Fuller was the precursor of the Women's Rights agitation of the last thirty-three years" (quoted in Urbanski 158).

The text in which those same conversational strategies were employed for *written* argument, however, continued to be regarded, in Dall's words, as "a complete, scholarly exposition" that provided much-needed intellectual grist for the movement's political aims (Dall 249). Like most other antislavery and women's rights activists, Dall credited Fuller with "the first clear, uncompromising, scholarly demand for the civil rights of her sex" (Dall 262). But she never suggested that *Woman in the Nineteenth Century* might also be read as a sourcebook of techniques for a feminist public discourse.

Understandably, the women who led the nineteenth-century movement pursued the forms of public advocacy that they had been taught in coeducational academies and female seminaries. But, as Fuller had so well understood, that was the problem. From personal experience she knew that, even at the best of these establishments, women were given "young men as teachers, who only teach what has been taught themselves at college." And even where "women are . . . at the head of these institutions," still Fuller objected that they were not generally "thinking women, capable to organize a new whole for the wants of the time" (83).

She herself had complained about being assigned Blair at Miss Prescott's School, and when she taught at Greene Street, the best Fuller could offer her senior girls was Whately. Within this delimiting educational context and absent Fuller's continued re-creation of her text as the ongoing conversation she hoped for, the general critical response that her treatise "lack[ed] method sadly" effectively discredited the book as a rhetorical model that women should seriously consider.

United States feminists have thus been caught in bifurcated discourses. The inclusive, collaborative, and searchingly open-ended discussions that sustained the conversationals in the nineteenth century and the consciousness-raising groups in the twentieth were only haphazardly translated into corresponding experiments in *written* forms of public argument, especially in the academy. Admittedly, feminist scholarship throughout the 1980s was diligent in scrutinizing its own premises and foundational arguments. And that scholarship also moved toward the inclusion of an ever widening variety of voices and "feminisms." Additionally, the renewed insistence in the 1990s that the writer identify a subject position certainly echoes Fuller's closing remark that she argued from the ground of maturity, "stand[ing] in the sunny noon of life" (163), neither naive from inexperience nor cynical from disappointments. Those innovations notwithstanding, even the boldest of feminist scholars for the most part continue to adapt themselves to the discourse behaviors of their chosen disciplines, eager to be persuasive in the ways that term is commonly understood.

But that practice has never been wholly satisfactory, and Gearhart and Elshtain have hardly been alone in their quest to locate discourse models appropriate to feminist ideals. Gearhart recommended "transactional" communication techniques (199), while Elshtain approved Jurgen Habermas's "concept of an ideal speech situation" as a precedent for "creating a feminist discourse that rejects domination" (620, 621). Each alternative incorporates much that Fuller attempted,[11] of course (though Fuller is never mentioned by transactional theorists or by Habermas), but neither specifically invokes that conversation through which women can "organize a new whole for the wants of the time" (83). Hirsch and Keller recommended no specific rhetorical strategies, but they invoked Fuller's spirit—if not her name—when they encouraged contributors to *Conflicts in Feminism* to engage in "dialogue and conversation among opposing factions" (370). Even here, however, "each of [their] authors expresse[d] increasing frustration at the way that disagreements lead to oppositional politics" (371). While Fuller provides no sure formula for resolving such oppositions, she does offer a play of strategies that ensures ongoing exchange and eschews overheated terminations.

To return to the quality of *that* conversation, we must read Fuller on her own terms, and *Woman in the Nineteenth Century* must be accepted as an intentional experiment in a feminist discourse that refuses premature closure. To put it another way, if we seriously re-engage the conversation that Fuller began in 1843 with the publication of "The Great Lawsuit," then we come to understand that that conversation *cannot* be brought to closure—not until, that is, "inward and outward freedom for woman as much as for man shall be acknowledged as a right, not yielded as a concession."

NOTES

A Beer Memorial Trust research grant from Rensselaer Polytechnic Institute in 1987–1988 supported the initial research for this essay, and a 1993–1994 sabbatical from the University of Arizona allowed its completion. As the research progressed, Joel Myerson was endlessly generous in supplying good advice and vital bibliographical material, including copies of crucial books and articles. At different stages, three outstanding scholars read drafts of the essay in progress and sent me back to the drawing board with a better understanding of rhetorical theory and new insights into Fuller: George D. Gopen, S. Michael Halloran, and Carolyn Karcher. Finally, this essay greatly benefited from the devotion, intelligence, and initiative of my research assistant, Ruthe Thompson. My heartfelt thanks to all.

1. In addition to the all-important influence of Wollstonecraft, Fuller was also aware of a growing body of United States literature on women's rights, including Charles Brockden Brown's *Alcuin: A Dialogue*, the first book by an American to reject the concept of *separate spheres*; Sarah Moore Grimké's *Letters on the Equality of the Sexes and the Condition of Woman, Addressed to Mary Parker, President of the Boston Female Anti-Slavery Society*, the first book by an American to argue for the legal emancipation of all women, both black and white; and Sophia Dana Ripley's essay on married women's rights, "Woman." (All quotations from *Woman in the Nineteenth Century* are taken from the facsimile edition, 1980.)

2. This charge was leveled in a number of critical reviews, but the phrasing here appeared in a letter from Elizabeth Peabody to her daughter, Sophia Peabody Hawthorne, and was included in Julian Hawthorne's *Nathaniel Hawthorne and His Wife* (Myerson 115).

3. Chevigny's *The Woman and the Myth* was instrumental in presenting a sympathetic overview of Fuller's life and works, but even Chevigny characterized *Woman in the Nineteenth Century* as "lack[ing] ... systematic analysis" (222).

4. As of 1993, the only edition still in print was the 1971 Norton edition with an introduction by Bernard Rosenthal, which reprints Arthur B. Fuller's 1855

edition. This edition is particularly troubling because it is prefaced by her brother's apologetic and sanctimonious assurance that, despite her intellectual pursuits, his sister had never "neglect[ed] the domestic concerns of life" (6). Happily, a selection of Fuller's work is now available that includes a reprinting of the original 1845 edition of *Woman in the Nineteenth Century* in its entirety, with all appendices (Kelley 228–362).

5. By 1837, when Fuller began teaching at the Greene Street School, Whately's third edition had become one of the standard rhetoric texts assigned in schools and colleges across the United States. The book was well enough known to be featured in an 1838 advertisement for Greene Street (see Albert 53), which suggests that it was also the text used for training the boys in rhetoric and public declamation.

6. While Elizabeth Palmer Peabody kept summary notes, and while some participants made general statements about the conversations in their journals and letters, only Caroline Healey [Dall] attempted to accurately record the actual give and take of discussion, noting who said what and incorporating her own candid impressions of the participants and their ideas.

7. It is entirely possible that Fuller prevailed upon her friend and bookstore owner Elizabeth Palmer Peabody to secure for her from London the revised and expanded sixth edition of Whately's *Elements of Rhetoric* (London: B. Fellowes, 1841); in that event, Fuller worked from a text with additional illustrative material—but its structure and arguments remained identical to the earlier third edition that she had taught at Greene Street. In fact, nothing substantive from the third edition was cut; more examples and an occasional clarification were simply added in the revised sixth edition.

8. Urbanski reminds us that Fuller was later vindicated when a young Boston woman, in the face of her husband's illness, captained a ship around Cape Horn en route to California in the 1850s. As Urbanski points out, this incident "caught the imagination of many people" and elicited more respectful responses to Fuller's original remark (161–62).

9. Evelina Metcalf's journal entry for December 12, 1838, records that "our Rhetoric lesson which was on Persuasion to-day was very well recited. It spoke of the province of the orator and the requisites of a perfect orator" (in Shuffelton 38).

10. While Whately employs occasional martial imagery throughout his text, such images are never as brutal, nor as concentrated and as elaborate, as those in pt. 2, 117–67.

11. Although Fuller is never cited as a source, recent work in rhetoric and composition theory has reconsidered the meaning of *conversation* as a formal discourse, including most notably Clark's *Dialogue, Dialectic, and Conversation*.

REFERENCES

Albert, Judith Strong. "Margaret Fuller's Row at the Greene Street School: Early Female Education in Providence, 1837–1839." *Rhode Island History* 42.2 (May 1983): 43–55.

Briggs, Charles F. "Review of *Woman in the Nineteenth Century.*" *Broadway Journal* 1 (March 1, 1845): 130–31; (March 8, 1845): 145–46; (March 22, 1845): 182–83. Rpt. in *Critical Essays on Margaret Fuller.* Ed. Joel Myerson. Boston: G.K. Hall, 1980. 8–15.

Brown, Charles Brockden. *Alcuin: A Dialogue.* Philadelphia, 1798. Rpt. with introduction by LeRoy Elwood Kimball. New Haven: Yale UP, 1935.

Brownson, Orestes A. "Miss Fuller and Reformers." *Brownson's Quarterly Review* 7 (April 1845): 249–57. Rpt. in Myerson. 19–25.

Capper, Charles. *Margaret Fuller, An American Romantic Life.* 2 vols. New York: Oxford UP, 1992.

Chevigny, Belle Gale. *The Woman and the Myth: Margaret Fuller's Life and Writings.* New York: Feminist P, 1976.

Child, Lydia Maria. "Woman in the 19th Century." *Broadway Journal* 1 (February 15, 1845): 97. Rpt. in Myerson. 7.

Clark, Gregory. *Dialogue, Dialectic, and Conversation: A Social Perspective on the Function of Writing.* Carbondale: Southern Illinois UP, 1990.

Dall, Caroline Healey. *Historical Pictures Retouched: A Volume of Miscellanies.* Boston: Walker, Wise, 1860.

Elshtain, Jean Bethke. "Feminist Discourse and Its Discontents: Language, Power, and Meaning." *Signs* 7.3 (spring 1982): 603–21.

Emerson, Ralph Waldo. "Self-Reliance." *Selections from Ralph Waldo Emerson.* Ed. Stephen E. Whicher. Boston: Houghton Mifflin, 1957. 147–68.

Emerson, Ralph Waldo, William Henry Channing, and James Freeman Clarke, eds. *Memoirs of Margaret Fuller Ossoli.* 1852. 2 vols. Boston: Brown, Taggard and Chase, 1860.

Fergenson, Laraine R. "Margaret Fuller in the Classroom: The Providence Period." *Studies in the American Renaissance 1987.* Ed. Joel Myerson. Charlottesville: UP of Virginia, 1987. 131–42.

Fish, Stanley E. *Self-Consuming Artifacts.* Berkeley: U of California P, 1972.

Fuller [Ossoli], Margaret. *Woman in the Nineteenth Century and Kindred Papers Relating to the Sphere, Condition, and Duties of Woman.* Ed. Arthur B. Fuller. Boston: John P. Jewett, 1855. Rpt. as Fuller, S. Margaret. *Woman in the Nineteenth Century.* New York: Norton, 1971.

Fuller, S. Margaret. *Woman in the Nineteenth Century.* New York: Greeley and McElrath, 1845. Facsimile Edition rpt. as S. Margaret Fuller. *Woman in the Nineteenth Century.* Ed. Joel Myerson. Intro. Madeleine B. Stern. Columbia: U of South Carolina P, 1980.

Gearhart, Sally Miller. "The Womanization of Rhetoric." *Women's Studies International Quarterly* 2.2 (1979): 195–201.

"The Great Lawsuit. Man versus Men. Woman versus Women." *Dial* 4.1 (1843): 1–47.

Grimké, Sarah Moore. *Letters on the Equality of the Sexes and the Condition of Woman; Addressed to Mary Parker, President of the Boston Female Anti-Slavery Society.* Boston: Isaac Knapp, 1838.

Hawthorne, Julian. *Nathaniel Hawthorne and His Wife.* 2 vols. Boston: Houghton Mifflin, 1884. Excerpted in Julian Hawthorne, "Margaret Fuller and Hawthorne." In Myerson. 114–16.

Healey, Caroline W. *Margaret Fuller and Her Friends, or Ten Conversations with Margaret Fuller upon the Mythology of the Greeks and Its Expression in Art.* Boston: Roberts Bros., 1895.

Hirsch, Marianne, and Evelyn Fox Keller. "Practicing Conflict in Feminist Theory." *Conflicts in Feminism.* Ed. Marianne Hirsch and Evelyn Fox Keller. New York: Routledge, 1990. 370–85.

Hudspeth, Robert N., ed. *The Letters of Margaret Fuller.* 3 vols. Ithaca: Cornell UP, 1983–1984.

Huntington, Frederic Dan. "Review of *Woman in the Nineteenth Century.*" *Christian Examiner* 38 (May 1845): 416–17. Rpt. in Myerson. 26–27.

Johnson, Harriet Hall. "Margaret Fuller as Known by Her Scholars." *Christian Register* (April 21, 1910): 427–29. Rpt. in Myerson. 134–40.

Kelley, Mary, ed. *The Portable Margaret Fuller.* New York: Penguin, 1994.

M., A. G. "The Condition of Woman." *Southern Quarterly Review* 10 (July 1845): 148–49.

McKerrow, Ray E. "Richard Whately's Theory of Rhetoric." *Explorations in Rhetoric: Studies in Honor of Douglas Ehninger.* Glenview, IL: Scott, Foresman, 1982. 137–55.

Myerson, Joel, ed. *Critical Essays on Margaret Fuller.* Boston: G.K. Hall, 1980.

Parrington, Vernon L. *Main Currents in American Thought: The Romantic Revolution in America 1800–1860.* 3 vols. New York: Harcourt, 1927.

Poe, Edgar A. "The Literati of New York City.—No. IV. Sarah Margaret Fuller." *Godey's Magazine and Lady's Book* 33 (August 1846): 72–75. Rpt. in Myerson. 35–39.

Ripley, Sophia Dana. "Woman." *Dial* 1 (January 1841): 362–67.

Robinson, David M. "Margaret Fuller and the Transcendental Ethos: *Woman in the Nineteenth Century.*" *PMLA* 97.1 (January 1982): 83–98.

Scheick, William J. "The Angelic Artistry of Margaret Fuller's *Woman in the Nineteenth Century.*" *Essays in Literature* 11 (fall 1984): 293–98.

Shuffelton, Frank. "Margaret Fuller at Greene Street School: The Journal of Evelina Metcalf." *Studies in the American Renaissance 1985.* Ed. Joel Myerson. Charlottesville: UP of Virginia, 1985. 29–46.

Urbanski, Marie Mitchell Olesen. *Margaret Fuller's "Woman in the Nineteenth Century": A Literary Study of Form and Content, of Sources and Influence.* Westport, CT: Greenwood, 1980.

Whately, Richard. *Elements of Rhetoric . . . from the Third English Edition.* Boston: Hilliard, Gray, 1832.

9

To Call a Thing by Its True Name: The Rhetoric of Ida B. Wells

Jacqueline Jones Royster

Ida B. Wells was born a slave in Holly Springs, Mississippi, on July 16, 1862, the daughter of a carpenter and a cook. By 1890, she had moved to Memphis, Tennessee, and become the editor of the *Evening Star*, a regular contributor to the *Living Way*, co-owner of the *Free Speech*, and a nationally syndicated columnist. In writing about those early years, Wells indicated her surprise at her recognition and popularity as a writer since she was not formally trained as a journalist and had not thought of herself as particularly gifted in the literary arena. She explained what she perceived to be her strength:

> I had observed and thought much about conditions as I had seen them in the country schools and churches. I had an instinctive feeling that the people who had little or no school training should have something coming into their homes weekly which dealt with their problems in a simple, helpful way. So in weekly letters to the *Living Way*, I wrote in a plain, common-sense way on the things which concerned our people. Knowing that their education was limited, I never used a word of two syllables where one would serve the purpose. I signed these articles "Iola."
> (Duster 23–24)

For the next forty-one years, Wells would cut a broad path across the national and international landscape. She would carve out a unique space for herself within the public discourse of her day as a journalist, a clubwoman, a public speaker, and a community activist. Perhaps more important for this analysis, by doing so she would be among the vanguard of African American women who would hold in their hands a new claim within the world of rhetoric to the art of speaking and writing effectively.

Over the course of her public life as a speaker and writer, Wells was extraordinarily productive. As an active participant in the Black Club-women's Movement, Wells spoke frequently in the United States and Great Britain to varied audiences about race matters in general and the evils of lynching in particular. As a journalist, she had weekly columns in the African American periodical press (including the various news-papers and newsletters that she owned, edited, and published herself), and she contributed occasionally to the white periodical press, for ex-ample her column "Ida B. Wells Abroad," a series of articles published by the *Chicago Inter-Ocean* that focused on her British antilynching cru-sade. Her essays were published in African American magazines and occasionally in white magazines. In addition, Wells also published three pamphlets on lynching, *Southern Horrors*, *A Red Record*, and *Mob Rule in New Orleans*; wrote an autobiography, *Crusade for Justice*, which re-mained unfinished and unpublished until 1970, when it was edited by her daughter, Alfreda M. Duster; and kept diaries, one of which has been edited by Miriam DeCosta-Willis (1995).[1]

By general accounts, then, from 1884 when she first began writing and speaking publicly until her death in 1931, Wells created a remarkable record of active participation as speaker, writer, and activist within the public arenas that were available to her. For many decades after these accomplishments, however, her place within the fray of progress and change in the United States was set aside. She was not lauded in public annals of the life and times of her era or her profession. Her name was not on the tongues of those who studied American history or American literature. Despite the centrality and longevity of her involvement with issues of national and international concern, neither this African Ameri-can woman's contribution to history nor her contributions to the making and shaping of public discourse were recognized. Like too many other women whose contributions have been both singular and noteworthy, Wells fell victim to the muck and mire of racism and sexism.

Recent research and scholarship in feminist studies and African American studies, however, have made it possible for many women's stories to be recovered. For Wells, the result is that her place as a his-torical figure of note has become clearer. She has now received greater public recognition than ever before with the existence of specific re-sources that document her footprints as a courageous standard bearer for equity and justice (see, for example, DeCosta-Willis; Duster; Giddings; Lerner; Loewenberg and Bogin; Thompson). Her image is preserved on a stamp by the United States Postal Service. Her story as a journalist and social activist has been immortalized in a documentary, *The American Experience: Ida B. Wells, A Passion for Justice* (1990). Her essays and pamphlets have been made available through reprinted editions (e.g., *On Lynchings: Southern Horrors, A Red Record, Mob Rule in New Orleans*, 1990; *The Antilynching Campaign of Ida B. Wells-Barnett*, forthcoming), and she has been included in various books and articles, especially those that chronicle the participation of African American women in American culture (e.g., Hine, ed., *Black Women in America: An Historical Encyclopedia*, 1993).

For those interested in rhetoric, however, Wells has another place that deserves more public acknowledgement and preservation. Wells was not just a woman of distinction who led an active public life. Wells was a rhetor, a speaker and writer whose use of language in public arenas had a significant impact on the thinking and behavior of the audiences of her day and on the application of law.[2] While she spent little or no time discussing abstract notions of the ways and means of rhetorical effectiveness, as philosophers of rhetoric have done, she did spend considerable time engaging in rhetorical acts and demonstrating rhetorical eloquence and expertise. Wells had her eyes on action, and she seemed much more inclined to practice rather than preach the rhetorical arts. She accomplished this task with flair and style, leaving behind a provocative image of language well used. Ida B. Wells engaged in writing as swordsmanship, demonstrating that in the right hands the pen can indeed become a mighty sword.

As suggested in her autobiography, *Crusade for Justice* (1970), and in Mildred I. Thompson's analysis (*Ida B. Wells-Barnett: An Exploratory Study of an American Black Woman, 1893–1930*, 1990), from the beginning of her career as a journalist, Wells evidenced a tendency to be bold and outspoken on sensitive issues. An article in the *Living Way*, in which she chronicled her suit against the Chesapeake, Ohio and Southwestern Railroad for refusing to honor her first-class ticket and forcibly removing her from the train, was the first to bring her significant public attention. The turning point in Wells's career as a journalist came, however, on March 9, 1892, when three men, including one of Wells's closest friends, were lynched in Memphis.

Before this incident, Wells had abhorred lynching but had accepted the idea that it was the horror of rape and other crimes that incited such violence. With this lynching, however, of men whom she knew to be leading citizens of Memphis, her eyes were opened to the truth of lynching as an act of terror perpetrated against a race of people in order to maintain power and control. Lynching, she began to see, was an instrument used to retard the progress of African Americans in their efforts to participate more fully in social, political, and economic life. With this insight, she was energized to begin a campaign to counter misconceptions and to encourage the application of justice, a campaign that would result ultimately in a dramatic decrease in this type of lawlessness and disorder, especially in the city of Memphis.

Wells's immediate response to the lynchings was to write editorials that encouraged African Americans in Memphis to leave a city that offered no protection of their rights of citizenship and to go West to Kansas and Oklahoma. Her editorials were quite successful, affecting in a significant way the migration of thousands of African Americans to the West (see *The American Experience*). Wells also began collecting data on other lynchings, and on May 21, 1892, she wrote an editorial that served as the springboard to catapult her onto the national scene. She stated:

> Eight Negroes lynched in one week.... Nobody in this section of the country believes the old thread-bare lie that negro men rape white women. If Southern white men are not careful they will overreach themselves, and public sentiment will have a reaction. A conclusion will then be reached which will be very damaging to the moral reputation of their women. (Thompson 177)[3]

When the editorial was published, Wells was traveling in the Northeast. The response of the white community in Memphis was to use this moment as an excuse to silence a discordant voice. They destroyed her press, attempted to kill her partner, and let it be known that if Wells ever set foot in the state of Tennessee again, she would be killed. Instead of silencing her, however, these actions provided an opportunity for Wells to intensify and direct her campaign much more freely away from the immediate terror of the South and much more effectively in terms of the people she could influence to bring about change.

As an exile, Wells was able to bring African American women together for their first collective response to a political cause, an event that became a crystallizing moment for the emerging national Black Clubwomen's Movement. She was also able to reach across the Atlantic Ocean to London where she was instrumental in establishing the first antilynching society. This springboard became the launching pad for an antilynching campaign that she sustained for over forty years. Much of this Wells was able to do with the power of her pen.

In analyzing the nature of this power, two intriguing points emerge. First, Wells's particular uses of verbal strategies situate her very well within traditions of leadership among African American women. Second, a basic analysis of her rhetorical choices reveals not only that she operated as a rhetor with skill and eloquence but also that she, like other African American women rhetors, did so with what must clearly be recognized as "amazing grace," given her position as speaker within a complex sociopolitical environment.

The Intersection of Leadership Styles and Rhetorical Prowess

Despite being confronted by personal danger, as speaker and writer Ida B. Wells acted boldly and tenaciously in the interest of social change. What is striking about her courage is that her perceptions of what she was trying to do can be contextualized within traditional patterns of leadership among African American women, patterns that directly connect language use and action.

In her autobiography, Wells stated:

> Having lost my paper, had a price put on my life and been made an exile from home for hinting at the truth, I felt that I owed it to myself and to my race to tell the whole truth now that I was where I could do so freely.
>
> (Duster 69)

This statement, in concert with the self-assessment of her strengths quoted earlier, illustrates that Wells embraced what appears to be a habit among African American women, i.e., the use of whatever literacy skills they were able to acquire and exercise in the interest of making life better for themselves and for others.

In her own words, Wells wanted to write in a "plain common-sense way on the things that concerned our people." She wrote: "[I] owed it to myself and to my race to tell the whole truth." Her basic goal was to tell the truth, to tell it simply, to tell it directly. She obviously felt that, in that way, she could help her people to understand more clearly what was happening to them and around them. She also felt that such an understanding was important, in keeping with the general belief that knowledge is power. By this reckoning, if African Americans had knowledge, they would also have the option, the wherewithal, to act. So Ida B.

Wells set as her goal speaking the truth as she saw it, and did so despite threats to her life.

To accomplish this rhetorical goal, Wells had to fashion her own vision of womanhood, since the prevailing image did not encourage public roles for women, and certainly not for African American women. Telling her simple truth would therefore mean assuming a public role. She needed to resist prevailing sociopolitical realities, since these conditions urged conformity to a status quo that sought to constrain her within specified racial and gendered boundaries. Speaking out would entail questioning values and assumptions that others were not questioning. Wells needed to defy opinions within her immediate community that had internalized race and gender boundaries and that urged her to silence. In speaking out, Wells would be assuming privileges that at the time women and people of African descent were not entitled to assume.

In keeping with a pattern of behavior that Audre Lorde explained a century later, Wells needed to be willing to stand alone. In the poem "A Litany for Survival" (*The Black Unicorn* 32), Lorde articulates a path to voice that has served as a prescription for many African American women who recognize themselves as "standing upon the constant edges of decision/crucial and alone." In this poem, Lorde presents a gripping image of African American women's lives, capturing the enduring pain, fear, and frustration of those who are disempowered by life's circumstances. She captures abiding fear, the sense of being damned if we do and damned if we do not. She lays open with considerable passion and remarkable clarity conditions that would rob those without power and without choices of the ability to speak. She allows the reader to see and feel the lives of African American women as the heavy hands of oppression seek to strip quietude, voice, joy, possibility, even life.

At the end of this poem, however, Lorde articulates most provocatively a seemingly inevitable recognition, given the course that she charts for the poem. She leads us to understand that under such circumstances, African American women are brought by necessity and by uncommon sense, perhaps, to action. She says:

> So it is better to speak
> remembering
> we were never meant to survive.

The statement from Wells's autobiography indicates that Wells understood, as Lorde would later articulate it, that considering the likelihood that she was not meant to survive, she might as well speak the truth: in fact she "owed" it to herself.

In *Sister Outsider* (1984), a collection of essays, Lorde continues to analyze survival and to see language as a tool of activism. In "The Master's Tools Will Never Dismantle the Master's House," Lorde talks insightfully about the tools of racism and patriarchy, and in doing so offers a springboard for rethinking what seems a basic legacy of nineteenth-century African American women writers like Ida B. Wells. In this essay, Lorde raises questions about the role that the personal point of view plays in the illumination of choices and in an individual's ability to bring herself to positive action. She suggests the possibility that self-definition and self-activation are inextricably connected. When we raise the possibility of self-definition, we carve out a space from which we can understand that Wells looked closely at her life, named herself, claimed her own vision of reality, claimed her own authority to speak the truth that she saw, entitled herself to this authority, and made the decision to use the tools of rhetoric and composition to bring about what she perceived to be much-needed social change.

As for other African American women, speaking and writing became for Ida B. Wells very much an act of defiance.[4] In defiance of the world around her, Wells chose to be an instrument of her own survival, and she committed herself to the survival of her people as well. However, surviving so defiantly ultimately means, as Lorde says, "learning how to stand alone, unpopular and sometimes reviled, and how to make common cause with those others identified as outside the structures in order to define and seek a world in which we can all flourish" ("The Master's Tools" 112). Seemingly, Ida B. Wells took passionately to standing alone.

As a self-defined crusader for justice, Ida B. Wells was defining and seeking a world in which we, African Americans included, could all flourish. Wells chose to make this cause, i.e. her cause, a common one for others like and unlike herself, through the power of her pen. As a journalist, she built a reputation, according to Mildred Thompson, as "a radical race woman, who had risked alienation among blacks and stirred up sentiments of outrage among whites. She was not a new black woman; she was a militant black agitator" (Thompson 24). Wells observed conditions and circumstances around her. She called what she saw by its name, whether the name was pleasant or not, whether those around her affirmed her efforts or not; and she directed her audiences toward action. Wells was an independent thinker, a skilled businesswoman, uncompromising in her beliefs and in her strategies for action, unrelenting in her efforts to bring about meaningful change. She was a catalyst, sometimes welcome, sometimes not, always sharp-tongued and always sharp-witted.

In an early essay she wrote:

> I am before the American people today through no inclination of my own, but because of a deep-seated conviction that the country at large does not know the extent to which lynch law prevails. . . . I can not believe that the apathy and indifference which so largely obtains regarding mob rule is other than the result of ignorance of the true situation. And yet, the observing and thoughtful must know that in one section, at least, of our common country, a government of the people, by the people, and for the people, means a government by the mob; where the land of the free and home of the brave means a land of lawlessness, murder and outrage. (Thompson 171)

In calling the act of lynching by its true name, an act of terrorism, an outrage, a crime, a sacrilege against "truth, justice, and the American way," Wells established herself as a bold, outspoken woman, a woman who was willing to risk everything for the sake of her principles, for the sake of truth.

In choosing this path, Wells provides evidence, not just of the resonance of her life with other African American women's lives over time, but also of her connectedness with a tradition of leadership among African American women. In an ethnographic study of three contemporary women, Jacquelyn Mitchell delineates specific characteristics of this brand of leadership. She reports her findings in an issue of *Sage: A Scholarly Journal on Black Women* (5.2) that focused on the cultural and political context of leadership among black women from various backgrounds. The issue gave particular attention to the ways in which women exercise power and authority, gain autonomy, and operate with vision, self-esteem, and confidence in taking care of their responsibilities and in addressing immediate and long-term needs within their communities.

In "Three Women: Cultural Rules and Leadership Roles in the Black Community," Mitchell reports that the women in her study mastered the informal rules of their culture and developed skills that allowed them to "teach." Each of the women had a remarkable ability to garner and sustain authority by helping others to see their own realities for themselves. She discovered that these women all used verbal strategies to get the people around them to hear themselves, to see their situations, and as a result to use what they had come to understand in solving problems. Mitchell concludes that

—They insist on calling things by their true names.

—They articulate the fears that inhibit others from acting responsibly.

—And they prescribe courses of action that focus not on what others have done to them, but on what the individual can do. (Mitchell 9–18)

In drawing these conclusions, Mitchell also suggests that the similarities in behavior among the women in her study are likely, based on general observation and anecdotal evidence, to characterize many women in African American communities and thereby to constitute a vibrant tradition of leadership[5]

In the case of Ida B. Wells, there is more than anecdotal evidence to support Mitchell's theory.[6] Through her articles, essays, pamphlets, and speeches, Wells broke the silence on lynching. She articulated for a race, a nation, and a world the complexities of this problem so that those with the power to do so could act responsibly, and she pointed her readers toward what for her was the obvious thing to do:

Such attacks imperiling as they do the foundation of government, law and order, merit the thoughtful consideration of far-sighted Americans; not from a standpoint of sentiment, not even so much from a standpoint of justice to a weak race, as from a desire to preserve our institutions. (Thompson 171)

The institutions which she urged her audiences to preserve were those that constitute the founding values of the nation itself: law and order, freedom, justice, and equality for all citizens. Even further, however, she asserted her authority by claiming all of these institutions, not just for white people, but for African Americans as well. In her words, the nation is "our common country," and the institutions, she says, are "our institutions," not just "yours" but "ours." And, of course, she assumed that knowing the truth about lynching would demand action.

To summarize this first point about the nature of Wells's rhetorical power I am arguing that, in general, rhetorical prowess for African American women gains its deepest meaning and clarity within the context of their particular brand of community leadership. I recognize that the essence of our sense of what rhetoric is is deeply rooted in a public sphere, a space that we recognize in contemporary scholarship as historically highly gendered. Making a claim for African American women as rhetors in such a space demands understanding how they have participated in, negotiated, and redefined the "public" sphere (an overwhelmingly "male"-defined arena) and the "private" sphere (an overwhelmingly "female"-defined arena). It demands also that we understand the ways in which women rhetors, including African American women, have been compelled to "dance" without a net along a rhetorical tightrope between these two spaces.[7]

. . . . . .

For African American women, rhetorical expertise can be significantly defined by their abilities to use language imaginatively, creatively, and effectively in their efforts to assume a subject position. An enabling strategy with these rhetors has been to place themselves in a position, not always to act on their own, but more often than not to influence the power, authority, and actions of others. For them, rhetorical prowess has been intertwined historically with the artful ways in which they have participated as agents of change in community life. A few women, like Ida B. Wells, have been able to stretch the range of their influence to audiences outside their immediate community. As a journalist, public speaker, and community activist, Ida B. Wells had a forum in the public sphere.

Social and Cognitive Dimensions of Rhetorical Competence

In coming to appreciate the abilities of Wells and other nineteenth-century African American women leaders to operate within the highly charged sociopolitical environment in which they lived and worked, I have constructed a matrix of concepts that seem particularly relevant for understanding their ways of being and doing.[8] Among these concepts are: (1) language development as a lifelong learning process; (2) communicative competence as it includes both social and cognitive dimensions; (3) the role of literacy in the development of communicative competence; and (4) a reconsideration of rhetorical competence within the framework of an understanding of both social and cognitive dimensions of communicative competence.

While a short essay does not provide adequate opportunity for a detailed explanation of each of these concepts, the point to emphasize here is that our ability to understand the rhetorical strategies of Ida B. Wells and other African American women rhetors rests to a great extent on the task of thinking more deeply and broadly about more traditional definitions of rhetoric as a "public" enterprise, about the acquisition of rhetorical competence, and about the ways in which we analyze rhetorical events. An initial step toward greater understanding is the recognition that rhetoric, as a use of language and as both a social and a cognitive process, occurs through the internalization of a complex system of understandings that provide the context within which we decode and encode texts, make meaning, and operate with autonomy, power, and authority. Using this perspective, Wells's antilynching campaign becomes a remarkable rhetorical event. The pivotal questions are simplified: How did Wells use language? What did she use it to do? What did her uses of language indicate about the eyes, the mind, even the passions behind the rhetor's hand?

As a core example of her rhetorical style, Wells's antilynching campaign demonstrates that she was an astute writer who had an expert understanding of a complex rhetorical task. As stated earlier, Wells's purpose was to tell the truth, to tell it simply, to tell it directly, and to push her audiences toward actions that would bring about social change. Beyond her impassioned commitment to this purpose, however, Wells's rhetorical prowess can be illustrated in other ways. In her essays (a genre she used frequently, in addition to newspaper articles), Wells was able to use her sociocultural knowledge and understanding, as well as her abilities as a thinker, language user, problem finder, and problem solver with artistry. She used these rhetorical competences to engage in the process of creating and transmitting meaning. Her essays, then, as a manageable and available set of texts, provide an opportunity to analyze the ways in which Wells was able to capture the conscience of a nation and to push that conscience so that the nation might be primed to act responsibly.

An excellent example is the essay from which I have been quoting. One of Wells's earliest essays on lynching, "Lynching in All Its Phases" first saw public light as a lecture on February 13, 1893, in the Boston Monday Lectureship. Later, in May of the same year, it was published in *Our Day: A Record and Review of Current Reform*, a monthly periodical that had debuted in January 1888. This periodical included among its illustrious editors the internationally renowned reformist and president of the Women's Christian Temperance Union, Frances E. Willard. According to its prospectus in the opening volume (January 1888), *Our Day* had as its mission to provide a record that would "form a comprehensive register of Criticism, Progress, and Reform, secular and religious, national and international." It also took as its special task the publication of the Boston Monday lectures that were delivered in February and March of each year. According to the prospectus, these lectures "which for several seasons have had a circulation of a million copies at home and abroad, will discuss, as they have done for the last twelve years, whatever is at once new, true, and strategic in the relations of Religion to Science, Philosophy, and Current Reform."

This information was apparently not lost on Ida B. Wells. Take note again of her opening sentence:

> I am before the American people today through no inclination of my own, but because of a deep-seated conviction that the country at large does not know the extent to which lynch law prevails in parts of the Republic, nor the conditions which force into exile those who speak the truth. (Thompson 171)

Wells begins humbly, befitting her station as a female who would have no inclination on her own to speak, and as victim who has been unjustly forced into exile for being truthful. At the same time, however, Wells also extends this definition of herself by invoking an image of one who is compelled by "deep-seated conviction" to speak the truth (whether she was to be punished for it or not) and by portraying herself as a patriot among American peers who believe in truth and justice as strongly as she. She explains the genesis of her authority to speak, claims that authority, levels the distance between herself and the audience, and proceeds to weave her tale convincingly and authoritatively. In other words, Wells creates a comfortable seat for an audience with Christian and American values who happen (by whatever circumstance) not to know the truth, and she invites them to sit and to listen—all in one sentence. In doing so, Wells ties her audience swiftly and directly to a set of historical values and to a set of companion obligations, and thereby engages them interactively in a process of creating meaning, in an exchange that she expects will result in action.[9] Wells situates this audience within the concreteness of their shared values and anchors them immediately to her point of view and to her experiences. Consider, in this regard, the second and third sentences:

> I can not believe that the apathy and indifference which so largely obtains regarding mob rule is other than the result of ignorance of the true situation. And yet, the observing and thoughtful must know that in one section, at least, of our common country, a government of the people, by the people, and for the people, means a government by the mob. (Thompson 171)

Wells moves obliquely to an implied rhetorical question that in effect is a thinly veiled indictment, increasing her momentum and invoking the beginnings of moral outrage. She says, in effect, that if righteous people are not acting against this horror, it has to be because they do not know; but the question is how could they not know, these people who are so observant of progress and reform, who are so thoughtful and intelligent. With this strategy, Wells subtly encourages the audience not to delay any longer in doing what must inevitably be done. She encourages them rhetorically to take a noble stance, to listen, and to ready themselves for appropriate action.

At this point in the essay, Wells moves to an antithetical listing of national values alongside specific injustices: "A government of the people, by the people, and for the people, means a government by the mob"; "land of the free and home of the brave . . . a land of lawlessness, murder and outrage"; "liberty of speech . . . license of might to destroy." These juxtapositions lead climactically toward the proposition:

"Repeated attacks on the life, liberty and happiness of any citizen or class of citizens are attacks on distinctive American institutions" (Thompson 171).

Here, Wells subtly shifts the focus of the sentences from incidents of injustice to the citizens against whom these injustices are perpetrated. In one sentence she declares lynching to be an injustice. In the next, she embodies the victims by making them the subject of the sentence. The structuring of these sentences encourages the audience to notice that acts are not just being perpetrated, but that "citizens" are being wronged—not mere random victims, but citizens with rights and privileges that are guaranteed by their citizenship. The audience, then, as fellow citizens, as compassionate and intelligent people who believe in the rights and privileges of citizenship must act, not just to save these victims, but to preserve the law and order and the values of the nation:

> Such attacks imperiling as they do the foundation of government, law and order, merit the thoughtful consideration of far-sighted Americans; not from a standpoint of sentiment, not even so much from a standpoint of justice to a weak race, as from a desire to preserve our institutions. (Thompson 171)

To repeat an earlier point, Wells also reminds her audience that the institutions are "ours," not just "yours," but "ours." This paragraph, as the opener of a rhetorically powerful essay, is densely crafted. Wells establishes an interactive space between the audience and herself, and then proceeds to lay out, piece by piece, a politically charged message that stings the conscience.

In the next section of the text, Wells tells a story of hard work, commitment to the values of good character, education, and economic opportunity, a story of racial uplift, a story of confidence in the law. She gives a step-by-step chronology of the events that led to the lynching of her three friends and the subsequent events leading to her exile. In journalistic style, she lays out the scene of a crime, uses her oppressors' own words as reported in white newspapers (the *Daily Commercial* and the *Evening Scimitar*) to support her claims of oppression, and clearly indicates where she believes the many injustices rest. Wells crafts her argument from good sense, reason, and logic, and she documents her account through sources that her audience would find reliable, more reliable than the word of a young black woman.

At that point, Wells makes a rhetorical change and ends her chronology with a breathless flair:

> I have been censured for writing that editorial, but when I think of the five men who were lynched that week for assault on white women and that not a week passes but some poor soul is violently ushered into eternity on this trumped-up charge, knowing the many things I do, and part of which I tried to tell in the *New York Age* of June 25, (and in the pamphlets I have with me) seeing that the whole race in the South was injured in the estimation of the world because of these false reports, I could no longer hold my peace, and I feel, yes, I am sure, that if it had to be done over again (provided no one else was the loser save myself) I would do and say the very same again. (Thompson 180)

This paragraph is one sentence, one long sentence fired with passion and determination, a sentence that builds and builds and builds, and in this sentence she underscores the idea, "I said it, and by the powers of truth and justice, I'd do it again."

The next section of the essay extends the arena for lynching beyond the single incident of her friends or the state of Tennessee, giving a specific accounting of the pervasive nature of the problem throughout the South. Wells spends time defending her view of lynching, not just with her own investigations but with the investigations of the Chicago *Inter-Ocean*, a white newspaper. She then refutes excuses for inaction, and ends with a question:

Do you ask the remedy? A public sentiment strong against lawlessness must be aroused. . . . The voice of the people is the voice of God, and I long with all the intensity of my soul for the Garrison, Douglas, Sumner, Wittier, and Phillips who shall rouse this nation to a demand that from Greenland's icy mountains to the coral reefs of the Southern seas, mob rule shall be put down and equal and exact justice be accorded to every citizen of whatever race, who finds a home within the borders of the land of the free and the home of the brave. (Thompson 185–87)

According to Wells, who re-invokes images of basic American values, images of men of character and people of conscience, the answer to the problem of lynching is to garner righteousness and to bring power and influence to bear so that there will be no more lynching. Her voice, then, becomes the voice that she calls for, the voice "who shall rouse this nation." Further, in the way that she has previously detailed the numbers of atrocities, she communicates also an ever present danger and a sense of urgency.

The Laying of a Foundation

Ida B. Wells was a wonder, personally and rhetorically. She was a small, attractive woman who, if we accept stereotypical images of race and gender, belied in outward appearance the substance of the person within. By all accounts, Wells had a remarkable intellect and passion for truth and justice. As Paula Giddings states, however, "Her entire life, it seemed, had prepared her not only to understand but to confront the broader issue head on—despite the consequences" (Giddings 20).

Wells's parents, politically active in Holly Springs, provided her with strong role models for activism and social consciousness. At sixteen, responsibility was thrust upon her when her parents died suddenly of yellow fever and she had to take care of herself and five younger siblings. She did so by teaching in the public schools of Mississippi and Tennessee, moving to Memphis to better their circumstances.

Wells took with her to Memphis a sense of righteous indignation which she was called upon to demonstrate again and again. By the age of twenty-two, as indicated, she had sued the Chesapeake, Ohio and Southwestern railroad and won the suit, after being evicted from the ladies' coach. The railroad company appealed to the Tennessee Supreme Court and the decision was overturned. In addition, Wells had campaigned in her editorials at the *Free Speech* against the Board of Education in the interest of better teachers and better school facilities for African American children, an effort for which she lost her teaching position. Undaunted, she turned an African American newspaper into a financially stable enterprise and continued to build a reputation for herself as a bold woman who spoke the truth (see Duster; Giddings; Thompson; Royster).

Ida B. Wells accomplished many remarkable feats during her lifetime and was instrumental in bringing about changes that made a difference in people's lives. Most remarkable among those accomplishments was the central role she played in reducing the rising tide of atrocities occurring at the end of the nineteenth century. Her efforts were catalytic in bringing the issue of lynching to the attention of the nation and the world. As evidenced by the essays and other texts she has left behind, Wells's primary weapon in these causes was her pen, a pen that she used as a mighty sword to slash across the American scene a new pathway toward truth and justice.

Wells's analytical abilities were distinctive, a strength she used well in her texts as she analyzed the sociopolitical contexts within which she wrote, and as she used an insightful awareness of language to construct meaning and inspire change. Amazingly, she wrote with total regard for truth and justice and little regard for personal affirmation or for personal safety during an era when both were at great risk.

Our rediscoveries of Wells allow us to say, as Thomas T. Fortune said in 1893 and as Mildred Thompson repeated in 1990:

> There is scarcely any reason why this woman, young in years and old in experience, shall not be found in the forefront of the great intellectual fight in which the race is now engaged; ... if she fails to impress her personality upon the time in which she lives, whose fault will it be? (Thompson 1)

The truth of this statement still rings in our ears some one hundred years later. Clearly, we are just coming to know Ida B. Wells. She, however, is the tip of an iceberg of other notable African American women whose lives and work have been muted and displaced. In the essayist tradition alone, we should know more about Maria Stewart, Anna Julia Cooper, Gertrude Mossell, Josephine St. Pierre Ruffin, Amy Jacques Garvey, Josephine Silone Yates, Nannie Helen Burroughs, and so many others. Individually, these women provided distinctive examples of language imaginatively and interestingly used. Collectively, they opened for generations to come new pathways for the participation of African American women in public discourse.

The resounding message is that if, in the times in which we live, we fail in our processes of recovery to reestablish a place of respect within the rhetorical domain for Ida B. Wells and for a number of other discarded women, we will know whose fault it is. The fault will be with us. What will remain, I imagine, given the possibilities of African American cultural traditions, is the chance for some bold woman with pen in hand to call us and our deeds by their true names.

NOTES

1. For a more complete review of the works of Ida B. Wells, see Thompson.

2. Analyses of Ida B. Wells as a speaker and writer, rather than a community activist, for example, are still very few. Two dissertations (Hutton; Humrich) are representative of what is currently available.

3. All quotations from Wells's essay "Lynch Law in All Its Phases" are from Thompson.

4. See hooks for a more extended explanation of this notion of defiance.

5. This tradition is documentable at least as early as the mid-nineteenth century, as illustrated, for example, by the fact that Isabella Van Wagener changed her name to Sojourner Truth as a declaration of the activist path she had chosen for herself.

6. For another example of similar habits of action among African American women, see the second chapter of hooks, in which she explains the terms "back talk" and "talking back," both of which are applied to a child (especially a female child) and also a woman in southern African American communities who speaks "as an equal to an authority figure . . . daring to disagree" (5).

7. The seminal text for the historical position of African American women on this issue is Cooper.

8. This theoretical frame is part of my work in progress, *Traces of a Stream: Literacy and Social Change among African American Women*. In addition, the works of Andrews, Campbell, Hymes, Romaine, Saville-Troike, Lane, and Vygotsky offer other points of departure for examining these concepts.

9. See Brandt for a detailed discussion of the ways in which writers forge social, interactive relationships with readers through the language of texts.

REFERENCES

The American Experience: Ida B. Wells, A Passion for Justice. Prod. William Greaves. Video Dub, 1990.

Andrews, James R. *The Practice of Rhetorical Criticism*. 2d ed. New York: Longman, 1990.

Brandt, Deborah. *Literacy as Involvement: The Acts of Writers, Readers, and Texts.* Carbondale: Southern Illinois UP, 1990.

Campbell, Karlyn Kohrs. *The Rhetorical Act.* Belmont: Wadsworth, 1982.

Cooper, Anna Julia. *A Voice from the South.* 1892. New York: Oxford UP, 1988.

DeCosta-Willis, Miriam. *The Memphis Diary of Ida B. Wells.* Boston: Beacon, 1995.

Duster, Alfreda M., ed. *Crusade for Justice: The Autobiography of Ida B. Wells.* Chicago: U of Chicago P, 1970.

Giddings, Paula. *When and Where I Enter: The Impact of Black Women on Race and Sexism in America.* New York: Morrow, 1984; Bantam, 1985.

Hine, Darlene Clark, et al., eds. *Black Women in America: An Historical Encyclopedia.* 2 vols. Brooklyn, N.Y.: Carlson P, 1993.

hooks, bell. *Talking Back: Thinking Feminist, Thinking Black.* Boston: South End, 1989.

Humrich, Shauna Lea. "Ida B. Wells-Barnett: The Making of a Reputation." Diss. U of Northern Colorado, 1990.

Hutton, Mary Magdalene Boone. "The Rhetoric of Ida B. Wells: The Genesis of the Anti-Lynching Movement." Diss. Indiana U, 1975.

Hymes, Dell. *Foundations in Sociolinguistics.* Philadelphia: U of Pennsylvania P, 1974.

Lane, Vera W. *The Dynamics of Communicative Development.* Englewood Cliffs: Prentice, 1982.

Lerner, Gerda. *Black Women in White America.* New York: Pantheon, 1972; Vintage, 1973.

Loewenberg, Bert James, and Ruth Bogin, eds. *Black Women in Nineteenth Century American Life.* University Park: Pennsylvania State UP, 1976.

Lourde, Audre. *The Black Unicorn.* New York: Norton, 1978.

———. *Sister Outsider: Essays and Speeches.* Freedom: Crossing, 1984.

Mitchell, Jacquelyn. "Three Women: Cultural Rules and Leadership Roles in the Black Community." *Sage: A Scholarly Journal on Black Women* 5.2 (1984): 9–18.

Romaine, Suzanne. *The Language of Children and Adolescents: The Acquisition of Communicative Competence.* New York: Blackwell, 1984.

Royster, Jacqueline Jones, ed. *The Antilynching Campaign of Ida B. Wells-Barnett.* Boston: Bedford, 1995.

Saville-Troike, Muriel. *The Ethnography of Communication: An Introduction.* New York: Blackwell, 1982.

Thompson, Mildred I. *Ida B. Wells-Barnett: An Exploratory Study of an American Black Woman, 1893–1930.* New York: Carlson, 1990.

Truth, Sojourner. *Narrative of Sojourner Truth.* 1878. Salem: Ayer, 1988.

Vygotsky, Lev S. *Mind in Society.* Ed. Michael Cole et al. Cambridge: Harvard UP, 1978.

10

"Intelligent Members or Restless Disturbers": Women's Rhetorical Styles, 1880–1920

Joanne Wagner

I

In 1891 A. Wetzell, a writer for *The Mount Holyoke*, commented on Olive Schreiner's first book,[1] which Schreiner had published under a male pseudonym:

> It was only necessary to read a very few pages to discover that it was undoubtedly the work of a woman, so please you, the strong work of a strong woman. Following the example of many talented women, Olive Schreiner, an ardent champion of the increased freedom and larger rights of womankind, sent out the firstling of her pen under a man's name. (Wetzell 1)

Despite her confidence that Schreiner's style infallibly revealed her gender, Wetzell also recognized that a strong woman's style might be better received if it seemed to come from a man. Women speaking and writing publicly in the late nineteenth century were constantly faced with this tension between developing a personal style in language and accommodating society's stylistic expectations. In particular, instruction in rhetorical style at women's colleges presented conflicting ideals to women students studying to participate in public discourse. On the one hand, practical rhetoric courses reified the notion of plain and correct language as the way to enter educated society. On the other hand, increasing emphasis on belletristic models showed women how a personal and powerful voice could be achieved, even as society limited their opportunities to define themselves through their style. The instruction in rhetorical style at four of the Seven Sisters colleges—Smith, Vassar, Wellesley, and Mount Holyoke[2]—demonstrates how these choices were reflected in pedagogy and practice. Because they had strong women faculty with influential pedagogical theories that stressed the importance of rhetoric, these four schools provide evidence of how style was understood and taught—and how women saw its implications for themselves and their academic and professional companions.

By most accounts, the formal study of rhetoric, on the decline since the Renaissance, reached a low point in the nineteenth century, with "no intellectual, philosophical, or theoretical center" (Stewart 136).[3] One sign of this malaise was the omission of *invention*, the act of discovering what to say on a particular topic, from the domain of rhetorical studies (Berlin 146). As a result, rhetoric was most often reduced to the process of skillfully ornamenting already developed thoughts. For instance, when describing Daniel Webster's oratory in 1889, Wellesley rhetoric professor Louise Manning Hodgkins presents rhetoric as a weak relative of more serious truth-seeking projects: "There is [in Webster] always the same consistent subservience of the expression to the thought, always the same dependence upon the certain foundations of logic rather than the uncertain flights of rhetoric" (9). Webster's effective language choices were always based on the logical progression of thoughts rather than any rhetorical decoration. Since rhetoric was seen as merely the arrangement of knowledge generated in other contexts, unlike the logical results that emerged from philosophy and science, at best it could only enhance the conclusions of "real" methods for seeking truth.

This diminished view of rhetoric as style, and style's further reduction to ornamentation, was reflected in the content of *practical rhetoric*, one of the strands of nineteenth-century rhetoric identified by modern commentators.[4] By 1880, practical rhetoric entailed a set of rules and standards prescribed by textbooks and enforced through a first-year class like Rhetoric I (which became the ubiquitous English Composition I, or Freshman Composition, in the next decade). In the last quarter of the nineteenth century, the practical rhetoric course also became a method for enforcing the dialect of the "professional class," those educated according to certain standards (Berlin 72). If women wanted to join the ranks of the educated, they had to learn the standards of usage and grammar that had become central to rhetorical instruction. At their simplest, these rules included the topics covered by Frances Perry, a Wellesley rhetoric instructor, in her *Punctuation Primer* (1908): general punctuation, bibliographies, and forms of epistles. More inclusive rhetoric texts covered the parts and forms of discourse. A typical text discussed words, sentences, paragraphs, and whole compositions, including exposition, argument, description, narration, and letter writing (Bascom). Although the initial class in rhetoric was often derided because it dictated stylistic rules without any theoretical basis, the class served the important function of standardizing the accepted manners of expression. Such courses continued to act as the academic gatekeeper well into the twentieth century.

Herbert Spencer's *The Philosophy of Style* (1852) was the basis for much of the practical instruction in style in women's colleges, both as a primary source and as interpreted through textbooks. Spencer's theory was popular because it gave simple psychological backing for his extremely prescriptive rules. He attempted to justify the plain style by supporting it with "scientific ordination," showing that "economy" is the great underlying principle of all communication (6). Diction, syntax, figures of speech, and rhythm are all justified insofar as they serve the principle of economy, and in turn economy in speech and writing ensures that an audience's mental faculties will not be overloaded by a segment of discourse. While Spencer's view of human communication was based on overly narrow conceptions of the motives for language use, his appeals to efficiency and science made his work attractive to late nineteenth-century teachers of rhetoric. Thus *The Philosophy of Style* served the purposes of a practical rhetoric while justifying its exhortations with a rationale based on principles of human cognition.

While rhetorical style was being reduced to simplistic rules for composition, another view of style—style as personality—was maintained in the *belletristic rhetoric* of literature-based courses (Stewart 140). Even if style was not seen as part of an epistemic process, it still could give force to and express personality in discourse, becoming part of the ethos rather than the logos of the text. That is, style could illustrate the persona of the speaker rather than serving merely as decoration for the argument of the text. The most influential belletristic stylist was Thomas De Quincey, whose distinction between "literature of knowledge" and "literature of power" was analogous to the distinction between the practical rhetoric of those seeking to convey knowledge and the belletristic rhetoric of those interested in the expressive power of discourse.

Practical rhetoric, then, placed its faith in the effect of unadorned messages. Belletristic rhetoric applauded the force of style in discourse and yet limited its domain to fiction and essays where its persuasive aspects were masked. By the 1890s, courses with "rhetoric" in the title usually included practical stylistic training, so that at the beginning of the twentieth century, when style began to be the concern of literary studies, literary scholars used the words "prose style" to distinguish their object of study from the texts used in skill-oriented practical rhetoric courses.

Both strains of rhetorical instruction served a larger goal: preparing women to shape their discourse for an educated, public audience. Through their training women were being prepared to emulate the men they would have to persuade. An observer of the first women's intercollegiate debate between Wellesley and Vassar in 1902, remembering the event later, commented on how the women spoke in a style that would be familiar to their future audiences:

> The quality of the speaking was not greatly unlike that in men's college debates. . . . The young Dianas utilized the crossbow of factual exposition, not the longbow of perfervid oratory. . . . [Vassar] spoke as easily and authoritatively as if admonishing an underclassman—or does one say girl?—for breach of a college rule, instead of, as the fact was, trying to convince an audience of a thousand—including three male judges. (Seasongood 6)

Indeed, in some areas—elocution, delivery, and technique—this observer judged the women better than college men in debating, although "in substance . . . the debate compared less favorably with the Yale-Princeton contest of the previous year, on the same subject" (Seasongood 5). But no matter what the debate's substance or style, the very act of public speaking in male terms was preparation for entrance into a society that many women hoped would see them as fully participating citizens first and women second.

II

Rhetoric classes at Wellesley, Vassar, Smith, and Mount Holyoke used both practical rules and belletristic models to teach style, although concern for style as such increasingly became a feature of literature classes after 1890. At Wellesley, as at many other colleges, Spencer's text initially provided the main set of principles for evaluating style. An 1884 senior rhetoric exam tested Wellesley students on their knowledge of Spencer's principles with questions such as: "What is the general law which governs effective writing?" and "In what way is the Metaphor superior to the Simile?" The test also asked for a stylistic analysis of a passage, showing "the manner of building up the thought" ("Senior Class Rhetoric Examination").

Another essential part of stylistic instruction at Wellesley, as at the other schools, was diction, and diction involved choosing not only the most economical word but a socially acceptable word as well. Thus there were many exercises in choosing a particular word over its synonyms, and much was said about barbarisms and solecisms. In 1892, in the class in rhetoric and English composition, Wellesley students were asked to "define a Barbarism; an Impropriety; an Idiom" and give two examples ("Rhetoric and English Composition Hour Examination"). Most test questions about style asked for definitions like these, or required analyses of passages using stylistic precepts learned in class.

By 1904 Wellesley students were being asked questions more in keeping with belletristic rhetoric: "What is style?" "Locate and explain . . . le style c'est l'homme." By 1916 the ascendancy of belletristic rhetoric was clear in these questions from English Composition 2:

1. Criticize in detail the cited passages in the light of the following possible interpretations of style:
   a. "Style is personality, and therefore various."
   b. "Style consists in finding and keeping the right tone."
   c. "Style is 'proper words in proper places' or 'pattern in words.' "
   ("June Examination")

Here, Spencer's notions of "economy" and "clearness" are no longer mentioned as possible interpretations of style, and "proper words in proper places" is only one possibility. The "cited passages" were works of literary criticism, emphasizing the extent to which the study of style was considered appropriate almost exclusively in literary contexts.

Vassar had a similar sequence of rhetoric offerings, beginning with a first-year rhetoric course that emphasized style. The 1879 Vassar catalog stated the English department's pedagogical aims:

This department aims to teach, theoretically, the laws of thought, expression, and utterance, by a thorough course in Logic, Rhetoric, and

Elocution; to train the student practically in a good style of writing, reading, and speaking the English language (206).

The parallel sequences of "thought, expression, and utterance" and "Logic, Rhetoric, and Elocution" show the extent to which rhetoric was considered training in appropriate "expression," or style. In 1902 the department was reorganized, and although department chair Laura Wylie was committed to maintaining the connections between rhetoric and literature, the catalog shows rhetoric losing ground as a formal discipline. In the same way, style became an explicit part of literature rather than rhetoric classes. In 1909, "The nature and function of style" is included as a topic of literary theory at Vassar. Belletristic discussions of style gained new prominence and authority with the increasing formalization of literary criticism, while advanced courses in rhetorical practice and theory were eliminated.

From 1880 to 1920 Smith College offered the same kind of first-year classes in rhetorical style and form. In addition, from 1883 to 1893 it also offered an upper-level elective on style, focusing on men such as Thomas Carlyle and Hugh Blair as stylistic exemplars. The course also discussed how the writers' styles were an integral part of their style in life, emphasizing the extent to which style expressed not linguistic propriety but the balance between social norms and personal expression (Wallace class notes).

By the first decade of the new century, Smith's rhetoric classes, like those at Wellesley, focused more on literature. Characteristic course titles include "Development of English Prose Style" and "Elements of Power in Literature," a "study of subject-matter, spirit and technique." The move from a class on "style" to a class on prose style emphasized the change from the study of style in all discourse (a rhetorical focus) to style within a particular genre (a literary focus).

Mount Holyoke's curriculum reflected the influence of belletristic rhetoric earlier than the other women's colleges, partly because the study of literature was an important feature of rhetoric from the earliest days of the college (Snell 1942). During the 1880s a required practical rhetoric course was taught by instructors who often taught in other departments such as chemistry and math. The texts for this course emphasized usage and correctness as the main features of style. Specialized rhetoric courses at Mount Holyoke, added in the 1890s, showed more skepticism about some of the stylistic rules of the nineteenth century. Professor Margaret Ball's course on "Prose Style" pointed out fallacies in Spencer's theories and compared his ideas of economy to those of other authors on style.

Thus, during the years from 1880 to 1920 stylistic study was moving from rhetoric classes with a practical emphasis to literary classes with a belletristic emphasis. For women who went to college during those years, the two kinds of style represented two options for public and private discourse. Practical rhetoric recommended the kind of unadorned, clear speech and writing that would pass muster in any group of educated people. In contrast, belletristic rhetoric provided the stylistic options that could give women the power to express their personalities and their thoughts distinctively.

What these two approaches to style had in common was the prominence of male models and texts. The women's textbooks, and indeed, sometimes even the exercises they used, were similar or identical to those used in men's colleges. While there is ample evidence that women in rhetoric departments had a special and strong investment in the education of their women students, their special sense of community rarely displayed itself in explicit exhortations to women to adopt a woman's style of discourse. At a time when popular magazines urged women to adopt feminine mannerisms, and much of society still worried about the masculinization of educated women, female rhetoric instructors at the Seven Sisters assumed that, as far as stylistic strategies went, women educated in rhetorical style should learn what men learned. And once women had learned to express themselves as men did, it would be difficult to convince them to limit their discourse to "appropriate" subjects and socially sanctioned settings.[5] Thus, what might be seen as a conservative use of male-authored materials becomes radicalized in the context of a woman's community.

III

Although the belletristic emphasis on a self-expressive style gained prominence after the turn of the century in women's colleges, the tension between a correct, plain style and a forceful personal style was always part of the rhetoric curriculum. Janet Wallace's notes from Smith College's "Style" course make this tension between the plain style and the powerful individualistic style clear:

> Blair—first teacher of rhet[oric] at Edin[burgh]—formal tho[ugh] elegant style. His influence [was] counteracted by Reviewers—Jeffreys,

Smith, Wilson—against formality; letting individual personalities show. Review[ers] mimicked the conflict going on in politics. Powerful minds expressing themselves on topics of the day with as much clearness & lucidity as poss[ible]. In Blair's class of writing there [was] little opportunity for aught but that. R[eviewers] made style a forcible means of exp[ression]. (Wallace class notes)

Hugh Blair's formal, clear, lucid writing was described as a contrast to "letting individual personalities show," which created a "forcible means of expression." Although Blair's clarity was "elegant" and effective, the most powerful writing was the product of unique and truly authentic voices. Insofar as the plain style was conventional, it could not be the height of stylistic mastery. This tension between personal emphasis and conventional clarity occurs throughout men's and women's rhetoric but is especially problematic for women, since the forceful presentation of personality represents a substantial risk when the personality is female and the models to be imitated are male.

Course materials represented this ambivalence about women's style, as in this 1916 Mount Holyoke exam:

What should be the conversational aim of an intelligent student of prose style who is not in any sense a prig, in her relation with her fellow-students in college? Do you think that such an aim is followed by any appreciable number of students here? (Examination in English XIV)

The fact that the author of the exam had to specify that the hypothetical student was "not a prig" suggests that readers might assume that the narrow moral standards of a prig applied unless explicitly denied. This suggestion in turn indicates that feminized constraints on language use could hamper the "conversational aims of an intelligent student." Given such constraints, women may have felt obligated to adopt a plain style, revealing, insofar as possible, nothing of their personalities so that their gender would not be considered a mark against them in sensitive discussions.

In contrast to the plain style, which trusted the content of a speech or essay to speak for itself, a powerful style was often attributed to the writer's voice or personality as it was manifested in the text. For example, an 1888 Wellesley handout listed "the writer's own earnestness" as one of the major determinants of force ("Rhetoric 1"). More broadly, style as the expression of personality was a theme that ran through many composition texts of the late nineteenth century, especially those focused on belletristic rhetoric. For example, Charles S. Baldwin's *A College Manual of Rhetoric* (1902), used at Wellesley and Smith, elaborated the familiar theme "the style is the man" in three ways.

First, according to Baldwin, style is a true expression of personality, an authentic form of self-expression, "the personal use of language" (196). Second, the quality of style is a measure of overall aesthetic sensibility. Baldwin notes, "Most men have not the creative assertion of individuality which we call the artistic impulse; and without that, style can no more be learned or taught than it can be translated" (198). In other words, style can be learned, but the genius that allows the highest forms of style cannot. This sort of elitism limits the range of people who can use style effectively, since the rhetor must have the kind of personal freedom of expression that allows a "creative assertion of individuality." Indeed, the word "men" in that sentence, even as it denies most males an artistic impulse, can be read as gender-specific, speaking as it does only to the members of society who have the freedom to use style as they choose.

Finally, says Baldwin, style involves sincerity, and forms of expression bring up questions of ethics and not just aesthetics:

> For words are so far the necessary expression of all men, they involve so much of life, that what in other arts is bad taste, in literature is bad morals. To study style as a mechanism of extraneous ornament would be both futile and insincere. (229)

Style builds ethos, the credibility or character of the rhetor. Such credibility was of special importance to women who had to gain acceptance not just for what they said but for their right to speak at all. If their style could build their credibility and support their moral relation to their subject, then it was worth studying.

Women's rhetoric classes included discussions of how style revealed sensibility and created ethos, but when applied to women the process of defining a self through writing was not so clear-cut. Women attending college from 1880 on had grown up reading books written for women by women, a genre which, according to historian Ann Douglas, "dominated the literary market in America from the 1840s through the 1880s" (62). From these books students saw that women could write successfully and popularly, but they were also most likely aware of the attacks on "those scribbling women" in the press. Women had to contend with the stereotypes of women's writing developed from years of critical disdain for popular women authors (Tompkins 82–83). When young women reached college, the popular women authors were not part of their curriculum; their serious stylistic models were written by men, with a few exceptions made for women novelists in belletristic classes.[6]

Margaret Ball's experience as a student and professor at Mount Holyoke exemplifies the conflicting messages women received about style. As an undergraduate in 1898, Ball (who would later become a professor emeritus in the English department) took the following notes in a course on journalism: "How are we to write forcefully? Vital thought; accurate words; illuminating figures; logical thought-subordination" (Ball, class notes).

Here aspiring students were given the tips they needed for a forceful journalistic style, a style seemingly accessible to women. But students also received some discouraging advice from Mrs. Whiting of the *Springfield Republican* on the skills required for journalism:

> As a reporter on a daily [the woman] has no proper place. Almost impossible except for one extraordinarily constituted. . . . Book reviewing often done by women. This often mushy, using personal style. One must know subject, use author's p[oint] of view, feel yourself in his place, especially where his personality is shown. (Ball, class notes)

Mrs. Whiting neatly re-creates the familiar conflict for women students. Wary of their own potentially "mushy" style, women might use a forceful style to make themselves heard, a style presumably inauthentic and therefore suspect. But even forcefulness would not make a place for them on a daily newspaper where they had "no proper place." At the same time, they were expected to identify forcefulness in the authors they read, and to identify with the male personalities that generated forceful writing. Twenty years later, when Margaret Ball taught her own course in prose style, she was more openly optimistic about women putting the styles they learned into practice, as her exam question shows: "Have you gained any new ideals for your own style or any new methods of revision from the study done in this course? Explain" ("English XIV Examination").

Women could base their ideals for style on the canonical works (in Ball's course, texts by men such as Sidney and Bacon, and the Bible) and were implicitly encouraged to do so. But underlying this goal was the dilemma of how, and whether, their own stylistic constructions would be accepted. Using a more characteristic and personal style was further complicated by the growing rift between literary and rhetorical discourse. Style was studied in literature classes as a literary device, rather than as a rhetorical method for moving audiences to proper action. So although women rhetors were increasingly public and visible in the first decades of the twentieth century, the important connection between women's ethos and their styles was not studied in the context of public discourse.

IV

Successful rhetoricians in women's colleges were able to develop rhetorical theories that integrated the rules of public discourse with ways to fulfill the need for personal expression. Two of these women, Gertrude Buck at Vassar and Mary Jordan at Smith, are especially noteworthy not only because of their long years of dedicated scholarship and pedagogy but also because of the way their theories transcended narrow definitions of style to synthesize language use with human and social possibilities.

No matter what approach was taken to style—the practical or the belletristic—it was rarely suggested that style, conceived as choices in language, might actually be an essential part of the process by which human thought is realized in language. In this sense Gertrude Buck, an instructor and professor at Vassar for twenty-five years, was far ahead of her time in anticipating the enormous importance that twentieth-century theorists would place on metaphor. In current theory, metaphor is not just a way of arranging or juxtaposing words but is in fact a method of creating knowledge through expanding the boundaries of human language and hence meaning (Lakoff and Johnson; Sacks). In the figures of speech that nineteenth-century rhetoric attempted to classify and regulate, Buck saw essential evidence for the evolution of human cognition. Her explanation of metaphor was significantly more powerful and complex than Spencer's theory that the power of metaphor arose from its brevity. One historian has called Buck's book, based on her Ph.D dissertation, "the only serious attempt" in the late nineteenth century to explain "the nature and function of figurative language" (Kitzhaber 281–82).

Buck's study explained metaphor as arising from the state of human consciousness before language. In her view, before humans were able to distinguish between like things, they spoke of those things as the same, in what we would now see as metaphoric terms. Later, when humans were able to better discriminate, they began to use the poetic met-

aphor, and then the simile, both of which require a recognition of difference. Buck's crucial point was that the metaphor does not bring pleasure
because it "economizes" the reader's energies by being concise; rather,
metaphor elicits pleasure because it "incites the reader to reconstruct
the mental process by which it came into being" (Buck, *Metaphor* 62).
This idea that stylistically interesting language creates an experience of
identification between the rhetor and audience is lost in practical rhetorics, and only rarely discussed in more belletristic studies.

In fact, Buck's whole plan of rhetoric was based on nineteenth-
century psychological principles. Her method of "exposition of the qualities of style" was part analytic and part inductive, but always directed
toward understanding how the writer's act of creation is reenacted by
the reader ("The Study of English on Psychological Principles"). Style
was a crucial part of making sure the author's intentions were understood. For instance, Buck asked students to write an "exposition of the
character of a cook from her dress," showing that even as observers they
had to be sensitive to style ("The Study of English" 1). Further, Buck
recognized that the cook's dress was her style and that she would be
judged accordingly. As a teacher of writing, Buck was sensitive to how
outward symbolic acts were used to judge the inner person.

Buck used the metaphor to demonstrate that style had power to create meaning among communities of people who could share in the author's experience. For the author, style could guarantee not only that a
message was transmitted but also that the experience of that message
was understood. And yet Buck considered herself a practitioner of "the
modern science of rhetoric" ("What Does Rhetoric Mean" 200) and in
her own academic writing she adopted a plain style, presumably to guarantee acceptance in the rhetoric community and secure her image as a
scientific researcher. Buck's success as a rhetorician was due partly to
her ability to present herself conventionally, but one of her unique contributions was to recognize that the nineteenth-century focus on cate-
gorizing rather than understanding style limited appreciation of how
choices in language—style—could create meaning.

In contrast to Buck, Mary Augusta Jordan, a longtime teacher of
rhetoric at Smith, argued against the plain style in both her writing and
practice. She sought to protect the rhetor from stylistic excess through
the combined constraints of intellect and ethos. She allied her views of
rhetoric not with science but with a precise and rigorous form of humanism for which she thought women especially suited.

Mary Augusta Jordan graduated from Vassar and taught at Smith College from 1884 to 1921, leaving a deep and idiosyncratic mark on the college. In her eyes, a well-educated woman had learned to see the value of things in the world, not just their intellectual relations. In a treatise on higher education, Jordan observed, "It is all a question of social proportion and individual responsibility, in which women, as long as they remain the great incentives to effort, must do the bulk of the work" ("Concerning the Higher Education" 12). Later, she suggests what educated women's responsibility is when she questions the notion of political "neutrality": "Do the social and economic relations of sewing women and mill girls owe nothing of their hardships to the neutrality of educated women?" (14). While Jordan did not support suffrage for women, she did see educated women as social leaders who should exercise their moral influence outside of corrupt, male-controlled politics.

Jordan's specific prescriptions for women appear in her 1904 book, *Correct Writing and Speaking*. With its introduction by Margaret Sangster, a Christian women's leader and editor of *Harper's Bazaar*, the book is obviously directed at educated women, and in various ways it seeks to free them from strictures against certain kinds of self-expression. Jordan says that good speaking and writing are not natural, and not always easy: "Choice and exclusion are not among the easy-going, hospitable virtues" (80). But this process of choice and exclusion makes one a better, more effective manipulator of style. Such criticism "must make the pragmatic mind over into the sympathetic mind. It must convert the demand for easy rules and heavy weights and measures into intelligent interest in plotted curves and barometers, atmospheres, and cloud currents" (72). Jordan is here arguing for a continuum for judging style, rather than the correct/incorrect dichotomies of the "easy rules and heavy weights."

Obviously, Jordan's own style is not particularly plain, nor does she recommend plain style for her readers. The best style is determined by audience, said Jordan, but more than that, by an appropriate mental attitude. "To speak and write correctly, one must think, feel, and act correctly" (229). As Jordan makes clear in her other writings, "acting correctly" means acting with feeling controlled by intellect and will. Thus, style cannot be separated from the person who creates it. Moreover, a proper style is determined not by reference to fixed standards but by an alert and open mind. According to Jordan, "The charms of grace, flexibility, and variety can not be had except as the expression of constantly renewed comparison of one's own methods with those of all sorts and conditions of men," (81) and such comparisons will necessarily require changes that might horrify the writers of rule books. Jordan does not appear to adhere to the notion that style is the woman, but rather that a woman must cultivate her self, and then let her style rest on choices made with intelligent feeling. This broader attitude toward style represents her sense that women had a part to play in society as "intelligent members or restless disturbers" ("The Higher Education a Social Necessity"). As intelligent citizens, they could influence public decisions through speaking and writing; as restless disturbers, they should agitate for moral solutions to social problems.

Above all, Jordan did not advocate rules for their own sake in stylistic training or in any other endeavor, because she knew that strong intelligence could always find good reasons to disregard them. Cheris Kramarae documents how, for 150 years, women have been instructed to avoid slang, and how this advice has kept women bereft of power over one segment of language (60). Practical rhetoric courses, with their emphasis on correctness, instructed women (and often men) to avoid barbarisms and impropriety. But Jordan, always iconoclastic, recognized the power of slang, a power that women might use if they were intelligent about their choices:

> The only safe course for timid, and irresolute, and irresponsible, but sensitive souls is never to use slang, if they know it; and for stupid and brutal persons, never to joke, if they know themselves. For the rest, it must be remembered that slang is adventure and experiment in words; that a joke is art suddenly confronting life. . . . For the present it is perhaps wise to stop experiment in words and in vivisection at the same place. (184)

Style has gone too far when it gives pain to the audience, because causing such pain violates Jordan's ethical standards for "acting correctly." Still, stylistically inventive language involves "adventures" and "experiments"; as such it is worth the risk.

In encouraging women to learn when to break the rules of style, Jordan taught that women could not only learn the discourse conventions of a male world but could also master them. Further, women did not need to adopt a plain style, bereft of the feelings that gave their speech power, but instead could speak forcefully and still maintain credibility. Women needed judgment "at once autocratic, instructive and sympathetic" to speak for their own and society's good, and such speech was not only their right but their responsibility.

Women such as Buck and Jordan represented the strongest elements of rhetorical instruction at women's colleges. Supportive teachers, imaginative scholars, and social activists, they provided models for both academic and more public styles of rhetoric. In their own ways, they resolved the tension between the communicative and expressive functions of language so that their rhetoric was distinctively their own and yet spoke to their audiences as well. But even they could not overcome the constraints on how women's speech would be heard.

No matter how women planned to use their education, graduates expected to become participants in literate society. They expected the world to ask for their opinions, and they wanted to be able to reply in style. Edith Metcalf (Wellesley, class of 1880) wrote back to her alma mater to support the value of extracurricular rhetorical training in "this 'cold world,' which on general principles expects a college graduate to know all about it and tell it immediately." But the question was: How to "tell it immediately"? Rhetoric courses exposed women students to two opposed stylistic options: the plain, correct, unemotional on the one hand and the personal, vigorous, perhaps controversial on the other. Students might even have seen themselves according to Mary Jordan's categories: "intelligent members" or "restless disturbers" of society, each identity manifested by the styles of speaking and writing they chose.[7] Intelligent members could argue lucidly toward desired ends, but restless disturbers also had their place, bringing an audience to focus on issues through the powerful appeals of heartfelt language.

Made in the cloistered atmosphere of women's colleges, these stylistic choices would have real implications for women who went on to have careers or other positions in the public eye and to participate in the public conversation. Many women would be discouraged from their aspirations. As Lynn Gordon notes of the girl who went to the women's college during the Progressive era, "Higher education and campus experiences prepared her to do whatever men did; society permitted her few options" (Gordon 226). But some women would not be discouraged and would go on to prominence in professional careers as well as in the suffrage debate, reform movements, and other political and social movements.

This entrance, then, this open door into the waiting world of public discourse, was the goal of the women who studied style and those who taught it. Trained in both the plain style and the methods by which style could be given unique force, women of Wellesley, Vassar, Smith, and

Mount Holyoke could choose how best to speak and write in any given situation. Even with the limitations imposed on them by rhetorical and social orthodoxy, they made up a generation of women armed with strategies for joining in public discourse and making their voices heard. As we move towards a new century, one in which women's unique and widely various voices may at last be fully heard, we have much to learn from our Seven Sisters foremothers.

NOTES

1. Schreiner's first book was *The Story of an African Farm* (1883), published under the name of Ralph Iron. Her second book, the one being reviewed here, was *Dreams* (1891).

2. The Seven Sisters colleges were founded exclusively for women. In alphabetical order, with founding dates, they are: Barnard College, in New York City, 1889; Bryn Mawr College, in Bryn Mawr, Pennsylvania, 1889; Mount Holyoke College, in South Hadley, Massachusetts, 1888; Radcliffe College, in Cambridge, Massachusetts, 1879; Smith College, in Northampton, Massachusetts, 1875; Vassar College, in Poughkeepsie, New York, 1865; and Wellesley College, in Wellesley, Massachusetts, 1875.

Helen Lefkowitz Horowitz explains in *Alma Mater* that although these women's colleges did not receive the nickname Seven Sisters until after the Seven College Conference held in 1926, they were "a small network of colleges which shared early commitments" (xvi–xvii).

3. For an alternative to this view see Kathryn Conway's article "Woman Suffrage and the History of Rhetoric at the Seven Sisters Colleges: 1865–1919" (this volume), as well as Nan Johnson's *Nineteenth-Century Rhetoric in North America*.

4. Other strands identified are classical, elocutionary, psychological-epistemological, and belletristic rhetoric.

5. While women may have thought that using male models would make their curriculum unimpeachable, many commentators were not pleased about women styling themselves after male patterns. According to Horowitz, many of the objections to isolated women's colleges centered on the fear that, separated from men, women would take on men's roles. For instance, E. A. Andrews, head of Boston's Mount Vernon School for Girls, worried in 1887 that at the women's colleges, "In place of all which is most attractive in female manners, we see characters expressly formed for acting a *manly part upon the theatre of life*" (emphasis in the original; *Alma Mater* 58).

6. Women who wrote textbooks placed slightly more emphasis on female writers, although they were not always portrayed in flattering terms. Shackford and Johnson, for instance, use women's writing in some exercises, and in examples of personal description. However, an odd passage from Bret Harte's "A Sappho of Green Springs," used as a writing sample, reveals common prejudices about women's style.

In "Sappho," the "Stranger" tells the "Editor" his ideas about the authorship of a piece of writing: "No . . . it wasn't no man. There's ideas and words there that only come from a woman: baby-talk to the birds, you know, and a kind of fearsome keer of bugs and creepin' things that don't come to a man who wears boots and trousers" (531–32).

7. An interesting version of the combination of style and women's political activity comes from W. C. Brownell's *The Genius of Style*. Brownell sees in reform movements of the 1920s a "radical and adventurous element" that has made the "business of propaganda practical, productive—and remunerative" (155). When women entered this radical element, they "opened the cell doors" of the social proprieties and, by extension, the limitations on polite discourse (157). While Brownell is sympathetic to the "equality" of women, he sees all radicalism as a threat to the style of society; women and other malcontents disguise their bad taste in an appeal to "natural" style. Brownell's book was used during the 1920s at Mount Holyoke.

REFERENCES

Baldwin, Charles Sears. *A College Manual of Rhetoric*. Norwood, Mass.: Longman, Greens & Co., 1902.

Ball, Margaret. Margaret Ball's papers, Series 4, Box 10, Folder 4. Mount Holyoke College Library/Archives.

Bascom, John. *Philosophy of Rhetoric*. New York: G.P. Putnam's Sons, 1883.

Berlin, James. *Writing Instruction in Nineteenth Century American Colleges*. Carbondale: Southern Illinois UP, 1984.

Brownell, W. C. *The Genius of Style*. New York: Charles Scribner and Sons, 1924.

Buck, Gertrude. *A Course in Argumentative Writing*. New York: Henry Holt and Company, 1901.

———. *The Metaphor: A Study in the Psychology of Rhetoric*. Ann Arbor: Inland Press, 1899; Folcroft Library Editions, 1971.

———. "What Does 'Rhetoric' Mean?" *Educational Review* 22 (1901).

Douglas, Ann. *The Feminization of American Culture*. New York: Anchor Press/Doubleday, 1988.

"English XIV examination," June 1919. English Department Box. Mount Holyoke College Library/Archives.

"Examination in English XIV," June 1916. Mount Holyoke College Library/Archives.

Gordon, Lynn D. "The Gibson Girl Goes to College: Popular Culture and Women's Higher Education in the Progressive Era, 1890–1920." *American Quarterly* 39.2 (summer 1987).

Hodgkins, Louise Manning, ed. *Webster's First Bunker-Hill Oration*. Boston and New York: Leach, Shewell & Sanborn, 1889.

Horowitz, Helen Lefkowitz. *Alma Mater: Design and Experience in the Women's Colleges from Their Nineteenth-Century Beginnings to the 1930's*. New York: Alfred Knopf, 1984.

Johnson, Nan. *Nineteenth-Century Rhetoric in North America*. Carbondale: Southern Illinois UP, 1991.

Jordan, Mary. "Concerning the Higher Education: An Address Before the Western Association of Collegiate Alumnae, Oct. 30th, 1886, Chicago." Mary Jordan folder, The Library, Vassar College.

———. *Correct Writing and Speaking*. New York: A.F. Barnes & Co., 1904.

———. "The Higher Education a Social Necessity for Women." Paper presented to the Rhode Island branch of the Association of Collegiate Alumnae at Brown University, Providence, Rhode Island, November 4, 1892. Mary Jordan folder, Smith College Archives.

"June Examination," 1916, English Composition 2. Box 3L, Department of English Composition, English Composition 2 folder, Wellesley Archives.

Kitzhaber, Albert R. "Rhetoric in American Colleges, 1850–1900." Diss. University of Washington, 1953.

Kramarae, Cheris. "Proprietors of Language." In Sally McConnell-Ginet, Ruth Borker, and Nelly Furman, eds. *Women and Language in Literature and Society*. New York: Praeger, 1980.

Lakoff, George, and Mark Johnson. *Metaphors We Live By*. Chicago: U of Chicago P, 1980.

Metcalf, Edith. "Phi Sigma, 'Though Dead, Yet Speaketh.' " *The Courant College Edition* (February 1, 1889).

Perry, Frances M. *Punctuation Primer*. New York: American Book Co., 1908.

"Rhetoric I handout." Rhetoric I, II, III. Box 3L, Department of English Composition. Wellesley College Archives.

"Rhetoric and English Composition Hour Examination," October 28, 1892, Box 3C, Curricular Material, Department of English Composition. Wellesley College Archives.

Sacks, Sheldon, ed. *On Metaphor*. Chicago: U of Chicago P, 1978.

Seasongood, Murray. "Wellesley vs. Vassar: The First Women's Intercollegiate Debate." Box 6S, Debating Club. Wellesley College Archives.

"Senior Class Rhetoric Examination," March 1884. Box 3C, Curricular Material, Department of English Composition. Wellesley College Archives.

Shackford, Martha Hale, and Margaret Johnson. *Composition—Rhetoric—Literature*. Chicago: Benjamin H. Sanborn and Co., 1917.

Smith College Catalogs, Smith College Archives.

Snell, Ada L. F. *History of English Studies in Mount Holyoke Seminary and College 1837–1937*. Unpublished manuscript in Mount Holyoke College Library/Archives, 1942.

Spencer, Herbert. "The Philosophy of Style." *The Westminster Review* 57 (October 1852).

Stewart, Donald C. "The Nineteenth Century." In Winifred Bryan Horner, ed. *The Present State of Scholarship in Historical and Contemporary Rhetoric*. Columbia: U of Missouri P, 1983.

"The Study of English on Psychological Principles—The Required Work at Vassar College." Periodical unknown, 1898. The Library, Vassar College.

Tompkins, Jane. "Sentimental Power." In Elaine Showalter, ed. *The New Feminist Criticism*. New York: Pantheon Books, 1985.

Wallace, Janet M. Notes from Summer Rhetoric course, 1890. From Janet M. Wallace box, Smith College Archives.

Wetzell, A. "The Work of Olive Schreiner." *The Mount Holyoke* (1891): 1–3.

11
· · · · · · ·

Woman Suffrage and the History of Rhetoric at the Seven Sisters Colleges, 1865–1919

Kathryn M. Conway

The woman suffrage movement was the first public campaign for women's rights in the United States launched and sustained by women who had received formal rhetorical training. These women pioneered both in higher education and in public speaking; they were among the first women to attend college in the United States, and many put their education to work as pro- and antisuffrage speakers. In particular, alumnae of the Seven Sisters colleges gained prominence in this public debate.[1] Their rhetorical preparation included classes in argumentation, elocution, composition, and criticism. These subjects were offered with both oral and written components by the English departments of the Seven Sisters colleges.

In particular, four aspects of rhetorical education for women highlight the connection between rhetoric and suffrage. First, the teaching of rhetoric gave women unprecedented access to the study and practice of oratory. While training in oratory had been a traditional prerequisite for men entering political life, Kennedy and O'Shields note that women in the mid-nineteenth century were "beginning to awaken to their rhetorical potential," and thus eagerly sought this training, too. To engage in public debates on the same basis as men, women had to become convincing and persuasive public speakers. Skill in oratory and familiarity with argumentation were especially important for women who sought to demonstrate that women could be full "political persons": women not only wanted to vote, they also intended to hold political office.[2]

Second, rhetoric was a required subject at all of the Seven Sisters colleges. Thus, all the thousands of women who graduated from these schools were trained in an essential activity of participatory democracy: the practice of informed discourse. Rhetoric courses instructed students in methods of logical thought, which could be expressed in either written or oral form. Thus, the ancient art of oratory, heretofore reserved exclusively for men, became the object of women's study. In the spirit of Greek and Roman orators, young women learned how to construct and deliver convincing and persuasive arguments in their argumentation classes. Rhetoric courses encouraged women to explore, develop, and articulately express their own ideas on many subjects, particularly public policy topics. Because the students lived at single-sex colleges, suffrage was an obvious and appropriate concern to be raised in rhetoric classes. As a complex topic, woman suffrage offered the student of rhetoric a challenge: whether she was for, indifferent about, or against suffrage, she had to state her position clearly, research the changes that the adoption of suffrage promised, and subsequently present her views to her professors and classmates in a structured argument. In retrospect, we can see that rhetoric classes made an important contribution to the intellectual growth of the suffrage movement: they provided a means for developing both arguments and audiences.

The college audience was strategically important because a significant number of these young women became leaders in the suffrage movement (Scott and Scott 164). Others became leaders in science, government, and social reform movements, and carried their knowledge of and commitment to women's rights to these fields. (See, e.g., Solomon; Ware; Rupp and Taylor; Kraditor; Cott; Brown).

Third, the ambitious young women of the Seven Sisters colleges created community forums. Classroom training alone did not give students sufficient practice in addressing an audience to make them confident orators. So, on their own initiative, some students formed extracurricular groups, called "literary societies" or "debate societies," in which they discussed and practiced their rhetorical skills. These self-governed societies organized oratorical events wherein students spoke publicly, both to other societies and to the college community. Woman suffrage was of particular interest to debating societies, as documented by the extant records of these groups, and by the letters and autobiographies of students. Many alumnae later praised the direct contribution that rhetorical training had made to their careers.

Fourth, many of the women who took full advantage of the excellent rhetorical education offered at the Seven Sisters colleges also participated in local, state, and national suffrage organizations, such as the National College Equal Suffrage League. With both an academic and a practical background, these young women graduated as orators and activists rather than as novices. Women faculty in the English departments and professors from other departments were also active in the suffrage movement, and so stood as an inspiring example to their students. Whether a mentor was a pro- or an antisuffrage activist, she guided and encouraged her students to apply their study of rhetoric to their own political goals.

A few outstanding women who successfully drew upon their training in rhetoric were: Harriot Stanton Blatch (Vassar, class of 1878 and 1894), daughter of Elizabeth Cady Stanton and member of the Congressional Union for Woman Suffrage; Susan Walker Fitzgerald (Bryn Mawr, class of 1893), recording secretary of the National American Woman Suffrage Association; Harriet Burton Laidlaw (Barnard, class of 1902), author and member of the Woman Suffrage Party; and Lucy Burns (Vassar, class of 1902), assistant to Alice Paul, the militant founder of the Congressional Union for Woman Suffrage.[3] These women and hundreds of other alumnae of the Seven Sisters colleges shared two strong bonds: their training as orators and their campaigning as suffragists.[4]

I

A brief look at women's severely limited access to rhetorical education in the first half of the nineteenth century provides a stark contrast to what was available by the end of that century. Prior to 1835, seminaries offered education beyond grammar school, but no college programs were available to women. For example, the Troy Female Seminary, founded by Emma Willard in 1821, offered a "curriculum similar to that of the contemporary men's colleges" (Scott 3) as did The Mount Holyoke Female Seminary, founded by Mary Lyon in 1838 (which became Mount Holyoke College in 1888). Both schools included basic rhetorical instruction in their curricula; however, they emphasized writing rather than oratory.

In 1835, Oberlin College became the first college in the United States to welcome women, an opportunity that Lucy Stone recollected with no little gratitude: "Men came to Oberlin for various reasons; women because they had nowhere else to go" (Hosford 107). Stone and her classmate Antoinette Brown Blackwell struggled at Oberlin to gain the right to speak publicly, an act then forbidden to women. As historian Frances Juliette Hosford observed, nineteenth-century women were told "not to appear before a mixed audience and were to utter no word in the churches" (50). Men were assumed to be preparing for the ministry, law, or politics and so received training in oratory and debate in the form of weekly declamations and discussions. The women, in contrast, were instructed in essay writing because they were expected to become teachers. Hosford comments that "in sentiment, Oberlin was pathetically anxious to preserve the conventions of female modesty, while making certain concessions to the female brain" (50).

Stone and Blackwell, frustrated in the rhetoric classroom because they were expressly forbidden to debate, joined with a few other women students in a secret debating society.[5] Stone recalled that they met off campus, where they discussed "educational, political, moral & religious questions." No doubt they addressed woman suffrage as one of these "questions," because they discussed "Women and Politics," and the resolution that "ladies have a right to debate and declaim in public" (Seidman 15). Reminiscing, Stone wrote to Blackwell that their most significant activity was learning "to stand and speak, to put motions, how to treat amendments, &c [sic]" (Lasser and Merrill 263). Her confidence secured by practice, Stone had boldly asked the Oberlin administration for permission to read a commencement address. Graduating men presented their essays orally at commencement, but in 1847 Oberlin was not ready for women to do the same. The rebellious Stone refused even to write hers, because she had been denied the right to read her own work. Not until 1874 did Oberlin grant its women students the privilege to "engage in the same Rhetorical Exercises as the gentlemen." In so doing, Oberlin finally permitted the long-sought equality of rhetorical education, but even then did not wholly sanction women orators, for the conservative faculty remarked that "the appearance of young ladies in public orations is not in the best of taste, or desirable" (Hosford 105).

Stone, Blackwell, and the classes of women who followed after them worked for decades to garner respect for women orators. Their efforts attested to the intense desire of women to gain the practical speaking and leadership skills that men cultivated in rhetoric classes. The debating society that Stone and Blackwell had participated in furtively in 1846 was later officially recognized as the Young Ladies Literary Society. Blackwell was compelled "to immortalize that primary woman's Club," for she recognized women's laying claim to language as a historically and politically significant act. The stated goal of the society was "to improve its members in writing, speaking, and Discussion" (Seidman 14). Blackwell knew that women were empowered by their collective study of oratory in societies and clubs. As one of her student successors at Oberlin commented, "society" was one place where women could discover their "hidden oratorical powers" (Seidman 15). She witnessed the proliferation of women's clubs during the latter part of the nineteenth century, and recognized that these clubs were crucial to the success of the suffrage movement (Lasser and Merrill 233). Oberlin women pioneered, setting educational and social precedents for the women who would attend the Seven Sisters colleges.

II

By 1865, when Vassar College opened, state universities and a few other colleges accepted women students. Some women graduates from these institutions and some women without formal schooling were by now familiar figures on public platforms as activists in the abolitionist movement and in various post–Civil War reform movements. Stone, Blackwell, and a subsequent generation of women introduced and thus began to articulate and debate the issues of women's rights, and like Sojourner Truth, they eventually gained public respect as orators and leaders.

The accomplishments of these exceptional women orators notwithstanding, women's intellectual abilities still were questioned publicly by conservative critics. Following the 1868 campus visit of the well-known speaker Anna Dickenson, Matthew Vassar responded with exasperation to criticism of women's education:

> The truth is it is all nonsense and irreconcilable with Divine truth in regard to the Mental Capacity of Woman, nothing but long prejudice with the dominering [sic] spirit of Man has kept Woman from occupying a higher elevation in literature & art, but mans tyrany & jelousy [sic], and wilfull usurpation of her normal rights &c. (Haight 184–85)

Vassar was keenly aware of the disadvantages against which women toiled, and had established the first women's college so that "our Fair sex" could gain an education as excellent as men's. Vassar's letters to the first trustees, administrators, and students of the college affirm his confidence in women and reveal his commitment to women's rights. Moreover, unlike the administrators of Oberlin College, he clearly advocated oratorical training for women in his curriculum preferences and his encouragement of extracurricular activities.

By inviting women's rights activists to speak on campus, the founder and the faculty encouraged students to respect and emulate women orators. Writing home to her parents in 1869, a young woman enthusiastically described the politically conscious environment in which she studied: "Really the large view we get of national problems interests me more than any other subject unless it is 'the woman question'! I expect yet to be the assistant editor of the 'Revolution' in collaboration with Mrs. Stanton and Susan B. Anthony" (*Letters* 130–31). She was inspired directly by her professors and their friends, for some of whom women's rights represented a lifetime commitment.

At Vassar, faculty and students frequently dined together, and in some cases were housed together.[6] In *The Earliest Days at Vassar*, Frances Wood speaks of a community of professors and students devoted to political change, describing her memories of the world-renowned Vassar astronomer Maria Mitchell:

> However interested you might have been in woman suffrage and all the other subjects concerning the "cause," you felt that in comparison with this great woman you hardly knew the alphabet. She judged everything from the standpoint, "How is this going to affect women?". . . Every woman speaker of note in that day,—Julia Ward Howe, Anna Dickinson, Mary Livermore, Elizabeth Cady Stanton, Ednah D. Cheney, were personal friends of Miss Mitchell, and at various times her guests. (82–83)

Vassar told a student who attended the prosuffrage lecture by Dickinson that his "300 Daughters" (the students at the college) should be fully aware of the "shamefull" categorization of themselves in New York state law: at that time, women were excluded from suffrage, as were "criminals, paupers, Idiots &c." Vassar urged his students to apply "the remidy" to this situation (82–83).

One aspect of "the remidy" was self-improvement. As an incentive, Vassar wrote in 1867 that he would sponsor debates four times a year for the "encouragement of 'Gifts or Talents' of the young lady pupils in public speaking." He further suggested that this series of debates be the basis for the founding of a "Vassar College Offhand Speaking Society," so called because the debates were to be extemporaneous, rather than prepared in advance (Debate Folder, Vassar College Special Collections). Vassar was well aware that young men prepared themselves for citizenship by joining such societies, and he wished to extend their benefits to women. In effect, Vassar created a setting geared toward educating the "good woman" orator, much as Quintilian had outlined the rhetorical education of the "good man" (Meador). Vassar sought the best available teachers for his students and engaged them to teach the subjects studied by classical orators: philosophy, logic, history, religion, and rhetoric.

Each of the Seven Sisters colleges required students to follow a prescribed program of rhetoric courses, offered by the English departments, which also offered elective courses and lectures. Notably, the colleges did not introduce courses designed especially for women: the programs did not differ markedly from the standard fare at men's colleges, in that they utilized the same texts and had similar requirements. Yet, the number and depth of courses differed among the seven institutions. The strength of the departments varied, too, and reflected the relationship between the college's administration and the department's faculty. Thus, the core curriculum, electives, and faculty determined the different character of rhetorical education at the colleges.

The first rhetoric courses at Vassar included lessons on grammar, composition, elocution, and analysis, all devised with the goal of improving the students' writing, reading, and speaking of the English language. The junior year was devoted to the study of Richard Whately's *Elements of Rhetoric* and to the use of syllogisms in argument. Classical texts concerning rhetoric were studied in other courses, in the original Greek or Latin. Two of Plato's dialogues, *Phaedrus* and *Gorgias*, along with Aristotle's *Rhetoric* and *Poetics*, were studied in Greek, while Cicero and Quintilian were studied in Latin. For centuries, knowledge of Latin and Greek had been reserved for the socially elite group of the educated men who governed Western society. When women acquired these languages and studied the masterworks of rhetoric that had previously served as models for male orators, they initiated a significant new tradition.

Three other women's colleges opened soon after Vassar: Smith and Wellesley in 1875, and Radcliffe in 1879. A decade later, the remaining three "sisters" further increased women's access to higher education: Mount Holyoke in 1888 and Barnard and Bryn Mawr in 1889. All their students participated, willingly or not, in the required writing of "daily themes," a practice originally instituted in rhetoric courses at men's colleges.

Professors assigned literary topics and encouraged their students to work on personal topics, too. Professors and assistants read and corrected themes for grammar, composition, style, and clarity. The 1876–1877 Vassar annual catalog stated that the criticisms of these themes were "minute, personal, and free, being made in private interviews between the teacher and the students individually" (Vassar 18–19). The

constant quest for material to use in themes led Barnard graduate Alice
Duer Miller to remark, "Nothing is sacred; your hat, your diction, your
anecdote about your maiden aunt—all may serve as copy for the vora-
cious 'daily-themer' " (221). Always in need of material for a daily theme,
students found Maria Mitchell's question, "How is this going to affect
women?" to be a continually useful device for generating topics. Often,
the question resulted in essays that expressed how the student, as a
woman, was affected by her academic experiences.

Students crafted their themes in the form of short essays or verses,
and although most themes had a serious tone, some had a self-reflective,
satirical slant. The 1895 Barnard annual included such a poem, which
strongly resembles Miller's later published work, *Are Women People? A
Book of Rhymes for Suffrage Times.*

> "Why can't I write as others do?"
> She sighed—then wrote her daily page;
> The subject of her essay was
> "The Voting Woman of Our Age."
> Friday she seized her weekly pack,
> To find this theme she glanced it through;
> "It's marked 'Conventional!' " she cried,
> "Why do I write as others do?" (77)

Through the use of antimetabole, or the "turning about" of words, the
author cleverly presented the rhetoric teacher's comment, "Conventional," as ambiguous. Was the reader to think that the daily-themer
wished to emulate her peers' manner of writing, their interest in suffrage,
or both? Furthermore, did the phrase, "Voting Woman of Our Age," refer
to the women outside of New York state who were already enfranchised,
or did it refer to the author's classmates who would work toward that
goal? The ambiguity might have been a humorous ploy, or quite possibly,
a sincere attempt by the author to camouflage her own political stance.

In that case, the author chose to remain anonymous, but for most
students, writing was a public act: a student had to contend with the comments not only of her classmates but of her professors as well. In the
classroom professors read, or requested students to read aloud, both
"good" and "bad" themes. In a letter written to her parents in 1869, a
Vassar student reported on one of her recent themes: "When Prof. Backus
praised it highly and said it was better than the others because I used
purer Saxon language and my essay was a fine example of the easy, flow-

ing, graceful, and simple style (he used all those adjectives)—I nearly died the death of the righteous" (*Letters* 32–33). For young women, the first experiences of baring their inner thoughts to the public criticism of peers and professors created anxiety at best and trauma at worst.

Radcliffe student Abby Parsons MacDuffie worried, "I am afraid my poor composition will be badly treated. You know that ridicule is the Harvard College theory" (20). A woman suffrage advocate during college, MacDuffie struggled to reconcile the value of rhetorical training with the everyday conflicts engendered by her harsh professor, Adams Sherman Hill, the influential holder of the Boylston Chair of Rhetoric and Oratory at Harvard and author of the textbook that was adopted by most colleges during the 1880s. To her, he was "simply dreadful" (18). When he read one of her essays aloud, "Slash, bang, went his caustic criticism, while slow, infinitesimal tears wet my cheeks" (11). For four years she and her classmates endured the notorious rhetorician's remarks, painfully conscious of his scorn, which MacDuffie reported in letters to her family: "Mr. Hill said the other day that I was the most cheerful person he knew. I hope he doesn't think I am an idiot and therefore cheerful" (24). Although she felt "very much taken down" by this treatment, she persisted, regarding Hill's rhetoric text as "valuable" (16).

By the turn of the century, rhetoric programs had adopted a standardized sequence that typically included description, narration, exposition, argumentation, and criticism.[7] In the first year, the student took "Rhetoric and English Composition," a survey and theme-writing course. In subsequent years, she studied criticism, style, and argumentation. The latter courses involved both the written and the spoken word, with the emphasis varying from one school to another. Argumentation was especially important for women with political aspirations, because their success depended upon well-reasoned thought. For instance, in 1892 Wellesley offered a rigorous course entitled "Argumentation and Persuasion," which included "a brief based on some skillful argument; three forensics, preceded by briefs, discussion of briefs and of forensics; debates once a week; criticism of the speakers" (Wellesley 1892–1893).[8] This type of course opened a practice that had been of long standing in men's colleges to women. Donald Hayworth, in "The Development of the Training of Public Speakers in America" concludes from the history of men's education that "undoubtedly the Wednesday Afternoon Forensicks' were highly significant in the training of all college and academy students, and especially for those with political ambitions" (492). So, too, were the women's forensics.

Those women who sought more training in rhetoric than was offered in the required courses continued their studies through electives. Barnard, Bryn Mawr, and Radcliffe offered some electives of particular interest to future orators, such as "Oral Discussion and Platform Reading" (Radcliffe 1902), but by far the widest range of options was offered at the remaining schools.[9] Wellesley, Mount Holyoke, Vassar, and Smith all presented advanced courses in argumentation, such as one taught by Mary Jordan in 1900: "Exposition in Oratory, Science, Philosophy." The first section of the course focused on debate and argument, parliamentary procedure, study of speeches and debates, and "Practice in writing and delivering arguments." The second part required an "Argumentative Paper, written after consultation with instructors, preparation and criticism of trial briefs, and proper use of reference material" (Smith College 46–47). Smith students remembered Jordan's pedagogy in vivid terms: "Her method was to take something and tear it to pieces," said Mildred Scott Olmstead, class of 1912, an influential feminist who subsequently abandoned writing in favor of public speaking (van Voris 30). Pulitzer Prize winner Constance McLaughlin Green, class of 1919, found the rigor of Jordan's rhetoric, and Jordan's insistence that students express their ideas in "lucid English" the best thing that happened to her in college (Van Voris 45).

Alumnae letters and memoirs reveal that although the Seven Sisters colleges generally supported the right of women to speak publicly, the faculty and administrators were by no means unified in their individual encouragement of women as speakers or as potential voters. Annie Winsor Allen observed that Radcliffe students were not at ease in rhetoric class. Although Harvard rhetoric classes provided male students with a comfortable forum in which to speak, women who studied with the same professors at Radcliffe remained silent. Outside the classroom they told each other that they disagreed with the professor, but in the classroom the professor so intimidated them that they could not speak. Allen found her classmates' ideas "original" and she understood why they hesitated to stand up to older academicians. In a daily theme written in 1887, Allen asserted:

I think women, besides really lacking independence, add to their apparent servility by their timid silence. Women students often disagree radically and emphatically with their instructor's statements and opinions, often have independent sensible notions of their own, but they do not dare to express their dissent, or knowing themselves ignorant they do not feel justified in propounding original theories to men who have spent years in study. They are not the mere receptacles which they seem to be. (Allen 1)

On the verso of this theme, her professor, Barrett Wendell, wrote, "Clever, Thoughtful," an incongruous comment when reviewed in light of his later scathing remarks about Radcliffe students.[10]

If a woman dared to voice an "independent sensible notion" in support of suffrage, she risked censure at Radcliffe because the administration and many of the faculty members were adamantly opposed to universal franchise. The historian Barbara Miller Solomon points out that Radcliffe was the only college of the Seven Sisters to have an organized antisuffrage club (237). In this atmosphere, young women who were prosuffrage, or even undecided, were set apart as dissenters. Solomon found that in 1895, when a Harvard rhetoric professor asked his Radcliffe students to compose a theme concerning woman suffrage, only "two nonconformists wrote in its favor (out of almost seventy students)" (111). The two women brave enough to speak their mind were Maud Wood Park and her friend Inez Haynes Irwin, both of the class of 1898.

In contrast to Radcliffe's English department, which drew its all-male faculty from Harvard, the predominantly female faculty of the English department at Mount Holyoke supported students' prosuffrage activities and guided them in articulating their views. For instance, at the turn of the century, Clara Stevens offered courses in rhetorical theory, structure, style, and journalism, all of which permitted students to research and develop arguments concerning suffrage. In 1902 Beth Gilchrist, one of Stevens's journalism students, entered her essay, "Equal Suffrage as an Influence on the Individual and on the Race," in a Press Club contest and subsequently won the then sizable sum of $75 (Gilchrist 1902). While the coincidence of a student's viewpoint on suffrage with that of her professor did not guarantee harmony, it may well have allowed the student easier access to constructive criticism.

Wellesley's women faculty members were well known for their activism, which they did not hesitate to carry into the classroom. This was demonstrated by the predominantly female English Composition department, which required all students to take "Critical Exposition and Argumentation." In 1906 the second question on the Midyear Examination for this course instructed each student to arrange twenty-one statements concerning "Woman Suffrage in logical, brief form under an appropriate propositional heading." If a student altered the order or rejected any of the statements, she needed to justify her decision. This question allowed students to apply the skills of argument that they had learned in class to a familiar debate, the outcome of which could affect their lives profoundly. To complete the task, the student first categorized the statements as evidence ("The only other disenfranchised classes are idiots, criminals and children"), assertion ("Suffrage is a natural right"), irrelevant ("Women are interested in the education of children"), or objection ("Women are represented by men"). Because the content of the given statements was such that only an affirmative case could be made, the student then arranged the statements in a logical form that would convince her audience of the necessity of woman suffrage. The positive emphasis on suffrage in this exam question was a conscious rhetorical choice made by members of the department.

A similar decision was made by Sophie Chantal Hart, chair of the English Composition department, when she approved the use of a lesson book from Harvard's introductory composition classes. Hart modified the content of the book to make it more appropriate for Wellesley women. Originally, "English A: A Manual of Instructions and Exercises for 1914–15," written by a Harvard professor, contained no references to suffrage.[11] However, the Wellesley version of the same manual, which was used during World War I, contained six suffrage topics as suggestions for themes, as follows:

—Suffrage in My Home Town

—Why I am a Baptist, democrat, antisuffragist (or anything else you
    really are).
—The Militant Suffrage Movement in England
—The Status of Women's Suffrage at the Present time—Particularly in
    its relation to the peace movement
—Reply to J. S. Mill's "Subjection of Women" or Frederick Harrison's
    "The Future of Woman." (English Composition 21, 23–24)

In her own teaching, Hart attempted to guide each student in her writing "to possess the content of her mind, to correlate ideas, [and] to discover her reactions to ideas and connection between things which have just begun to dawn, enchantingly, on the horizon of the mind" (Hart 373). Obviously, the Wellesley rhetoric professors considered woman suffrage to be one such idea on the political horizon, and Hart and her colleagues made special efforts to awaken their students to this issue.

III

Young women at the Seven Sisters colleges organized literary and debating societies, as Stone and Blackwell had done at Oberlin, and as men had done for decades (Hayworth). Mount Holyoke and Wellesley had active literary and debate societies as early as the 1880s. Often the societies included a woman professor as adviser or honorary member. Rhetoric professor Clara Stevens sponsored "The Reading Circle" so that Mount Holyoke students could practice literary and social criticism on an informal and regular basis outside of the classroom, much as Oberlin students had done in the Ladies Literary Society.

Suffrage was a favored topic of discussion and debate "in society." Writing home from Mount Holyoke in 1895 to describe her debate society activities, Matilda S. Calder reported "a great deal of excitement" in a letter to her parents: "Our side for Woman's Suffrage held the rally on Saturday night. The speeches were very good and we had some patriotic songs." Two weeks later, the entire college gathered to hear the debate teams: "All the good arguments were on our side—for it." As was customary in such debates, the members of the audience cast ballots on the resolution debated. Calder's confidence notwithstanding, the negative side won. She also noted that Wellesley held a similar debate on the same night and that the affirmative side won (Calder, letters of Oct. 27, Nov. 9, 1895).

Clearly, women valued their literary and debating societies as training grounds for their eventual participation in public discourse. Wellesley's Phi Sigma literary society member Edith Metcalf argued in 1889, "Have not our oral debates, discussion of papers, conversation upon current affairs, and above all, that impromptu critique . . . vindicated their value repeatedly?" She continued in praise of the group's activities, asking, "Where else were we taught the laws and etiquette of criticism?" and "Where else did we gain any true hint of parliamentary usage?" She concluded her argument for the practice of rhetorical skills by noting that college graduates "forcible in business or the professions, speak with unbounded gratitude of their society training." She foresaw that women schooled and practiced in rhetoric who found themselves in "a knot of floundering women frantically trying to organize into something" would know just what to do to bring about order and facilitate communication (Metcalf 1889). The "societies" section of the 1900 Vassar yearbook includes an illustration of one such well-prepared student calling her colleagues to order: she holds a gavel in one hand and *Roberts Rules of Order* in the other.

Vassar College was recognized as "the pioneer in debating for women" (Yost 129). The "T&M" society was formed in 1879 and included all the students in the odd-year classes, while "Qui Vive" was formed in 1882 and included all the students in the even-year classes. The societies' foremost function was to "train the individual member in habits of logical thought and forceful expression" (Colton 145). Each society held three debates per year among its own members. At the end of each year the societies debated each other in the "Intersociety Debate." Topics for all the debates were chosen by the students themselves, and focused on state- and national-level economic and political policies.

Although the debate societies were a time-consuming extracurricular activity, students on each campus participated in them with great enthusiasm. To prepare for a debate, a student carefully researched her topic, consulted with her teammates to choose appropriately persuasive strategies, arranged a convincing argument in the form of a written, forensic brief, and finally, practiced the oral delivery of her argument. All of these steps were taught in argumentation class.

Gertrude Buck, professor of English at Vassar College, co-authored *A Handbook on Argumentation and Debating* with her former student Kristine Mann in 1906.[12] The handbook contained detailed guidelines and suggested topics for debate, including suffrage. In one exercise, the authors instructed the student to "write a three minute speech to persuade women who believe in suffrage, that suffrage would not be a good thing for women" (12). This exercise gave the antisuffrage student practice in articulating her views in an efficient and persuasive manner. Alternatively, the exercise alerted the prosuffrage student to the possible arguments of her adversaries, to which she might prepare rebuttals. In another exercise, the student had to "suggest three ways of wording a question for debate on women's suffrage, showing the change of emphasis corresponding to the wording" (44). Manipulating emphasis prepared students to analyze arguments and taught them how to control the direction and the extent of an argument.

Suffrage was distinguished as the only topic out of more than fifty debated more than once in a ten-year period at Vassar, demonstrating both Buck's influence and the students' sustained interest. When the Qui Vive Society debated the resolution, "That women should have an equal voice with men in municipal government" in 1899 (Buck's second year at Vassar), both the issue in question and the affirmative team lost the debate, which was decided by a vote of the judges and the audience (1900 *Vassarion* n.pag.). Four years later, a new crop of Qui Vive members debated the resolution, "That full suffrage should be extended to the women of the United States." This time, the affirmative won (Colton 169). In that same year, students dedicated their yearbook to Buck, who instructed the debate teams. The decision for the 1909 T&M Society debate on the resolution, "That New York State extend the suffrage to its women" was not recorded (Colton 168).

A growing acceptance of women as public speakers had taken place during the latter half of the nineteenth century, as noted by Mary Jordan in *Correct Writing and Speaking* (1904).

> The old teaching that women should not be heard in the congregation has given way before necessity. Probably few women who speak in public began by choosing to do so as the gratification of any taste or desire for publicity. But circumstances forced the effort upon them, repetition made its difficulties less formidable, and gradually the feeling has grown in the community that women ought to be able to do what public speaking naturally comes their way. (66–67)

Bolstered by this trend, Wellesley and Vassar staged the first women's intercollegiate debate in 1902, before a public audience. This event and others like it gave the young women access to a wide and appreciative audience, a stepping-stone to some of the more difficult audiences they would face as suffrage activists. As World War I escalated, so did the suffrage movement. According to E. R. Nichols, "During the war the debating interest [in the nation] was sustained in large part by women students ("Historical Sketch III" 259). This gave women the necessary leverage to gain entrance to men's forensic honor associations, such as Pi Kappa Delta ("Historical Sketch II" 601). With an increased sense of power, women spoke out of what they saw as necessity, and went further to capture public speaking opportunities than what "naturally" came their way. As a senior at Smith in 1920, Katherine Graham Howard did "good hard digging for source material" as a member of the debate team. Standing in public to debate at this early stage of her life was "a tremendous help" to a woman who later became the secretary of the National Committee of the Republican Party, and who held many other high-ranking political appointments (Van Voris 48).[13]

IV

Some students who eagerly absorbed their lessons in rhetoric, argumentation, and oratory also debated, and they went beyond the campus environment to join local and national suffrage organizations before they graduated. The administrators and faculty at the Seven Sisters had a dual impact on this phase of a student's involvement with the suffrage movement: they were both academic and political mentors. The combined contributions of these individuals, added to the other consequences of rhetorical education, produced outstanding leaders for the movement. Solomon asserts that "most women's colleges . . . were not potent breeding grounds for the cause," basing her conclusion on the results of polls conducted in the early 1900s, which revealed that the majority of students at all-woman colleges did not favor the extension of suffrage to their own sex (112). Nonetheless, the large number of leaders who graduated from these colleges points to a different interpretation of the colleges' influence on the movement: the Seven Sisters colleges furthered the suffrage campaign greatly by educating its future leaders, who had responded to both positive and negative campus experiences as they matured. These leaders followed a pattern in their affiliations: as students, they belonged to college suffrage clubs; as graduates, to national suffrage groups; and after suffrage was won, to national political parties.

In several cases, the college administration discouraged or forbade prosuffrage speeches and meetings on campus: Radcliffe, Smith, and Vassar had antisuffrage administrators. At Smith, Mary Jordan, chair of the Department of Rhetoric and Old English, agreed with the administration, whose policy was "to refuse any form of recognition to woman suffrage." Jordan spoke at large rallies and also authored "Noblesse Oblige," an antisuffrage pamphlet published by the Massachusetts Association Opposed to the Further Extension of Suffrage to Women (Jordan n.d.). Although students were fond of Jordan, who was a powerful speaker and administrator, they regarded her political beliefs as "quite old fashioned," and questioned Jordan publicly, asking, "How can you help college girls discussing what they will?" (Newspaper clipping, n.d., Jordan Papers). One student, Mildred Louise Colton, boldly did prosuffrage research for Jordan's "Junior Argumentative Paper" course (Colton Papers).

Indeed, college women did discuss suffrage, even if they had to do so in secret: some went so far as to hold meetings in a graveyard, as did Inez Millholland, a debater at Vassar (Solomon 112–13). She resorted to this off-campus rendezvous because Vassar's President Taylor forbade suffrage meetings. Despite the ban, Millholland successfully started the Vassar chapter of the National College Equal Suffrage League, which had one hundred members by 1917, according to the 1918 *Vassarion*. She later undertook an exhausting cross-country speaking tour on behalf of the cause (Fortieth Anniversary Report 11). Taylor also had refused to allow Jane Addams to speak on campus because of her prosuffrage position (Taylor). In a turnabout for Vassar, Taylor's successor in 1915, Henry Noble MacCracken, favored suffrage. MacCracken, who had taught previously at Smith, became a member of Vassar's English department, which housed a large number of suffrage advocates, including its chair, Laura Wylie, and the well-known rhetorician Gertrude Buck. The department's faculty welcomed this change of presidents and the subsequent policy changes.

The presidents of Mount Holyoke and Bryn Mawr Colleges, Mary Woolley and Martha Carey Thomas, joined with other colleagues to form the National College Equal Suffrage League (NCESL) in 1906. Thomas became president of the organization in 1908, and also traveled widely, speaking on behalf of NCESL and NAWSA (Bacon 198–99).

Students started suffrage clubs on every Seven Sisters campus. Most often, these clubs were affiliated with NCESL. At Vassar, the club members took an active part in working for the passage of a full-suffrage constitutional amendment, proposed to the New York state electorate in a 1917 referendum. This was a pivotal vote, because with its success, "victory throughout the nation was assured" (Kraditor 6). Alice Snyder directed the activities of the club in the Poughkeepsie area. Snyder was well prepared for the job, for in addition to her rhetorical studies, she had debated suffrage in 1909 as a member of the T&M debate team (1918 *Vassarion*). Club members worked doggedly, "circularising the voters, house-to-house canvassing and watching the polls Election Day." During the second semester they prepared to send out workers to non-suffrage states (1918 *Vassarion*). To learn more about political organizing, the students relied upon materials provided by their national association, and may well have consulted "Organizing to Win by the Political District Plan: A Handbook for Working Suffragists," written in 1914 by Harriet Burton Laidlaw, a Barnard College alumna. Laidlaw urged her coworkers: "At every political meeting, and in every political committee, the Women Suffrage Party's voice must be heard in undeviating demand for the submission of the woman suffrage amendment to the voters" (Laidlaw n.p.). The author herself spoke fervently at massive street gatherings in immigrant neighborhoods of New York City, answering opponents' challenges with arguments that she had outlined in another publication to which she contributed, "Twenty-Five Answers to Antis" (111). These women built upon the wave of activity in New York state that had been generated by yet another graduate of the Seven Sisters: the daughter of Elizabeth Cady Stanton, Harriot Stanton Blatch, class of 1878 and 1894, who had earned bachelor's and master's degrees from Vassar (Kraditor 268–69). Inspired by the suffragists with whom she had worked during her twenty-year residence in England, after her return to the United States, Blatch formed the Women's Political Union in 1907. By organizing labor workers and by tapping into Inez Millholland's newly formed New York state affiliate of the NCESL, Blatch's group grew to over nineteen thousand members in just one year (Flexner 253). Blatch brought oratory out of the confines of the meeting room and into the street, creating a massive and mobile outdoor forum for women speakers.

   In the first two decades of the twentieth century, most suffragists belonged to the National American Woman Suffrage Association (NAWSA), led by Anna Howard Shaw, who until 1915 "devoted her truly great oratorical powers to the suffrage cause" (13). Alice Paul and other militants founded the Congressional Union for Woman Suffrage in 1912 and broke from NAWSA in 1914. Paul's sister Helen, a Wellesley graduate, wrote of the Englishwomen who inspired this new group in an article entitled "A Glimpse of the Suffragette movement" (*Wellesley College News* 1914). Other Seven Sisters alumnae joined this radical organization, which merged with the Women's Party in 1917 to become the National Women's Party (NWP). Lucy Burns, who had debated suffrage questions at Vassar was "Miss [Alice] Paul's chief lieutenant" (Kraditor 280).[14] In *The Story of the Woman's Party*, Inez Haynes Irwin observes that Burns "speaks and writes with equal eloquence and elegance. Her speeches before suffrage bodies, her editorials in the *Suffragist* are models of clearness; conciseness; of accumulative force of expression" (16–17). In sum, the training common to all Seven Sisters alumnae gave Irwin the authority to recognize and praise Burns's rhetorical excellence.

   Most activists remained with NAWSA and bitterly opposed the NWP's tactics, which included inflammatory oratory and civil disobedience. Despite the rifts in the movement, suffrage became a political reality in 1919. In the aftermath of the struggle, the women orators who had contributed zealously to the cause found or created new and related pursuits. For example, Marguerite Hickey Lawler, class of 1912, one of Jordan's students at Smith, continued to press for the extension of suffrage by educating immigrants. She knew that by studying the English language, rhetoric, and civics, hundreds of thousands of women and men in New England could acquire the communication skills required for citizenship. With her own strong background in rhetoric, Lawler secured an appointment as Connecticut State Agent of Americanization. She traveled and lectured widely to promote the state's program, and also applied her mastery of rhetoric to the writing of a textbook for Americanization instructors, *Lessons for New Americans: Advanced Course* (1923). Her choice of materials included excerpts of speeches by well-known United States orators, which she recommended as oral and written models for women and men students (Conway 1986).

As members of the League of Women Voters, Seven Sisters alumnae and faculty members turned their prosuffrage energies toward registering and educating women as voters. Maud Wood Park, the "nonconformist" student at Radcliffe, progressed from her membership in NAWSA to become the first president of the League of Women Voters. Others, like Martha Carey Thomas, followed Alice Paul's lead in pressing for the passage of the Equal Rights Amendment. In 1909 an optimistic Vassar student penned "A Suffragist Soliloquy." In verse, she dreamed of a woman who would ascend to the top of the political hierarchy in the United States.

> To take the stump, to vote, perchance be President
> . . . . .
> Yet who can bear the calm of household life,
> A voteless year, the proud world's contumely,
> Pangs of despised franchise, the law's defect,
> The politician's scorn and cruel jokes
> That earnest suffragettes from voters take,
> When they might rulers make
> With "Votes for Women?"
>
> *(1909 Vassarion 206)*

She and her college-educated sisters before her had proudly gained access to the ancient, male-dominated tradition of rhetoric, and had used what they learned in rhetoric classes to speak out on behalf of women. Having successfully argued for the privilege of participating in a political state far more democratic than those inhabited by the Greek and Roman masters of oratory, these women continued to work collectively to empower women as fully realized political persons who could skillfully and persuasively engage and inform public discourse.

The history of rhetoric at the Seven Sisters colleges reveals three key factors in the lives of the suffragists who contributed to the eventual success of the movement. First, as a group they were uniformly well educated in rhetoric: they studied the same classical texts and benefited from the same oratorical training as did their male contemporaries, and thus were the first women in the United States who were purposefully educated to be full "political persons." Second, they became deeply involved in organizing themselves into "societies" during college, an activity that gave them great confidence in their own ability to be effective public speakers and political leaders. Third, and finally, they forged lifelong associations with mentors, peers, and successors in academia and in state and national women's organizations—connections that proved to be invaluable for coordinating a national political movement.

NOTES

Research and travel for Kathryn M. Conway's chapter was provided in part by grants from the Reader's Digest Foundation and the United States Department of Education.

1. The Seven Sisters colleges were founded exclusively for women. (For names, dates of founding and further discussion, see Wagner, Notes, this volume.) Although the twentieth-century stereotype portrays a woman at one of these colleges as a rich white woman of a Protestant religion, many students were middle class, some were poor, some were black, Hispanic, or Asian, and the students represented many religions. The archives of each college preserve student records that supply this biographical information. See also Barbara Miller Solomon's *In the Company of Educated Women: A History of Women and Higher Education in America*, chap. 5, "Who Went to College."

2. "Political persons" was the phrase used in 1911 by Lorna Birtwell, a pro-suffrage Radcliffe student. Quoted in Solomon 113.

3. For the names of other Seven Sisters graduates who were suffrage leaders see Kraditor; Solomon; and Flexner. Oates and Williamson document the important role of the Seven Sisters colleges in producing women leaders, in "Women's Colleges and Women Achievers" and "Comment on Tidball's 'Women's Colleges and Women Achievers Revisited.' "

4. Throughout the later decades of the nineteenth century and into the twentieth, increasing numbers of students lobbied for suffrage. By 1918 the Vassar Chapter of the National College Equal Suffrage League reported a membership of over one hundred persons, most of them students. Six of the Seven Sisters colleges formed chapters of this organization, while Barnard students formed the "Suffrage Club" in 1914 and the "Feminist Forum" in 1916. This information can be found under various listings in the archives of each of the colleges, such as "suffrage," "student clubs," and the specific names of the individuals and organizations.

5. Cazden writes in "Antoinette Brown Blackwell: A Biography" that Stone and Blackwell did debate once in class, with the encouragement of their rhetoric professor, James Thome. Their brilliance in the debate resulted in an outcry from the rest of the faculty and from the Ladies Board of Oberlin College (28–29).

6. According to Horowitz, in the earliest days, unmarried women faculty members lived in apartments in the students' dormitories.

7. The popularization of Adams Sherman Hill's teachings led to this reduced notion of the domain of rhetoric. For various accounts of the history of rhetorical instruction in men's colleges, see: William Riley Parker, "Where Do English Departments Come From?" and Ronald F. Reid, "The Boylston Professorship of Rhetoric and Oratory, 1806–1904." In "Two Model Teachers and the Harvardization of English Departments," Donald C. Stewart mentions Gertrude Buck, Helen Mahin, and Ruth Mary Weeks, who were all students of Fred Newton Scott, a "model teacher" of rhetoric. But Stewart fails to give these women any further credit for their subsequent careers as educational leaders. Buck created an innovative rhetoric department at Vassar College and was the author of over twenty textbooks and articles on rhetoric. According to *The University of Michigan: An Encyclopaedic Survey*, Mahin became professor of journalism at the University of Kansas and Weeks "became a distinctive leader in the liberal movement in language matters" (562). James Berlin gives more attention to Buck in his books *Rhetoric and Reality* and *Writing Instruction in Nineteenth-Century American Colleges*.

8. In "Rhetoric in the American College Curriculum" S. Michael Halloran argues that "the classical art of oral public discourse" that predominated in late eighteenth-century men's colleges underwent a "severe eclipse" in the late nineteenth century, never to reemerge, even in today's rhetoric programs. A consideration of the emphasis placed on oratory and the focus on public issues in the rhetoric programs of the Seven Sisters colleges at the turn of the nineteenth century could lead to a different reading of the history of rhetoric in the United States.

9. Barnard relied upon Columbia for many of its professors, especially in rhetoric. Radcliffe drew its English department faculty members entirely from Harvard. The limited offerings in rhetoric may be linked to the male domination in these departments. Formidable women rhetoricians such as Sophie Chantal Hart at Wellesley, Mary Jordan at Smith, Clara Stevens and Margaret Ball at Mount Holyoke, and Gertrude Buck at Vassar developed their own theories of rhetoric, some of which drew heavily upon classical rhetorical theory rather than on Hill's theories.

10. Wendell wrote a caustic attack on Radcliffe College women twelve years later, in 1899, claiming that they were a corrupting threat to "the pure virility of Harvard tradition." He wished to protect the university which was to him, "even more profoundly than it seems, an institution of learning, a traditional school of manly character" (4, 6).

11. The book was written by C. N. Greenough. A newly hired Harvard graduate, P. W. Long, suggested the use of Greenough's book to Hart, as documented in Hart's personal copy of the book (Wellesley College Archives, English Department Files).

12. This handbook was an outgrowth of Buck's 1899 textbook, *A Course in Argumentative Writing*. Buck, a pedagogical innovator, believed that students should learn how to argue by means of the inductive method: each student would examine her "own unconscious reasonings" for evidence of "logical formulae." Other authorities began by teaching what Buck called the "maxims and formulae

regarded by the learner as malign inventions of Aristotle" (Buck and Mann iii–v). Furthermore, she advised students to work on topics of current interest about which they already held strong convictions (3).

13. Mary W. Dewson, Wellesley, class of 1897, led a similar life, first as an active suffragist and then as the vice chairman of the Democratic Party National Committee (Ware 146).

14. Burns participated in an intersociety debate in March 1902 on the resolution "That legislation against Negro suffrage is justifiable" (Colton).

REFERENCES

Allen, Annie Winsor. "Women," an essay in "1887 Daily Theme Book." Radcliffe College Archives.

Bacon, Margaret Hope. *Mothers of Feminism: The Story of Quaker Women in America*. San Francisco: Harper, 1986.

Berlin, James A. *Rhetoric and Reality Writing Instruction in American Colleges, 1900–1985*. Carbondale: Southern Illinois UP, 1987.

———. *Writing Instruction in Nineteenth-Century American Colleges*. Carbondale: Southern Illinois UP, 1984.

Brown, Dorothy. *Setting a Course: American Women in the 1920s*. Boston: Twayne, 1987.

Buck, Gertrude, and Kristine Mann. *A Handbook of Argumentation and Debating*. Orange, NJ: Orange Chronicle, 1906.

Calder, Matilda S. Matilda S. Calder Letters. Mount Holyoke College Archives.

Cazden, Elizabeth. *Antoinette Brown Blackwell: A Biography*. Old Westbury, NY: Feminist P, 1983.

Colton, Mildred Louise. Colton Papers. Sophia Smith Collection. Smith College.

Conway, Kathryn M. "Marguerite Hickey Lawler: Agent of Americanization." Unpublished manuscript, 1986.

Cott, Nancy F. *The Grounding of Modern Feminism*. New Haven: Yale UP, 1987.

English Composition 1. 1915–1916. Wellesley College, 1915.

Flexner, Eleanor. *Century of Struggle: The Woman's Rights Movement in the United States*. Cambridge: Belknap P of Harvard UP, 1959.

Fortieth Anniversary Report of the Arthur and Elizabeth Schlesinger Library on the History of Women in America. Cambridge: Radcliffe College, 1983.

Gilchrist, Beth. In "1902 Press Club Notebook." Mount Holyoke College Archives.

Greenough, C. N., et al. *English Composition Notebook*. Boston: Ginn, 1907.

Haight, Elizabeth Hazelton, ed. *The Autobiography and Letters of Matthew Vassar*. New York: Oxford UP, 1916.

Halloran, S. Michael. "Rhetoric in the American College Curriculum: The Decline of Public Discourse." *PRE/TEXT* 3.3 (fall 1982): 245–69.

Hart, Sophie Chantal. "English Composition—An Interpretation." *Wellesley Magazine* (June 1937): 372–74.

Hayworth, Donald. "The Development of the Training of Public Speakers in America." *QJS* 14.4 (November 1928): 489–502.

Horowitz, Helen Lefkowitz. *Alma Mater: Design and Experience in the Women's Colleges from Their Nineteenth-Century Beginnings to the 1930s.* New York: Knopf, 1984.

Hosford, Frances Juliette. *Father Shipherd's magna Charta: A Century of Coeducation in Oberlin College.* Boston: Marshall Jones, 1935.

Irwin, Inez Haynes. *Angels and Amazons: A Hundred Years of American Women.* Garden City: Doubleday, 1934.

———. *The Story of the Woman's Party.* New York: Harcourt, 1921.

Jordan, Mary A. *Correct Writing and Speaking.* New York: A.S. Barnes, 1904.

———. Jordan Papers. Sophia Smith Collection. Smith College.

———. "Noblesse Oblige: Why Women Do Not Want the Vote." Pamphlet 36 of the Massachusetts Association Opposed to the Further Extension of Suffrage to Women (n.d.): 1–7. Sophia Smith Collection, Suffrage, Box 19. Smith College.

Kennedy, Patricia, and Gloria Hartmann O'Sheilds. *We Shall Be Heard: Women Speakers in America, 1828–Present.* Dubuque: Kendall/Hunt, 1983.

Kraditor, Aileen S. *The Ideas of the Woman Suffrage Movement: 1890–1920.* New York: Norton, 1981.

Laidlaw, Harriet Burton. *Organizing to Win by the Political District Plan: A Handbook for Working Suffragists.* 1914. Microfilm 949, no. 1908, History of Women Series.

Lasser, Carol, and Marlene Deahl Merrill, eds. *Friends and Sisters: Letters between Lucy Stone and Antoinette Brown Blackwell, 1846–93.* Urbana: U of Illinois P, 1987.

Lawler, Marguerite Hickey. *Lessons for New Americans: Advanced Course.* Hartford: Connecticut State Board of Education, 1923.

Letters from Old-Time Vassar: Written by a Student in 1869–70. Poughkeepsie, N.Y.: Vassar College, 1915.

MacDuffie, Abby Parsons. *The Little Pilgrim: An Autobiography.* N.p., 1938.

Meador, Prentice A. "Quintilian and the Institutio Oratoria." *A Synoptic History of Classical Rhetoric.* Ed. James J. Murphy. Davis: Hermagorus P, 1983.

Merrill, Marlene Deahl. "Justice, Simple Justice: Women at Oberlin 1837–1987." *Oberlin Alumni Magazine* (fall 1987): 11–16.

Metcalf, Edith. "Phi Sigma, Though Dead, Yet Speaketh." *(Wellesley) Courant College Edition* (February 1, 1889): n.p.

Miller, Alice Duer. *Are Women People? A Book of Rhymes for Suffrage Times.* New York: Doran, 1915.

Newcomer, Mabel. *A Century of Higher Education for Women.* New York: Harper, 1959.

Nichols, Egbert Ray. "A Historical Sketch of Intercollegiate Debating: II." *QJS* 22 (December 1937): 591–602.

———. "A Historical Sketch of Intercollegiate Debating: III." *QJS* 23 (April 1937): 259–78.

Oates, Mary J., and Susan Williamson. "Women's Colleges and Women Achievers." *Signs* 3.4 (summer 1978): 795–806.

———. "Comment on Tidball's 'Women's Colleges and Women Achievers Revisited.'" *Signs* (winter 1980): 342–45.

Parker, William Riley. "Where Do English Departments Come From?" *College English* 28.5 (February 1967): 339–51.

Radcliffe College. *Catalog.* Cambridge, MA: 1902.

Reid, Ronald F. "The Boylston Professorship of Rhetoric and Oratory, 1806–1904: A Case Study in Changing Concepts of Rhetoric and Pedagogy." *QJS* 45.3 (October 1959): 240–57.

Rosovsky, Nitza. *The Jewish Experience at Harvard and Radcliffe.* Cambridge: Harvard UP, 1986.

Rupp, Leila J., and Verta Taylor. *Survival in the Doldrums: The American Women's Rights Movement, 1945 to the 1960's.* New York: Oxford UP, 1987.

Scott, Anne Firor. "The Ever Widening Circle: The Diffusion of Feminist Values from the Troy Female Seminary, 1822–1872." *History of Education Quarterly* (spring 1979): 3–25.

Scott, Anne Firor, and Andrew MacKay Scott. *One Half the People: The Fight for Woman Suffrage.* Urbana: U of Illinois P, 1982.

Seidman, Rachel F. "The Ladies Literary Society: Oberlin's Early Feminists." *Oberlin Alumni Magazine* (fall 1987): 14–15.

Shaw, Wilfred B., ed. *The University of Michigan: An Encyclopedic Survey.* Vol 2. Ann Arbor: U of Michigan P, 1951.

Smith College. *Annual Catalog.* 1900–1901.

Solomon, Barbara Miller. *In the Company of Educated Women: A History of Women and Higher Education in America.* New Haven: Yale UP, 1985.

Stewart, Donald C. "Two Model Teachers and the Harvardization of English Departments." In *The Rhetorical Tradition and Modern Writing*, ed. James J. Murphy. New York: MLA, 1982. 118–29.

Taylor, President of Vassar College. Letter to Jane Addams. Presidents' Papers, Special Collections, Vassar College Library.

"Twenty-five Answers to Antis: Five-Minute Speeches on Votes for Women by Eminent Suffragists." New York: National Woman Suffrage Publishing Co., n.d.

Van Voris, Jacqueline, ed. *College: A Smith Mosaic.* West Springfield: Smith College P, 1975.

Vassar College. *Annual Catalog.* 1876–1877.

Vassar Debate Folder. Vassar College Special Collections.

Vassarion. Vassar College Archives.

Ware, Susan. *Beyond Suffrage: Women in the New Deal.* Cambridge: Harvard UP, 1981.

Wellesley College. *Annual Catalog.* 1892–1893.

Wellesley College News. No. 4, January 1914.

Wendell, Barrett. "The Relations of Radcliffe College with Harvard." *Harvard Monthly* 29.1 (October 1899): 1–10.

Wood, Frances A. *The Earliest Years at Vassar: Personal Recollections.* Poughkeepsie, NY: Vassar College P, 1909.

Woody, Thomas. *A History of Women's Education in the United States.* New York.: Science, 1929.

Yost, Mary. "The Intercollegiate Debate." *Vassar Quarterly* (May 1916): 128–29.

Sojourner Truth: A Practical Public Discourse

Drema R. Lipscomb

At a time when it was uncommon for women—and in particular black women—to speak publicly, Sojourner Truth was a major force in speaking on pressing matters of public policy. Much has been written about her as an abolitionist and as a champion of women's rights in the nineteenth century. To date, however, no research has focused on her oratory as deliberative rhetoric[1]—the sort of rhetoric that many theorists place in "settings mainly civic" (Bitzer 71) and that "gives primary emphasis to communication on public problems" (Halloran 246). A former slave who remained illiterate all her life, Sojourner Truth commanded large crowds in an effort to arouse public action on *the* two most crucial political and social issues of her day—slavery and suffrage.

Sojourner Truth was born a slave in upstate New York sometime around 1797. She was given the name Isabella by her owner, Charles Hardenberg, a wealthy Dutch landowner; the first language she learned to speak was Dutch. After passing through the hands of several owners, Isabella served from 1810 to 1827 in the household of John J. Dumont of New Paltz, New York, where she bore at least five children by a fellow slave named Thomas. After learning that Dumont intended to renege on his promise to grant her freedom prior to the 1828 mandatory emancipation of slaves in New York state, Isabella fled Dumont's household in 1827. She found refuge nearby with a Quaker family whose surname she took; Isabella remained with them until emancipated.

As Isabella Van Wagener, she arrived in New York City with her two youngest children around 1829 and secured domestic employment. Although she joined several churches, she did not find the religious satisfaction she sought until she aligned herself with Elijah and Sarah Pierson, wealthy patrons who had undertaken a widespread mission of conversion in New York City, especially among prostitutes. The Piersons and Van Wagener preached on the streets and attracted much attention; Van Wagener also assisted in the religious services of the Retrenchment Society, an organization that Elijah Pierson founded. Sometime between 1829 and 1831, she joined the Piersons' private household, where they "prayed together interminably and fasted for three days at a stretch" (*Notable American Women* 479–80).

For eight or nine years following her association with the Piersons, Van Wagener lived quietly in New York, maintaining a home for her two children, earning her living as a cook, maid, and laundress, and regularly attending the African Zion Church. Intensely religious but unhappy in New York City, she left her home in 1843 and set out to preach at camp meetings and private residences in New England and cities west of New York. Since she was leaving behind her years of servitude and making a fresh start, Isabella Van Wagener felt she needed a new name—one more reflective of her "calling." According to her autobiographical narrative, she prayed for instruction (Gilbert, *Narrative of Sojourner Truth* 100; hereafter cited as *Narrative*) and the Lord commanded her to take the name "Sojourner." Sometime later she decided that having a second name would be appropriate. "Afterwards I told the Lord I wanted another name, cause everybody else had two names; and the Lord gave me Truth, 'cause I was to declare the truth to the people" (*Narrative* 164).

Sojourner Truth spent the summer of 1843 walking through Long Island and Connecticut, sleeping wherever she found shelter and working when she needed food. She sang and spoke at camp meetings, in churches, on highways, and in the streets of towns. By the winter of 1843 Truth had made her way to Northampton, Massachusetts. She became a member of a communal farm and silk factory, the Northampton Association of Education and Industry, which had been founded by George W. Benson, brother-in-law of William Lloyd Garrison. Encountering the abolitionist movement for the first time, Sojourner Truth became an enthusiastic convert. When the association collapsed in 1846, she remained in the Benson household as a guest and continued to speak periodically throughout the state. The abolitionist leaders recognized her unique gifts for engaging crowds and publicized her travels in their periodicals.

Around 1850 Sojourner Truth traveled west, her growing reputation as a public speaker having preceded her. "She had a personal magnetism that drew great crowds, which were held by her homely, trenchant, seemingly random remarks, her gift for repartee, and her gospel songs" (*Notable American Women* 480). In Ohio the office of *The Salem Anti-Slavery Bugle* was her headquarters, and from there she toured Indiana, Missouri, and Kansas, at times sharing platforms with abolitionist leaders such as Frederick Douglass and Parker Pillsbury. She supported herself by selling the *Narrative of Sojourner Truth* (1850).[2]

To appreciate fully the significance of Sojourner Truth's voice in the nineteenth century, one must understand the historical context in which she functioned. Janey Weinhold Montgomery describes the rhetorical setting from 1850 to 1875 as "characterized by an expression of rights. Continual controversy over slavery involved the right of the federal government to prohibit slavery, and the right of the states to protest in defense of their sovereignty" (12). The period preceding the outbreak of the Civil War in 1861 was politically characterized by sectional controversy: the South was engaged in debate over expansion, a thinly veiled disguise for the acquisition of more slave territory in the West, while the North—not uniformly abolitionist—was strongly against the South's extension of slavery into Western territories. Meanwhile, Congress found that "efforts to enforce the newly enacted Fugitive Slave Law added to the difficulties of the situation" (Hicks et al., in Montgomery 13).

Another issue whose time frame closely paralleled abolition was women's rights. Women's conventions and public meetings in the 1850s were held in Ohio, Pennsylvania, New York, Maryland, Maine, Massachusetts, and elsewhere, but most of these gatherings were segregated by race. Because many nineteenth-century white women's rights advocates were active in the abolitionist movement, it is often assumed they were also antiracist. bell hooks claims that the first white women's rights advocates were never seeking social equality for all women, but only for white women (124). When white women reformers in the 1830s chose to work to free the slave, says hooks, they were motivated by religious sentiment. On a moral platform they attacked slavery, not racism.[3] While these white women strongly advocated an end to slavery, they never advocated social or political change that would allow the status of blacks to be equal to their own (125). In the 1850s, when many white female reformers complained that the issue of slavery and women's rights were being confused as one, most black abolitionists split from the white women's movement. Few black women seem to have been welcomed at white women's rights meetings. Sojourner Truth's presence at the second women's rights convention in Akron, Ohio, in May 1851, was thus exceptional.

Frances D. Gage, who presided over the 1851 convention, relates this account of Truth's presence at that meeting:

> The cause was unpopular then. The leaders of the movement trembled on seeing a tall, gaunt, black woman, in a gray dress and turban, surmounted by an uncouth sun-bonnet, march deliberately into the church, walk with the air of a queen up the aisle, and take her seat upon the pulpit steps. A buzz of disapprobation was heard all over the house, and such words as these fell upon listening ears—"An abolition affair!" "Woman's rights and niggers!" "Don't let her speak, Mrs. Gage, it will ruin us. Every newspaper in the land will have our cause mixed with abolition and niggers, and we shall be utterly denounced." (*Stanton 1:115–16*)

Gage replied, "We shall see when the time comes" (115). Sojourner Truth did not speak that day, but in the succeeding days of the 1851 convention and in the many years that followed, her voice became a formidable force in deliberating both the issues of slavery and equal rights for women.

II

Historians often describe nineteenth-century American rhetoric as a classical tradition derived primarily from ancient Greek and Roman sources. This tradition is also depicted as a continuous thread, surviving without a break from ancient to contemporary times. For example, writes Christine Oravec, Marie Hochmuth Nichols and Richard Murphy sketch a scenario in which rhetoric changes, shifts, but grows ever "stronger" throughout the nineteenth century: "Through the age, now swift flowing, now quiescent, continued the main channel of classical rhetoric. Many tributaries fed it, and at times, indeed, rivaled the main stream in size and momentum—the science of voice, the quasi-scientific elocutionary system . . . the Delsartian systems. But the stream flowed on, and gathering momentum, at the end of the century cascaded into what we now know as the modern department of speech" (395). More recent scholarship argues that a "severe eclipse in the tradition occurs during the nineteenth century which accounts for the decline of rhetoric in American culture."[4] However, according to Oravec, both interpretations assume the continuity of a single, specifically classical rhetorical tradition.

Significantly, then, the classical or classical–belles lettres tradition described by many scholars resides primarily in the native textbooks, pedagogical practices, and curricula of universities and colleges. Hence, the dominant assumptions about American rhetorical theory are based upon the legitimacy of certain formal institutions. But, says Oravec, significant rhetorical theory may well have emerged in a much more responsive and politically volatile arena than in the textbooks and the curriculum (396). Alternatives to what we see now as an established tradition may have resided implicitly in the practical public discourse of the age.[5] While Oravec maintains that "a well-articulated theoretical alternative to the classical-belle lettres tradition" emerged in nineteenth-century periodicals (397), I am suggesting that an alternative practical public discourse emerged in another form during this period. At no time, perhaps, in the history of American speech and amidst mass social turmoil was there a period more conducive to a rhetoric of practical public discourse.

Sojourner Truth offered such an alternative in her "practical public discourse," a deliberative discourse that sought to inspire human action on the issues of slavery and women's rights. The ultimate goal of her practical discourse was to enact legislation, considered to be the most critical subject for deliberation because "it reflects and preserves the character of the regime, regulates the lives of all who live under its authority; and the ends of legislation encompass all the ends of human action, a category so broad as to include the final end of all action— happiness" (Arnhart 57). Implicit in Truth's rhetoric was the notion that if everyone in a democratic society were allowed to contribute, then the whole of society would benefit. Although she was not trained in formal rhetorical strategies, and although her platform style may have seemed "random" and extempore, Sojourner Truth nonetheless commanded sophisticated rhetorical strategies and knew quite well what she was doing. Nothing of hers was wholly unplanned or accidental. She had a goal— to effect action on suffrage and slavery. Her rhetorical strategies were consciously designed to help her achieve that goal. Her rhetoric was thus deliberative, and her religious beliefs were always at the helm of these strategies.

While Sojourner Truth's association with the Quakers and the African Zion Church played a significant role in her rhetorical training, her religious instruction can be traced back to her youth. "In the evening, when her mother's work was done," Truth recalled in her *Narrative*, her mother "would sit down under the sparkling vault of heaven, and calling her children to her, would talk to them of the only Being that could effectually aid or protect." Her mother's teachings were in Low Dutch and, according to Olive Gilbert, the English translation "ran nearly as follows—'My children, there is a God, who hears and sees you and when you are beaten, or cruelly treated, or fall into any trouble, you must ask help of him, and he will always hear and help you' " (*Narrative* 17). She taught them to kneel and say the Lord's Prayer.

Truth never forgot these instructions from her mother, and while she never learned to read, she always managed to have someone read to her. It is important to note that whenever she employed someone to read the Scriptures to her, she wished to hear passages without commentary. If adults read to her and she asked them to repeat a passage over and over again, many invariably began to explain by giving their version of it. This tried her patience exceedingly; consequently, she ceased asking adults to read to her and substituted children. Children, as soon as they could read distinctly, would reread the same sentence to her, as often as she wished, and without comment. In that way she could hear—and memorize—without interruption. She did not want the explications of others; she wanted to interpret the scriptures as she saw them (*Narrative* 108–09). Crucial to her being able to draw her own interpretations was the emphasis she placed on memorizing; this process—a conscious effort—was central to her ability to incorporate biblical precedents and biblical passages into her speeches.

Truth's independence of mind continued to play a major role in her activities when, in 1843, she met William Lloyd Garrison's brother-in-law and joined the abolitionist movement. She immediately aligned herself with members of major antislavery organizations. The aim of such societies was to develop a systematic program of agitation to bring about emancipation and full citizenship for Negro freedmen. Major antislavery societies employed agents, or public speakers, who toured the North and West promoting abolitionism. Some of the speakers were designated "local" agents and served part-time, usually speaking within a restricted geographical locality. Other speakers were designated "regular" agents and were employed on a full-time basis (Kennicott 18).

Initially, black speakers were not a part of the agent corps but, once employed, fugitive slaves were the most sought-after group of antislavery agents. A letter published in Garrison's newspaper, the *Liberator*, commented in 1842: "The public have itching ears to hear a colored man speak, and particularly a slave. Multitudes will flock to hear one of this class speak" (quoted in Kennicott 19). Henry Bibb, a Kentucky fugitive, began his speaking career in 1844 by telling an Adrian, Michigan, audience of his harrowing escape to freedom, his return to the South to rescue his wife, and his subsequent recapture and second escape. By 1844, Lewis and Milton Clark were touring the North and West with moving testimonies of the cruelties of captivity (19).

Among the other popular slave speakers, according to Patrick Kennicott, was Isabella Van Wagener who, "upon becoming an antislavery lecturer, adopted the name Sojourner Truth, the name she claimed God had given her" (19). Kennicott and Sojourner Truth's biographers place her with William Lloyd Garrison, fugitive slave agents, various antislavery societies, and antislavery activity (Gilbert; Fauset; Pauli). Her association with the antislavery societies provided Truth the opportunity to observe many polished religious and civic speakers who undoubtedly served as rhetorical models. Since she was not book-trained in rhetorical devices, she adapted the speaking techniques of the platform and pulpit orators of the early period of the antislavery movement: namely, establishing one's own good character (ethos), exhibiting biblical knowledge and moral rationale (logos), and relating one's personal trials (pathos). Indeed, these were the three means she utilized to establish her authority as a platform speaker in nineteenth-century America.

III

The convention atmosphere during the early platform period often produced hostile audiences. In fact, much of the time the audience was filled with hecklers provoked by the clergy and the press. Elizabeth Cady Stanton and Susan B. Anthony, authors of the *History of Woman Suffrage*, reported: "Gentlemen and ladies alike who attempted to speak were interrupted by shouts, hisses, stamping, cheers, rude remarks and all manner of noisy demonstration" (1:547).

During her address to what later became known as the "Mob Convention" in New York City on September 7, 1853, Sojourner Truth encountered one of the most hostile crowds imaginable. According to Stanton and Anthony, Truth "combined the two most hated elements of humanity: she was black and she was a woman, and when she spoke all the insults that could be cast upon color and sex were hurled at her" (1:567). In response, her opening remarks attempted to establish her own character as a good citizen:

> Is it not good for me to come and draw forth a spirit, to see what kind
> of spirit people are of? I am a citizen of the State of New York; I was born
> in the State of New York; and now I am a good citizen of this state. I was
> born here, and I can tell you I feel at home here. (Stanton 1:567)

By opening with a rhetorical question, Truth established an intimacy
with her listeners and reassured them that she intended them no harm.
By declaring herself a citizen of the state of New York, she was also
identifying with the audience—she was more like than unlike them.

To further establish her ethos and moral authority to speak, Sojourner Truth often cited stories and passages from the Bible. At the
Mob Convention, she told the story of Queen Esther, who "came forth,
for she was oppressed, and felt there was a great wrong, and she said,
'I will die or bring my complaint before the King.'" Sojourner Truth
explained that women in the United States wanted their rights, just as
Queen Esther had demanded hers. "The King raised up his sceptre and
said, 'Thy request shall be granted unto thee—to the half of my kingdom
will I grant it to thee!'" "Should the king of the United States be greater,
or more crueler, or more harder?" asked Truth. "Women do not ask half
of a kingdom, but their rights, and they don't get 'em" (1:568).

In addition to establishing her ethos with the audience, Truth also
developed logical forms of argumentation. Montgomery demonstrates
how Truth, never having studied logic, "amazed her audiences with her
refutation and constructive efforts" (55). Since Sojourner Truth had no
formalized training in refutation, she listened to her opponent and applied what she heard to her own experiences or her knowledge of the
Bible. This tactic amounted to "turning the tables," a strategy she likely
mastered from listening to polished black orators such as John Mercer
Langston, a lawyer educated in Europe, Dr. James McCune Smith, a
prominent New York physician, and the well-known abolitionist Frederick Douglass.

When "turning the tables," Truth would repeat her opponent's statement and then use it to her own advantage. In her speech to the Women's
Convention in Akron, for example, she heard a minister advance the
argument that superior rights and privileges were claimed for males
because of the "manhood of Christ" (Stanton 1:115). Truth replied:

> Den dat little man in black dar, he say women can't have as much rights
> as men, 'cause Christ wan't a woman! Whar did your Christ come from?
> Raising her voice still louder, she repeated, Whar did your Christ come

from? From God and a woman! Man had nothin' to do wid him! (Stanton 1:116)

Without introducing any other type of evidence, Truth had effectively rebuked her opponent. According to Truth, nothing more needed to be said. As Sojourner Truth stood there with "outstretched arms and eyes of fire, rolling thunder couldn't have stilled that crowd as did those deep, wonderful tones" (Stanton 1:116).

As part of her rhetorical strategy, Truth often used humor in her logical appeals. The humor of the argument was enough to destroy the effectiveness of her opponent's point. In her speech delivered to the Equal Rights Association Convention, Truth was advocating woman suffrage. She stated her opponent's stand as:

I am sometimes told that "Women ain't fit to vote. Why don't you know that a woman had seven devils in her; and do you suppose a woman is fit to rule the nation?" Seven devils ain't no account; a man had a legion in him (great laughter). The devils didn't know where to go; and so they asked that they might go into the swine. They thought that was as good a place as they came out from (renewed laughter). They didn't ask to go the sheep—no, into the hog, that was the selfishest beast; and man is so selfish that he has got women's rights and his own too, and yet he won't give women their rights, he keeps them all to himself. (Stanton 2:222)

By continuing the argument and introducing humor into the story, she was able to "minimize" the effect of the original argument (Montgomery 56).

As these examples illustrate, Sojourner Truth had a strong sense of self and always spoke in the first person; she was never afraid to call attention to herself when advancing any argument. Arguing from example as a rhetorical strategy, she often exposed various parts of her body for dramatic effect: "Look at me! Look at my arm! . . . I have ploughed, and planted, and gathered into barns, and no man could head me!" In addition to body parts, Sojourner Truth used her physical stature to her advantage as well: "Sojourner stood nearly six feet high, head erect and eyes piercing the upper air like one in a dream" (Stanton 1:115–17). No doubt her physical characteristics impressed her audience while enhancing the effectiveness of her speeches.

Whereas argument from example, rhetorical induction, is "the foundation of reasoning," rhetorical deduction uses the enthymeme, an abbreviated syllogism based on probabilities. Sojourner Truth often used the enthymeme in refutation as a constructive means of proof. When men claimed superior rights due to their superior intellect, Truth replied with this observation: "If my cup won't hold a pint and yourn holds a quart wouldn't it be mean not to let me have my little half measureful?" The implication here is that since the men claimed superior rights based on their superior intellect, then women with some intellect, even if just a "pint," should have some rights. According to one observer, the audience responded with long and loud cheering (Stanton 1:116).

There are many accounts from contemporaries who witnessed the power Sojourner Truth wielded over hostile crowds. Her use of wit and her own life experiences were consistently effective. Speaking of Truth's address at the 1851 Women's Convention in Akron, Ohio, Frances Gage made these observations:

> The tumult subsided at once. . . . At first word there was a profound hush. She spoke in deep tones, which, though not loud, reached every ear in the house, and away through the throng at the doors and windows. . . . The speaker had taken us up in her strong arms and carried us safely over the slough of difficulty, turning the whole tide in our favor. (Stanton 1:116–17)

In other words, with "the tender-skinned among us" quickly losing dignity in an atmosphere which "betoken[s] a storm," Sojourner Truth had rescued the women too timid to speak and those whom the "boys in the galleries were getting the better of" (Stanton 1:115). In what had become an unruly situation, Sojourner Truth, with her quiet reserve and deep voice, had calmed the noisy crowd and rescued the women who were not accustomed to speaking publicly.

Frances Titus also relates the following story about Sojourner Truth. In a large reform meeting, Truth sat among many able public speakers. One man, a lawyer speaking against the rights of women, in defiance of propriety, was wasting time by "distasteful and indelicate declamation." Some, thinking he would never end, left the meeting. Others, "distressed and mortified," silently endured. Just at the point when he was finally forced to pause to draw new breath, Truth, "groaning in spirit, raised her tall figure before him, and, putting her eyes upon him said, '*Child*, if de people has no whar to put it, what is de use? Sit down, child, *sit down!*' The man dropped as if he had been shot, and not another word was heard from him" (*Narrative* 149).

Titus tells another anecdote reported to her by a friend. In the period of the antislavery movement, Sojourner Truth was in the presence of a speaker whose address "appealed to the lowest sentiments of scurrilous and abusive" racial superlatives. "Alluding to the black race, he compared them to monkeys, baboons, and ourangoutangs [*sic*]." When he was about to close this inflammatory speech, Truth quietly drew near to the platform and whispered in the ear of the advocate of her people, "Don't dirty *your* hands wid dat critter; let *me* tend to him!" (149). The speaker knew it was safe to trust her. Straightening herself to full height, Truth said:

> Children, I am one of dem monkey tribes. I was born a slave. I had de dirty work to do—de scullion work. Now I am going to reply to dis critter (pointing her long, bony finger with withering scorn at the petty lawyer). Now in de course of my time I has done a great deal of dirty scullion work, but of all de dirty work I ever done, dis is de scullionist and de dirtiest.

She had taken the crowd by storm. "The whole audience shouted applause, and the negro-haters as heartily as any" (*Narrative* 149).

Sojourner Truth's public work included speeches for abolitionism, women's rights, and economic assistance for freed slaves after the war. She employed moral arguments, legal arguments, and used herself as example when discussing the condition of slaves, women, and former slaves. By critically examining these strategies in what exists as a fragment of her most famous and oft-quoted speech, "Ain't I A Woman," we can see how her rhetoric worked not as "seemingly random remarks," but as a well-integrated whole.

IV

Sojourner Truth delivered her most famous speech at the Women's Rights Convention in Akron, Ohio, on May 29, 1851. As previously noted, few black women were welcomed at these meetings, and Truth's presence was exceptional. She approached the platform before a hostile crowd of white men and white women, and employed all the available means of persuasion within her power.

Sojourner Truth began her speech by setting the tone with humor and goodwill; she presented herself as a calming mother figure: "Wall, children, whar dar is so much racket dar must be somethin' out of kilter."

As Karlyn Kohrs Campbell observes (435, emphasis in original), at the outset of her speech Sojourner Truth "acknowledged the potent combination abolitionism and woman's rights represented for white males": *"I tink dat 'twixt de niggers of the Souf and de womin at de Norf, all talkin' 'bout rights, de white men will be in a fix pretty soon."* Says Campbell, "As a whole, that speech was refutative, a response to claims that: (1) Women suffer no ill effects under current laws; (2) Women are intellectually inferior to men, thus requiring fewer opportunities; and (3) Woman's limited sphere was ordained by God. Her responses illustrate the power of enactment,[6] the force of metaphor, and the use of theology to respond to biblical justifications for woman's inferior position" (435).

Campbell continues the discussion by emphasizing what Sojourner Truth's biographers have already illustrated: she was herself an immediate and dramatic proof of the ills resulting from woman's position. Like other poor women, particularly poor slave women, Sojourner Truth's life had never been consonant with traditional nineteenth-century concepts of "womanliness" or "femininity." *"Dat man ober dar say dat womin needs to be helped into carriages, and lifted over ditches, and to hab de best places everywhar. Nobody eber helps me into carriages! And A'n't I a woman?"* She drew attention to herself: *"Look at me!"* she exclaimed. *"Look at my arm!"* "Moreover," says Campbell, "her life demonstrated women's physical prowess—she had done the most backbreaking farmwork so well that no man could do it better." *"I have ploughed and planted, and gathered into barns, and no man could head me."* For emphasis and dramatic effect, she repeated her refrain, *"And a'n't I a woman? And a'n't I a woman?"* "She called attention to the contradiction at the heart of slavery—the treatment of slave women, which wholly ignored their status as women and treated them as chattel, as breeding stock" (Campbell 435). *"I have borne thirteen childern, and seen 'em mos' all sold off to slavery, and when I cried out with my mother's grief, none but Jesus heard me! And a'n't I a woman."* By describing her experience as not just that of a slave, but also of a slave woman and slave mother, Sojourner Truth aroused the passion of her listeners. She appealed to the audience members—to their emotions—not as persons who held the reins of social power and justice, but as parents who would feel the same grief were their own children taken away. By including the reference to Jesus, she further established her Christian ethos. And according to Campbell, "Her response to claims of woman's intellectual inferiority evaded argument about women's mental capacity to affirm the right to equality of opportunity" (435). *"If my cup won't hold but a pint, and yours holds a*

quart, wouldn't you be mean not to let me have my little half-measure full?"
"Her response to theological justifications for 'woman's place' was
equally apt," says Campbell, "a dramatic version of the theological notion
that Mary wiped out Eve's curse": *"Then that little man in black there he
says women can't have as much rights as men, 'cause Christ wasn't a
woman! Where did your Christ come from? . . . From God and a woman!
Man had nothing to do wid Him."*

Truth ends the speech with what she considers a logical explanation
of women's entitlement to rights. "If de fust woman God ever made was
strong enough to turn de world upside down all alone, dese women
togedder ought to be able to turn it back, and get it right side up again!"
This is an abbreviated syllogism, which demonstrates Truth's wit as she
poked fun at the obvious weakness of man in the very "beginning." If
Adam let Eve "turn de world upside down all alone," then perhaps man
has never been as strong as he thinks he is, and women can't possibly
be as weak as men think they are. After all, Sojourner Truth boasted,
she was equal in strength and intellect to any man.

Sojourner Truth became extremely skillful in using ethos, logos, and
pathos along with her wit and straightforward manner to engage and
soften hostile crowds. Although she did not read or write, we know from
the fragments of her extant speeches and from the various documented
accounts of audience responses that Truth's practical public discourse
was effective, that her rhetoric did work as a unified whole.

On May 9, 1867, Sojourner Truth gave the third of her extant
speeches. It was a major address to the American Equal Rights Association in New York City. This was the post–Civil War period, a time of
division and regrouping in the women's movement. With the outbreak
of hostilities between North and South, northern prosuffrage women had
suspended activities on their own behalf to devote full energy to the
Union cause. In addition, the National Woman's Loyal League was
formed under the leadership of Susan B. Anthony, Elizabeth Cady Stanton, and others, in effect functioning as an arm of the Republican Party's
radical wing. In this capacity, the Woman's Loyal League collected hundreds of thousands of petition signatures calling for the immediate abolition of slavery.

However, when enfranchisement of black men only became the policy of the very faction of the Republican Party that the League had
worked to strengthen, the women's movement became bitterly divided.[7]
The proposed Fourteenth Amendment to the Constitution—adopted in
1866—gave Negroes the vote but omitted any reference to women, and

in its second section, actually introduced the word "male" into the Constitution for the first time. Stanton and Anthony felt betrayed, but their former abolitionist allies for the most part seemed resigned. It was widely held at the time that this was "the Negro's hour," and that women had no decent course available but to stand aside and wait their turn (Schneir 128).

Stanton and Anthony would not accept this premise and openly opposed the constitutional amendments that guaranteed suffrage to black men but not to women. Observes Miriam Schneir, "Both believed that this position was the only consistent one with their feminist principles" (129). Stanton, who had never before argued for women's rights on a racially imperialistic platform, expressed outrage that "inferior niggers" should be granted the vote while "superior" white women remained disenfranchised. So strong was her rage that she argued:

> If Saxon men have legislated thus for their own mothers, wives and daughters, what can we hope for at the hands of Chinese, Indians, and Africans? . . . I protest against the enfranchisement of another man of any race or clime until the daughters of Jefferson, Hancock, and Adams are crowned with their rights. (quoted in hooks 127)

Into this strife-torn atmosphere came Sojourner Truth to stand alone for the all but forgotten black woman. Her dedication to feminism and her political acumen were demonstrated in the speech she delivered in 1867 before the Equal Rights Association.

> There is a great stir about colored men getting their rights, and not a word about the colored women; and if colored men get their rights, and not the colored women theirs, you see the colored men will be masters over the women, and it will be just as bad as it was before. So I am for keeping the thing going while things are stirring; because if we wait till it is still, it will take a great while to get going again. (Quoted in Stanton 2:193)

Truth was intelligent enough to understand that in a society built on both racial and sexual hierarchy, the only way black males would ever feel they had any real power would be to exercise control over black women. Furthermore, history proved Sojourner Truth correct in her second assertion, "If we wait till it is still, it will take a great while to get going again." It was not until 1920 that women were finally granted the right to vote in this country.

Other topics dominated Sojourner Truth's later career. She was very much concerned with the fate of freed Negroes after the Civil War—where would they live and how could they become self-sufficient? During the Civil War she witnessed the "affliction of her people" in Washington, D.C., and "desiring to mitigate their sufferings," she found homes and employment for many in Northern states" (*Narrative* 191). However, while working for the Freedman's Bureau (1864–1866) in Arlington, Virginia, she decided that the federal government should play a more significant role in reconstruction than it was doing. As Olive Gilbert paraphrased Sojourner Truth's views in the *Narrative*, "Justice demanded that government take efficient legislative action in the interest of these people. Nations anxiously watching the scales in which this government and its dependent millions must be weighed, waited to render their verdict" (193).

As she looked upon the imposing public edifices that graced the District of Columbia, all built at the nation's expense, Sojourner Truth noted that blacks had helped to pay the cost. The slaves had been a source of wealth to the republic.

> Our labor supplied the country with cotton, until villages and cities dotted the enterprising North for its manufacture, and furnished employment and support for a multitude, thereby becoming a revenue to the government. Beneath a burning southern sun have we toiled, in the canebrake and the rice swamp, urged on by the merciless driver's lash, earning millions of money; and so highly were we valued there, that should one poor wretch venture to escape from this hell of slavery, no exertion of man or trained blood-hound was spared to seize and return him to his field of unrequited labor. (*Narrative* 197)

According to Truth, one solution to Washington's problems of high unemployment, a growing welfare system, crime, and poverty—exacerbated by the influx of freed slaves from neighboring Virginia and Maryland—was to designate lands "out west" for the Negro. She knew that the United States owned countless acres of unoccupied land, which by cultivation would become a source of wealth to the nation. She was also aware that some of the land was being used to build railroads, and that large reservations had been apportioned to the Indians. "Why not give a tract of land to those colored people who would rather become independent through their own exertions than longer clog the wheels of government?" (197). Sojourner Truth felt that if the freed slaves could be educated and trained to support themselves, there eventually would be no need for large welfare payments. The government could put "welfare" money to other, more productive, use in rebuilding the country after the Civil War.

In her last years of traveling and lecturing, Truth canvassed the nation, gathering signatures for a petition (which she would later submit to Congress) in support of legislation that would give the freed slaves land out west. It was this concern that she brought before the public on January 1, 1871, at the Commemoration of the Eighth Anniversary of Negro Freedom in the United States. This speech, given at Tremont Temple in Boston, is recognized as her last extant address. Sojourner Truth was now more than eighty years old, and while Janey Montgomery claims that Truth never used pathos as a means of persuasion, we see in this speech her use of pathos at its best.

> I was born a slave in the State of New York, Ulster County, 'mong de low Dutch. W'en I was ten years old, I couldn't speak a word of Inglish, an' hab no education at all. When my master died we was goin' to hab an auction. We was all brought up to be sole. My mother an' my fader was very ole, my brudder younger 'em myself, an' my mother took my hand. Dey opened a canopy up even, and my mother sat down and I and my brudder sat next to her. We were they only two children left, for dere was a great number ob us, an' was all sole away befor'. . . . I know what it is to be taken into the barn an' tied up an' de blood drawed out ob yere bare back. . . . Now this is de question dat I am here tonight to say. Colud people been degraded enough. Dat de colud pepul dat is in Washi'ton libin on de government dat de United States ort to giv' 'em land and move 'em on it and it would be a benefit for you all. (*Narrative* 213–15)

After stirring the emotions of the crowd, playing on its sympathy in an effort to get signatures, Sojourner Truth concluded her speech by announcing that she had spoken these words because she wanted everyone to know exactly why they should sign the petition when it came around. Olive Gilbert explains, "Being convinced of the feasibility and justice of this plan, she hastened to present her petition to the public, and solicit signatures" (*Narrative* 198).[8]

VI

Sojourner Truth's public speaking career was extensive: it took her from New York as far west as Kansas and from Maine as far south as Virginia. Her efforts to free southern slaves, procure rights for women, and improve the lot of freed slaves spanned some forty years. She met many people and touched many lives in her unique way. Since she never learned to read or write, we are grateful for the *Narrative of Sojourner Truth*, which is the only known collective personal account of her life's work. With its publications in 1850, 1853, 1875, 1887, 1881, and 1884, it has been instrumental in assuring her immortality.

Sojourner Truth's life was founded on her own concepts of moral character and Christianity as she interpreted the Scriptures. As a skilled practitioner in the art of public speaking, she did not develop a formal theory of language; she did, however, call for a spirit that was uniquely woman's. When retelling the following story about Mary near Jesus' tomb, she related the message to all women.

> And when the men went to look for Jesus at the sepulchre they didn't stop long enough to find out whether he was there or not; but Mary stood there and waited and said to Him, thinking it was the gardener, "Tell me where they have laid him and I will carry him away." See what a spirit there is. Just so let women be true to this spirit and the truth will reign triumphant. (Stanton 2:222)

Truth deeply believed that women had by nature a kind and patient spirit. Women were not greedy, but wanted only what was due them. "We are trying for liberty that required no bloodshed—that women have their rights—not rights from you" (Stanton 2:225).

Sojourner Truth was not simply a ceremonial speaker—a preacher, an evangelist—as some have described her. She was, instead, speaking to bring about social and political change for slaves, women, and former slaves through legislation. Her practical public discourse, her lifelong commitment to communication on public problems, has justly earned Sojourner Truth a place in the history of deliberative rhetoric.

NOTES

1. In a 1968 dissertation, Janey Weinhold Montgomery does attempt a rhetorical analysis of parts of Sojourner Truth's speeches. Montgomery does not,

however, forthrightly conclude that Sojourner Truth was a rhetorician, one skilled in the art of persuasion.

2. Although Sojourner Truth lectured over a forty-year period, no complete texts exist. Only four fragmentary texts of her speeches are extant. Her early speeches against slavery were not recorded, and the speeches that are extant primarily represent Sojourner Truth's views on women's rights. They are: (1) 1851, Address to the Women's Rights Convention, Akron, Ohio; (2) 1853, Address to the Mob Convention, New York City; (3) 1867, Address to the American Equal Rights Association Convention, New York City; and (4) 1871, delivered in Boston, an Address of Commemoration on the Eighth Anniversary of Negro Freedom in the United States.

3. While bell hooks makes this strong claim, the attitude was not held by all white women of the period; women such as Lydia Marie Child and others had a different view on this issue.

4. S. Michael Halloran, "Rhetoric in the American College Curriculum," 257. Other examples of histories that assume a "break" or "decline" of the classical rhetorical tradition in the nineteenth century include Robert J. Connors, Lisa S. Ede, and Andrea A. Lunsford 1–15. But see also Nan Johnson for a different view.

5. Increasingly, rhetorical theorists and historians have begun to acknowledge the importance of understanding implicit theories residing in the communication practices of nonacademicians (for a thorough listing, see Oravec 396–97).

6. Enactment is a reflexive rhetorical form in which the speaker incarnates the argument, is the proof of what is said. For a more detailed discussion, see Campbell and Jamieson 9–11.

7. Giddings notes that the feminist and abolitionist camps were not neatly divided. Leading white feminists such as Lucy Stone and Julia Ward Howe did not believe that the world would come to an end if black men—whose leadership was sympathetic to woman suffrage and promised to work toward that end—were enfranchised first.

8. A highlight of Sojourner Truth's career was her interview with Abraham Lincoln. Although she allegedly addressed the Senate at this time, no speech was recorded in *The Congressional Globe*. There is no evidence that Congress ever acted on her petition to move freed slaves to lands out west.

REFERENCES

Arnhart, Larry. *Aristotle on Political Reasoning*. DeKalb: Northern Illinois UP, 1981.

Baskerville, Barnet. "Principal Themes of Nineteenth-Century Critics of Oratory." *Speech Monographs* 19 (March 1952): 11–26.

Bitzer, Lloyd. "Rhetoric and Public Knowledge." *Rhetoric, Philosophy, and Literature*. Ed. Don Burks. West Lafayette: Purdue UP, 1978.

Campbell, Karlyn Kohrs. "Style and Content in the Rhetoric of Early Afro-American Feminists." *QJS* 72 (1986): 434–45.

Campbell, Karlyn Kohrs, and Kathleen Hall Jamieson, eds. *Form and Genre: Shaping Rhetorical Action.* Falls Church, VA: The Speech Communication Association, 1978.

Chambers, Stephen, and G. P. Mohrmann. "Rhetoric in Some American Periodicals." *Speech Monographs* 37 (June 1970): 111–20.

Connors, Robert C., Lisa S. Ede, and Andrea A. Lunsford. *Essays on Classical Rhetoric and Modern Discourse.* Carbondale: Southern Illinois UP, 1984.

Fauset, Arthur. *Sojourner Truth, God's Faithful Pilgrim.* Chapel Hill: U of North Carolina P, 1938.

Giddings, Paula. *When and Where I Enter: The Impact of Black Women on Race and Sex in America.* New York: Bantam, 1984.

Gilbert, Olive. *Narrative of Sojourner Truth.* Boston, 1850.

Halloran, S. Michael. "Rhetoric in the American College Curriculum: The Decline of Public Discourse." *PRE/TEXT* 3 (1983): 245–69.

hooks, bell. *Ain't I A Woman: Black Women and Feminism.* Boston: South End, 1981.

Johnson, Nan. *Nineteenth-Century Rhetoric in North America.* Carbondale: Southern Illinois UP, 1991.

Kennicott, Patrick. "Black Persuaders in the Anti-slavery Movement." *Speech Monographs* 37 (March 1970): 15–24.

Montgomery, Janey Weinhold. *A Comparison of Two Negro Women Orators.* Diss. Fort Hays Kansas State College, 1968.

Notable American Women, 1607–1950. Cambridge: Bellknap Press, 1971.

Oravec, Christine. "The Democratic Critics: An Alternative American Rhetorical Tradition in the Nineteenth Century." *Rhetorica* 4 (fall 1986): 395–422.

Pauli, Hertha. *Her Name Was Sojourner Truth.* New York, 1962.

Schneir, Miriam, ed. *Feminism: The Essential Historical Writings.* New York: Random House, 1972.

Stanton, Elizabeth Cady, et al. *History of Woman Suffrage.* 6 vols. Rochester, 1887.

Titus, Frances W. *Narrative of Sojourner; With a History of Her Labors and Correspondence Drawn from Her "Book of Life."* Boston: Published for the Author, 1875.

13

The Telling: Laura (Riding) Jackson's Project for a Whole Human Discourse

James Oldham

What is not clear is what is clear.
—Laura Riding, "Cure of Ignorance"

One of our primary "discoveries" in the late twentieth century has been the ultimate dependence of human beings and their activities upon language. Language has come to be seen as the medium in which human intercourse is conducted, its sheer power determining not only our conceptions but also our perceptions. In the most extreme versions of this story, language itself, or its persona, "text," becomes the sole agent of human activity, endlessly flowing through human subjectivities that feel they exist but are "really" only the artifacts of language. The Cartesian formula for this might be, "Language thinks me, therefore 'I' is not," language taking the place of Descartes's evil tempter who, from some obscure motive, sought to fool the philosopher into believing that the philosopher's mind, and the world that mind perceived, actually existed. In the bleakest view, the human (so called) is a fiction inscribed by language upon hapless, animate slates.

Relatively unscathed by the discovery of this intertextual polyverse, rhetoric lately has been recovered as a way of understanding how people do things, and have things done to them, with words. As rhetoricians have known since they first named their art, it is possible for a skilled speaker to persuade an audience that the worse case is the better and the better case the worse. To put it more bluntly, rhetoric can make the false seem true. While some rhetoricians have rejoiced at the license rhetoric apparently affords them, others, including some who would reject the title "rhetorician," have sought to discipline rhetoric and make it solely a tool for presenting Truth. Interpreted as a discussion of rhetoric, Laura (Riding) Jackson's *The Telling* (1972) provides a powerful example of this tendency to yoke human language to truth telling. Expanding on an earlier essay on human language and discourse, in *The Telling* Jackson presents her view that human language is not only the messenger but also the message; according to Jackson, "telling" is the only means by which we can preserve our own integrity and the integrity of the world. While Jackson does not identify *The Telling* as a rhetoric, I argue here that her work offers the ground for a strong theory of epideictic rhetoric, understood not as empty display but as the ground of human discourse.

I

Born in 1901 in New York City, Laura (Riding) Jackson began publishing poetry, fiction, and criticism in the 1920s. She published Gertrude Stein, was published by Djuna Barnes, and was quickly recognized by peers such as Allen Tate and W. H. Auden. Auden called her "the only living philosophical poet," a remark she received less as a compliment than as a pigeonhole (*Poems* 410). A brilliant critic, she deserves at least partial credit for developing the method of close reading employed by William Empson in *Seven Types of Ambiguity* and generally adopted by the New Criticism.[1] Her critical work, together with her poetry and fiction, await sustained scholarly attention.[2]

During the 1920s and 1930s, Jackson developed a theory of poetry as the ultimate medium for the expression of truth. "A poem," she wrote in 1938, "is an uncovering of truth of so fundamental and general a kind that no other name besides poetry is adequate except truth" (*Poems* 407). Jackson later renounced poetry because she felt that it distracted from truth through its focus on the author's unique personality and on its properties of style and form. Jackson saw this renunciation as a positive step through which she could further "the general human ideal in speaking ... [and solve] the universal problem of how to make words fulfill the human being and the human being fulfill words" (Riding, *Selected*

15). To this end of fulfilling human language and human being, Jackson wrote *The Telling*.

"The Telling" was first published as an essay in *Chelsea* in 1967. In 1972 that essay was republished (with revisions) in a book of the same title, this time with additional material, including a "Preface for a Second Reading" and material based on Jackson's correspondence with readers of the *Chelsea* essay. "The Telling" consists of sixty-two numbered sections, each one a single paragraph generally less than a page in length. This sequence is preceded by a two-paragraph preface, entitled "Nonce Preface," and is followed by four paragraphs, each one enclosed within parentheses. These four final paragraphs are followed in turn by the "Preface for a Second Reading" and the other material Jackson added in 1972, which approximately triples the length of the text.[3]

While Jackson's reputation is based primarily on her literary works of the 1920s and 1930s, in *The Telling* she presents a vision of human discourse that has parallels with other modern theories of language and rhetoric. She adopts a broadly philosophical view of language, placing it at the center of our identity as human beings. In her view, language is central to what we know as the human; in this, she seems to be in broad agreement with many modern thinkers. She distinguishes herself, however, by calling on us to exercise self-discipline in our use of language and by asserting that language has a purpose, which we should recognize, respect, and seek to fulfill, namely, "the articulation of our humanness" (70). In Jackson's view, language is neither a solipsistic trap nor a prison that cuts us off from reality. Instead, it is the means by which human beings can tell the story of their own Being and of their place in the larger reality that engenders and sustains them. For Jackson, it is not enough simply to accept the idea that we are defined as human beings by our use of language. Beyond that bald fact, she insists, we are both able and obligated to use language honestly and well, and language is the only means we have to keep faith with one another and with our common being.

In correspondence of 1988 and 1989, Jackson indicated to me that she would not herself term *The Telling* a rhetoric. In fact, in the book she uses "rhetoric" in the pejorative sense common in our culture.[4] Such critiques of deceptive persuasion are an integral part of the rhetorical tradition. In the *Phaedrus*, one of the earliest and most widely known of these critiques, Plato condemns the rhetorical practice of his time as a false art, even as he reaches out for a discourse that would avoid the perceived distortions and dangers of rhetoric by grounding the rhetor in perfect knowledge of an absolute, incorruptible reality. Like Plato, Jackson envisions an absolutely true mode of discourse. Her view is distinguished from Plato's, however, both by her fundamental optimism about the value of our language and by her sense that something crucial is at stake in the human use of language, both for human beings and for the larger reality from which human existence derives.

Certainly *The Telling* is not a rhetoric in the Aristotelian model, a handbook for finding all the available means of persuasion in a given situation. It has more in common with Isocrates's approach, in which rhetoric is viewed as fundamental to human judgment and action. Although it differs from these and other rhetorics on various questions, *The Telling* is concerned with issues fundamental to rhetoric: the centrality of language to human existence, the problem of the rhetor's character and method, the role of values in rhetoric, and the problems raised by specialist discourses for any general theory of human discourse. In Jackson's thought, all these topics are related to her understanding of gender and her vision of a world in which women and men are collaborators in the project of telling.

II

In *The Telling*, Jackson writes: "We have language, all, as a gift from one another for going apace with one another in advancing into our Subject" (70). This statement contains three ideas about language that are essential both to *The Telling* and to Jackson's thought in general. First, there is the immanence of language in human culture. Second, there is the purpose of language: its proper use, according to Jackson, is to improve our collective understanding by "advancing into our Subject," that of Being, including human being.[5] Third, there is the appreciation we owe one another for the gift of language and thus of our humanity, an appreciation Jackson believes we can best express through discourse that affirms our existence and our integral role in Being. These points are axiomatic for Jackson; she neither apologizes nor directly argues for them, although she does criticize discourses she sees as violating or undermining these principles.

In *The Telling*, Jackson assumes that all human beings derive ultimately from the same source, a source she terms "Being." Being, for Jackson, is not a transcendent entity or realm, as it is, for example, in Plato's work. Instead, Jackson's concept of Being is generally synonymous with the universe (understood as all that exists), a physical universe whose animating spirit is manifest in the human mind (28). Finding ourselves in possession of these spiritual manifestations of Being, it is our responsibility to recognize and articulate it, its value, and our place within it. Jackson calls this activity of recognition and expression "telling"; human beings, as recipients of Being and the creators of language, are the only real candidates for telling. Jackson concurs with other contemporary theorists in seeing discourse as a powerful influence on human beings, but she differs from many of her contemporaries in asserting not only that there is a single, comprehensive reality, but also that our experience of that reality is not determined by language and that our primary obligation as human beings is to ensure that our use of language is true to that reality. As I interpret Jackson, the highest human calling is to experience truth and to reflect that truth to other human beings through language. Rather than declaring the world itself a fiction and human experience nothing more than a web of words, Jackson assumes that we shape our own and others' understanding of the world through the fictions we create. She asks, however, that we make our fictions true to Being, and her standards for those fictions are high.

III

At the center of Jackson's rhetoric in *The Telling* is what I will call here a philosophical view of ethos: the way a speaker presents herself and the effect that presentation has on an audience. Rhetoricians have long recognized the crucial role that the speaker's character, as perceived by the audience, plays in influencing that audience. Rather than making a trivial contribution to persuasion, according to Aristotle, ethos can "almost" be called the most important means of persuasion when compared with logos, the appeal to reason, and with pathos, the appeal to emotion (25). Rather than appealing to the audience's reason or emotions, ethos persuades by meshing the audience's values with the speaker's apparent character. A cynical speaker who understands an audience's values can deliberately present a "self" that will persuade, even when that speaker knows that the presented self is at odds with the real self. For what I will call here strategic rhetoric, it is enough, as Nan Johnson puts it, that the speaker project "the appearance of goodness"; for philosophical rhetoric, on the other hand, "the reality of a speaker's virtue is . . . a prerequisite to effective speaking" (99).[6]

For Jackson this debate over ethos is not a particularly complex problem. While she rejects the idea that the self should be manipulated in order to persuade an audience, this is only secondarily because such manipulation is "unethical." For Jackson, the primary reason that a speaker's ethos should not be willfully distorted is that telling can occur only if the speaker recovers and expresses her essential self. This essential self Jackson terms the self of the "Whole," the self that is shared with all other selves and that contains a knowledge of its own Being (24). Within Jackson's system, a new effort at "telling" is necessary because the true self has already been distorted. For human beings, such distortion is the fundamental problem and the root of all other problems that human beings face. From Jackson's point of view in *The Telling*, further distortion of that true self could never lead to a positive outcome.

This self-distorting self is analogous to the manipulative view of ethos recognized by strategic rhetoric. According to Jackson, such a self does not identify with all other human beings; instead it sees its own needs and even its own identity as self-generated, autonomous, and opposed to any common good. In her "Outline," which immediately precedes "The Telling" proper, Jackson distinguishes sharply between this greedy, "self-claiming" self and its opposite, a "human-souled," "speaking self" of Being, one that is conscious of its common identity with other selves (6). Both types of selves speak, but the greedy self is "garrulous" and speaks to satisfy its needs, while the human-souled self speaks because it recognizes both Being's need to be spoken of and our need to so speak. In Jackson's view, the self a speaker presents must be one with the speaker's true self; any dissembling for the ends of persuasion is playing that true self false.

The greedy self Jackson describes is "selfish" in the common sense of the word; as a type, it recognizes neither the good of the whole nor the importance of its own speech. It uses words simply to get things. The human-souled self is aware not only of its own being, but also of the larger Being that extends beyond itself; in "telling," it seeks to articulate the larger Being on which its own being depends. To speak to another from within this ethos is not to conceal one's true nature but to reveal it by addressing, within oneself and within one's audience, the Being that speaker and audience share. For Jackson, speaking from one's true self is essential to effective discourse.

IV

Jackson does not set out in *The Telling* to offer a systematic rhetorical method, yet the idea of method is integral to what she intends: "The method [of telling] is in the assumption by each of the task" (59). Given her view of the task, rhetorical method is both essential and superfluous. Method is superfluous because the primary content of the discourse already exists: it need not be created but only remembered. Method is essential, however, because the speaker must articulate these memories through language, and language can be mismanaged and thereby distort one's meaning (59–62). The teller's method must also help her to recover and represent her memory of original Being, and it should help her to avoid competing with others to tell better than they do. Jackson admits implicitly that there is some art of rhetoric that allows individuals to "prevail" in "catching the ears of others" (55); she suggests that such individuals are blinded by selfish ambition. Jackson's method is not intended to gain fame for the speaker at the expense of the audience and the subject.

As in many discussions of rhetoric, the most important part of Jackson's method is invention, the discovery and development of the matter of the discourse. In telling, the sought-after content is the story of human beings' origin in the origin of all Being and of their ongoing existence. Jackson's means for recovering this story are memory, imagination, and reason. Of the three, memory is primary, with imagination and reason serving to balance it. Invoking an ideal realm similar to that portrayed in Socrates's second speech in the *Phaedrus*, Jackson asks us to remember what she calls "the Before," a time "back beyond one's physical ancestors, and beyond the entire material ancestry of our bodies" (25). By recovering this origin, Jackson says, we will be able to overcome false stories of our Being, stories that begin not in unity but in separation, stories that divide and that end in division. "In describing the memory, I refer to what I find in me that belongs to me not in my simple present personhood but in my intricate personless identity with all that has preceded me to the farthest, timeless reach of not-me" (25). Each of us, Jackson says, contains an individual vestige of this original identity, but before we can tell it, we must recover it through memory. "To save ourselves we must save our souls, to save ourselves we must *find* our souls" (35).

Memory is not wholly adequate for telling, however; according to Jackson, attention to our past must be balanced with imagination and reason so that we do not miss the present and the future. By imagination, Jackson seems to intend the common sense of the word, the ability to envision what is not immediately visible or empirically verifiable; deserted by reason, imagination leads to delusion (59–60). By reason, she seems to mean human intelligence in general rather than any external technique; for her, the primary evidence and exercise of reason resides in our understanding and use of language (35–36). For Jackson, both imagination and reason are native faculties, part of our essential humanity, and not to be distrusted.

She herself identifies her method as diction, a term she employs in a broader sense than that in common use. For Jackson, "diction" is "the use of words with attentive regard for their individual rational nature" (70); neither obeying nor flaunting grammarians' rules will produce good diction.[7] The meanings of words can be rationally understood, Jackson says, and since reason is universal, a product of our being, it is at least within our power to arrive at common definitions of words and to use them so that others understand them. It is important to recognize that Jackson is not claiming that a word's meaning is immanent within the word. To use language truly is an ongoing effort, but this effort is certainly worthy of our attention. If our foremost intention is to be understood and to understand, Jackson insists, we will find ourselves capable of expressing meanings and receiving meanings through words. By using our words in accordance with their rational meanings, we fulfill the human rationality that lies immanent in human language. For Jackson, language is both the beginning and the end of rationality. By using words rationally, we can fulfill reason and thereby achieve the good (69–70).

V

In his lectures on rhetoric, Aristotle named a set of three contrasting kinds of rhetoric: forensic, deliberative, and epideictic. It is epideictic rhetoric that I believe is most usefully illuminated by *The Telling*. Defined narrowly, epideictic rhetoric has been limited to ceremonial discourse of praise and blame, speeches appropriate for ceremonial orations such as funeral orations or speeches promoting or criticizing public figures (Woodson 21). Defined more broadly by several modern rhetoricians, epideictic discourse focuses on the moment in which the speaker and audience find themselves joined, a moment for taking stock and celebrating the communal values present in the occasion—or, when appropriate, for decrying their absence. In the sense in which I apply the term to *The Telling*, the "epideictic" is the discourse that calls us to remember our common origin, common being, and common destiny. Because epideictic rhetoric makes it possible for us to share our awareness of common Being, it offers a foundation for all of our discourse.

Within Aristotle's framework, the "epideictic" serves as the temporal complement of forensic and deliberative discourse. Forensic rhetoric, the discourse of the courtroom, takes as its temporal focus the events of the past and argues about their meaning. Deliberative rhetoric, the discourse of the legislature, focuses on the future, arguing about what policies should be pursued. Within Aristotle's system, at least as it has generally been interpreted, epideictic rhetoric is denigrated as discourse that is relevant to neither past nor future and that consists of speeches that are ceremonial, empty of content, and "rhetorical" in the most pejorative sense of the word.

The term "epideictic" itself has been translated as "display," and is commonly understood as the orator's self-display of her own rhetorical powers, but the suggestion of self-aggrandizement and empty puffery is unnecessary, as several rhetoricians have recently pointed out. According to Kenneth Duffy, epideictic rhetoric was for Plato not trivial but was rather the mode of discourse that demonstrates the possibility of combining philosophy and rhetoric (87). Christine Oravec, in her essay on Aristotle's theory of the epideictic, argues that epideictic oratory displays not only the speaker's skill but also the speaker's virtue and the quality of the subject itself (168). The speaker acknowledges, praises, or possibly disparages the subject's qualities, bringing them into relation with values which are, or should be, held by the audience. In Oravec's view, the epideictic has a significant public function, that of bringing to the audience's attention both their common values and their community as locus of those values (172–73). In this view, the epideictic becomes the necessary basis for all other forms of discourse, since neither forensic nor deliberative rhetoric can be effective unless the speaker and audience share a set of basic values that motivate them to evaluate the past or to create a plan for the future. According to Aristotle, the basic value and ultimate motivation for any audience is the Good, the meaning of which is located in the individual's happiness (37). For Jackson, our ultimate motivation should be the happiness of the Whole, a happiness we can achieve only through bringing our attention to Being, the only source of the Good. We can bring our attention to Being only by telling; Jackson's concept of telling, as I interpret it here, proposes that the epideictic be adopted universally as the foundation of all discourse.

Tracing the history of the term, Lawrence Rosenfield suggests that epideictic discourse, the "speech in honor of excellence," should be redefined. More than conferring value upon the subject, the epideictic orator acknowledges the essential value of the subject and calls upon the audience to join in recognizing that value. According to Rosenfield, true epideictic rhetoric refuses the temptation to cater to the audience's assumptions and never simply repeats the obvious. Instead, it attempts to bring the audience to recognize anew "Being's radiance." Rosenfield argues that such an approach to discourse may be antiagonistic and antipragmatic, but it is not therefore meaningless, for nothing can be more important to humanity than recognition of existence and our place in it. "A life consumed in projects prevents us from glimpsing the eternity of ever-present (though veiled) Being" (Rosenfield 137). Rosenfield's essay shows that there is space within rhetorical theory for an expansive, ontologically based view of the epideictic and of rhetoric as a whole. Within Aristotle's triad of the forensic, the epideictic, and the deliberative, for example, both the first and the last modes refer necessarily to the present and to the audience's common values to create arguments and to establish their appeals. There is no reason to punish a crime or initiate a policy unless the speaker, the audience, and the society at large share allegiance to concepts that justify these actions. In epideictic discourse, we are called upon as a community to remember what we have in common; the speaker speaks now for all of us, and, ideally, any of us might be the speaker.

The Telling is both a theory and an instance of epideictic rhetoric; that is, while Jackson defines and instructs us in telling, she is herself simultaneously telling. As a theory of epideictic discourse, *The Telling* suggests methods for invention and presentation, discusses a variety of appeals to the audience, and conveys an overall justification of its assumptions and values. As an instance of epideictic discourse, *The Telling* engages us in epideictic discourse in order to persuade us that we, too, should engage in epideictic discourse. Jackson addresses us on a subject of fundamental importance and tries to bring us to recognize the importance of that subject. She does not argue that we should adopt her whole understanding, but speaks to and for us, at the same time encouraging us to remember and recount our own stories of Being. If she succeeds in her purpose, Jackson will move us to recognize the importance of telling and enable us to adopt it ourselves.

VI

Even as epideictic discourse praises its subjects, it is also responsible for appropriately criticizing and disparaging those subjects, and in the epideictic of *The Telling* such criticism plays an important role.[8] Jackson criticizes the various special disciplines for being "man-minded" (18), bringing to her audience's attention the flaws and limits of what she terms the various "truth-telling professions": science, religion, history, poetry, and philosophy (11). A significant portion of *The Telling* is occupied by Jackson's critique of these discourses, and one basic internal pattern of the essay is a movement from positive statement about Being and the project of telling to disparagement or heavily qualified approval of each of these professional discourses.

While she treats each field individually, these professions share the fault of being "man-minded," Jackson says. Each of them sees itself as constituting, at least potentially, a complete statement of the truth, and each of them attempts to establish itself as the whole story of Being. None of these professions "gives us ourselves," however; "rather, each story-kind steals us to make its reality of us" (5). These discourses are more loyal to themselves than they are to the whole; all of them fail to recognize that they depend, radically and ultimately, on the human capacity to produce, understand, and care about discourse.

Science, for example, as the explanation of matter and life forms, "cannot be the explanation of ourselves," because we are qualitatively different from the topics it treats; rather than scientists' stories explaining human beings, Jackson says, the human story explains science (9). The success of science in gaining specialized knowledge has created the illusion that it can give us general knowledge of ourselves and our collective existence, or even that it can sweep away as illusory human experiences of meaning and value (2). Jackson's critique of science is to some degree a critique of the empirical method, but her primary challenge is to science's loyalty to that method, a loyalty that prevents it from recognizing that the knowledge it gains is inadequate to explain the spirit within us that finds current knowledge insufficient and that quests after further knowledge.

Traditional religious stories also fail to explain us, Jackson says, despite their appeal to many who are attentive to the question of our being, because these stories blindfold our reason rather than expanding it. While the men who told these stories were of "honest purpose," they were also "more man-minded than human-minded" (18). Nonetheless, Jackson says, we should be grateful to the religions for continuing to remind us that without knowledge of our origin in Being we will lose ourselves.

If religion falls short of explaining our existence, politics, especially antireligious politics, falls still shorter for Jackson. Discourses that locate the truth of our existence in some material-historical struggle lose sight of the "deep natural past" out of which we have come (19). Jackson is explicitly anti-Marxist on this point, arguing that the socioeconomic class to which one belongs is not the deepest identity one possesses. Such a limited identity can only make us forget our common origin in a deeper past (20). Neither can history clearly explain us: its deepest past is too shallow, and it offers no vision that can tell us truly what we are, where we come from, or where we will go. For many years Jackson believed poetry is, or should be, the perfect truth-telling discourse, and her argument with poetry and poets runs through many of her works. Poetry fails us, she says, because it draws our attention to the tellers and the forms of their telling more than to what they tell (11).

Philosophy, Jackson says, has made a worthy attempt at telling the story of our being in Being, a story that extends from the beginning, through the present, and beyond to whatever ultimate future will come. Each philosopher, however, has "the voice of *a* time," not the voice of all time (12). Jackson grants that philosophy has carried the impulse to speak truth, universal and eternal, but because the philosopher typically tries to create a coherent whole from his limited point of view and impose it on others through argument, rather than speak his sense as one to all, "the philosopher's whole is always a mortal enlargement of a mortal part" (12). Even the truest philosophers have been limited by insisting on the universal application of their personal insights.

Jackson holds up for special disparagement what she calls "the new hybrid scientific-philosophic thinking," a phrase that seems to refer to logical positivism and suggests modern linguistics in particular. This hybrid of science and philosophy, she says, "threw out the human substance in words and made them subject to a weird logic of physicality, as if we the speakers and orderers of words had died, all, but left the words behind; and then threw out philosophy itself, using against it to prove it foolish a false scientific sagacity in matters of words" (12). According to Jackson, such self-designated philosophers delude themselves into thinking that their denial of thought can be a triumph of thought when it is actually a refusal to think beyond the microcosmic and mechanical. Such "philosophy" denies the general breadth of human intelligence, including our imagination, intuition, sensibility, and the spirit that Jackson sees as vital to the ongoing human project of posing questions and seeking answers to them. The proposition, upheld by such self-designated "philosophers," that human beings can neither intend nor communicate meanings through language is, according to Jackson, a betrayal of the philosophical tradition, which, whatever its inadequacies, never attempted to substitute passive observation of phenomena for the effort to reason about philosophical problems and to communicate its insights clearly.

The attempt to use philosophy to deny linguistic meaning or to reduce human beings to mechanically determined objects is an evasion and a "counsel of sin," a "discontinuance of the journey to the meeting-point where beings have a debt to pay to Being in true words spoken of themselves to one another" (14). According to Jackson, there is something more to being than mere abject existence; there is articulation, representation, reiteration, remembrance of existence, and the expression of communal and whole joy. Any discourse that claims to present truth about humanity by stripping our humanity from us and reducing us to things must be false. None of the specialist discourses "gives us ourselves; rather, each story-kind steals us to make its reality of us" (11). The proponents of these discourses are more loyal to their own disciplines than they are to the whole human community.

The important role that Jackson's critique of various discourses plays in her own telling lends support to the idea, promoted by various poststructuralist thinkers, that no discourse can constitute itself as pure, positive assertion, isolated and insulated from other discourses and ideologies. If *The Telling* is itself an exemplary instance of telling, as Jackson apparently intends it to be, then telling, as a process of discourse, must be more complex than simply repudiating other discourses and asserting positive, unquestionable "truth." While Jackson does not explicitly recognize her indebtedness to the discourses she criticizes, her text is structurally dependent upon them. Without them to oppose, her positive assertions about telling and Being would lose much of their meaning and force; by bringing them into her discourse, she has added to their meaning and to her own. The overall sense of *The Telling* is that, fundamentally, we are more alike than different, that without common success no individual can achieve much, and that we cannot achieve this common success without using language in a mutual effort of understanding and support. Discourses that lose sight of our essential commonality will always be false to the community on which they depend for their existence.

VII

All genuine epideictic discourse, from Pericles's Funeral Oration to the Gettysburg Address to *The Telling*, is based on a speaker's felt need to urge an audience to recognize and return to lost or threatened values, to redouble our efforts, to become again our true or better selves. In the case of *The Telling*, Jackson urges us to recognize the threat to our own collective being that is perpetrated by "male-minded" discourses and to overcome the silence in which these discourses have wrapped our story. Here she speaks especially to women, who have been, she says, "most mute" (45). The story of women, according to Jackson, is a story within the story of Being; because of the way women have endured in silence, they are the personification of unrecognized Being. Jackson calls for women to turn toward Being and speech. Women, she says, have endured their silence because there was nothing in the discourses men created to draw them in. Women's silence paid more homage to Being than their participation would have done, although this silence, she adds, was no more adequate than the discourse of men.

If interpreted literally, the passivity that Jackson attributes to women is troubling, especially if read into the history of the feminist movement. In Jackson's account, having chosen their silence, women now wait passively for men to recognize the incompleteness of their own voices and to ask women to join in discourse. When read within or as a type of the larger story that Jackson describes in *The Telling*, however, women and men become figures of Being and human discourse, respectively. The healing act of telling then becomes a reunion of Being and discourse in which the "man-part" of ourselves finally understands the incompleteness of its discourse and lowers its voice to ask the woman-part to join it in discourse, and "thus shall the woman-part and man-part make each other free" (47).[9] This reunion will occur in what Jackson calls the "After," but in the interval those who understand will "[speak] to one another with the constant reason of confirming Being in one another" (52), because there is nothing else left to do. Jackson announces here, on the final pages of the essay, a great crisis in Being, one in which there are only two choices: to continue foolishly in inadequacy and falsity, or to join together with those who understand telling (52–54).

The Telling is a challenging work for a contemporary audience: this would probably be true in any time, and to no small degree Jackson wants it to be difficult. What is compelling about Jackson's project, however, is what it "tells": it reminds us of what we as a species need to believe, of what must be true, and of how we must meet one another if we are to overcome our habit of insisting on the triumph of our differences. If we do not believe that we are, at our core, one kind of being, one Being together, then we have only selfish reasons for survival, and no reason to be concerned for one another's existence. If we do believe that we are one people, and that our common good is the only good we can know, then we have a rational basis for discourse that confirms that universal value, rather than enslaving and silencing one another.

The Telling provides the thought and method for a rich new understanding of the value of the epideictic in human discourse. While critiquing the tendency in modern discourses to discard our humanity in our search for objectivity, Jackson tells us that, in our pursuit of knowledge about language, we have thrown out the understanding of ourselves that we can obtain only through language. Jackson reminds us that there is some general Good in our being, in our existence here together, and that it is up to all of us to tell the story of our commonality and to hear one another's telling. No one of us alone can tell the story completely, and there is neither competition for doing it better nor punishment for doing it worse. Together, we are apart, until we tell.

NOTES

I extend my gratitude to Hiroship Matsumoto and to Sigrid P. Perry of the Northwestern University Library Special Collections Department for their help in preparing this essay.

1. The question of who deserves credit (Jackson, Empson, and/or Robert Graves) for the method in question is well treated in Jacobs and Clark's essay on Jackson's (mis-)treatment by "Gravesians" and other literary scholars. For a bibliography of works by and about Jackson, see Wexler (1979).

2. Attention to Jackson's work from literary scholars has been limited, and much of it has focused on her life, particularly her relationship during the 1920s and 1930s with Robert Graves. Jackson herself seems to have discouraged others from writing about her work. Because she has been treated primarily as a literary figure, her renunciation of poetry has been understood, even by sympathetic writers, as a regrettable aberration whose probable explanation is emotional rather than rational. This should change as the considerable body of critical, linguistic, and philosophical work she produced receives more recognition and is better understood. Few of Jackson's works are currently in print, but most are readily available through interlibrary loan.

3. All references in this essay are to the book *The Telling*. The title essay appears pages 6–56. References to "The Telling" indicate the essay, while *The Telling* refers to the book as a whole.

4. This essay was largely completed before Jackson's recent death. My sense of her as a probable reader influenced my writing, and some signs of that influence may be apparent even to a casual reader. While I would write differently were I to begin now, it seems unnecessary to expunge all signs of my sense of her as a key member of my audience.

5. Jackson's use of the words *Being, Truth, the Whole*, and other terms makes summary of her work difficult, partially because she uses the terms without drawing on definitions from other texts, but primarily because the concepts themselves are difficult to define satisfactorily. The debate over "Being" must be as old as the concept itself, a knotty problem for Gorgias and Plato as well as for Heidegger, Sartre, and Derrida. But Jackson refers to such philosophers only occasionally and usually disparagingly. For Jackson, human language is one of the products of Being, not its producer; in philosophical terms, she is a realist rather than a nominalist or an idealist. In *The Telling*, Being is not a supernatural hierarchy, as it is for Plato, Hegel, Heidegger, and other idealist philosophers; there is no superior Mind apart from the human collective. Instead, Jackson's idea of Being appears to be virtually synonymous with physical reality, plus a spiritual affirmation of that reality. For Jackson, Being is good in itself and good for itself.

6. At the risk of oversimplification, I employ in this essay a dichotomy between strategic and philosophical approaches to rhetoric. While Nan Johnson does not employ this simple binary scheme, she does assert that "Aristotle's and Plato's different accounts of the role of the speaker can be traced to their different notions about what constitutes the 'Good' and what rhetoric owes the Good" (99).

7. Jackson refers to an unpublished work entitled *Rational Meaning: A New Foundation for the Definition of Words*, which she wrote in collaboration with her late husband, Schuyler B. Jackson. Even if the work were available to me, it would be beyond the scope of this paper to evaluate the Jacksons' linguistic studies.

8. Dale Sullivan points out that the epideictic is fundamentally concerned with unveiling the values implicit in a discourse. Arguing that literary criticism is properly understood as epideictic discourse, Sullivan views the critic as simultaneously audience and rhetor: "The critic can be said to be judging the text's depiction of reality and to be presenting a depiction of reality as well" (343). Although the two approaches are dissimilar in scale, Sullivan's view of the epideictic as a project of absorbing and reflecting the value of the subject is compatible with Jackson's project of telling.

9. The approaches to women's discourse proposed by such theorists as Irigaray, Cixous, and Kristeva have some affinities with Jackson's project of telling and would provide interesting contrasts with it. That discussion would require a separate essay, one that I look forward to reading, but am not now equipped to write.

REFERENCES

Adams, Barbara. "Laura Riding's Autobiographical Poetry: 'My Muse is I.' " *Concerning Poetry* 15.2 (1982): 71–87.

———. "Laura Riding's Poems: A Double Ripeness." *Modern Poetry Studies* 11.1–2 (1982): 189–95.

Aristotle. *Rhetoric*. Trans. W. Rhys Roberts. In *The Rhetoric and Poetics of Aristotle*. New York: Modern Library, 1984. 1–218.

Duffy, Bernard K. "The Platonic Functions of Epideictic Rhetoric." *Philosophy and Rhetoric* 16 (1983): 79–93.

Jackson, Laura (Riding). *The Poems of Laura Riding: A New Edition of the 1938 Edition*. London: Persea, 1980.

———. *The Telling*. London: University of London (The Athlone Press), 1972.

———. *The Telling*. New York: Harper & Row, 1972.

Jacobs, Mark, and Alan Clark. "The Question of Bias: Some Treatments of Laura (Riding) Jackson." *Hiroshima Studies in English Language and Literature* 21 (1976): 1–27.

Johnson, Nan. "Ethos and the Aims of Rhetoric." *Essays on Classical Rhetoric and Modern Discourse*. Ed. Robert J. Connors, Lisa S. Ede, and Andrea A. Lunsford. Carbondale: Southern Illinois UP, 1984. 98–114.

Masopust, Michael A. "Laura Riding's Quarrel with Poetry." *South Central Review* 2.1 (1985): 42–56.

Oravec, Christine. " 'Observation' in Aristotle's Theory of Epideictic." *Philosophy and Rhetoric* (1976): 162–74.

Riding, Laura. *Anarchism Is Not Enough*. London: Jonathon Cape, 1927.

———. *Contemporaries and Snobs*. London: Jonathon Cape, 1928.

———. *Experts Are Puzzled*. London: Jonathon Cape, 1930.

———. *Selected Poems: In Five Sets*. London: Faber, 1970.

Riding, Laura, and Robert Graves. *A Pamphlet Against Anthologies*. New York: Doubleday, 1928.

———. *A Survey of Modernist Poetry*. London: Heinemann, 1927.

Rosenfield, Lawrence. "The Practical Celebration of Epideictic." In White, Eugene E., ed. *Rhetoric in Transition: Studies in the Nature and Uses of Rhetoric*. University Park, PA: Penn State UP, 1980. 131–55.

Rosenthal, M. L. "Laura Riding's Poetry: A Nice Problem." *The Southern Review* 21.1 (1985): 89–95.

Sullivan, Dale L. "The Epideictic Character of Rhetorical Criticism." *Rhetoric Review* 11.2 (1993): 339–49.

Wexler, Joyce Piell. "Construing the Word: An Introduction to the Writings of Laura (Riding) Jackson." Diss., Northwestern University, 1974; UMI, 1977. #7713838.

———. *Laura Riding's Pursuit of Truth*. Athens: Ohio UP, 1979; Southern Illinois UP, 1984.

Woodson, Linda. *A Handbook of Rhetorical Terms*. Urbana: NCTE, 1979.

Susanne K. Langer: Mother and Midwife at the Rebirth of Rhetoric

Arabella Lyon

A woman can speak with innovation and precision, be heard by more than a million people, and still not be recognized. Due to a dramatic failure of attribution, the American philosopher Susanne Knauth Langer (1896–1985), a significant, early force in the revival of rhetorical studies, remains unacknowledged for her contributions to contemporary thought. Langer developed and popularized a vision of language as emotive, creative, and multifarious: as structuring our perceptions, expressing our experiences, creating and communicating knowledge within a community. She presented this celebratory view of language with a clarity and fervor that guaranteed its acceptance. There can be no doubt of her influence when all but one of her nine philosophy books are still in print decades after publication, and most are in multiple editions. *Philosophy in a New Key* (1942) alone has sold over 500,000 copies (Hall 79).

While Langer's innovative ideas have been heard and are prevalent in modern rhetorical theory, philosophers and rhetoricians have not credited her as a significant early theorist in rhetorical epistemology (the study of how we know through language) or as a primary source for the modern perception of knowledge as a cultural construct. Prior to this century, the Western tradition of rhetoric had linked speech, community, and individual thought. And certainly throughout history, small, quiet statements suggesting a rhetorical epistemology have been made by rhetoricians and philosophers such as Isocrates, Vico, Blair, and Peirce. What Langer did, so essential to the rebirth of rhetoric, was to demonstrate the primacy of symbols to knowledge and to represent meaning as both constructed within culture and the individual, and thus as achieved collaboratively between a speaker and listener. Now, of course, scholars as diverse as the rhetorician Wayne Booth, the literary theorist Stanley Fish, and the anthropologist Clifford Geertz explore the epistemic nature of communities. Prior to Langer, however, no one coherently, clearly, and consistently argued that all knowledge was based in the symbols of a community, symbols that—be they art, myth, ritual, or science—were equally valuable. In addition, she described a dynamic community capable of change, one where meaning is placed within praxis, where meaning is achieved in a collaborative dialogue between the expressive, feeling self and the community's stable, preserving structures. Langer's formulation of meaning making is so powerful that it can still instruct us.

In this essay, I will demonstrate that Langer, in giving birth to a new conception of language and culture, is the mother of contemporary rhetorical theory and, through the wide reception of her work (or labor), is also a midwife at rhetoric's rebirth. To demonstrate her double role, I will establish that Langer's texts—though widely read—are scarcely acknowledged, that her philosophy is, in fact, rhetorical and still profoundly telling, and finally that her theories—complete, compelling, and accessible—prefigure those of later rhetoricians who are prominently connected to rhetoric's rebirth, rhetoricians such as Kenneth Burke or Chaim Perelman and Lucille Olbrechts-Tyteca.

I

Susanne Langer labored and delivered her theory in comparative silence; despite the overwhelming demand for her books, required reading in fields as diverse as semantics, general philosophy, English, aesthetics, music, and dance (Hall 79), she has never been adequately acknowledged in philosophy or rhetoric. Langer herself would deny that she was isolated or hindered by her gender, maintaining that she "always had what she needed" and "did what she wanted" (letter, Houghton Library). Still, her career path suggests otherwise. Langer did not start college until she was twenty. Her father discouraged his daughters from seeking higher education, and only after his death and through her mother's help was she able to attend Radcliffe ("Profiles"). Langer obtained her Ph.D. in philosophy from Harvard University in 1926, studying with Alfred North Whitehead, and continued there as a *tutor* for *sixteen* years. Even after her divorce from Harvard historian William Langer in 1942, she held only temporary appointments, in at least five colleges, teaching on both coasts. Finally, in 1954—after publishing four well-received books and only six years prior to her appointment to the American Academy of Arts and Science—Langer received her first tenured appointment, at Connecticut College, then a women's college.

Her books, despite wide readership, receive hardly better recognition in the academy. From the initial publisher's review of *Philosophy in a New Key* until now, Langer's intellectual contributions have been minimized and denigrated. In his evaluation of the manuscript for the Harvard press, William Ernest Hocking, chair of the Harvard philosophy department, wrote, "I am prejudiced against books on philosophy by women: according to this prejudice no woman could write as good a book as she has written" (80); while he acknowledges the quality of the book, Hocking is willing to do so only within the limited framework of gender. Several years later, the review of *Philosophy in a New Key* in *Mind*, the premier journal of philosophy, takes note of the quality of the book, but responds in the same denigrating tone and apparently responds only when the book's importance could no longer be ignored; the review's first paragraph reads:

> This review must begin with an apology for its long delay owing to great pressure of work upon the reviewer. I am sorry that a book of such exceptional interest and merit as Mrs. Langer's should have had its official introduction to readers of *Mind* so long postponed. (Reid 73)

The review's very first line draws attention to the reviewer's work and explicitly gives his other work privilege over any professional obligation to Langer's book. Fortunately, despite this consistent willingness on the part of reviewers to dismiss or ignore Langer's labor, the consequence of *Philosophy in a New Key* demanded that it be read. As Max Hall observes in his history of the Harvard University Press, "hardly anyone, woman or man, has ever written a Press book that attained a larger total sale than Susanne Langer's" (79).

Philosophy in a New Key and her other books may have won a wide readership and forced disciplinary acknowledgement of their "exceptional interest and merit," yet today one can go to any university library, review a dozen histories of philosophy, and not find even her name. As a rare exception, Bruce Kuklick may include Langer in his history of Harvard philosophy and lament that "Harvard was never kind to women"

(590), but, with what can only be conscious irony, he places this discussion of her in the last of four appendices, "Women Philosophers at Harvard."

One might hope that Langer would receive more appropriate acknowledgment outside philosophy; after all, if her concerns are rhetorical, traditional philosophers may avoid her theories. In fact, outside philosophy, a few scholars do acknowledge her significance to their thinking; Clifford Geertz, for example, quotes her extensively in *The Interpretation of Cultures*. His recognition of her position, however, is unusual. More frequently, theorists, even when they find it necessary to reference her work, dismiss or diminish her scholarship. Wayne Booth is typical in his approach. In a lengthy *footnote* in *Modern Dogma and the Rhetoric of Assent* (1974), Booth writes: "The literature on signs and symbolic languages is immense, but the relatively popular account by Susanne Langer, based in part on Cassirer, is still perhaps the best introduction (*Philosophy in a New Key*)" (113). While he acknowledges Langer as a force in introducing many to a theory of symbols, his footnote diminishes her accomplishments by its pejorative qualifiers—"relatively," "popular," "perhaps"—and by its reduction of a major work of philosophy to an "account" and "introduction." His need to mention Cassirer in this brief note is puzzling. Langer's philosophy has been related to the work of the neo-Kantian Ernst Cassirer (1874–1945), and, certainly, she translated his work and built her philosophy of symbolic forms on his initial investigations, as he built his on Kant's. Even so, if one reads the work of both scholars, one discovers that Langer's philosophy is anything but derivative or imitative; it both elaborates and diverges from Cassirer's philosophy in important ways.

Booth's need to call attention to Langer's precursor is especially disquieting because his pages are filled with echoes of Langer's labor, ideas now considered common currency and passed without a thought about the mint. For example, a reader of Langer hears echoes of her theories of community-based knowledge and the genesis of language in Booth's discussion of persuasion as mutual inquiry. Booth writes: "Our rhetorical purpose must always be to perform as well as possible in the same primal symbolic dance which makes us able to dance at all" (137).

That "primal symbolic dance" is the conceptual breakthrough in understanding that allowed Langer to link language, meaning, subject, and society. Thirty-two years after her well-read speculation, the idea reappears as a metaphor the writer can expect an academic audience to understand. Because of the wide acceptance of Langer's discussions of feeling, art, myth, and ritual, we nod and accept Booth's assertion: "But the rules for good discourse or clear thinking can no longer be confined to logical prose—we must take in the proofs of personal appeal and commitment, of art and myth and ritual" (203).

Since Langer's call to hear the new key, logic no longer rules rhetoric, and the value of all symbolic transformations grows. Booth benefits, as do all rhetoricians, from having Langer as a common source of knowledge within the community. Still, the rhetorical community needs to understand the particular worth of her books and to acknowledge her as its intellectual mother.

II

Langer always worked as a philosopher, and while she never wrote a rhetoric, her philosophy of language and aesthetics is easily translated into a complex theory of rhetoric. Translating Langer's work from philosophy to rhetoric is possible because many of the concerns of philosophy and rhetoric intertwine. Both describe discourse and systems of knowing. Throughout most of its history, Western civilization has valued philosophy's claims to knowledge through logical argument above rhetoric's strategies for public persuasion. Except in a few democracies such as the Roman Republic, philosophy has dominated rhetoric in the study of language and meaning. Within this tradition, philosophers sought rational truths while rhetoricians sought only political consensus through social appeal.

In the twentieth century, philosophers following Langer, such as the later Wittgenstein, Jacques Derrida, and Richard Rorty, abandoned the fruitless tasks of determining truth and finding absolute foundations for all human knowledge. Some philosophers in the last half of this century have moved to examine the traditional concerns of rhetoric: mediating between competing knowledge claims, describing the nature of language, making competing discourses commensurable. Rather than seeking universals, these philosophers examine language and its relationship to a specific community or context. In the same way, twentieth-century rhetoricians have both reexamined classical rhetoric and developed new theories that emphasize language's socially unifying role. In the first half of this century, rhetoric was reborn, and Langer's *Philosophy in a New Key* was both the birth announcement ("a new generative idea has dawned" [21]) and the first analysis of its implications.

Langer began her career with a traditional view of the relationship between logic and feeling and, therefore, with a traditional view of the relationship between philosophy and rhetoric. At first, she saw feeling and logic as separate, with logic dominant. For instance, in 1937, she published her second book, *An Introduction to Symbolic Logic*, a textbook that explores "the science of logic." As always, Langer was concerned with forms of symbolization, but in this early text, she examined the "shortcomings of natural language" and taught "the simpler and more consistent medium of ideographic symbols" (61). She discarded the individual's "subjective and incommunicable mental pictures" (65) and focused on the communicative "concept" (79, 313), which she described as the piece of an idea that two people can share without context. For an example of the relationship of a concept to "subjective pictures" or conceptions, she used absolute zero, which one might imagine as "dark void" or as the bottom of a long thermometer (65–66). These images are personal conceptions, but in order to talk with each other two people would have to share the same central concept, a scientific definition of absolute zero. At this point in Langer's career, she did not mention feeling as a force in the creation of knowledge, but instead attempted to describe a knowable world.

A reductionist theory of symbols and a communicative model of language did not satisfy her for long, however. Within five years of the publication of *Symbolic Logic*, Langer was mapping frontiers both in the mind and in the discipline, developing a philosophy that founded all symbolic transformations in feeling rather than logic. She proclaimed as intrinsically human the constant and necessary transformation of sensual experience into personal symbols. From the flux of sensations felt by our bodies, our eyes, our ears, our mouths, and our noses, our minds abstract what is significant—the forms that affect us. Every act of thinking is an act that expresses these feelings by transforming them into symbols, insists Langer. In privileging feeling over logic in meaning making, Langer defied the mainstream of her discipline. She created and nursed this theory at a time when philosophers such as Bertrand Russell, Rudolph Carnap, and A. J. Ayer were enthralled by logic and enunciating positivist interpretations of the world.

In 1942, Langer presented "the unrecognized fact" that philosophy was changing its questions (*Key* xiii) and taking "the study of symbols and meaning" as its "starting-point" (xiv). She struck a new key and argued for a theory of meaning founded on an innate human need to make symbols of experience. First in *Philosophy in a New Key*, where she outlined her insights, and then in *Feeling and Form*, where she developed the details of her aesthetic, she argued for a primary understanding of language as the symbolic transformation of sense-data. No longer did she focus on concepts and the things that they refer to, but instead on the mind's process of symbolizing the world. She observes, "Symbols are not proxy for their objects, but are *vehicles for the conceptions of objects. . . . It is the conceptions, not things, that symbols directly 'mean'* " (*Key* 60–61). Because all human beings appreciate form, we recognize repeated patterns in different sensuous experiences and find recurring conceptual patterns in the world. Individuals constantly abstract and form their conceptions out of a chaotic world, insists Langer. Furthermore, she shows that symbols are more than simply a means of communication: "Symbolization is both an end and an instrument" (51). It is an end in that the symbol expresses the individual's conception; it is an instrument in that it allows human beings to share meaning. For human beings to understand one another, our individual conceptions must have a common concept, but our personal symbolization of experience is unique. Necessarily, primally, innately, all people construct the world through abstraction; they abstract symbols from sense experience, from feelings (21).

This ability to symbolize, according to Langer, did not evolve as a higher-level social tool for meeting the physiological needs common to all animals. Instead, she declares, symbolization *is* the primary human need. Our minds demand dreams, rituals, art, myths, language, and finally even science. Thus, Langer observes that "if our basic needs were really just those of lower creatures much refined, we should have a more realistic language than in fact we have" (36). For Langer, language does not just communicate, or even primarily communicate, but instead makes symbols. The symbols then construct our reality.

Embedded in this view of an expressive, symbol-making *Homo sapiens* is a more emotive mind. Repudiating her earlier work, Langer asserts that "a philosophy that knows only deductive or inductive logic as reason, and classes all other human functions as 'emotive,' irrational, and animalian" dismisses "all other things our minds do . . . as irrelevant to intellectual progress" (292–93). In other words, a philosophy of just logic dismisses symphonies and sonnets as nonintellectual. When Langer classified all symbolic transformations as rational and intellectual (sonnet and song as well as science), she legitimized the study of the emotional and moral aspects of language, the traditional territory of the rhetorician.

III

Having deposed logic from its throne, Langer approached human meaning as the relationship between a community, its discourse, and the individual. Once Langer had based human expression in feeling and described the nature of meaning in symbolic transformation rather than in the objects in the world, her philosophy came to examine the concerns of rhetoric and social change: the motivation of the speaker, the powerful aspects of language that affect people, and the relationship between the speaker and her community. Thus, Langer's philosophy of symbolic transformation can easily be read as a rhetoric.

Langer's theory is so holistic as to start at the origin of human culture. Langer placed social order and shared meaning at the first moment of speech (*Key* 128–38; *Sketches* 26–53). She posited that prior to symbolic forms as complex as speech or music, hominids must have developed a "*sense of significance*" and attached importance to certain objects and sounds, a pattern of behavior discernible in modern apes. She further speculated that language developed concomitantly with dreams, superstition, and ritual, and that language had its ancient origins in the dancing and voice play of a hominid tribe. Elaborate ululation coupled with gesture and dance bonded the tribe. In ritualistic group behavior, meaning accrued to sounds that accompanied actions, so that the entire tribe shared in concept formation. While individuals may have had unique conceptions, the group concept of the action was uniform. The chant that accompanied the act of shaking a stick at the moon acquired the meaning, "Shake a stick at the moon." Song and ritual, repeated rhythm and pattern, thus precipitated language.

This positing of a communal origin of language and the theory of symbolic transformation enabled Langer to demonstrate that thinking, feeling, society, and language are all inseparable. Her work forges the links of this complex relationship and tests the movement possible in this bond. She also explores the significance of context to all communication of meaning. Langer believes a speaker and her listeners make meaning most naturally in an interactive context where their individual meanings or conceptions are created and reinforced by the concepts of common experience and common articulation (*Key* 240). The context (verbal or practical) and the novelty (what the speaker is expressing) combine to create discourse. If expression of the novelty is ambiguous or completely new, the shared context molds the meaning (139).

Context is created not only by the moment but also by society in the larger sense. Langer remarks upon the implications of this for the individual speaker:

> No matter how original we may be in our use of language, the practice itself is a purely social heritage. But discursive thought, so deeply rooted

in language and thereby society and its history, is in turn the mold of our individual experience. (*Feelings* 220)

When a speaker uses language, even for private purposes, she must use a language formed through history by society's needs. Therefore, even our individual thoughts tie us to our society. As Langer writes:

> The formulation of thought by language, which makes every person a member of a particular society, involves him more deeply with his own people than any "social attitude" or "community of interests" could do; for this original mental bond holds the hermit, the solitary outlaw, and the excommunicate as surely as the most perfectly adjusted citizen. Whatever brute fact may be, our experience of it bears the stamp of language. (220)

Audience members can hear and interpret a speaker's language, in short, because their experience has been stamped in this shared symbolic form. Meaning thus is created through the interactions and mutual interpretations of a speaker and a listener—whose thoughts and language are pinioned by their society. In many ways, her subversion of the humanist subject foreshadows that of Julia Kristeva (Clark, this volume).

According to Langer, many mechanisms within a society control individuation and keep the group's members interdependent. Social groups use rituals, or "formalized gestures," which articulate feelings and common thinking. A regularly performed rite of action or of speech becomes "a disciplined rehearsal of 'right attitudes'" (*Key* 153). Since society works toward uniform belief, even a singularly effective speaker cannot dictate or prescribe meaning. The individual may express her conceptions, but the meaning is determined in and by communal attitudes.

While many theories of communally constructed meaning have evolved since Langer's original insights, Langer remains among the few theorists to discuss the dynamics of change in a community. In Langer's holistic rhetoric, the pieces—text, speaker, audience, logic, and feeling—can create meaning only in cooperation with one another. Thus, they can create change only in cooperation. In consequence, new ideas enter any community with great difficulty. Acts or rites that violate the community's system of belief undermine the shared beliefs and concepts of their members, so a community discourages change. Resistance to change is so strong that the members of a community will resist performing alien rites or speaking alien languages, even as "lip service." Langer explains this recalcitrance, observing that "it takes a strong mind to keep its orientation without overt symbols, acts, assertions, and social corroborations; to maintain it in the face of the confounding pattern of enacted heresy is more than average mentality can do" (291). Thus, to maintain a consistent system, society demands adherence to rituals and repetitive rhetoric, which reinforce the desired patterns.

Even so, change can occur when an individual suddenly conceives experience in a new formulation. From "fulness of experience" and more important, the mind's "wealth of formulative notions," an individual asks a generative question or forms a generative idea—a thought that so intrigues active minds that it cannot be denied (8, 23). *Humans, then, are motivated by both their individual conceptions (differences) and their need to function within the boundaries of society.* Langer explicitly attributes both motives to us as symbol users. In 1942, she addressed the first motive, writing that "the transformation of experience into concepts . . . is the motive of language" (126). In 1953, she addressed the second when writing of the "biological" motive for poetic language and noting that "we are driven to the symbolization and articulation of feeling when we *must* understand it to keep ourselves oriented in society and nature" (*Feeling* 253). Therefore, language keeps constant and communal our interpretation of experience and our orientation within experience. We are motivated to express our experiences in order to "make sense out of emotional chaos," to function both in nature and culture.

As early as 1942, Langer described three sources for change within discourse: the potential power of an individual's questions, the metaphor, and the subtexts within any discourse. Unlike later theorists, such as Kuhn, Foucault, or Rorty, who see the social institution as dominating thinking and thus allowing few routes to change, Langer, even in her incipient theory, sees the need to describe the resources for change and to describe them as multiple. Overcoming internal resistance to change, new questions and new ideas will always enter communities, observes Langer.

First, Langer argues that while a society constrains a member, the individual's strength of conception can formulate new insights. The insightful discoverer may witness a common event but dress it in the uniqueness of private conception (*Key* 8). If her new insight gives rise to new questions and excites other members of the community, her idea may generate change within a community. Langer herself provides an apt example: she saw old evidence in a new light. Rather than accepting symbols as simply the evolution of an animal signal system, she perceived them as a basic human *need* that ordered a social reality out of a chaotic world. When members of her community read her, they asked their own questions about language in society and formed theories of contextual knowing.

Second, Langer writes that people can create and communicate the new insight through the power of metaphor or, as she expands the concept, "logical analogy." If language originated in the repetition of ritual, then it grows and changes as a result of new relationships made through metaphor (*Key* 139–40). A word can function in many contexts, even creating new meaning through new contexts. As Langer saw it, metaphor is the mind's primary tool for discovering new meaning. "Language, in its literal capacity, is a stiff and conventional medium, unadapted to the expression of genuinely new ideas, which usually have to break in upon the mind through some great and bewildering metaphor" (201).

The discoverer uses metaphor to express the concept to herself, but she must also use metaphor and the concepts shared in the analogy to express the new idea and her private conception to another person. After this burst of individual insight mediated by metaphor, society, as always, controls the formation of theories from these insights.

Third, Langer exposes the richness within any discourse: "There is always new life under old decay" (17). In her view, the dominant culture is far from the only layer of meaning: for instance, underneath experimental science and philosophical empiricism lies the purely symbolic mathematics, "the boldest, purest, coolest abstractions mankind has ever made" (18). The cue for philosophy's symbolic turn was already present in philosophy's empirical epoch (21). Even within the science of the atomists and positivists lay a symbolic core, and in time, mathematics reshaped the problems of observation and sense-data to problems of meaning.

For Langer, then, change is always possible, always a mediated product of the existing culture and the individual impulse, always facilitated in some way by questioning, metaphor, and the complex layers of discourse existing already in the epoch. In 1942 this was a complex statement of knowledge change.

Echoing a more traditional notion of rhetorical theory, Langer also discusses technique, that is, how language can be used most effectively in shaping change. Like her contemporary Louise Rosenblatt, Langer saw all literary forms as intersecting: "All writing illustrates the same creative principles" (*Feeling* 213). Her ideas on poetry and her discussion of nonfiction or "applied art" (301) show us her view of effective rhetorical techniques; Langer wrote that the successful writer creates an illusion that "effects the break with the reader's actual environment" (214). The perception of art cuts through the experience of the moment and presents "united" and "vivid" feelings. The feelings expressed by a successful poet or writer create the "semblance of events lived and felt" (212). In effect, the shared feelings of the writer and the reader carry the argument. To cause a change in the reader or listener's thinking, the felt experience should initiate "studious thinking," develop an "impatience" for solution, and celebrate "the cadential feeling of solution" and the expanded "consciousness of new knowledge" (302). To produce this powerful influence, the language's tempo, rhythm, sound, word association, and the sequence of ideas and images (*Key* 260–61) must be balanced to create experience, not simply assertion. It is this close linking of text to the physical feeling of thought and experience that makes artistic language untranslatable. Abridgement, paraphrase, or interpretation would destroy the unique union of sense and form.

The rhetoric abstracted from Langer's work contradicts conservative readings of Aristotle—that is, it diminishes persuasion and logic—but the ascension of expression and feeling over persuasion and logic is a small part of the difference. Langer placed meaning within the context of a complex and diverse social system: Language forges a fluid creative system, one that forms our entire reality. In his discussion of persuasion, Aristotle, through his fascination with taxonomies and hierarchies, fragmented the complexity of meaning. Langer never broke the complexity of meaning into small, easily defined pieces. Within her theory, shared meaning is not based in the speaker, created by textual technique, or targeted at an audience. With revolutionary vigor, Langer located *individual* expression within the *social* context of shared ethics, and argued that discourse is formed by the sensory experience we share. Meaning comes into being through the symbols constructed by both the speaker and the hearer, and the speaker and the hearer are unified through social activity. In *Philosophy in a New Key*, Langer portrayed an intimacy between speaker and audience that rhetoricians—still working out of a traditional Aristotelian or, perhaps, a positivistic concern with understanding and interpretation—had not yet perceived. Yet soon they would come to echo her, to sound her new key.

IV

Langer's readers were exposed to ideas that came to be at the core of contemporary rhetorical theory: some used her ideas as a basis for forming their own systems of rhetoric, while others used them to understand and evaluate the theorists who came later. Granted that this century's revival of rhetoric is no monolithic phenomenon, its scholars nevertheless share in refocusing rhetoric from a concern with style, argumentation, and speaker-based language to a concern with a system that recognizes knowledge as negotiated meanings in the context of a community. To put it another way, they are developing the details of a rhetorical epistemology whose origins are evident in Langer's early writing.

Any argument for motherhood within the history of ideas is a labyrinthine undertaking, and necessarily incomplete. But in the case of Langer, it is an obligatory undertaking because the earlier neglect requires that her labor now be reconceptualized in relationship to its precursors in philosophy and its progeny in rhetoric. Langer's ideas, of course, reflect earlier work: she writes as part of the new philosophical concern with symbolism in the last fifteen to twenty-five years, and her list of references is very long: A. J. Ayer, Rudolph Carnap, Ernst Cassirer, H. Noack, C. K. Ogden, I. A. Richards, A. N. Whitehead, the early Wittgenstein, and so on (21–22). Unfortunately, *despite* her movement away from her colleagues' positivistic concern with individual words and from their fantasies of complete communication (at least within scientific disciplines), her work often is subsumed under earlier, less developed theories of social construction, and consequently, her theoretical innovations are lost.

For example, too often her theories have been characterized as a popularization of Cassirer's work (clearly Booth is guilty of this). While the differences between these two prodigious writers are numerous, a brief outline of some differences relevant to this essay should help us understand each of the philosophers and distinguish between their positions. First, Ernst Cassirer's theory of symbolic transformation does not have a theory of art; in fact, he barely wrote about art as a symbolic form. In *Feeling and Form*, Langer develops an aesthetic theory. Second, while both philosophers have a developmental model of symbolic forms and both address the evolution of science, Langer's system is far less hierarchical than Cassirer's. She values art as highly as science and sees feeling at the core of *all* human activity. Cassirer acknowledges sensation and feeling in language, but he describes language and knowledge as evolving to leave emotion behind: we move from myth and "subjective feeling" to scientific thought where "all elements arising from the sphere of feeling and even the images, the pure schemata of intuition, are progressively excluded" (*Symbolic Forms* 3:424). He goes so far as to value numbers over language. Specifically, he writes that "in language, we find the first efforts of classification, but these are still uncoordinated. . . . For the symbols of language themselves have no definite systematic order" (*Essay* 211). In contrast, numbers have a system and "a clear and definite structural law" (212). Third, Cassirer does not explicate the complex relationship between society and language or explain how that relationship affects knowledge. Rather, Cassirer believes the primary purpose of language is communication (*Essay* 224). Langer minimizes communication, describing language's "essence" as "the formulation and expression of conceptions rather than the communication of natural wants" (*Key* 118). Fourth, Cassirer is suspicious of tropes and describes emotionless scientific language as precise and free of metaphor and allegories, "obscure language" (*Essay* 215). As we know, Langer sees metaphor, "logical analogy," as the vehicle for new insights; "It is the force that makes (language) essentially *relational*, intellectual, forever showing up new, abstractable *forms* in reality" (*Key* 141).

Clearly, Cassirer most esteems the symbolic forms (science and number) that are not subject to critique by large audiences, that are reduced in ambiguity (for whatever reason), and that are subject to explicit laws and rigid criteria of judgment. His work is concerned most with the efficiency of communication and the avoidance of misunderstanding. Furthermore, his hierarchical view reflects a commitment to the concept of progress. This clearly contrasts with Langer's sense that symbols are fortuitously unstable, mutable, emotive. She affirms aspects of symbolic processes other than clarity, hierarchy, and explicit criteria for interpretation, and this is what makes her work so significant.

Langer's theoretical advances, then, are significantly more rhetorical in nature than those of her philosophical contemporaries. Her contributions in many ways form the bridge between the limited textual concerns of philosophers and New Critics and the social, knowledge-producing vision of mid-twentieth-century rhetoricians. The popularity of Langer's contribution, in effect, suggests that the formalization of rhetoric in the 1950s is as much the daughter of philosophy's concern with symbols as it is of Aristotle's *Rhetoric*.

Rhetoric's slow movement toward Langer-like insights is visible in a chronologically sensitive examination of the theoretical developments of the recognized rhetoricians Burke, Perelman, and Olbrechts-Tyteca. In their work, we can see both how Langer's insights precede theirs and how theirs evolve in the direction she describes.

Closest to Langer in thought and chronology, Kenneth Burke drew relationships between the individual, society, and language in the 1930s—first in his 1931 book *Counter-statement,* then more explicitly in *Permanence and Change* (1935) and *Attitudes Towards History* (1937). This early in his career, however, as important as Burke was even then, he was defining relationships common to the rhetorical tradition in terms that minimized the interaction between individual and society. And he certainly lacked the coherent and developed insights of Langer. In these early books, his view was fragmentary and concerned with logos, individualism, manipulation, and war/conflict. For example, in *Counter-statement,* over and over again, the powerful artist controls the masses. Here, Burke makes such statements as:

> The artist's manipulations of the reader's desires involve his use of what the reader considers desirable. . . . The Symbol may also serve to force patterns upon the audience. . . . By an ideology is meant the nodus of beliefs and judgements which the artist can exploit for his effects. (146, 154, 161)

At this time, Burke simply did not show the interplay of the forces and sources of meaning as Langer did. In *Permanence and Change,* emphasizing the rhetor's power and aggression, he writes that speech "has elements of exhortation and threat which guide and stimulate action" and that "the moral elements in our vocabulary are symbolic warfare" (192). Rather than seeing meaning as collaborative, he sees it as aggression. Finally, in *Attitudes to History,* when Burke began to consider consistently the interaction between an individual and society, he writes that the individual joins society through a process of individual death, that "the individual must 'die,' with relation to autistic and intimate frames, to fit himself for identification with the more 'abstract' frame of 'the city' (as extended to either religious or historical notions of community)" (288). But, according to Burke (at this point), even after individuals die, they are in some way separate from language and society, not quite embedded. And because of his evolving view, Burke writes odd sentences that place individuals both in society and language, and at the same time outside them, as judges of their discourse. For instance, he writes:

> The "social" aspect of language is "reason." Reason is a complex technique for "checking" one's assertions by public reference. And insofar

as one forms his mind by encompassing such linguistic equipment, he learns to use this technique of checking "spontaneously," with varying degrees of accuracy and scope. (341–42)

As important as he was to the rebirth of rhetoric, Burke did not precede Langer in describing the epistemic unity of community or in depicting interpretation as an act between speaker and listener. Seemingly, in these early works, Burke believes language is a violence that we use on one another: his early position is far removed from Langer's vision of communities creating complex and changing meanings.

By 1950, eight years after the publication of *Philosophy in a New Key*, Burke was asserting a position closer to Langer's. In *A Rhetoric of Motives*, he wrote that the relationship between community members, "identification" or "consubstantiality," is the unity people share through "joined interests" (20). He had come to believe that "in acting together, men have common sensations, concepts, images, ideas, attitudes that make them *consubstantial*" (21). By this time, like Langer, Burke saw common sensations (feelings) and ideas as existing in the individual as well as within human communities; the shared activities contribute to "social cohesion." He described "belonging" as "rhetorical" and "the use of language as a symbolic means of inducing cooperation in beings that by nature respond to symbols" (43). Like Langer, Burke came to know that the individual and society need symbols for identification, unity, and cooperation.

Communities of collaborative meaning and discourse, presented by Langer in the 1940s, became part of rhetoric in the 1950s. Chaim Perelman and Lucille Olbrechts-Tyteca's *The New Rhetoric: A Treatise on Argumentation* (1958) provides an example of how prevalent Langer's ideas had become. Perelman and Olbrechts-Tyteca presented a rhetoric apparently focused on logic and persuasion, Aristotelian concerns. Their initial statement of rhetoric's purpose—"to induce and to increase the mind's adherence to the theses presented for its assent" (4)—seems to deny the sense of communal knowledge so essential to modern rhetoric. But as they elaborate their theory, the necessity of a communal setting for knowledge becomes obvious. These rhetoricians see argumentation as aimed "at gaining the adherence of mind" through the existing "intellectual contract" (14). This contract or "community of minds" occurs in a social setting, demanding a common language and a set of norms (15). In *The New Rhetoric*, adherence actually implies the glue between language and society.

The epistemic theory of Perelman and Olbrechts-Tyteca closely echoes Langer's. They also distinguish societies or "social circles" by specific knowledge—the "unquestioned beliefs" and "dominant opinions" that are reinforced by ritual. Like Langer, they note that society's integral beliefs are reinforced by epideictic discourse—ritual and ceremonial speech—which "strengthens the adherence to what is already accepted" (54). Like Langer's rituals, epideictic speeches reinforce the individual's participation in a society. As a consequence of seeing knowledge as constructed within culture, they are led to describe the indivisible relationship of each society to its speech. Perelman and Olbrechts-Tyteca point out that the relationship of society's knowledge and language is so close that we can rely on speeches and texts for "considerable knowledge of the character of past civilizations" (21). Langer contemplates a similar point in a more complex manner at the start of *Philosophy in a New Key* (4–8).

No evidence exists that Burke, Perelman, or Olbrechts-Tyteca read Langer, but the wide acceptance of her earlier work must have eased the delivery of their ideas. Scholars and students in philosophy, rhetoric, and literature already had heard large parts of the rhetoricians' arguments expounded by Langer a decade earlier, and they were ready to acknowledge the progeny of a multitude of rhetorical theorists.

V

If it remains a great scandal that Langer can be so widely read and so disregarded in the history of ideas, the situation need not continue. Langer's work is rich enough to assist our investigations into many contemporary issues. Given the nature of the volume in which this essay appears, I have chosen to examine her relationship to contemporary feminism. In no way, however, do I see that as the only place where she can be reread and used both to gain a divergent perspective and to unsettle current assumptions.

Although Langer would deny feminist aspects in her thinking or connections to it, much of her work figures and prefigures insights associated with contemporary feminism. Her recognition of feeling as prior to logic and just as valid, her emphasis on the social construction of knowledge and action, and her refusal to privilege any one symbol system as more truthful than the others are all positions commonly ascribed to feminist theories. Even her balancing of the individual and the social reflects women's common concern for balancing the private sphere and the once forbidden and still dangerous public sphere. Because her ideas are so basic to feminist thought, and so well integrated into it, it is conceivable that her theoretical developments, uniquely critical of the prevailing paradigm in masculine philosophy, were aided by her gender. Although—as I believe—her gender hindered their reception, it may have helped their invention.

Langer's desire to have her work judged as scholarship, not as a woman's scholarship, is understandable, especially given the open hostility toward women's writing expressed by philosophers such as William Ernest Hocking, Harvard's chair of philosophy, who reviewed her work. Even so, her process of invention seems to echo the process of some earlier women writers. In *Madwoman in the Attic*, a relatively early theory of feminist Poetics, Sandra M. Gilbert and Susan Gubar write of "the woman writer's quest for her own story" and "the woman's quest for self-definition" (76). For the nineteenth-century woman writer to invent her story, they argue, she must shatter male images of woman—as angel and monster—and thus be "concerned with assaulting and revising, deconstructing and reconstructing those images." That is, a woman writer must create a space, a place in the world where her experiences exist and are valued. Langer, unlike Gilbert and Gubar's literary writers, did not face an explicit patriarchal *image* of angel or monster to destroy: instead of facing a mutilation of herself, she confronted a logocentric, individualistic model of philosophical thought, a model that did not reflect her experience of human relations. To construct a more total view of what it means to speak as a human being, to find within discourse theory her woman's experience, Langer responded by developing a concept of the symbolizing human being who could be said to destabilize the duality of gender and to assert the values commonly attributed to women. Applying her understanding that "the transformation of experience into concepts . . . is the motive of language" (*Key* 16) and her concern with the change in discursive systems, she worked towards describing a semiotic model that privileged her experience.

The androgyny implicit in Langer's work is complex in that it implicitly denies duality by not acknowledging gender, but at the same time privileges the values associated with feminine experience. We know that the move to valorize woman's difference can be dangerous. Catharine A. MacKinnon, for instance, argues that the socially defined aspects of difference reflect patriarchal forces of dominance. She writes, "When difference means dominance as it does with gender, for women to affirm differences is to affirm the qualities and characteristics of powerlessness"

(51). According to MacKinnon, when feminists such as Carol Gilligan emphasize the significance of gender difference, they potentially rein- scribe the position forced upon women in this society. Langer's work begins to answer the question of difference as powerlessness by trans- forming attributes of women's difference into the basis of all human sym- bolic processes. In her denial of a gender basis for innate caring and social dependency, in her balance of individual and society, and in her emphasis on shared feelings as basic to all speech, interaction, and in- vention, she describes feminine values in the symbolic processes of all people. She creates a space removed from oppression in her narrative of human action where depreciated and denied feminine activities are given power as the fundamental characteristics of us all. The destruction of difference, so often seen as the colonizing strategy of those in power, is used here as a subversive strategy. Langer reinvents philosophy as rhetoric and as valuing the feminine; in doing so, she conceals the oth- erness (the radicalness) of her work by claiming the universality of sym- bolic processes that are feminine and rhetorical. With that subtle gesture, she fertilizes what was then a masculine and positivistic discipline.

Langer's writing, then, is subversive, placing rhetorical concerns and feminine values above the tradition of logocentric, masculine philosophy. She replicates the masculine move that denies difference, but in doing so, she moves what has traditionally been conceptualized as the margin to the center. *Philosophy in a New Key* is thus more than the announce- ment of a concern with symbols; rather, it creates the space for the rebirth of Rhetorica. In giving birth to the new rhetoric and fostering its reception across disciplines, Langer reclaims feeling and shared expres- sion as not only the maternal providence but also the most valuable, unique, and essential of human activities.

REFERENCES

Aristotle. *The Rhetoric and the Poetics of Aristotle*. Trans. W. Rhys Roberts. New York: Modern Library, 1984.

Booth, Wayne C. *Modern Dogma and the Rhetoric of Assent*. Chicago: U of Chi- cago P, 1974.

Burke, Kenneth. *Attitudes Towards History*. 1937. 3d ed. Berkeley: U of California P, 1959.

———. *Counter-statement*. 1931. 2d ed. Chicago: U of Chicago P, 1953.

———. *Permanence and Change*. New York: New Republic, 1935.

———. *A Rhetoric of Motives*. Berkeley: U of California P, 1950.

Cassirer, Ernst. *An Essay on Man*. New Haven: Yale UP, 1944.

———. *Language and Myth.* Trans. Susanne K. Langer. New York: Dover, 1946.

———. *The Philosophy of Symbolic Forms.* 3 vols. Trans. Ralph Manheim. New Haven: Yale UP, 1953, 1955, 1957.

———. *Symbol, Myth, and Culture: Essays and Lectures of Ernst Cassirer, 1935–1945.* Ed. Donald Phillip Verene. New Haven: Yale UP, 1979.

Gilbert, Sandra M., and Susan Gubar. *The Madwoman in the Attic.* New Haven: Yale UP, 1979.

Greer, William R. "Susanne K. Langer, Philosopher, Is Dead at 89." *New York Times* (July 19, 1985), A12.

Hall, Max. *Harvard University Press: A History.* Cambridge: Harvard UP, 1986.

Kuklick, Bruce. *The Rise of American Philosophy, Cambridge, Massachusetts 1860–1930.* New Haven: Yale UP, 1977.

Langer, Susanne K. *Feeling and Form: A Theory of Art.* New York: Scribner's, 1953.

———. *An Introduction to Symbolic Logic.* 1937. 2d ed. New York: Dover, 1953.

———. Letters and note cards. Harvard University. Houghton Library. Uncatalogued.

———. *Philosophical Sketches.* Baltimore: Johns Hopkins UP, 1962.

———. *Philosophy in a New Key: A Study in the Symbolism of Reason, Rite, and Art.* 3rd ed. Cambridge: Harvard UP, 1979.

MacKinnon, Catharine A. *Toward a Feminist Theory of the State.* Cambridge: Harvard UP, 1989.

Perelman, Chaim. "Rhetoric and Philosophy." *Philosophy and Rhetoric* 1(1968): 15–24.

Perelman, Chaim, and L. Olbrechts-Tyteca. *The New Rhetoric: A Treatise on Argumentation.* Trans. John Wilkinson and Purcell Weaver. Notre Dame: U of Notre Dame P, 1969.

"Profiles." *New Yorker* (December 3, 1960): 24.

Reid, Louis Arnaud. "Critical Notices." *Mind: A Quarterly Review of Psychology and Philosophy* 54 (1945): 73–83.

15

A Rhetoric for Audiences: Louise Rosenblatt on Reading and Action

Annika Hallin

When she was teaching at Barnard College in the 1930s, Louise Rosenblatt became involved in the publication of a series of books by the Commission on Human Relations, which was part of the Progressive Education Association. The books were one way that the commission met its assigned responsibility of "helping young people with the urgent problems of personal and social living today," as Alice Keliher, chair of the commission, explained (xi). Rosenblatt's contribution to the book series was *Literature as Exploration*, published in 1938. In *Literature as Exploration*, she directed attention to the audiences of literary texts—especially student audiences in literature courses—usually unacknowledged by literary theorists of the day. According to Rosenblatt, the kind of literary study that current theory considered to be valid permitted readers neither flexibility nor autonomy, because it sought from them not their own responses but only supposedly correct readings of texts. Rosenblatt argued that readers should participate in, and not merely receive, discourse, and she challenged current mainstream literary theory for its lack of sound pedagogy in reading.

Rosenblatt's immediate argument was with literary theory and its attendant teaching methods, but her work has significant implications for rhetorical theory and pedagogy as well. Her critique of how literature was taught in the college English class was also a critique of what she saw as literary theory's refusal to acknowledge the persuasive dimension of all literature. Rosenblatt repudiated the premises of so-called objective criticism on many of the same grounds as rhetoricians who, decades later, drew connections between literature and rhetoric. Rhetorical criticism of literature has hinged on the idea that literary discourse works to convince audiences in much the same way as rhetorical discourse. Rosenblatt also argued that literary texts can affect readers' beliefs and judgments. Furthermore, she averred that it is the intrinsic nature not only of literature but also of the classrooms in which it is taught to request the audience's assent on various issues. While theorists of rhetorical criticism have argued that literature is like rhetoric because it, too, persuades its audience, Rosenblatt focused less on the qualities of texts and more on the responses of readers, whom she wanted to steer away from being persuaded unawares.

In her 1938 book, Rosenblatt developed an alternative method for teaching literature, arguing that existing literary education tended to foster not awareness but ignorance and passive reception of the persuasive capacity of fiction, drama, poetry, and other literary works. Her pedagogy strives to prepare audiences to meet the suasive aspects of the texts they read. According to Rosenblatt, the legitimate goal of literary study was not to interpret literary texts as isolated linguistic phenomena but to become alert to one's individual engagement with language. At stake, then, was more than better reading practices. Central to Rosenblatt's work was an idea that our perception of literary works cannot be separated from everyday discourse and everyday experience and that, ultimately, literary education ought to help students integrate their linguistic competence with their sense of who they are as persons.

Toward this end, Rosenblatt offered a unique theory that we can think of as an audience's rhetoric. Since classical times, theorists have discussed rhetoric primarily as an art by which speakers or writers can influence audiences, but rhetorical theory has been much more invested in speakers and writers than in audiences. Rhetoricians have argued that it is important for orators and authors to be aware of their auditors and readers, and of how they present themselves in their compositions. Although these theories assume that rhetoric speaks to an audience and seeks action, they often ignore precisely the person in the audience, the person who might take action. When they have considered audience, theorists of rhetoric have tended not to emphasize anything hearers and readers themselves might do but what speakers and writers do, or should do, with respect to audience. Rosenblatt's work of the 1930s broke the convention of literary theory to focus on texts and authors as the sole allocators of meaning, and her theory has promise for reconfiguring how rhetorical theory portrays the relations between participants in discourse.

I

Rosenblatt does not call herself a rhetorician, nor do others refer to her as one, but she shares many of the concerns of theorists who have linked rhetoric and literary theory, such as Wayne Booth, Donald Bryant, and Lynette Hunter, whose relation to Rosenblatt's work I will consider later in this essay. With the exception of a brief comment on Wayne Booth's book *The Rhetoric of Fiction*, Rosenblatt never explicitly places her work in the context of rhetorical theory (*The Reader* 93n). It is worth mentioning in passing, however, that in a footnote in her second book, *The Reader, the Text, the Poem* (1978), Rosenblatt identified a weakness in Aristotle's conception of rhetoric that she associated with a persistent weakness in contemporary reading pedagogy (89n). Both, she argued, sought only minimal involvement from the audience.

While no extensive discussion exists of the value of Rosenblatt's work for rhetorical theory,[1] her books and articles have received considerable attention in recent years. Most significant is John Clifford's 1991 collection of essays devoted to her work, *The Experience of Reading: Louise Rosenblatt and Reader-Response Theory*. Both Clifford's introduction and Carolyn Allen's essay in the book discuss the phenomenon that the recognition Rosenblatt has received is divided (Clifford 1; Allen 16–20). On the one hand, Rosenblatt's theoretical work was largely unknown to other literary theorists until the 1980s. On the other hand, there is evidence that since the late 1930s Rosenblatt has had continual influence as a teacher of English who is vocal on issues of teaching and involved in reshaping curricula at the national as well as the local level. Carolyn Allen has attributed literary theorists' sluggish reception of Rosenblatt in part to a division between pedagogy and theory within the field of English studies (16–20). As Allen shows, Rosenblatt's pedagogical concerns were a reason for literary theorists to dismiss rather than credit her work (15). Although Allen's description of Rosenblatt as having "two reputations" is accurate (16), Rosenblatt's literary and pedagogical contributions should be regarded as interdependent.[2] Rosenblatt never considered the relationship between theory and pedagogy to be paradoxical, as a recent retrospective comment of hers makes clear. Referring to her move, at an early stage in her career, from a position in a traditional English department to a post in English education, Rosenblatt claims she found expression for her theory in the school of education: "The programs reflected my theoretical approach more fully than anything that I had published" ("The Transactional Theory" 379). Theory reflected in teaching approaches is no less theoretical for being pedagogical.

Attesting to Rosenblatt's steady presence on the academic scene in the United States is her record of professional activities from the 1930s on (Rosenblatt, "What We Have Learned"). Soon after the publication of *Literature as Exploration*, Rosenblatt became active in professional organizations, and especially in their efforts to create a curriculum suited to meet students' needs. The same year the book was published, members of the Modern Language Association (MLA) asked Rosenblatt to join them in writing a statement on "The Aims of Literary Study," and the National Council of Teachers of English (NCTE) asked her to address its 1939 General Session. Rosenblatt's initial involvement with the MLA and NCTE in 1938 and 1939 was followed by more committee service and other keynote addresses. In the 1950s and 1960s, she was a member of the Commission on English of the College Entrance Examination Board, the NCTE's Committee on Literature in the First Two Years of College, the National Conference on Research on English, and the Ad Hoc Committee on the Impact of Literature and Art, among other groups. Rosenblatt's later keynote addresses include the 1976 NCTE Conference and the 1985 Conference on College Composition and Communication. In addition to this visibility, Rosenblatt published actively and her 1938 book appeared in three editions after its initial publication (1968, 1976, and 1983).[3]

In spite of Rosenblatt's professional involvement, several decades passed after the publication of *Literature as Exploration* before literary theorists cited Rosenblatt in their writing.[4] Susan Suleiman, for example, included Rosenblatt in a footnote to her 1980 introduction to *The Reader in the Text*, unable to give her more attention because she only discovered Rosenblatt shortly before the volume went to press (45n). Wayne Booth, whose treatment of the question of readers in *The Rhetoric of Fiction* was considered innovative in 1961, also did not cite Rosenblatt in his text; in the second edition (1983), he added a parenthetical reference to "the unfortunately neglected works of Rosenblatt" (442).[5] In her introduction to *Reader-Response Criticism* (1980), Jane Tompkins credited Rosenblatt as this country's first reader-response critic but muted the significance of the claim by placing it, again, in a footnote (xxvi). Indeed, Rosenblatt was not a figure of focus in any scholarly publication until Elizabeth Flynn's 1983 article "Women as Reader-Response Critics." Flynn also provided the initiative for a 1988 issue of the journal *Reader* devoted entirely to Rosenblatt, an issue that was guest-edited by John Clifford and which he later expanded into the collection cited above.

Even though Rosenblatt has rejected being characterized as a reader-response critic, she certainly deserves credit for anticipating the concerns of reader-response theory.[6] To extract a theory of interpreting texts while overlooking the pedagogical concerns of Rosenblatt's work is, however, to ignore the acute sense of social responsibility in which her theory is embedded.

Rosenblatt broke new theoretical ground with her work in reading, but her theory grew out of a commitment to what she saw as the common work of all teachers of English: to enable students to "enter as fully as possible into the potentialities of language" ("What We Have Learned" 88). If they are to contribute to this primary goal, according to Rosenblatt, none of the specialties within the field of English studies can separate theory and pedagogy.

Rosenblatt's writing focuses specifically on literary theory and education, but her intention was never to isolate literary study from other kinds of language study. Even though she has acknowledged that individual teachers and scholars might properly become specialists, to value specialization for its own sake is, in Rosenblatt's view, improper.

Rosenblatt addressed this issue in a 1977 address she delivered to the NCTE, entitled "What We Have Learned: Reminiscences of the NCTE." Looking back on the previous forty years of education, Rosenblatt commented that, in 1945, members of committees of the NCTE Commission on the English Curriculum were set up to encourage communication between specialties and grade levels. The commission recognized that individuals were often "experts in some discipline, be it linguistics or stylistics or literary history, but these were not seen as ends in themselves" (88). According to Rosenblatt, she, along with other NCTE members, felt that the legitimate aim of teaching English was to "help people acquire the capacity to use language in all its modes, to organize their sense of their worlds, to communicate it to others, and to participate in the experiences and ideas of others" (88). Ultimately, the purpose of scholarly expertise in the "disciplines" of discourse was not simply to advance specific kinds of knowledge but to give students opportunities to become accomplished with language in varied ways. Shared responsibility for this goal—rather than her own particular interests in subject matter or approach—convinced Rosenblatt of the value of teaching English. This "vision of the profession," she said, "inspired my allegiance" (88).

II

Believing, prior to her involvement with the NCTE, that education must allow students to "achieve a philosophy, an inner center from which to view the shifting society about [them]," Rosenblatt founded a critical theory conducive to this goal in her first book, *Literature as Exploration* (3).[7] In this book, Rosenblatt did not start out with a question about reading per se but rather with a question about the contribution of literary study to the important educational goal of developing students' competence with language. While she sought to activate and legitimize readers, her object was never simply to demonstrate that the reader plays a role. "In searching for a theoretical basis for the teaching of literature," Rosenblatt has said, "I found I had arrived at a general theory of the reading process" (*Literature* viii). Rosenblatt found literary study's potential value curtailed by narrow conceptions both of literary language and of teaching. The first two parts of *Literature as Exploration* she devoted to overcoming these inadequate conceptions by redefining literature and teaching.

Rosenblatt rejected both the dominant literary theory of the time and what she perceived as typical classroom approaches to literature, which were not necessarily steeped in any definite literary theory, at least not consciously. She criticized the dominant literary theory for its treatment of literary works as self-contained aesthetic objects, arguing that literature should not be isolated from ethical and social considerations. Created within societies—whose members hold beliefs and have opinions and make assumptions—any literary work of art contains "implied moral attitudes and unvoiced systems of social values" (*Literature* 8). By ignoring such systems of values, Rosenblatt argued, teachers tacitly reinforce them. She wrote, "teachers of literature . . . have not always realized that, willy-nilly, they affect the student's sense of human personality and human society" (*Literature* 4).

Even though Rosenblatt wanted to make readers both wary and aware of literature's persuasiveness, she did not want to eliminate the potential of texts to sway minds, nor would she argue that this was even possible. She saw suasive power neither as necessarily harmful nor inherently undesirable, but she was not content with a pedagogy—itself suasive—that failed to require, or allow, students and teachers to acknowledge and even challenge the belief systems inherent in any use of language.

Rosenblatt questioned her contemporaries' notion that literary texts should, or even could, be interpreted objectively, but she was ultimately more troubled by the attitude toward student readers that their method implied. By focusing exclusively on the properties of texts, Rosenblatt argued, literary education tended to treat students' contributions—their personal responses to literature—with skepticism. Students' chances to articulate their responses to literature were preempted by questions such as, "What is the name of this kind of poem?" or "What is the effect of the refrain?" (*Literature* 69). Rather than encouraging students' active contributions, such questions gave students the comparatively passive task of finding correct answers. In another example, Rosenblatt cited a collection of literary texts intended for secondary education; in reference to Hawthorne's *Scarlet Letter*, it asked students, "Which in your opinion is the guiltiest of the three: Hester Prynne, Arthur Dimmesdale, or Roger Chillingworth? Which suffered most?" (*Literature* 17). Rather than being an issue students proposed as a result of their own evaluations of the literary work, the characters' relative guilt was here identified for students as a topic of discussion. The question moved quickly to requesting an appropriate answer and took precedence over readers articulating their own range of responses to the text. Questions such as this "impose a set of preconceived notions about the proper way to react to any work" and do not let students "be free to grapple" with their own responses (*Literature* 66). To place the reader in the role of someone who answers these kinds of questions encourages the student only to gather information or arguments from texts. "Teachers," Rosenblatt wrote, "frequently approach a book or poem as though it were a neatly labeled bundle of literary values to be pointed out to the student" (*Literature* 58). Instead of inviting debate and discussion, discursive acts—literary or pedagogical—become indisputable.

To make reading a process of deriving correct answers is to adopt what Rosenblatt in *The Reader, the Text, the Poem* called the "efferent stance," an approach whose aim is not audience participation but audience persuasion. In efferent reading, readers' goals are to arrive at certain convictions that they can take from the poem—the Latin word "effere" means "to carry away" (*The Reader* 24). The reader retains some presupposed truth about a refrain or the knowledge that a certain text is a ballad or a sonnet. Although in 1938 Rosenblatt had already identified the efferent stance as the unfortunate rule in literary education, she continued to see it as a persistent problem both in and after the 1978 publication of *The Reader, the Text, the Poem*. In "What Facts Does This Poem Teach You" (1980), for example, she held that "both the learning environment and teaching approaches have tended to inculcate a predominantly efferent stance toward all texts, even those presumably 'literary'— poems, stories, or plays" (389). As Rosenblatt wrote in a 1981 essay, students have been asked to respond to literature with the same kind of interest that they would bring to reading the label on a medicine bottle or the list of ingredients in a recipe ("On the Aesthetic as the Basic Model" 21).

As an alternative to the efferent stance, Rosenblatt posited what she called the "aesthetic stance." Contending that capable and responsible participants in discourse must have self-conscious linguistic awareness, Rosenblatt proffered this alternative as a model for teachers who wanted to encourage involvement with texts rather than the reception of them. Although Rosenblatt did not use the specific phrases "efferent reading" and "aesthetic reading" until she wrote *The Reader, the Text, the Poem*, already in *Literature as Exploration* she argued for the importance of what she called the aesthetic experience. An aesthetic experience does not spontaneously result from reading particular "artistic" or "aesthetic" texts. Not the text but the kind of attention the reader gives it makes the experience "aesthetic." Furthermore, Rosenblatt's criterion for literariness would not conventionally be considered aesthetic. Rosenblatt regards as "works of literature" not only poems, short stories, novels, or plays canonized as works of art but also all texts in which the reader perceives "a mind uttering its sense of life" (*Literature* 6). This idea that any text, even a literary text, is created by an author with a point of view on the world is more familiarly rhetorical than aesthetic. For Rosenblatt, a perceivable point of view is partly what defines literature. Under this conception, Rosenblatt included both biography and essay as literary forms (*Literature* 6). She also included, for example, Darwin's *On the Origin of Species* and Adam Smith's *Wealth of Nations*, as well as William James's *Principles of Psychology* (*Literature* 134n). She even saw the category as encompassing visual media, including "the moving picture" and, by the second edition of *Literature as Exploration*, television (1st ed. 214; 2d ed. 181). These and other works that can be read aesthetically put forth "some approach to life, some image of people working out a common fate, or some assertion that certain kinds of experiences, certain modes of feeling, are valuable" (*Literature* 20).

Whether the reader's experience of these "literary works" will be aesthetic depends on how she or he reads. While efferent reading requires the skill to "[focus] our attention . . . on the information or ideas or directions for action that will remain when the reading is over," aesthetic reading allows students to notice and pause for the experience evoked in them while reading (*Literature* 33). In a recent formulation of the aesthetic stance, Rosenblatt wrote, "In this kind of reading, the reader adopts an attitude of readiness to focus attention on what is being lived through during the reading event" ("Writing and Reading" 159). Drawing on John Dewey and Arthur Bentley's *Knowing and the Known*, Rosenblatt has also used the word "transaction" to convey the sense that in aesthetic reading the reader and the text exist in a reciprocal relationship to one another (*The Reader* 16–19; "Writing and Reading" 154).

As an example of a classroom practice that asks students to draw on their experiences of reading, Rosenblatt described a class of first-year college women discussing Ibsen's *A Doll's House*. Students were given free range to respond and began by disagreeing over how to judge the character Nora. One student claimed that "Nora was a fool to have become so dependent on her husband," while others argued that Nora had no choice (*Literature* 122). From there the students moved to a discussion of what criteria of judgment were fair given the difference between the time in which the play is set and their own 1930s. The women then wanted to learn about the history of women's legal and political rights in the nineteenth century. In the process, they managed not only to gain an understanding of the play in its historical and cultural context but also to assess the "extent of woman's emancipation" in their own time (*Literature* 122).

Teachers can expect a class discussion that draws on students' aesthetic reading to begin with any of a variety of topics, and it may not always begin felicitously. Rosenblatt states that students "are often insecure and confused when given the opportunity and responsibility to express their own honest responses to the work," and she cites I. A. Richards's *Practical Criticism* (1929) as demonstrating this (*Literature* 63). While Richards dismissed many readers' discussion of literature, admittedly often inadequate and unsophisticated, as drawing on "mnemonic irrelevances" and "stock responses" (15–16), for Rosenblatt such responses are neither irrelevant nor undesirable. A student may initiate discussion of Keats's "The Eve of St. Agnes" by labeling it as "romantic love twaddle," as did one of Rosenblatt's students (*Literature* 97). Only by beginning with personal reactions, even those emphasizing "personal obsessions, chance associations, and irrelevant conventional opinions about poetry"—and then testing and developing these reactions—can a teaching method bring readers to come to terms with their responses to texts (*Literature* 64). Efferent questions, on the other hand, do not invite students to consider personal responses or to develop the kind of sophisticated understanding of their own reactions that would allow them to reckon with literature in a way that is genuinely meaningful to them.

Rosenblatt held that we are most powerfully affected by discourse when we can link the language to our own experiences—to our emotional reactions, to our assumptions about other people, and to our conceptions of logic. She also showed that readers actively seek such links between reading and experience. In *Literature as Exploration*, Rosenblatt cited empirical evidence that "to the great majority of readers, the human experience that literature presents is primary" (7). Having asked a class of first-year college women, "Why do you read novels, anyway?" Rosenblatt received answers revealing the "personal satisfactions" that readers pursue (35, 36). The responses included: "I like to read anything that is well written, in which the author gives you interesting descriptions and exciting adventures"; "I like to find out about the things that happen to people, and how they solve their problems"; and "I like to read about as many different kinds of situations as possible—just in case I, myself, might be in such a situation some day" (35–36). Even though readers' personal concerns are rarely integrated into classroom teaching, these responses indicate that readers nevertheless make judgments about the "sense of life" they perceive a book as presenting (*Literature* 6). Current pedagogy, Rosenblatt argued, did not allow judgments to be tried and developed in dialogue. Because their personal reactions were neglected, students did not learn to assess their reactions to a particular work's persuasiveness as responses to "a scheme of values, a sense of social framework, or even, perhaps . . . a cosmic pattern" from which an author has written (*Literature* 6). Under this pedagogy, readers' judgments remain only vaguely known to them.

III

The persuasive aspects of literary discourse that interested Rosenblatt have more lately been an object of debate among twentieth-century theorists who have established what they refer to as a rhetorical dimension in literature. Donald Bryant, Wayne Booth, and Lynette Hunter, among others, have argued that literature cannot be isolated from persuasive discourse and have linked the two concepts by focusing on audience. Bryant edited and contributed to a collection of essays, *Papers in Rhetoric and Poetic* (1964), based on conference papers presented by scholars in speech and English. Booth's book *The Rhetoric of Fiction* (1961) has long been recognized as a considerable contribution to rhetorical literary criticism. Appearing two decades after Bryant's and Booth's work, Hunter's book *Rhetorical Stance in Modern Fiction* (1984) was an effort to resolve issues of literature's power over readers. I will argue that, while Rosenblatt discussed the audience's role in discourse, these rhetorical theorists limited their discussion to the effects of language on audiences.

Note that, in contrast to these three theorists, Rosenblatt rarely employs the word "rhetoric" in her writing, and she does not generally refer to persuasive discourse as "rhetoric." In her 1978 book, *The Reader, the Text, the Poem*, Rosenblatt used the phrase "rhetorical terms" interchangeably with "critical terms" to refer to concepts such as form and unity. In the 1978 book, she also acknowledged that rhetoric historically has been associated with persuasive discourse. In a rather broad stroke, she addressed the thought and reception of one of traditional rhetoric's major theorists:

> It is perhaps regrettable that Aristotle did not prevail in his restriction of "rhetoric" to persuasive speech or writing. . . . This would reduce confusion between efferent and aesthetic reading. In persuasive speech or writing, the author seeks to act on the listener or reader through specific (rhetorical) uses of language. The aim is to lead the listener or reader to reach certain conclusions or engage in certain actions. Emotions are to be aroused, but in order to affect judgments and decisions. The listener or reader is being called upon to adopt a predominantly efferent stance, with the argument the focus of attention. (89n)

Rosenblatt did not elaborate further, and her purpose here was not to define rhetoric, or to either include or exclude any particular definition of it. Her interest was in the difference between a "static," efferent theory of reading and a "dynamic," aesthetic theory, a distinction she felt would have been easier to make had rhetoric consistently been identified as persuasive discourse.

Rosenblatt's link between rhetoric and efferent reading is pertinent, however, when her work is compared to that of rhetoricians who have argued that literature and rhetoric intersect. Bryant, Booth, and Hunter differ with Rosenblatt not in their rendering of literary texts as persuasive but in their acceptance of what is ultimately an efferent stance toward texts. In his article "Uses of Rhetoric in Criticism," Donald Bryant claimed that "much literature . . . characteristically encompasses ethical, and political or public events, and the instruments and dynamics which affect these events" (10). While Rosenblatt would agree that this is a plausible depiction of literary discourse, she would take issue with the adequacy of Bryant's characterization of literature's function. From his initial premise, Bryant argued that literature is rhetorical when it seeks "imaginatively to organize idea and emotion . . . toward political enlightenment or action, and not merely or solely to articulate idea and emotion" (13). Although Rosenblatt would agree that the purpose Bryant sees is rhetorical—i.e., persuasive, in the sense that he assumes an efferent stance toward such texts—she would not agree that the efferent stance should be recommended to or imposed upon readers of literature. Bryant does not differ from Rosenblatt in his description of literary discourse, but he depicts persuasion as its proper goal, while Rosenblatt urges readers to turn their analytical attention to the suasiveness of all literary works. Going beyond Bryant to address what ought to happen after the author releases a text, Rosenblatt presses readers to deliberately focus their critical abilities on a literary work's persuasive force, rather than simply accept it.

The implications for readers of the difference between Rosenblatt's and other theorists' views of audience is perhaps most visible when Rosenblatt's approach is compared to that of a critic whose work she has depicted as being similar to her own, Wayne Booth's approach in *The Rhetoric of Fiction*. In contrast to Bryant, Booth argues not that authors of fiction intend to affect their audiences' actions in the world, but that authors of fiction expect certain attitudes from audiences during the act of reading. Like Rosenblatt, Booth discusses the reading process, but he is interested in what he sees as contracts audiences must fulfill—rather than the contracts they choose to fulfill—in order to understand a particular text. In the preface to his book, Booth defines his subject as "the rhetorical resources available to the writer of epic, novel, or short story as he tries, consciously or unconsciously, to impose his fictional world upon the reader" (xiii). Booth's *Rhetoric of Fiction* is an extensive discussion of how readers encounter this wielding of power—but not of how they might successfully take it on.

Rosenblatt comments on Booth's work in *The Reader, the Text, the Poem*. While she sees it as approaching the spirit of her own thought, she is troubled, finally, by Booth's association of reading with the process of becoming persuaded. Rosenblatt describes *The Rhetoric of Fiction* as "deeply permeated by awareness of the reader" and feels that it "would be possible to rephrase many of Booth's points in transactional terms" (93n). Nonetheless, she concludes, "his ultimate concern is with the author's point of view and techniques, the production of a text that will have the desired 'effect' on the reader" (93n). Like Rosenblatt, Booth gives the reader an active role. Unlike her, he gives the author control over what constitutes appropriate reader behavior.

Closer to Rosenblatt's view is Lynette Hunter's *Rhetorical Stance in Modern Fiction*. Like Rosenblatt and Booth, Hunter sees all fiction as invested with perspective. Unlike Booth, Hunter does not restrict the audience to reading according to those perspectives . While Booth characterizes authors as controlling the audience, Hunter sees authors as having obligations toward audiences, even though some authors may fail to assume this responsibility. In Hunter's view, writers can make their purposes known, creating "positive rhetoric," or they can conceal them, creating "negative rhetoric." While the stance of negative rhetoric is to deny multiplicity of meaning, the stance of positive rhetoric is to admit to the existence of contradictory views (16–17). Hunter wrote that "an audience needs to learn how to assess stance . . . and to participate as fully as possible in the values it reveals" (64). She does not, however, discuss any specific actions audiences can take to assess the author's stance.

In contrast to Rosenblatt, Hunter, Booth, and Bryant ultimately say nothing to readers but only talk about them. Rosenblatt's theory not only extends to the audience some authority to establish meaning in texts and to judge their value, but also offers a pedagogy that empowers readers to assume this new authority in more than name. Opposite Rosenblatt's model for aesthetic reading is the efferent model, according to which the reader's activity is at best a quest to uncover a monologue. With its focus on the operations of texts and authors, rhetorical literary criticism to date has chiefly been concerned with monologues.[8]

IV

Rosenblatt's work is important to rhetoric not only because her theory has implications for rhetorical literary criticism but also because the connections she makes between texts and readers provide a strategy for teaching ethos, or character. In "Ethos and the Aims of Rhetoric," Nan Johnson addresses the difficulty of teaching students to assess how their personal character bears on their own writing and to judge the ethos presented in another's work. Johnson identifies two conceptions of ethos. One follows the tradition of Aristotle, where the rhetor presents her or his character in a particular way in order to make her- or himself believable to a specific audience. The other is Platonic, requiring that the speaker or writer possess moral goodness to begin with in order to be reliable. Johnson argues that the former view has dominated instruction in rhetoric in the past three centuries (112). Twentieth-century composition textbooks, Johnson shows, "[present] ethos as a skill of stylistic adaptability to mode and audience, and typically [eschew] moral implications" (113).

A theory of rhetoric that is oriented toward achieving writers' or speakers' goals may be completely inadequate for teaching ethos. Although rhetoricians have identified ethos as one means by which speakers and writers appeal to their audiences, they have not been concerned with teaching speakers and writers to develop character. They have concentrated on the effect that ethos has in making a speech or text convincing. Ethos has been treated as something a rhetor brings to—and might strategically present in—a composition. While rhetoricians have probably all assumed that successful speakers and writers do engage ideas, events, and previous discussion in dealing with issues, Rosenblatt is actively interested in how such engagement shapes opinions and persons.

Rosenblatt claims that "the insights attained through literature may be assimilated into the matrix of attitudes and ideas which constitute character and govern behavior" (*Literature* 274). She argues that becoming a theorist of one's own engagement with language can help the individual form a basis for sound judgment in life, although nothing in her theory suggests that this is a simple linear process. Rosenblatt's intention is not to deliver direct lessons to students through literary works. The belief that literature can present students with prescriptive models for their behavior, "the old notion of 'character building through literature,' " Rosenblatt describes as "completely alien" to her pedagogy (*Literature* 247). Rosenblatt does not hold up select literary works as models for imitation but defends the value of a critical process that enhances students' abilities to perceive and judge—and either act on or reject—assumptions about what is ethically or socially appropriate.

Students who develop "the habit of reflective thinking" in school may achieve intellectual certitude on various issues; furthermore, they can not only draw on previously acquired convictions in their own lives but, more important, can continue to use the responsive process (*Literature* 274). The purpose of teaching the aesthetic stance in reading—and an important overall goal in education—is to develop "individuals who will function less as automatic bundles of habits and more as flexible, discriminating personalities" (*Literature* 105). With her theory, Rosenblatt seeks to encourage students to take responsibility for their thoughts, words, and actions.

One of Rosenblatt's primary concerns in *Literature as Exploration* is how students act based on their perceptions of gender stereotypes and expectations of women's and men's behavior. Demonstrating a feminist orientation in numerous passages of the book, Rosenblatt argues, for example, that although the "young man at school or college" may have become aware of "woman's potential equality with man," his behavior might betray his learning (*Literature* 177).[9] For perception and action to come together in a desirable way, "intellectual convictions" must be "translated" "into emotional attitudes governing behavior" (*Literature* 178, 179). This translation requires personal commitment beyond mere reading of texts or response to events; tacit assumptions must become explicitly known.

Unless students are taught to detect the suasive gestures of texts, they may instead learn a discourse of mimicry, a potentially cruel language. As Rosenblatt says, individuals "often . . . seem unable to resist the pull of disingenuous slogans, specious appeals to emotion, or the contagion of mob hysteria" (*Literature* 177). To be defensible, a pedagogy that seeks only to transfer received knowledge to students would have to assume that what it communicates is intrinsically valuable, even good, and that it has no harmful potential. Fearing that the forces working to make us inflexible may dominate those that make us humanely discriminating, Rosenblatt argues that it is imperative that we engage ourselves personally in responding to communicative acts.[10]

Rosenblatt thus charts theoretical ground between the points of what rhetoric traditionally teaches and what it desires—between rhetoric's concern with composition and delivery and its goal of evoking audience response. Although they have often been overlooked, the human roles on which she focuses are pivotal to rhetoric: the person addressed—for Rosenblatt, the reflective thinker responding to literature—and the person who might be about to take action. "There is more than a verbal parallel between the process of reflective thinking arising from response to literature and the process of reflection as a prelude to action in life itself" (*Literature* 226). Not only does she claim that there is a similarity between the thinking that takes place in the wake of reading and that which takes place in anticipation of action but also that individuals' practice of aesthetic reading enhances their capacity to take responsible action.

For Rosenblatt, the crucial goal is not to get audiences to believe speakers or writers but to get all members of a rhetorical situation to trust themselves. Rosenblatt's conception of aesthetic response functions as a metaphor for many kinds of transactions in the world: " 'Literary judgment' or 'literary evaluation,' " she notes, "is more accurately viewed as the umbrella term under which all the various and varied scales of categories of criteria—from the technical to the moral and political and personal—are subsumed" (*The Reader* 155). Rosenblatt's pedagogy is not simply a process that allows people to understand literary texts. Rather, according to Rosenblatt, the engagement with language required when a reader "evokes . . . a literary work" is essential to developing linguistic awareness that can be fully integrated with a sense of self (*The Reader* ix). Readers—like all participants in communicative rhetorical acts—necessarily make choices about language. To be able to judge their choices, readers must be conscious of them. Training in the aesthetic stance develops their deliberate attention to their options.

NOTES

1. A few composition theorists have placed Rosenblatt in the context of rhetorical theory. Janet Emig (123) and Karen LeFevre (39) cite Rosenblatt's ideas that language is constructed through interactive processes. In *Rhetorical Traditions and the Teaching of Writing* (1984), Lil Brannon and Cy Knoblauch argue that writing teachers should adopt the kind of nonelitist stance toward their students' writing that Rosenblatt believed literature teachers should adopt toward students' reading (131).

2. For a discussion of ideological, institutional, and historical tendencies that separate theory and pedagogy—and how these tendencies figured in the reception of Rosenblatt's work—see Mariolina Salvatori's essay "On Behalf of Pedagogy."

3. During the four decades between her 1938 publication and the attention she won among literary theorists in the 1980s, Rosenblatt published articles both for the elementary school teacher reading *Language Arts* and the college English teacher reading the *English Journal* or *College English*, as well as for members of other disciplines reading *Educational Record* or the *Journal of Reading Behavior*. Sidney Ratner has compiled a bibliography of Rosenblatt's work through 1990.

4. While at least one literary scholar dismissed Rosenblatt because of her pedagogical concerns (see Carolyn Allen's discussion of David Bleich 15), others shifted wholly to literary theory, never noting Rosenblatt's concern with pedagogy. Jane Tompkins (xxvi) and Alan Purves and Richard Beach (2) have recognized Rosenblatt as one of the twentieth century's first reader-response theorists. Tompkins simply did not mention pedagogy, while, in their annotated bibliography of reading research (1972), Purves and Beach mentioned Rosenblatt's 1938 book in the section entitled "Studies of Response to Literature" but not in the section of their book addressing education. This tendency in some

recent scholarship on Rosenblatt to focus exclusively on her contributions to theory is in contrast to early reviews of *Literature as Exploration*. When the book first appeared, it was received as a publication of general importance for teachers of literature. Reviews in the *Nation* and the *New Republic* presented it as a work exploring the contributions of literary training to the overall goals of education, and articles in *Book Review Digest* and *Books* emphasized the work's discussion of the relation between the teaching of literature and theories of the social sciences.

5. In a later work, *The Company We Keep* (1988), Booth includes a discussion of Rosenblatt's work in his text proper (13–14).

6. In "The Literary Transaction" (1986), Rosenblatt distinguished herself from reader-response critics, whom she sees as concentrating on response from readers without attention to what it is that readers respond to (77). Rosenblatt raised this issue also in "Transaction versus Interaction—A Terminological Rescue Operation" (1985), where she took issue with criticism not only in reader-response theory but in information-processing theory as well (103).

7. All page references to *Literature as Exploration* are from the fourth edition, unless otherwise noted.

8. I realize that another sense of the term "rhetorical criticism" operates in the work of writers such as Terry Eagleton and Steven Mailloux. These writers treat rhetoric primarily as an ideological dimension of texts rather than an activity by which one person communicates with another. While their work is important to anyone wanting to place a text in its historico- political context, I have chosen here to focus not on this activity of interpretation but on the activity of communion, or communication, between author and reader or text and reader.

9. See Elizabeth Flynn, "Women as Reader-Response Critics" (23–25) for a discussion of feminism in Rosenblatt's reading theory.

10. The idea that readers shape—in a sense "write"—what they read points to the interdependence of reading and writing. Conversely, one would expect authors to "read" opinions, ideas, events, and so forth, prior to, or concurrently with, writing.

In her 1989 essay "Writing and Reading: The Transactional Theory," Rosenblatt discusses how the activities overlap but she also asserts that there are important differences between them.

REFERENCES

Allen, Carolyn. "Louise Rosenblatt and Theories of Reader-Response." *The Experience of Reading: Louise Rosenblatt and Reader-Response Theory*. Ed. John Clifford. Portsmouth, NH: Boynton/Cook, 1991. 15–22.

Booth, Wayne C. *The Company We Keep: An Ethics of Fiction*. Berkeley: U of California P, 1988.

———. *The Rhetoric of Fiction*. 1961. 2d ed. Chicago: U of Chicago P, 1983.

Brannon, Lil, and C[y] H. Knoblauch. *Rhetorical Traditions and the Teaching of Writing*. Upper Montclair, NJ: Boynton/Cook, 1984.

Bryant, Donald C. "Uses of Rhetoric in Criticism." *Papers in Rhetoric and Poetic*. Ed. Donald C. Bryant. Iowa City: U of Iowa P, 1965. 1–14.

Clifford, John, ed. *The Experience of Reading: Louise Rosenblatt and Reader-Response Theory.* Portsmouth, NH: Boynton/Cook, 1991.

———. "Introduction: Reading Rosenblatt." *The Experience of Reading.* Ed. John Clifford. 1–14.

Dewey, John, and Arthur F. Bentley. *Knowing and the Known.* Boston: Beacon, 1949.

Eagleton, Terry. *Literary Theory: An Introduction.* Minneapolis: U of Minnesota P, 1983.

Emig, Janet. "Writing as a Mode of Learning." *College Composition and Communication* 28 (1977): 122–28.

Flynn, Elizabeth A. "Women as Reader-Response Critics." *New Orleans Review* 20 (1983): 20–25.

Hunter, Lynette. *Rhetorical Stance in Modern Fiction: Allegories of Love and Death.* London: Macmillan, 1984.

Johnson, Nan. "Ethos and the Aims of Rhetoric." *Essays on Classical Rhetoric and Modern Discourse.* Ed. Robert J. Connors, Lisa S. Ede, and Andrea A. Lunsford. Carbondale: Southern Illinois UP, 1984. 98–114.

Keliher, Alice. Foreword to series. *Literature as Exploration.* By Louise M. Rosenblatt. New York: Appleton-Century, 1938. xi–xii.

LeFevre, Karen Burke. *Invention as a Social Act.* Carbondale: Southern Illinois UP, 1987.

Mailloux, Steven. *Rhetorical Power.* Ithaca: Cornell UP. 1989.

Purves, Alan C., and Richard Beach. *Literature and the Reader: Research in Response to Literature, Reading Interests, and the Teaching of Literature.* Urbana-Champaign: National Council of Teachers of English, 1972.

Ratner, Sidney. "Bibliography of Louise M. Rosenblatt." *The Experience of Reading: Louise Rosenblatt and Reader-Response Theory.* Ed. John Clifford. Portsmouth, NH: Boynton/Cook, 1991. 219–22.

Reader: Essays in Reader-Oriented Theory, Criticism, and Pedagogy 20 (1988).

Review of *Literature as Exploration* by Louise M. Rosenblatt. *Book Review Digest* (1938): 820.

Review of *Literature as Exploration* by Louise M. Rosenblatt. *Books* (October 16, 1938): 28.

Review of *Literature as Exploration* by Louise M. Rosenblatt. *Nation* 147 (August 6, 1938): 134.

Review of *Literature as Exploration* by Louise M. Rosenblatt. *New Republic* 95 (June 29, 1938): 231.

Richards, I. A. *Practical Criticism: A Study of Literary Judgment.* New York: Harvest-Harcourt, 1929.

Rosenblatt, Louise M. "The Literary Transaction." *The Creating Word: Papers from an International Conference on the Learning and Teaching of English in the 1980s.* Ed. Patricia Demers. Edmonton: U of Alberta P, 1986. 66–85.

———. *Literature as Exploration.* 1st ed. New York: Appleton-Century, 1938; 2d ed. New York: Noble, 1968; 3rd ed. New York: Noble, 1976; 4th ed. New York: MLA, 1983.

———. "On the Aesthetic as the Basic Model of the Reading Process." *Bucknell Review* 26 (1981): 17–32.

———. *The Reader, the Text, the Poem: The Transactional Theory of the Literary Work*. Carbondale: Southern Illinois UP, 1978.

———. "Towards a Transactional Theory of Reading." *Journal of Reading Behavior* 1 (1969): 31–47.

———. "Transaction Versus Interaction: A Terminological Rescue Operation." *Research in the Teaching of English* 19.1 (1985): 96–107.

———. "The Transactional Theory: Against Dualisms." *College English* 55 (1993): 377–86.

———. "What Facts Does This Poem Teach You?" *Language Arts* 57 (1980): 386–94.

———. "What We Have Learned: Reminiscences of the NCTE." *English Journal* 66 (1977): 8, 88–90.

———. "Writing and Reading: The Transactional Theory." *Reading and Writing Connections*. Ed. Jana M. Mason. Boston: Allyn, 1989. 153–76.

Salvatori, Mariolina. "On Behalf of Pedagogy." *The Experience of Reading: Louise Rosenblatt and Reader-Response Theory*. Ed. John Clifford. Portsmouth, NH: Boynton-Cook, 1991. 47–62.

Suleiman, Susan. *The Reader in the Text*. Baltimore: Johns Hopkins UP, 1980.

Tompkins, Jane P. "An Introduction to Reader-Response Criticism." *Reader-Response Criticism: From Formalism to Post-Structuralism*. Ed. Jane P. Tompkins. Baltimore: Johns Hopkins UP, 1980. ix–xxvi.

16

Julia Kristeva: Rhetoric and the Woman as Stranger

Suzanne Clark

In this essay I am going to return to the themes of otherness and colonial ideology with which this volume begins. Like Aspasia, Julia Kristeva is a stranger from the East; like Aspasia, she reminds us of an "Asian" rhetoric, a practice linked with excess, passion, and what Susan Jarratt and Rory Ong call a "dangerous femininity." The theme of strangeness marks the way woman unsettles language. But it is this very unsettling that has made rhetoric interesting again. Rather than reclaiming a place for women within a tradition of rhetoric that has excluded so many, the figure of Rhetorica gives rhetoric itself a new life, changing it from within to accommodate women and other strangers. Julia Kristeva argues in favor of a transformation in our ways of dealing with one another. According to her recent pleas on behalf of a more humane internationalism, we need to cease our struggles to eliminate or deny strangers; we need to acknowledge the strangeness within. And for Kristeva, woman is the prototypical stranger. She believes that the rhetoric against foreigners is a great danger to democracies in the West right now, and that the traditions of cultural and linguistic identity based on exclusion must be changed, at every level, from the personal to the international. There are high stakes involved in finding more inclusive forms of argument. It is Kristeva who first introduced the ideas of Mikhail Bakhtin to the West, in the Paris of the 1960s. The dialogism that has provided feminist rhetoricians such as Dale Bauer (as well as male rhetoricians such as Charles Schuster) with a more promising model for rhetoric has been elaborated in Julia Kristeva's theoretical works.

Julia Kristeva shows us how the very marginality of rhetoric in relation to truth and of woman in relation to power is important to poststructuralist philosophy and psychoanalysis. It is marginality that inaugurates the dialogic. She advocates a notion of cultural and personal identity which recognizes that the strangeness of the other is a strangeness within. At the level of the state, this implies the acceptance of foreigners. At the level of the individual, this implies the recognition of the unconscious. Identity, then, must be seen as provisional rather than exclusive, constructed as an effect of the heterogeneous processes of discourses. This unsettling of a singular and dominant ethos mitigates the way negativity functions in a purifying logic of either/or to create scapegoats and paranoia. As she brings these concerns together, Kristeva emphasizes the *ethical* dimensions of such a project.

Before I begin to explain, let me say a few words about Julia Kristeva's unusual history. She grew up in Bulgaria, the daughter of parents who did not belong to what she calls the "red bourgeoisie," so that she did not have access to the special education of the communist elite. Nonetheless, she went to a French *école maternelle* from an early age, and when she grew older, studied French at a second school that met after regular school hours. How did this education under the Bulgarian regime affect her perspectives? The freedoms afforded her by another language while she was under the constraints of a totalitarian society impressed themselves upon her, as she notes in an interview with me and Kathleen Hulley:

> The experience in Bulgaria permitted me at once to live in an extremely closed environment (which is called totalitarian for good reason, with enormous constrictions), to understand the weight of social life, and at the same time to try to find the small spaces of freedom, which are, for example: the arts, the interest in foreign languages, even religion. (172)

She went on to graduate school, to work on the "new novel," and won a scholarship sponsored by the French government to study in Paris. Nonetheless, she managed to get the opportunity to go only when the dogmatic director of the institute was out of town. She left precipitously and arrived in Paris in 1965, just before Christmas, with only five dollars in her pocket and no funds due for a couple of months. Fortunately, she fell upon an intellectual community there which welcomed her and found her work interesting. Soon she was giving a lecture in

Roland Barthes's seminar, and he was so impressed that he had it published.

She was only twenty-five, a foreigner, and a woman, but she brought with her the first understanding of Bakhtin's dialogism and a thorough grounding in Soviet linguistic research and Marxist scholarship. She had the perspective to reveal the inadequacies of structuralism at the very moment Paris was moving into the poststructuralist revolution. She became part of the avant-garde *Tel Quel* group; she married novelist Philippe Sollers; she participated in the great upheaval of French intellectual life marked by the events of 1968, along with Jacques Lacan, Louis Althusser, Jacques Derrida, Michel Foucault, and again Roland Barthes. This is to say that Julia Kristeva's work at once exemplifies poststructuralism and emphasizes the strangeness within it marked by her femininity and her foreignness. She both embodied and theorized the *difference* that entered French discourse.

Kristeva soon began to publish essays and books, working out a theory that brings together linguistics, semiotics, literary and cultural history, and psychoanalysis. Even her first works remain interesting for their innovative approach to thinking about woman and the subject of discourse (parts of *Polylogue, Semeiotike,* and *About Chinese Women* appear in translation in *Desire in Language* and *The Kristeva Reader*). In 1972 she published her doctoral thesis, *The Revolution in Poetic Language*, which developed a theory of how what she calls the *semiotic* and *symbolic* aspects of language interact. She argued that the historical crisis of modernity, with the old foundations no longer providing credible support to culture, requires not the repression of irrationality but a revolution in our language.

The theory set forth in *Revolution* privileges forms of discourse that are heterogeneous and dialogic, allowing subversive elements into play (for example, the elements Bakhtin called the "carnivalesque"). In *Revolution*, she focuses in particular on the poetic language of writers such as Mallarmé, a use of language that is not based on trying to exclude or constrain its gestural, rhythmic, repetitive component (the "semiotic"). Poetic language may be thought of as "revolutionary," according to Kristeva, not because it plays a direct part in politics, but because it changes the very forms of discourse, making new expressions possible, by liberating the "semiotic"—in Mallarmé's case, musicality—to rupture the constraining regularities of the "symbolic." Think of the "symbolic" as linguistic law and order, including not only the important conventions that make language seem *clear* but also the conventions that enforce ideology. Kristeva does not believe we can or should do away with the symbolic—that way is quite literally madness. However, she does show how the semiotic can interrupt the rigidities of language and open it to a subject in process, to the unsettling and nonlogical life of the body. As a psychoanalyst, she expresses a certain optimism about the crisis of discourses we experience, because the possibilities opened up may allow us to work at making progress.

In Kristeva's narrative of language acquisition, we begin—and we only know this in retrospect, as a function of entering into language—in a state of motility prior to identity or location, which she calls the "chora" of the semiotic. This space of gesture, rhythm, and repetition is not linguistic, but is marked by culture through an undifferentiated relationship to the maternal. We enter into culture, language, and the symbolic, but our discourse inevitably, and in different ways, always depends upon and interacts with the gestural materiality of the semiotic. We are never finished with this maturing identity. Thus Kristeva's theory gives us a rhetoric that is always in need of being situated and embodied, and a subject that is always a work in progress. This version of dialogism insists on the importance of the body.

In later books Kristeva has explored the ways that psychoanalysis and literature negotiate the historical crisis in our cultural discourses. *The Powers of Horror* introduces the notion of the *abject*; *Tales of Love* further explores love, narcissism, relationship, and identity; *The Black Sun* theorizes the melancholy of women and of modern history in relationship to the way we acquire language; *Strangers to Ourselves* argues that we—the modern nation-state as well as the individual—must acknowledge our own strangeness and unconscious to deal with the problem of foreigners; and a novel, *The Samouraïs*, tells the story of poststructuralism and its heroes, from Barthes to Derrida, in fictional form—and from the perspective of three women. In recent speeches and publications, Kristeva has frequently addressed the problems of foreigners and nationalism.

Kristeva is one of the most important poststructuralist theorists, and especially important for feminist rhetoricians. However, she is more likely to be called a philosopher or a psychoanalyst. But I believe that these designations have tended to obscure the way that Kristeva's work challenges philosophy from the position of rhetoric, and changes the psychoanalytic alliance with philosophy against rhetoric. When we read Freud, even as we recognize how indebted he is to a rhetorical understanding of the way the psyche works, and to a rhetorical understanding of therapy as well, we must nevertheless admit that his continuing appeal is to the truth of science. Freud does not present himself as a rhetorician, but as a scientist, and the truth he claims is the truth of philosophy. As Cynthia Chase has pointed out, this allegiance continues in the work of Jacques Lacan, when he locates psychoanalytic truth within language, pointing to the tropes and mathematical forms of language rather than acknowledging the persuasive appeal of identification with his words, or *transference*. So one of Kristeva's chief contributions is to bring psychoanalysis together with rhetoric and the study of language.

What Julia Kristeva helps us to see is the doubleness of how transference works—as rhetoric—both formally, as a trope, and affectively, as persuasion. Kenneth Burke argued in *A Rhetoric of Motives* that identification functions persuasively *before* any argument that might be advanced. Kristeva insists on the importance of identification, but also urges that we keep before us its *metaphoricity*—to transfer one's affective investment from one identity to another is to make a *metaphorical* identification between self and other. It is also the way the ego constructs its imaginary identity. Thus the purely rhetorical category of the ethos and its contingent relationship to pathos are not merely formal matters, but the very site of our identity in culture; the rhetorical situation is where we construct, again and again, the fragile truth of our relationships.

In other words, Kristeva theorizes a recovery of a relational, collaborative view of rhetoric which in *Tales of Love* she situates not in the necessities of opposition but in the necessities of mutuality. This will seem to American feminists congruent with the project of emphasizing interpersonal relationships, which appears in work by Carol Gilligan, Mary Field Belenky, and Deborah Tannen, among others. Kristeva would not fix this difference as "feminist," however. She worries that making gender differences into positive categories would reduce us to an oppositional logic—and to the rhetoric of dispute, antagonism, and hierarchy. She wants to avoid the feminist problem associated in the *Haraway too* United States with essentialism and identity politics, a problem many feminists would also like to avoid, but without giving up the possibility of feminism. However, I believe that Kristeva's work supports feminist projects, perhaps providing a way out of essentialist dilemmas for advocates of a dialogic rhetoric.

Kristeva's theory upsets the traditions of rhetoric in ways that extend feminist questioning and articulate that critique with poststructuralist philosophy. The social sciences in the United States and what poststructuralism calls "the human sciences," including also philosophy, literature, history, and linguistics, have taken a "rhetorical turn," with theorists such as Jacques Derrida, Michel Foucault, and Kristeva in France, and Richard Rorty and the anthropologist Clifford Geertz in the United States, arguing that knowledge is constructed by discourse. Following Nietzsche, poststructuralism posits that truth is metaphorical and figurative rather than prior to or outside language. However, there are traditions of rhetoric that are not at all compatible with the poststructuralist questioning of dominant discourses. This new interest in rhetoric sometimes ignores the historical connection of rhetoric with persuasion and with power. French critical theory, as it developed in the 1960s, when Kristeva had first arrived in Paris, sharply differentiated itself from what it saw as the "old rhetoric." This turn *against* a certain version of rhetoric in the history of poststructuralism is very likely to have been noted by Kristeva, since her chief mentor, Roland Barthes, discussed it at length.

In a seminar he gave in 1964–1965 ("The Old Rhetoric: An Aide-Memoire") Barthes specified in what seems to be loving detail the history of the old rhetoric he said he was leaving behind. Since he was a particularly strong influence in Kristeva's career—and she attended his seminar soon after she arrived in Paris from Bulgaria in 1965—his remarks may serve as a point of orientation to her situation within the critical discourse in France. Barthes dismissed classical rhetoric because he thought it functioned as a colonizing discourse of mastery, in the service of traditional conventionality. He resolutely left the tradition behind, in order to found the new semiotics, not because he believed that attention to the forms of rhetoric was misplaced, and not because he believed we should not learn these forms—indeed, he remarks that they now permeate our language, unbeknownst to us, an unconscious residue of past instruction. Barthes objects to the passing on of rhetorical doctrine because it pretends to control discourse and tries to eliminate whatever might upset order.

Nevertheless, he notes some elements in the history of rhetoric that will be of some importance to him, and to Kristeva. In particular he makes a very interesting distinction between "atticism" and "asianism" in rhetoric—between the "guardians of a pure vocabulary," the "castrating ethic of 'purity,' which still exists today" and "an exuberant style tending toward the strange, based, like mannerism, on the effect of surprise; here the 'figures' play an essential role" (29). The enduring classicizing aesthetic—which he goes on to call an ethnocentrism—involved not only racism but also classism, opposing the *classicus* author to the *proletarius*. This is a hint that has interesting affinities with Kristeva's later project in *Powers of Horror*, where she will specifically take up the problem of a rhetoric that purifies. Exclusionary rhetoric has served cultures and religions to distinguish between us and them, those who belong and those who are strangers. If by "rhetoric" we mean the project that would purify argument of its irrational elements, of whatever is foreign to reason, then neither Barthes nor Kristeva would want to be included in our list of rhetoricians. But, then, neither would most feminists, I think. Indeed, the critique of that ethnocentrism in rhetoric is of primary significance to Kristeva.

The way out of ethnocentrism is to pay attention to the interaction of subjects. Kristeva would be a rhetorician of what John Gage has called the "dialectic" rather than the technical. She is interested in a kind of knowledge that can only be rhetorical, the product of an exchange between speaking subjects. The situation of psychoanalysis is rhetorical, producing analytic knowledge in the only form that knowing can take. She does not, then, regard either writing or speech as a product representing some prior knowledge, but rather as a process, or "work in progress," that produces both the author and the audience in its text. Her special importance to women rhetoricians comes out of this attention to the *subjects* of rhetorical invention.

Kristeva proposes that we take up, through education and psychoanalysis, the insight that what we know in language, in ourselves as individuals, is a disquieting strangeness. This familiarity with the alien is what Freud called the sensation of the *uncanny*. In the practice of *disputatio*—where first one side, then the other, plays the game of claiming to be exclusively right, thus excluding contradiction—rhetoric takes its most foreign relationship to truth by excluding strangeness. Such agonistic discourse, by its insistence on absolute difference, practices an uncanny return of the truth of estrangement. Can this condition of estrangement in which humanity lives be cured? Is it not the condition of language itself? In her recent *Strangers to Ourselves*, Kristeva prescribes psychoanalysis and education not as a cure, but as a way to disseminate the understanding that we are, in fact, all strangers, without and within. Such a stance acknowledges the constructedness and fragility of individual and community identities. The ego, like the nation, should not be defended against otherness by paranoid exclusions; it should rather be conceived as a set of processes. To show what this might mean I need to address Kristeva's conception of the speaking person as a subject-in-process and on trial.

What does Kristeva tell us about the subject? She reminds us of the dialectic that always occurs between known and unknown in language, as between signs and affect, the symbolic and the semiotic. However, the problems for the contemporary subject are rhetorical in part, because we live in history and in a time of crisis. In another time we might have faithfully worked to reproduce the knowledge of our elders, within a stable set of conventions and beliefs regulated by religion and state—we might not even have recognized the rhetorical nature of our labor since its object would have been firmly bound within language and culture. Now we live in historical crisis, without the constraint (or the security) of institutions such as the Church; we live vulnerable to our own strangeness and faced with the task of finding ways to work together. This is both a crisis and an opportunity because the discourses of institutions of state and religion enforced sameness; they accepted the stranger only on condition that s/he be assimilated. The discourses of literature and psychoanalysis, on the other hand, provide models of a polylogic that incorporates strangeness into the language. Kristeva has argued throughout her career that the question of ethics, of horror but also of love—of human relationship—needs to be primary to the study of language.

What does Kristeva say about women as subjects? This has been a confusing question, because Kristeva has declared herself to be "anti-feminist." But the meaning of this, like Barthes's stance against rhetoric, has to be understood in terms of the cultural situation of feminism. Like other poststructuralists—in particular Althusser, Barthes, Lacan, and Derrida—Kristeva has worked to critique a positive notion of subjectivity, the humanist ideal of a free and singular individual. Therefore she fears that feminism simply resurrects the old identity together with the old problems positivism represents. This is especially important because Kristeva will go on to valorize not the state or other versions of social order but the individual—understood not as a fixed and fully conscious identity but as a subject-in-process—as the site for working through the historical crisis of modernity.

I will begin where Lacan seemed to end when he said that woman is not in language. This statement might seem like an example of wishful thinking on Lacan's part, but it might also be read as descriptive of the way language works in our culture, a location defined both by history and by community. Lacan did not invent this notorious exclusion: he rewrites Freud without escaping the history enclosing Freud. But this exclusion from the symbolic is something women have also noted, though, curiously, their objections have always seemed beside the point. Why is it impossible for women to simply speak up as women and offer a different opinion? The structuralist response and the Marxist response have shared a similarly deterministic characterization of the subject, explaining how we are subject *to* language and to history, but offering no sense of how we might be the subject *of* a productive discourse, or act as agents of change. This exclusion has been addressed by feminists in strategies that seem contradictory: first, by assembling an enormous quantity of writing by women which seems to write *woman*, to produce a gendered subject of writing; and second, by unsettling the apparent identity of the subject, which had seemed both unified and male, unwriting *man*. The two projects seem at odds, and indeed have resulted in contention within feminism. The notion of a female identity seems to require extremes of essentialism. And apolitical fragmentation seems to be the result of poststructuralist reflexivity and critique. However, the two have worked dialectically to produce a feminist subject which is both not an identity—not essentialist—and yet political.

Kristeva can be enormously helpful to feminism because she has helped to formulate the attack on the totalizing male subject, but she has also seemed frustratingly antifeminist in her refusals to take up the categories of gender. Furthermore, her work has been criticized by several feminists, such as Andrea Nye, Juliet Flower McCannell, Nancy Fraser, and Judith Butler, who have argued that it is consonant with oppressive systems, promoting traditional images of women, overemphasizing the maternal, and even revealing a bias in favor of heterosexuality. In particular, the writing since *The Powers of Horror* has seemed to formerly friendly critics such as Paul Smith a turn away from the leftist politics of her earlier work. Joan Brandt writes out of her interest in Kristeva's project: Kristeva, she says, is out to subvert the power of scientific discourse, the positivism of linguistics, "to show that the assumption of objectivity at the root of Western positivist thought is actually grounded in a subjectivity that orders and systematizes and that remains uncritical, indeed, unaware of the ideological underpinnings of its own constructs" (135–36). However, Brandt accuses Kristeva of the very binary thinking that her theory critiques. I believe that many of these critics are misreading a complex theory. Some may be promoting exclusivist ideas themselves. Kelly Oliver points out that critics of Kristeva read her in contradictory, sometimes opposite, ways. Oliver notes that this suggests a failure to take the tension among categories in her work into account. It also suggests that it is not so easy to write within a dialogic rhetoric, even when one is critical of positivist thought.

Far from contributing to the paranoia of exclusivist positions, Kristeva advocates—and practices—a rhetoric that is enabling for women and for men too, a healthy critique of obsessive certainties that makes philosophy more rhetorical. The move Kristeva wants to make, from language seen as a product to language seen as a process, overlaps with categories that are familiar to scholars and teachers involved in the recent history of American composition and rhetoric. For Kristeva, the crisis in political and philosophical foundations has accompanied the possibility of thinking about language itself, and the speaking subject, as a *process*. The subject-in-process is defined by a constant renewal of struggle, or crisis. This means that the speaking subject is deeply involved with the historical shifts experienced by contemporary Western cultures, and with the possibility of working out better ways of living together. She says "modernity . . . has rendered the crisis explicit. And . . . it has minimized the moments of equilibrium. One can think of it this way: previous social forms counted on a certain calm and the crisis came periodically, while now, an epoch has opened when we live in permanent crisis. And what is provisional is the moment of status-quo" ("Interview," 160).

The "status-quo" is provisional, and writing does not function merely to express fixities and identities (male or female). Writing works to *produce* these identities, often by repressing difference. Therefore Kristeva privileges not the generic language of clarity or of communication, but *poetic language*, by which she means a use of language that is genuinely dialogic, that allows the inclusion of the foreign, the strange, the unconscious—the woman. Yet to her critics, the idea that *art* can change the world by changing language has seemed naive, and the idea that woman is the most likely of marginal subjects, best witness to strangeness and difference, is nevertheless not connected to any positive notions of politicized gender. When Kristeva talks about "woman," she means to take up the Lacanian idea that woman is not *in* language and to valorize that very absence. Woman unsettles the repressive identity-making work of the language that would deny process. Rhetoric has itself repressed the rhetoricity of *all* discourse, working against itself. Kristeva opposes a feminism or a rhetoric that tries to deny marginality.

At the same time that many feminists are declaring the end of marginality for women, Kristeva is arguing that the crisis of modernity makes all of us marginal subjects. What Kristeva wants to emphasize is the importance of resisting the dominations of sameness and order. This resistance does not mean that Kristeva advocates a rhetoric of hysteria, which would *oppose* clarity and order in the name of the irrational. Instead she posits a kind of hysteria *within* the mastery of rational rhetoric, which would enable resistance to transform language from within. It is the woman not *in* language who provides the site of the strangeness that generates resistance, as she explains:

> I am very attached to this idea of the woman as irrecuperable foreigner. But I know that certain American feminists do not think well of such an idea, because they want a positive notion of woman. But one can be positive by starting with this permanent marginality, this motor of change. So I think that for me femininity is exactly this lunar form, like the moon is the inverse of the sun of our identity. From this point of view, perhaps we women have it more than the men, but the men have it also. And to try to preserve this part as unreconcilable permits us perhaps always to be what Hegel called the eternal irony of the community. That is to say, a sort of vigilance apart which keeps groups from closing up, becoming homogeneous and so oppressive. That is, I see the role of women as a sort of vigilance, a strangeness, always on guard and contestatory.
>
> In fact, it's the role of the hysteric, a little, but why not. I accept that altogether. We can play our hysterias without necessarily making a psychodrama and exposing ourselves to be the victims of the male order, but with great lucidity and ... great mastery and measure. That is, perverse hysterics. Very wise. ("Interview," 168–69)

If woman is an "irrecuperable foreigner," how does Kristeva theorize woman and the sign? In an early work, "The Bounded Text," she argues that the history of the sign has implications for the *subject*. Novelistic discourse constitutes the sign as "nondisjunctive," not allowing both sides of the dialectic, but rather insisting on identity and exclusion. Woman functions in this logic as a "pseudo-center" excluding the other, which is then constituted as the subject. In other words, the figure of woman as different defines the difference of the subject. We could see this in operation in Freud's text, where the sight of the little girl generates the little boy's sense of himself as well as his fear of castration. However, Kristeva does not read the Freudian text as altogether bounded, under the sign of absolute identity. She shifts her reading of Freud toward the importance of uncertainty in his texts. The Freudian discovery Kristeva emphasizes is the discovery of an unconscious that inhabits reason itself, that marks the crisis of the subject by producing a crisis within the identity of the nondisjunctive sign. Thus Kristeva's reading of Freud unsettles the absolute distinction of boy and girl, extending the Freudian thesis of bisexuality, and using Freud himself to oppose an absolutism of the Oedipal moment, a finality of the Oedipal cut. Kristeva's Freud is helpful to women in this sense *because* it is antifeminist. The production of a singular feminist identity (something in little danger of emerging, I might interject) would reproduce the logic of the sign, would reproduce, in fact, the female pseudocenter that mediates a return to the male as subject. Kristeva says: "I am afraid that, if we insist on the fact that the feminine differentiates the individual, we could arrive at a new form of homogeneity" ("Interview," 66).

Thus Kristeva brings to rhetoric a new insistence on the construction of ethos. Kristeva's concept of subjectivity in language, developed from Benveniste and from Bakhtin's dialogism, at once recognizes the constraints imposed on the subject that society defines through language, and also insists on the inventive agency of the subject as the speaker in discourse. Benveniste points out that the "I" refers to the exercise of discourse in a particular instance. The pronoun "I," that is, refers not to a particular individual but to the speaking subject of discourse. Subjectivity is not something separate from language but rather the effect of a rhetorical situation. This situation is always dialogic, constituted within dialogue. Thus the psychoanalytic dialogue represents the situation of the subject more accurately than the notion that the ego is an isolated individual.

Furthermore, for Kristeva, the dialogic that constitutes the subject is not an intersubjectivity of absolutely autonomous identities, but an *intertextuality that is dependent on bodies*. Thus the problem of isolation from history is an illusion produced by the failure to imagine the subject as text, but the problem of determinism is a failure to acknowledge how biology can make our social fate undecidable. Kristeva says:

> I think on the one hand, that we must maintain the autonomy of discourse with respect to social level, because it is a level of autonomy that guarantees freedom. We can speak in a different manner than our familial and social determination. There is an undecidable part which comes perhaps out of our biology, a certain number of determinations which escape us. But in any case which are not reducible to what we know of society. And if one does not keep this autonomy of discourse, one falls very quickly into a reductionist and sociological conception where all aesthetic or personal performances are explained by the social milieu or a similar fate: from the fact that you were born red, black, white, or poor. This said, there is nevertheless an incontestable interaction between discourse and society, and I myself would consider that the fact

of taking society as a generalized text permits us to see how, for example, a literary text does not live in an autistic fashion, closed on the interior of itself, but borrows at all times from the discourses of the press, from oral discourses, from political discourses, and from other texts which preceded it, which provide vehicles in their turn for these cultural and political texts of history. ("Interview," 175–76)

Kristeva's dialogism emphasizes her resistance to the reductiveness of identity politics. The "fact that you were born red, black, white, or poor" (or female) will not alone determine your fate, but become part of an interaction with other elements, including the unconscious. Kristeva's semiotic is to the symbolic as the unconscious is to the conscious, but also as the foreigner is to the nation. Freud is responsible for resolving the dualism of the rational and the irrational by locating the uncanny *within reason*, so we are all not only bisexual, both male and female, but also foreigners to ourselves, inhabited by otherness. Kristeva discovers an analogy between the state, which produces the foreign, and the ego, which produces the unconscious by the cut of the symbolic.

As an alternative to the subject of *understanding* assumed by rhetoric as the proper subject of argument, Kristeva proposes the *subject-in-process* of a dialogue that does not exclude the stranger. Kristeva proposes a model of female subjectivity that includes desire and estrangement, and that has the merit of acknowledging the extreme difficulties of relations between the sexes in our cultural history. As an alternative to the paranoia that Barthes associates with science, a paranoia embodied in the female referent, she proposes the position of the hysteric, embodying the feminine in the text as Hegel's eternal irony of the community, always apart from the closures of ideology. Kristeva has patiently adumbrated the limited but powerful concept of this negative, strange, uncanny, foreign subject-in-process, the subject of the global crisis, the subject to which women most easily have access. I believe this is a concept useful to feminism and to rhetoric.

Kristeva's view of society as a textuality returns us to rhetoric. In Kristeva's work, it is precisely the figurative nature of rhetoric's relationship to truth that would lead us to take up a rhetorical perspective. In place of the closed, bounded text with a subject that is inevitably male, Kristeva advocates a notion of discourse that is open, and a notion of the subject that escapes determinism by the immersion in struggle. The model of transference in psychoanalysis shows the doubleness of the rhetorical transaction, its persuasive and figurative nature. Thus Kristeva theorizes a view of the ethos of discourse that can return rhetoric to the use of women. Here is strangeness made familiar, an uncanny rhetoric indeed.

REFERENCES

Barthes, Roland. "The Old Rhetoric: An Aide-Memoire." *The Semiotic Challenge*. Trans. Richard Howard. New York: Hill, 1988.

Brandt, Joan. "The Systematics of a Non-System." *American Journal of Semiotics* 5.1 (1987): 133–50.

Chase, Cynthia. "Transference as Trope and Persuasion." *Discourse in Psychoanalysis and Literature*. Ed. Shlomith Rimmon-Kenan. London: Methuen, 1987.

Kristeva, Julia. *About Chinese Women*. Trans. Anita Barrows. London: Marion Boyars, 1977.

———. *Black Sun: Depression and Melancholia*. Trans. Leon Roudiez. New York: Columbia UP, 1989.

———. *Desire in Language: A Semiotic Approach to Literature and Art*. Ed. Leon S. Roudiez. Trans. Alice Jardine, Thomas A. Gora, and Leon S. Roudiez. Oxford: Blackwell; New York: Columbia UP, 1980.

———. "An Interview with Julia Kristeva." With Suzanne Clark and Kathleen Hulley. *Discourse* (fall–winter 1990–1991). 149–80.

———. *The Kristeva Reader*. Ed. Toril Moi. New York: Columbia UP, 1986.

———. *Powers of Horror*. Trans. Leon S. Roudiez. New York: Columbia UP, 1982.

———. *The Revolution in Poetic Language*. Trans. Margaret Waller. Intro. Leon S. Roudiez. New York: Columbia UP, 1984.

———. *La révolution du langage poétique: L'avant-garde à la fin du XIXe siècle: Lautréamont et Mallarmé*. Paris: Editions du Seuil, 1974.

———. *Les Samouraïs*. Paris: Fayard, 1990.

———. *Semeiotike: Recherches pour une sémanalyse*. Paris: Editions du Seuil, 1969.

———. "The Speaking Subject Is Not Innocent." Trans. Chris Miller. *Freedom and Interpretation: The Oxford Amnesty Lectures 1992*. Ed. Barbara Johnson. New York: Basic Books, 1993. 148–74.

———. *Strangers to Ourselves*. Trans. Leon S. Roudiez. New York: Columbia UP, 1991.

———. *Tales of Love*. Trans. Leon S. Roudiez. New York: Columbia UP, 1987.

Oliver, Kelly. *Reading Kristeva*. Bloomington: Indiana UP, 1993.

Smith, Paul. *Discerning the Subject*. Minneapolis: U of Minnesota P, 1988.

Afterword
· · · · · · · ·

"The strands of research and work and lived experience that have come together in *Reclaiming Rhetorica* seem so much a beginning, a portent of things to come, that we have attempted to resist any traditional sense of finished coherence, unified sameness, or full closure in this volume. In the spirit of ongoing collaboration, then, this work ends with a discussion of several questions I have raised for consideration, and with an open and enthusiastic invitation to readers to join in and thus continue the conversation. In the pages that follow, contributors to *Reclaiming Rhetorica* muse in print on some of the ideas that have animated our work on this project."—*Andrea A. Lunsford*

· · · · · ·

Is there a 'woman's' or a 'feminine' rhetoric? What issues does such a question raise?

"I am not persuaded that there exists a distinct women's rhetoric or feminine rhetoric (just as I doubt that there exists a single men's/masculine rhetoric). On the other hand, it is clear that women's voices have been deliberately stifled, that women have been barred from the study of academic rhetoric, and that the ways in which women have practiced and promoted rhetoric have not obtained canonical status in the places where rhetoric is studied. This book must be a sign of change in minds, the kind of change that rhetoric allows us to bring about in ourselves and others.

I think that rhetoric is most useful and interesting when seen as a bridge between differences in understanding, whatever the traces of such differences. I remain foolishly optimistic about the possibility of good faith between opposed partisans. —*James Oldham*

· · · · · ·

"[In the seminar on Women Rhetoricians] we tentatively began to suggest to one another that there were, after all, some common traits that seemed to cross time and place in women's formal use of language. We noted, for example, our authors' habitual reluctance to use violent or

319

coercive language; and we traced the rhetorical strategies used by so many of our subjects to create a sense of shared community in their audiences. Each of our subjects claimed language for herself as a powerful tool to make changes in the world. Yet, while public persuasion was certainly a goal for some—like Margaret Fuller and Sojourner Truth—more important, women's various discourses appeared to us to have been developed as a strategy for public survival rather than as a strategy merely for public persuasion. In other words, it seemed to us that the women we studied saw language as a way of imprinting their reality on a world in which they might otherwise remain invisible.

"[Nevertheless,] I have come away from the project skeptical about any claim to a unique or definable 'women's' rhetoric, and especially if such claims ignore the specificities of historical time frame, region, and cultural inflection. But I do think that most white women argue very differently from white men when they are addressing a mixed audience; and, again, I think white women participate in yet another discourse community when only other white women like themselves are present. Within Euro-American (educated) culture of the nineteenth and twentieth centuries, women have popularly been seen as irrational and illogical, appealing to emotion, when, in fact, my experience is that women are always more logical than men; and women only energetically appeal to emotion when addressing a mixed audience and attempting to evoke empathy in that audience. Indeed, if there is one salient difference in the way Euro-American men and women attempt to persuade one another, it is women's habitual reliance on the appeal to empathy as a way of asking an audience to consider radically new propositions by means of experiencing the world beyond their own skin. Men sometimes attempt this as well, but not as regularly."—*Annette Kolodny*

. . . . . .

"From what I read of the personal letters, public speeches, and curricular materials of the women who taught at women's colleges, I learned that they were fully conscious of themselves as women, women who chose to use and further develop a discipline academically attributed to men. They challenged their students to present themselves as women (but not necessarily *feminist*) speakers, debaters, and social changers. However, they did not suggest that women speak in one voice; rather, they respected and encouraged intellectual diversity . . . which we also agreed to do in working together as rhetoricians."—*Kathryn M. Conway*

"So far as a woman's, or a feminine, or a womanly rhetoric might go—I think the rhetoric of the disenfranchised and the disempowered is gendered feminine, which is different from "woman's rhetoric." Usually, such rhetoric comes out of the mouths of bodies sexed female, but it has surely come out of mouths of men as well: of African Americans, of political prisoners, of the poor, the uneducated, the weak. It's doubly ironic that the rhetoric of the (seemingly) disempowered could and does continually incite such powerful response (and overreaction) on the part of those who are in power. Those in power are all too often *enraged* by such rhetoric, and their overreaction manifests itself in shunnings, beatings, silencings, killings, tortures—punishments of all degrees and kinds.

"The enraged must be terrified and threatened. Otherwise, why would the powerful respond as they have to the Freedom Movement in Mississippi, the Kent State demonstrations (or the student demonstrations in China, Soweto, Germany, France), the antiapartheid movement in South Africa, the Salem witch trials, the McCarthy hearings? Why else would powerful men have responded so negatively to Aspasia (considered a courtesan), to Hypatia (stripped, skinned alive, chopped to bits, and scattered over Alexandria), to Heloise (violated, disgraced, discarded, hidden away), to Margery Kempe (shunned, beaten, jailed), to Anne Askew (burned)—and to all the 'madwomen in the attic,' all the 'crazy' women writers or speakers (Mary Wollstonecraft, Virginia Woolf)."—*Cheryl Glenn*

. . . . . .

"Yes, I think there is a women's rhetoric, one arising from women's experience in the private rather than the public sphere. I think it can be seen in selection of subject matter; in the relationship with the audience (communication rather then self-expression); in a conversational style; in a resistance to what Ong calls adversativeness, and to the hero as model for the writer; and in tact. Corresponding 'weaknesses' (from the more traditional point of view) are lack of force and lack of focus.

"The most important issue raised by this question is the danger of seeing a feminine rhetoric as exclusive to women, or, of course, a masculine rhetoric as exclusive to men. There have always been women who write in the masculine way, and men who write in the feminine. Moreover, as women increasingly move into the public sphere and as more men undertake child care, I think we may see a blending of masculine with feminine rhetoric."—*Christine Mason Sutherland*

"In these antiessentialist times, I would not be so bold or so co-optive as to imagine a women's rhetoric. Themes appear and disappear: ethos, ethics, caring, pathos, emotions, dialogue, community, difference, strangeness: but these are not themes unique to women's rhetoric. There is, however, one theme that 'stands out' in the frequency of its occurrence, and it is a theme seldom seen in traditional rhetoric. Writing on nineteenth-century women, Joanne Wagner in this volume observes that, for women, 'the process of defining a self through writing was not so clear cut,' and I believe that this difficulty in self-definition led women rhetoricians to reject individualist concepts of free will and to conceptualize a subject-in-process, a fragmentary psyche, and knowledge through sharing long before other rhetoricians. In turn, the subject-in-process suggests a very different rhetoric, one far more dynamic, interactive, and intertextual than those based on a Cartesian subject.

"Many of the figures here do describe the complexity of self-definition. If Aspasia invented the Socratic dialogue, she saw knowledge as existing within us but arrived at it in stages through a less than gentle dialogue. Kempe emphasizes the stages of her conversion, the changing of her costume, and the varieties of her devotion which put her at odds with others but allowed her to struggle toward a knowledge of her place in society. To write and teach, Christine de Pisan first had to imagine herself as a man; and in addressing women's needs, Wollstonecraft demanded 'the recontextualization of women inside the generally received notions of humans and their souls' (Barlowe). By the time we reach the twentieth century, we have Jackson telling of the woman-part and the man-part in need of reunion, and Kristeva developing an antihumanist subject. Even a rhetorician as removed from the psychological as Langer describes the mechanisms of creating change as a process between individual conception and social mediations.

"If self-definition is a major impetus in women's rhetoric, then rhetoric is as much directed at the speaker as the audience. A women's rhetoric would both accept and value that dialogue with the audience since it changes *both* the rhetor's and the audience's beliefs. We see hints of that here: none of these figures describes the activity of persuasion as simple or particularly desirable; at best, it is an act with ethical dangers. For instance, Ida B. Wells and other African American women leaders are not described as persuading (despite the righteousness of their causes), but rather as naming (truth telling), 'articulat[ing] the fears that inhibit others from acting responsibly,' and setting courses of action based on "what the individual *can do*," as Jacqueline Jones Royster puts it. The speaker describes a process of coming to self-awareness and yet does not dictate the audience's actions.

"In minimizing persuasion and emphasizing subjectivity both as discourse and as a process of negotiation, women's rhetorics may have the most insight as to the place of rhetorics in pluralistic societies. If these rhetoricians suggest that we are never simply women, men, philosophers, or African Americans, but rather multiple and changing, then implicit in their assumptions may be ways of revising a public discourse which for too long was based on exclusion, on the white man haranguing at the front of the room. This book can only begin to hint at what that revision might be, but it is important to begin that examination now in our postmodern world."—*Arabella Lyon*

. . . . . .

"Is there a women's rhetoric? It seems to me all of the women discussed in this volume spoke or wrote out of a sense of urgency. Several of them express both a genuine regard for the specificity of experience and a desire to make specific experience matter in, and contribute to, the world at large. Many encourage conversation, not as a way to pass the time, but as a matter of survival. They theorized about language chiefly to figure out how to solve problems through language, not so that they could create a map of language.

"As to whether there is a women's rhetoric, I believe there are probably a multitude of women's rhetorics. I want to be cautious about making generalizations before I have plenty of examples of female rhetoric— examples of rhetoric as practice and as theory (although I'm certain there is no definite line between these). My point is simply that I want us to look at what women have done and said rather than construct an idea of female rhetoric whose main purpose is to exist in contrast to male (traditional? classical?) rhetoric. I don't want to create a tradition of female rhetoric which then ends up excluding women who don't fit into it comfortably."—*Annika Hallin*

. . . . . .

"I like to view 'Dame Rhetoric' as the masthead on a ship filled with a number of women figures, their practices, and their understandings of rhetoric. In this context, then, yes, it is possible to speak of both 'women's rhetoric' and a 'feminine rhetoric,' even in the obligatory antiessentialist times Arabella Lyon refers to. I don't think these terms have to be avoided; they can be shaped as valid, valuable areas for inquiry. My

understanding of 'writing the body' and 'écriture féminine' is a reclamation and affirmation of women's speech patterns and practices that
have been suppressed, excluded, denigrated. Studies in sociolinguistics,
like Lakoff's *Language and Women's Place* and Deborah Tannen's deeply
funny *But You Just Don't Understand*, have defined tangible differences
in patterns of speech behavior and in perceptions and understandings of
interlocutional genres, which is a second level up—how a given speech
pattern is perceived and received—as feminine, masculine, strong, weak,
etc.—by men, by women, by the culture, in committee meetings, in public forums. Why does Hillary Clinton have to dress up like Barbie to
override the negative perceptions of her strength? A number of recent
studies, such as Hester Eisenstein's *The Future of Difference*, repeat the
warning that the study of difference is divisive and only reinstates binaries and polarizations that most feminists want to transcend. The problem with avoiding the study of difference is aptly defined by Deborah
Tannen in a dialogue with Robert Bly. For as long as there are perceived
and believed-in differences between men's and women's discourse practices, and demonstrably different receptions of the same practices—e.g.
assertive decisiveness, when practiced by men as opposed to women
(he's decisive; she's bossy, a control freak)—we cannot adopt a know-
nothing attitude toward such studies and toward the concept of difference itself."—*C. Jan Swearingen*

. . . . . .

"My feminist inclinations compel me to ask, 'Does anyone ever ask if
there is a *men's rhetoric?*' In my estimation, this is the question that
makes the doubting of a women's rhetoric make sense. After all, the
challenge is not, of course, whether there is such a thing as rhetoric.
The challenge is not whether rhetoric, as a human phenomenon, deserves attention. We answered those questions centuries ago. The challenge is really to the received understanding that rhetoric as a concept
has been encoded by images and experiences that are 'male,' so much
so in fact that, for some people, despite contemporary research and
scholarship that defies the exclusiveness of these images and experiences, women and rhetoric, like women and philosophy, or women and
intellectualism in general, seem antithetical at an essential rather than a
socially constructed level.

"Raising a question about 'women's' rhetoric, rightly or wrongly,
counters a deeply ingrained sense of what the very nature of rhetoric is
and inevitably meets walls of resistance. It is not surprising to me, then,

that questions emerge still that seem in some way essential. For example: How can you call what women do and have done 'rhetoric'?

"Beyond these culturally and historically defined constraints, however, I am reminded of earlier conversations in the 1970s and the early 1980s that focused on whether there is such a thing as 'women's' language. I was struck at the time by the research that pointed out the tendency of women to ask questions using the most polite form; by the features in 'women's' talk that seemed to receive affirmation and reward or denial and punishment in public discourse; by patterns in terms of the metaphors that women seemed to use more often to explain, instruct, or persuade. These discoveries pushed my thinking toward the social, political, and economic realities of language as a cultural phenomenon, and they seemed to have implications that were rhetorical, not just linguistic.

"Looking back on these conversations from the perspective of my having participated in this volume, I would say now that the question of a 'women's' language seems to become more suggestive when it is rephrased as a question of 'women's' rhetoric. Focusing on phonology, or morphology, or even on syntax and semantics strikes me as not offering quite as much distinctiveness for inquiry as does focusing on chunks of meaning beyond the sentence level that highlight sociological, or cognitive, or expressive dimensions of language. By contrast, a rhetorical perspective seems to underscore the notion that language use gains meaning not only in larger units but also in context rather than in isolation, and that the specifics of the context matter.

"My sense, then, is that if in the academy we can resist the tendency to set up nonproductive binary contrasts between women's lives and men's lives as the very first measure of validity, rather than one of many, then the question of 'women's' rhetoric can become a provocative entree for inquiry. Questions that come to mind are:

1. Have women artfully used language in the 'public' and/or the 'private' sphere (as we have come to understand these arenas as gendered spaces) to explain, inform, persuade, or activate? Have women demonstrated rhetorical competence?
2. Have women taught others to use language artfully? Have they participated in the enterprise of teaching and learning in terms of epistemic and/or pedagogical theory or in terms of innovative practice?
3. Have women thought, talked, and/or written about language as it intersects with knowledge and action? Have women participated

over time in ongoing philosophical, scholarly, or intellectual discourse about the art of writing effectively? Have women facilitated, extended, or affected in any way the discourse of others?

4. Who, in the specific, are these women—by race, class, ethnicity, historical place, training, profession, and so forth? What have they done? How have they done it? When? Where? Under what conditions? With what impact? At what costs?

5. Is the question of 'women's' rhetoric a question of the rhetoric of women (as an ordinary or extraordinary experience), or is it a question of women in rhetoric as philosophers, scholars, and/or practitioners, or are these other dimensions to what it means for rhetoric to have this particular modifier, as compared for example with having 'men's' as the modifier?

"At the very least, this volume suggests to me that each of the scholars here has answered a resounding "yes" to "women's" rhetoric as a valid area of inquiry. My sense, however, is that in the larger academic community we are just beginning to unlock thinking and just beginning to make a more fully developed case for the presentation of rhetoric in ways that make it possible for women to be perceived to be as naturally a part of this domain as anyone else. In my estimation, those of us with an interest in this area have much work to do, but my experiences also tell me that it can and should be done."—*Jacqueline Jones Royster*

. . . . . .

What are the major problems, questions, and/or issues facing scholars who want to pursue research on women and the history of rhetoric?

"There are a number of problems facing scholars who want to pursue research on women and the history of rhetoric. I've been involved in some very hostile exchanges with classicists and with postmodern theorists—two very different groups, obviously—who on different grounds and for different purposes quickly questioned or readily dismissed the (a) actuality and (b) discoverabilty of women in rhetoric. It is an exciting double challenge to draw on rediscovered women figures in recent classical scholarship and then to read that material with a rhetorician's eyes. Even our eyes are diverse, as this collection so splendidly illustrates, and that's great. A healthy tolerance for our burgeoning diversity and the goodwill that helps us define common goals are what I would put in my backpack for future expeditions. One favorite project: rereading the already amply read classical dramas to examine interpretations of women's political speeches, i.e. women's rhetoric, in the plays. Another place scholars need to look is to the religious side of reform movements. The place of women within that religious side, and the religious motivations of women reformers, is of great interest because it suggests another dinosaur about to fall—the notion that women weren't active outside the domestic sphere until very recently. There is a hidden history just getting uncovered, again. Histories of the ordination of women go back to the first centuries of the Church but are routinely suppressed. It was not until the 1240s that women were expressly forbidden to be ordained. Gerda Lerner has said in her most recent book that the historiographical problem is that we've had to recover our history each time a women's movement emerges: witness Christine de Pisan. Stretching back to antiquity, all the women in 'the tradition' know one another's names, but the official record kept bumping them out of the canon, or announcing they were 'fictions.' I'll borrow from George Kennedy's discussion of how rhetoric gets 'litteraturized' (*litteratuizzazione*) in various periods. Women have gotten fictionalized in a manner parallel to that by which, in Susan Jarratt's reasoning, the sophists were debunked—for being like women in certain ways. Here we are again, recovering what our forebears in each of the represented centuries also had to recover."—*C. Jan Swearingen*

. . . . . .

"There is a vast, unexplored history of women rhetors and rhetoricians (in every culture) who have constantly defined and redefined rhetoric as a discipline, a philosophy, a set of principles, and a diversity of methodologies. It becomes the responsibility—no, the imperative—of feminist scholars to unearth and examine these significant female contributors to intellectual and rhetorical history in order to rethink rhetoric as a living, breathing, vibrant process of inquiry, organizing, thinking, and dialogue, which includes rather than excludes and empowers rather than seeks power. In general, male academics have consistently viewed the inclusion of previously excluded women as a *loss* of tradition rather than a *gain* in terms of revitalizing that tradition. Thus, their resistance to current feminist scholarship, which pursues reclamation and revision, has mirrored the resistance that women have historically faced."—*Jamie Barlowe*

"Two major problems: one is the sliding definition of rhetoric. We (I include myself in this) have helped ourselves to a *very* wide definition of rhetoric. Like Burke's, it is sometimes in danger of being too wide to be useful. As more and more Foucauldian archaeology reveals more for-gotten texts, we may be able to tighten the definition without loss.

"The other problem is that in reaching out to women of earlier times, we sometimes evince a kind of historical naivete, neglecting to see them in their own context. We are so anxious to make common cause with these women that we tend to underplay views and values that differ sig-nificantly from our own. Mary Astell, for example, was conservative both in religion and in politics to a degree that many twentieth-century femi-nists might find disturbing. In order to do justice both to ourselves and to the women we write about, we must resist the temptation to 'rewrite' them."—*Christine Mason Sutherland*

· · · · · ·

"The major problem facing scholars who want to pursue research on women and the history of rhetoric is the fact that too few faculty mem-bers in this field have expertise or interest in women's materials. In this regard, the Department of Language, Literature, and Communication at Rensselaer Polytechnic Institute was not unique; it was typical. All of the experts in rhetorical history and rhetorical theory were men working on materials by and about men. None wanted to contemplate the paradigm shifts that might be required if women's materials were seriously en-gaged, and none had any interest in working with the students to develop expertise in women's materials. As a result, the students had to come to me—a faculty member whose field was really American literature and feminist literary criticism. It is imperative, therefore, that faculty mem-bers be given incentives to work on women's materials; and that these scholars be given the opportunity to offer courses which will radically alter the rhetoric curriculum."—*Annette Kolodny*

· · · · · ·

"The major problem facing all of us scholars is one best defined by Father Ong in his "Fighting for the Word": the masculinist, male need to contend, display, and dance with other men in public, a process that is equated with *rhetoric*. Any persuasive discourse other than that has been considered a quasi rhetoric, not the real thing. Of course, women have traditionally had little or no access to public display, to competition, to intellectual talk with other men. Women who wanted to contend with other women were most usually denied an audience; women who contended with men were denied respectability. No wonder so many women have resorted to the topoi of modesty and humility; to present themselves otherwise would be to present themselves sluttishly, brazenly.

"The point I want to make is that if rhetoric is defined strictly in terms of activities accessible only to public men-in-power, then how can we responsibly investigate women's role in the rhetorical tradition? Those of us working on related projects, by necessity, have expanded our definition of rhetoric.

"On the History of Rhetoric E-mail newsletter, men are discussing the various definitions of rhetoric. Some of the men agree that the Aristotelian definition of rhetoric, within the Ongian perimeters, should be/ is being expanded. But other men think that "standards are falling," that we're going "Burkean" (they invoke the rhetoric/persuasion/meaning/ definition of Burke), that true rhetoric remains undefiled by the unwashed and by washed-out definitions. Our biggest problem, then, as feminists, scholars, rhetoricians, is facing and accepting the plasticity of rhetoric, which some established scholars refuse to respect, condone, or support."—*Cheryl Glenn*

. . . . . .

"Despite the publication of this book, I feel that the problems facing feminist projects in rhetoric have changed only in degree since its inception. Initially, established rhetoricians discouraged us from pursuing the project; they expressed polite amusement at our claiming these women as rhetoricians and denied the interest inherent in the individual essays. Only senior women in the field were able to see the need for the project and the potential for individual research agendas, but given the scarcity of women working in the history of rhetoric, early on it was hard to find collaborators and supporters. The project, despite its academic origins and its liberal feminism, was treated as subversive and dangerous, and we began to call ourselves 'women rats' instead of 'women rhetoricians' (though I think that name, our name, rallied us).

"This project succeeded because of a long-term commitment of its contributors and a growing feminist community demanding attention, but many smaller projects continue to be marginalized and manipulated away from the mainstream. This book will go a long way toward legitimizing feminism within rhetoric, but the long need to justify feminist concerns and to engage men in our discussion remain major problems, perhaps not as overwhelming for us as they were for Wollstonecraft, but still a persistent problem."—*Arabella Lyon*

. . . . . .

What are your current thoughts on having worked on this project?
"The most exciting parts of this project have been working in a collective, getting work out that only recently had an audience, being exposed to the various methodologies employed by the contributors, and setting the stage for more and maybe even better work."—*Cheryl Glenn*

. . . . . .

"In working on this volume I have been most excited by seeing different kinds of inquiry and different stages of getting a handle on things and issues within different periods and even within single periods, for different groups of women, such as Euro-American and African American women in the nineteenth century. I think it is wonderful to have different undertakings sing together in this volume—very different notes; a true harmony. I like the tolerance for methodologies of finding or discovering alongside methodologies of interpreting, rereading. Both are important, as Annette Kolodny says very adroitly in 'Dancing Through the Minefield.' "—*C. Jan Swearingen*

. . . . . .

"Lack of financial support is a problem for nearly all rhetoricians, but it is magnified immensely for those who publicly choose women and women's texts. Not only are we subject to disbelief, ridicule, and faint praise, but we also find ourselves competing for monies meant for men. I know this full well, having dedicated my persuasive powers to fund-raising, with success several magnitudes greater for technology than for techne! Several of the original collaborators in this project found that the precious time and money that we devoted to women proved to be personally satisfying but professionally diverting. Feeding one's family is far easier to do while in the employ of industry rather than the academy. Nevertheless, we carry with us a positively subversive knowledge: women's rhetoric *does* empower us."—*Kathryn M. Conway*

. . . . . .

"I wanted to join this project from the first moment I heard about it, which was almost exactly the moment I heard someone say it was impossible. Those moments seem long ago, and I cannot separate what I now think about rhetoric from what I learned from my colleagues. I've learned a great deal from my colleagues' discoveries. I also learned to enjoy working on a highly collaborative project like this (my first time and perhaps my last). In addition, I learned that where conventional wisdom says there is nothing to discover, there is likely to be something very interesting that directly contradicts that conventional wisdom."—*James Oldham*

. . . . . .

"I have been reading and writing for this volume for virtually my entire professional career; I started reading Susanne Langer in my first graduate course with Anne Berthoff; I started researching my essay at the end of my first year of doctoral work. At various levels, this project shaped everything that I have learned about rhetoric: it has informed my thinking on the power within communities, the interactions between audiences and rhetors, the nature of strategies for effecting change, the dangers of persuasion, the limits of traditional representations of rhetoric, the narrative nature of history, the significance of theoretical bases for practice."—*Arabella Lyon*

. . . . . .

"What I most valued in working on this project has been the learning experience that all teachers dream about; my instructors were my students, and they taught me everything I know about women and rhetoric."—*Annette Kolodny*

. . . . . .

If Dame Rhetorica could join in this afterword, what might she say?

"If Dame Rhetoric could join the afterword, I would have her appear as a shape-shifter and take on all the different guises she's been given in past centuries and literatures, starting perhaps with Medusa, the Sirens, then the Eumenides, Cassandra, Esther, Diotima, Mary speaking prophetically in the Magnificat, and up through the many figures of the lofty medieval iconography, on into the bawdy harlot in Erasmus's *Praise of Folly*. Maybe she could include all those Renaissance images of Judith and Holofernes— were these guys feeling threatened, or what? Then up to Ann Lee, the founder of the Shaker religion, and the many seventeenth-century cartoon depictions of women in Quaker and Shaker dress that fed our 'witch' image—the woman with the puritan hat on—no one ever liked Rhetorica speaking, preaching, or otherwise being where she should not be. Right, Anita; right, Hillary? After she has done her shape shifting maybe she can resume as a real woman: Lily Tomlin, or in the manner of the Kathy and Mo duo, and just relax a bit."—*C. Jan Swearingen*

. . . . . .

"Dame Rhetoric might well resist the feminization of rhetoric in terms of its persuasiveness, its seductiveness, its direct connection with female flesh. It's no accident that the mistrust of rhetoric is equated with the mistrust of female flesh, that woman is the equivalent of the deception (and danger) of which language is capable, hence, 'Dame Rhetoric.'

"Also, she might want to comment on the use of silence, which in this collection is considered as the 'muted voice' of the disempowered. But Dame Rhetoric might force us to rethink such a position: after all, those in power can silence the disempowered; those in power can meet the words of the disempowered with silence, thereby disempowering those who want to be heard. Silence is tricky—it seems to remain powerful when used by the powerful, but to signify weakness when the weak are silent."—*Cheryl Glenn*

. . . . . .

"Dame Rhetorica would say, 'I carry a sword, but you may need an automatic.' "—*Arabella Lyon*

. . . . . .

"Dame Rhetorica might, at last, tell the Spartan to buzz off—to go get back in his own text (I'm thinking of the interpolation, Spartan versus Dame Rhetorica in *Phaedrus*, here)."—*James Oldham*

. . . . . .

"If Dame Rhetorica were with us, she would rejoice at having reclaimed some women's lost influence and ignored voices. And then she would turn her attention to the sisters who are living the history and continuing to shape the world as rhetors and rhetoricians. Most women work outside academia, where the influence of women's rhetoric is easily overlooked. Yet that power is there everyday, exercised more than ever before in the boardrooms, banks, labor halls, news media, courts, churches, legislatures, and administrations that tell us the boundaries of our lives. The Dame would remind us to pay attention to these women, too, so that their voices are not lost for yet another generation to come."—*Jenny R. Redfern*

. . . . . .

"If Dame Rhetorica could join in this afterword, she would ask that the afterword serve as an invitation for more such projects to follow. She would tantalize us with the hints that there are many surprises yet to be discovered and that women have been both persuasive speakers and theorists of rhetoric for a much longer history than we have dared to dream. I think, however, Dame Rhetorica would also warn us that—even after all these centuries—men still do not know how to hear, read, and decode women's discourses accurately. Or, perhaps, Dame Rhetorica might whisper that they do not *want* to."—*Annette Kolodny*

. . . . . .

"Dame Rhetorica would say—'Right on, girlfriends!' "—*Jamie Barlowe*

. . . . . .

"This volume closes, then, as James Murphy's preface began, with an invitation to future work: to continued commitment to making what bell hooks calls 'the liberated voice'—and for recovering, appreciating, and liberating voices long since silenced. Toward that end, we hope that readers will join us, that together we will continue to Reclaim the Dame."—*Andrea A. Lunsford*

Dame Rhetoric, *Margarita Philosophica*, 1515.

Index

Notes on Contributors

Index

· · · · · ·

abolitionist movement, 137, 142, 149, 161, 207, 228–30, 232–33, 237
About Chinese Women (Kristeva), 307
Acharnians (Aristophanes), 13
Adams, John Quincy, 151
Addams, Jane, 219
Ad Hoc Committee on the Impact of Literature and Art, 288
Aelders, Etta Palm d', 117
Aers, David, 54
Aeschines, 15
Aeschylus, 39–40
aesthetic stance, 292–93, 298
affective piety, discourse of, 54
African Zion Church, 228, 231
Agathon, 32, 33, 36
Akron Women's Convention (1851), 230, 234, 236, 237
Alcibiades, 29, 31–35, 38, 40, 41, 44–46
Alcott, Bronson, 141, 143, 147, 149
Alcuin: A Dialogue (Brown), 163n1
Alexander, Meena, 125
Allen, Annie Winsor, 212
Allen, Carolyn, 287
Allen, Hope Emily, 55
Althusser, Louis, 307, 312
American Academy of Arts and Sciences, 267
American Equal Rights Association, 235, 239, 240
Americanization, 221
analogy: argument from, 152–53; logical, 275
Anaximander, 10
Anaximenes, 10
Andrews, A. E., 200n5
androgyny, 282
Anne, Princess, 101
Anthony, Susan B., 208, 233, 239, 240
antimetabole, 210
Antiphon, 43
antiphrasis, 80–81

antislavery movement, *see* abolitionist movement
apologias, 80
Archimedes, 10
Are Women People? A Book of Rhymes for Suffrage Times (Miller), 210
Argives, 34
argumentation: Astell's use of, 101–05; college courses for women in, 211–14, 216; and communal knowledge, 280; Truth's use of, 234–35
Aristophanes, 13, 34
Aristotle, 26, 81, 150, 209, 250, 251, 254–56, 262n6, 276, 278, 295, 297
Arnauld, Antoine, 108
Art of Love, The (Ovid), 75
Art de parler, L' (Lamy), 109
Art de penser, L' (Arnauld and Nicole), 108
Askew, Anne, 321
Aspasia, 3, 9–22, 25, 26, 31–34, 47, 305, 321, 322
Astell, Mary, 3, 93–115, 328
Athenaeus, 32–34
attention, 109
Attitudes Towards History (Burke), 279–80
Auden, W. H., 248
audience: rhetoric of, 286, 294–97; style determined by, 197
Augustine, 74, 81, 112, 114–15
autobiography, 53–70, 76
autochthony, 18–19
Ayer, A. J., 270, 277

Bakhtin, Mikhail, 69n, 305, 307, 316
Baldwin, Charles S., 193
Ball, Margaret, 190–91, 194, 223n9
Ballard, George, 93, 97
barbarisms, 189, 198
Barnard College, 200n2, 205, 209, 210, 212, 219, 222n4, 223n9, 285

Barnes, Djuna, 248
Barthes, Roland, 307, 308, 310–12, 317
Bauer, Dale, 305
Beach, Richard, 300*n*4
Behn, Aphra, 109
Being, Jackson's concept of, 250–53,
    255, 257–60
Belenky, Mary Field, 113, 309
belletristic rhetoric, 185–91, 193, 194,
    195, 231
Benedict, Ruth, 48
Benson, George W., 228
Bentley, Arthur, 293
Berlin, James, 223*n*7
Berthoff, Anne, 331
Bibb, Henry, 233
Bible, 234
binary oppositions, refusal of, 119
Birtwell, Lorna, 222*n*2
Bizzell, Patricia, 6
Black Clubwomen's Movement, 168,
    170
Black Sun, The (Kristeva), 308
Blackwell, Antoinette Brown, 206, 207,
    215, 222*n*5
Blair, Hugh, 145, 146, 150, 162, 190–
    92, 265
Blake, William, 25
Blatch, Harriot Stanton, 205, 220
Bloedow, Edmund F., 16–18
Bly, Robert, 324
Boccaccio, Giovanni, 75, 77, 83, 84
Boethius, 80
Book of Rhetoric (Cappella), 79
Book of the City of Ladies, The
    (Christine de Pisan), 78–79, 80–83
Book of the Three Virtues, The, see
    Treasure of the City of Ladies, The
Book Review Digest, 301*n*4
Books, 301*n*4
Booth, Wayne, 59, 69*n*7, 266, 268–69,
    277, 287, 288, 294–97, 301*n*5
"Bounded Text, The" (Kristeva), 315
Brandt, Joan, 313
Brannon, Lil, 300*n*1
brevity, effect of, 155
Briggs, Charles F., 139
Broadway Journal, 139
Brody, Miriam, 6, 121
Brown, Charles Brockden, 163*n*1
Brownson, Orestes Augustus, 138–41,
    159, 160

Brownson's Quarterly Review, 139
Bryant, Donald, 287, 294–97
Bryn Mawr College, 200*n*2, 205, 209,
    212, 219
Buck, Gertrude, 195–96, 199, 216–17,
    219, 223*n*7, 223*n*12
Burke, Edmund, 117, 119, 120, 135
Burke, Kenneth, 5, 69*n*9, 266, 278–81,
    309, 328, 329
Burnet, Bishop, 101
Burns, Lucy, 205, 220, 224*n*14
Burroughs, Nannie Helen, 182
Butler, Judith, 313
Butler-Bowdon, W., 55, 57, 70*n*11
But You Just Don't Understand
    (Tannen), 324

Calder, Matilda S., 215
Callicles, 29
Campbell, George, 5, 150
Campbell, Karlyn Kohrs, 6, 238, 239
Cappella, Martianus, 79
Capper, Charles, 140, 146, 147
Carfania, 26
caring, principle of, 113–14
Carlyle, Thomas, 190
Carnap, Rudolph, 270, 277
Carr, Thomas M., 109
Cassirer, Ernst, 268, 277–78
Cato, 81
cause-to-effect argument, 153–54
Cazden, Elizabeth, 222*n*5
Chambers, R. W., 57, 70*n*11
Changes of Fortune, The (Christine de
    Pisan), 76, 77
Channing, William Ellery, 151
Channing, William Henry, 156, 160
Charles II, king of England, 104
Charles V, king of France, 76, 77
Chase, Cynthia, 309
Chaucer, Geoffrey, 53, 55
Chelsea, 249
Cheney, Ednah D., 208
Chesapeake, Ohio and Southwestern
    Railroad, 169, 181
Chevigny, Belle Gale, 163*n*3
Chicago Inter-Ocean, 168, 180
Child, Lydia Maria, 139, 156, 244*n*3
Christian Examiner, 139
Christianity, 53–68, 94, 95, 112–14,
    238–39, 243; revealed truths of,
    150

Christine de Pisan, 73–91, 321, 327
Cicero, 15, 111, 146, 150, 209
Cistercians, 54
Civil War, 229, 241, 242
Clark, Alan, 261n1
Clark, Gregory, 164n11
Clark, Lewis, 233
Clark, Milton, 233
class: Jackson on, 258; professional,
    dialect of, 186; Wollstonecraft on,
    119, 126
Cleobulina, 26
Clifford, John, 287–88
Clinton, Hillary, 324
close reading, method of, 248
closure, lack of, 160, 163
Col, Gontier, 82
Col, Pierre, 82
Coleridge, Samuel Taylor, 147
collaborative thinking, 48
College English (journal), 300n3
College Entrace Examination Board,
    Commission on English of, 288
College Manual of Rhetoric, A
    (Baldwin), 193
Colton, Mildred Louise, 218
Columbia University, 223n9
Commemoration of the Eighth
    Anniversary of Negro Freedom in
    the United States, 242
Commission on Human Relations, 285
communicative competence, 176
community-based knowledge, 266,
    268, 269, 280–81
confirmatio, 100
Conflicts in Feminism (Hirsch and
    Keller), 138, 162–63
confrontation, tradition of, 112–13
Congress, U.S., 229, 242, 244n8
Congressional Union for Woman
    Suffrage, 205, 220
Connecticut College, 267
Consolation (Boethius), 80
Constitution, U.S., Fourteenth
    Amendment to, 239–40
contextual knowledge, 275
conversation, art of, 111
conversational strategies, 147–50, 155–
    56, 158–59, 161–63
*Conversations with Goethe in the Last
    Years of His Life* (Eckermann), 146
Cooper, Anna Julia, 182

Cornford, Frances, 43
Correct Writing and Speaking (Jordan),
    197, 217
Counter-statement (Burke), 279
courtly love, 75, 81–82
critical theory, 310
Critobolus, 32
Crusade for Justice (Wells), 168, 169

Dall, Caroline Healey, 147, 149, 161,
    164n6
Danaids, 39–40
Dante, 77, 78
Darwin, Charles, 292
De claris mulieribus (Boccaccio), 75,
    83
De Quincy, Thomas, 187
debate, 188, 204, 206, 208–09, 211–12,
    215–17
decision making, art of, 86
Declaration of Independence, 156
DeCosta-Willis, Miriam, 168
Deipnosophistae (Athenaeus), 32
deliberative rhetoric, 254–56
Delsartian systems, 230
democracy: Greek, 13, 14, 17, 18;
    participatory, informed discourse
    in, 204
Democratic Party, National Committee
    of, 224n13
Democritus, 25–26
Derrida, Jacques, 262n5, 269, 307, 308,
    310, 312
Descartes, René, 106–09, 112, 115, 247
Desire in Language (Kristeva), 307
Despres, Denise Louise, 66, 68n1
Dewey, John, 293
Dewson, Mary W., 224n13
Dial (journal), 139–41, 143, 149, 150,
    154, 155, 160
dialectic: of conversation, 159; of
    Kristeva, 311–12; masculine, 67; of
    Socrates, 15
dialogics, 59, 67, 305–07, 316–17; of
    Wollstonecraft, 117–36; *see also*
    conversational strategies
Dickenson, Anna, 207, 208
diction, 189, 254
didactic works, 74
Diogenes Laertius, 12
Diotima, 3, 25–49

discourse: of affective piety, 54; in belletristic rhetoric, 188; double-voiced, 67; feminist, 137–63; informed, in participatory democracy, 204; literary, 80, 286–300; love and, 28–49; of medieval women, 83, 86, 88, 90; practical public, 227–43; in practical rhetoric, 187; sources for change within, 274; whole human, 247–61
Discourse on Method (Descartes), 108, 109
dispositio, 99
dissoi logoi (contradictory propositions), 15
Doll's House, A (Ibsen), 293
Douglas, Ann, 193
Douglass, Frederick, 229, 234
Dreams (Schreiner), 200n1
duBois, Page, 18, 19
du Castel, Etienne, 76
Duffy, Kenneth, 255
Duke of True Lovers, The (Christine de Pisan), 89
Dumont, John J., 227
Dunton, John, 98
Durkheim, Emile, 48
Duster, Alfreda M., 168

Eagleton, Terry, 301n8
Earliest Days at Vassar, The (Wood), 208
Early English Text Society, 55
Eckermann, Johann Peter, 146
economy, principle of, 187
education: of African Americans, 181–82; Fuller and, 143–47, 161–62; higher, for women, 185 (*see also* Seven Sisters colleges); Kristeva on, 311; modern, sexism in, 134–35; of immigrants, 220; Wollstonecraft on, 120–22; *see also* pedagogy
Educational Record (journal), 300n3
efferent stance, 291–93
Eisenstein, Hester, 324
Eleans, 34
Elements of Rhetoric (Whately), 143–47, 149–60, 164n7, 209
elocutio, 99
eloquence: of Astell, 93, 96–99, 101, 102, 105–06; of Christine de Pisan,

80, 90; of Fuller, 139; of Wells, 169, 171
Elshtain, Jean Bethke, 138, 162
Emerson, Ralph Waldo, 140, 141, 146, 148, 149, 159
Emig, Janet, 300n1
Empedocles, 35–38
empiricism, 275
Empson, William, 248, 261n1
English Journal, 300n3
English Mystical Tradition, The (Knowles), 56
English Reformation, 56
Enlightenment, the, 10
enthymeme, 235–36
Ephialtes, 14
epideictic rhetoric, 83, 86, 248, 254–56, 259–61, 281
epistemology, 113; rhetorical, 265, 277
epitaphioi (funeral orations), 16–21
Equal Rights Amendment, 221
Erasmus, Desiderius, 331
ethics: based on language, 47–48; and quality of caring, 113; style and, 193
ethnocentrism, 311
ethos: of Astell, 102, 112; of Christine de Pisan, 78, 81, 82, 85–86; of Jackson, 251–52; of Kempe, 59, 62–65, 68; of Truth, 233, 234, 238, 239; strategy for teaching, 297–98; style and, 193, 196
"Ethos and the Aims of Rhetoric" (Johnson), 297–98
"Eve of St. Agnes, The" (Keats), 293
Evelyn, John, 97
example, argument from, 153, 235, 237
exclusionary rhetoric, 311, 314
exordium, 102
Experience of Reading, The (Clifford), 287

Faust (Goethe), 42
Feeling and Form (Langer), 270, 272–75, 277
feminism: application of postmodern theory to, 29; Astell and, 93, 113–15; Fuller and, 137–63; Jackson and, 260; Kristeva and, 308, 309, 312–16; Langer and, 281–83; Rosenblatt and, 299;

Wollstonecraft and, 117–36; *see also* woman suffrage movement
Ferguson, Moira, 127
Ferrar, Nicholas, 99
Fish, Stanley E., 159, 266
Fitzgerald, Susan Walker, 205
Flynn, Elizebeth, 288–89
Fogarty, Daniel, 5
forensic rhetoric, 86, 112, 254–56
Fortune, Thomas T., 182
Foss, Sonja, 6
Foster, Abigail Kelley, 137, 142
Foucault, Michel, 274, 307, 310
Franciscans, 54, 64, 68*n*1, 70*n*13
Fraser, Nancy, 313
Freedman's Bureau, 240
French Revolution, 117
Freud, Sigmund, 308–09, 311, 312, 315–17
Fugitive Slave Law, 229
Fuller, Arthur P., 141, 144, 163*n*4
Fuller, Hiram, 143, 146
Fuller, Margaret, 122, 137–64, 320
Fuseli, John Henry, 122
Future of Difference, The (Eisenstein), 324

Gage, Frances D., 230, 236
Gage, John, 311
Garrison, William Lloyd, 228, 232, 233
Garvey, Amy Jacques, 182
Gawain poet, 55
Gearhart, Sally Miller, 137, 162
Geertz, Clifford, 266, 268, 310
gender: in Greek religion, 27, 39–40, 43; hierarchies of, 75, 138; in *Menexenus*, 18–20; and philosophy, 282–83; and project of telling, 250; proprieties of, in nineteenth century, 146; style and, 185, 192; Wollstonecraft on, 126
Gere, Anne Ruggles, 6
Gerson, Jean, 82
Gettysburg Address, 259
Giddings, Paula, 181, 244*n*7
Gilbert, Olive, 232, 241, 242
Gilbert, Sandra M., 282
Gilchrist, Beth, 213
Gilligan, Carol, 67, 283, 309
Glorious Revolution, 104
Godwin, William, 117, 129

Goethe, Johann Wolfgang von, 141, 147
Gordon, Lynn, 199
Gorgias, 9, 16, 17, 27, 29, 31, 209, 262*n*5
Gouges, Olympia de, 117
Graff, Gerald, 134
grammar, 111; in practical rhetoric, 186
Graves, Robert, 261*n*1
Greeley, Horace, 161
Green, Constance McLaughlin, 212
Greene Street School (Providence), 141, 143–47, 149, 152, 156–57, 159, 162, 164*n*5
Greenough, C. N., 223*n*11
Grimké, Angelina, 137, 142
Grimké, Sarah Moore, 163*n*1
Gubar, Susan, 282
Gunpowder Plot, 99

Habermas, Jurgen, 162
Hall, Max, 267
Halloran, S. Michael, 223*n*8
Handbook on Argumentation and Debating, A (Buck and Mann), 216
Hardenberg, Charles, 227
Harper's Bazaar, 197
Harrison, Frederick, 214
Harrison, Jane Ellen, 39, 40, 42, 43, 47–49
Hart, Sophie Chantal, 214–15, 223*n*9
Harte, Bret, 200*n*6
Harvard University, 211–14, 223*n*9, 223*n*11, 266, 282; Press, 267
Hastings, Lady Elizabeth, 96, 101
Hawthorne, Nathaniel, 291
Hayworth, Donald, 211
Hedge, Frederic Henry, 141
Hegel, Georg Wilhelm Friedrich, 317
Heidegger, Martin, 262*n*5
Heilbrun, Carolyn, 54, 70*n*17
Heloise, 321
herethics, 48
Herzberg, Bruce, 6
heteroglossic self, 59
Hildegard von Bingen, 66, 70*n*16
Hill, Adams Sherman, 211, 223*nn*7, 9
Hirsch, Marianne, 138, 162–63
Historical and Moral View of the Fench Revolution, A (Wollstonecraft), 127
historiography, 9

History of Woman Suffrage (Stanton and Anthony), 161, 233
History of Women Philosophers (Waithe), 10
Hocking, William Ernest, 267, 282
Hodgkins, Louis Manning, 186
Holbrook, Sue Ellen, 6
Hollis, Karyn, 6
Homer, 12
hooks, bell, 229, 244*n*3
Horowitz, Helen Lefkowitz, 200*nn*2, 5, 223*n*6
Hosford, Frances Juliette, 206
Hostmen, 94
Howard, Katherine Graham, 217–18
Howe, Julia Ward, 208, 244*n*7
Hulley, Kathleen, 306
humanism, 74–76, 196;
    poststructuralist critique of, 312
humor, Truth's use of, 235, 237, 239
Hundred Years War, 94
Hunter, Lynette, 287, 294–95, 297
Hypatia, 321
hysteria, 57, 314–15

Ibsen, Henrik, 293
ideology, colonial, 17, 20–22, 305
Imlay, Fanny, 126, 131, 132
Imlay, Gilbert, 117, 118, 126–33
implied author, 59–61, 64
individualism, social construction of, 48
Inferno (Dante), 78
Interpretation of Cultures, The (Geertz), 268
Interregnum, 95
Introduction to Symbolic Logic, An (Langer), 270
inventio, 99, 108
invention, 186, 253
Irigaray, Luce, 18, 262*n*9
irony, 122–24
Irwin, Inez Haynes, 213, 220
Isocrates, 250, 265

Jackson, Laura (Riding), 247–62, 322
Jackson, Schuyler B., 262*n*7
Jacobs, Mark, 261*n*1
James, William, 292
James II, King of England, 104
Jamieson, Kathleen, 102
Jarratt, Susan, 305

Jesus: historical, 28; Kempe and, 54, 55, 57, 58, 61–64; Truth on, 234–35, 238–39; as vernacular voice, 87
John the Fearless, 84
Johnson, Margaret, 200*n*6
Johnson, Nan, 6, 251, 262*n*6, 297–98
Jones, Lady Catherine, 96
Jordan, Mary Augusta, 195–98, 212, 217, 218, 220, 223*n*9
Journal of Reading Behavior, 300*n*3
Julian of Norwich, 66, 68*n*3,69*n*4, 70*n*16

Kant, Immanuel, 268
Keats, John, 293
Keliher, Alice, 285
Keller, Evelyn Fox, 138, 162–63
Kempe, Margery, 3, 53–70, 321, 322
Kemys, Anne, 99
Kemys, Mary, 99
Kennedy, George, 327
Kennedy, Patricia, 203
Kennicott, Patrick, 233
Kingston, Maxine Hong, 70*n*17
Knoblauch, Cy, 300*n*1
Knowing and the Known (Dewey and Bentley), 293
Knowles, David, 56
Korzybski, Alfred, 5
Kramarae, Cheris, 198
Kristeva, Julia, 3, 262*n*9, 273, 305–18, 322
Kuklick, Bruce, 267–68

la Barre, Poulain de, 106
Lacan, Jacques, 307, 309, 312, 314
Lacedaemonians, 34
Laidlaw, Harriet Burton, 205, 219–20
Lamentations (Matheolus), 75, 82
Lamy, Bernard, 106, 109, 113–14
Langer, Susanne K., 265–83, 322, 331
Langer, William, 266
Langston, John Mercer, 234
language acquisition, 308
Language Arts (journal), 300*n*3
language development, 176
Language and Women's Place (Lakoff), 324
Laud, William, 94
Lawler, Marguerite Hickey, 220
leadership styles, 174–76
League of Women Voters, 221

Lectures on Rhetoric and Belles Lettres (Blair), 145, 150
Lee, Ann, 331
LeFevre, Karen, 300*n*1
Le Fevre de Ressons, Jean, 83
Lerner, Gerda, 327
Letters on the Equality of the Sexes and the Condition of Woman (Grimké), 163*n*1
Letters Written During a Short Residence in Sweden, Norway, and Denmark (Wollstonecraft), 127, 128
Lettice, Lady, Viscountess of Falkland, 99
Leuba, J. H., 62–63
Liberator, 232
Lincoln, Abraham, 244*n*8
linguistics, 258, 307
"Litany for Survival, A" (Lorde), 172
literacy: among African American women, 171, 176; in Greece, 14; in Middle Ages, 76
literary theory, 285, 287
Literature as Exploration (Rosenblatt), 285, 288, 290–94, 298–99, 301*n*4
Livermore, Mary, 208
Living Way, 167, 169
Livre de Leesce, Le (Le Fevre de Ressons), 83
Locke, John, 5, 6
logical positivism, 258
logos, 251; Truth's use of, 233, 239
Long, P. W., 223*n*11
Loraux, Nicole, 21
Lorch, Jennifer, 117, 125, 127
Lorde, Audre, 172–73
Lorris, Guillaume de, 81
Louis of Guyenne, 84
love: of audience, 114–15; courtly, 75, 81–82; Diotima on, 28–49; of God, 97
lynching, campaign against, 168–71, 174, 175, 177–82
Lyon, Mary, 205

McCannell, Juliet Flower, 313
McCarthy, Mary, 70*n*17
MacCracken, Henry Noble, 219
MacDuffie, Abby Parsons, 211
McKerrow, Ray E., 145–46
MacKinnon, Catharine A., 282–83

Madwoman in the Attic, The (Gilbert and Gubar), 282
Mailloux, Steven, 301*n*8
Mallarmé, Stéphane, 307
Malory, Thomas, 55
"man-minded" disciplines, 257, 260
Mann, Kristine, 216
Mantineans, 34
Marguerite of Burgundy, 84, 87–88
Maria (Wollstonecraft), 117, 125
Marriage of Mercury and Philology, The (Cappella), 79
Marxism, 307, 313
Mary (Wollstonecraft), 117, 123–25
Masham, Damaris, 109
Maslow, Abraham, 48
Massachusetts Association Opposed to the Further Extension of Suffrage to Women, 218
Matheolus, 75, 82
matriarchy, 27
Mazarin, Duchess of, 103
meaning: as aggression, 279, 280; collaborative, 265–66, 270–73, 276, 280; creation and transmission of, 177; metaphor in, 195, 196
Meech, Sanford Brown, 55
Meilleraye and Mayenne, Duke of, 103
Memphis Board of Education, 181–82
Memphis *Evening Star*, 167
Memphis *Free Speech*, 167, 181
Menexenus (Plato), 10, 15, 18–22, 32, 33
metaphor, 195–96, 274, 275, 309
Metcalf, Evelina, 164*n*9, 199, 215–16
Meun, Jean de, 75, 80
Miletus, 10
Mill, John Stuart, 214
Miller, Alice Duer, 210
Miller, Susan, 6
Millholland, Inez, 218, 220
Milton, John, 104
Mind (journal), 267
Mitchell, Jacquelyn, 174–75
Mitchell, Maria, 208, 210
Mob Convention, 233–35
Mob Rule in New Orleans (Wells), 168
Moderate style, 101
Modern Dogma and the Rehtoric of Assent (Booth), 268
Modern Language Assocation, 288
Modest Proposal, A (Swift), 100

Mondini, Tommaso, 76
Montagu, Lady Mary Wortley, 95, 96
Montgomery, Janey Weinhold, 229,
    234, 242, 243n1
Montreuil, Jean de, 80, 82, 91n3
Mossell, Gertrude, 182
Mount Holyoke, The, 185
Mount Holyoke College, 186, 188,
    190–92, 194, 200, 205, 209, 212,
    213, 215, 219, 223n9
Murphy, Richard, 230

Narrative of Sojourner Truth (Gilbert),
    229, 232, 243
Nation, 301n4
National American Woman Suffrage
    Association (NAWSA), 205, 219–21
National College Equal Suffrage
    League (NCESL), 205, 218, 220,
    222n4
National Conference on Research on
    English, 288
National Council of Teachers of
    English (NCTE), 288–90
National Woman's Loyal League, 239
National Women's Party (NWP), 220
Necker, Suzanne, 151
neo-Kantians, 268
New Criticism, 248
New Republic, 301n4
New Rhetoric, The (Perelman and
    Olbrechts-Tyteca), 280
New York Age, 180
New York Tribune, 161
Nichols, E. R., 217
Nichols, Marie Hochmuth, 230
Nicole, Pierre, 108
Noack, H., 277
Noddlings, Nel, 113
Norris, John, 97, 98
Northampton Association of Education
    and Industry, 228
Nussbaum, Martha, 35, 44
Nye, Andrea, 313

Oberlin College, 205–07, 215
objective criticism, 285–86, 291
Ogden, C. K., 277
Olbrechts-Tyteca, Lucille, 266, 278,
    280–81
Oliver, Kelly, 313
Olmstead, Mildred Scott, 212

Ong, Rory, 305
Ong, Walter, 106, 321, 328–29
On the Origin of Species (Darwin), 292
oratory: training of women in, 203–04,
    206, 212; of woman suffrage
    movement, 219–21; *see also* public
    speaking
Oratory, the, 107, 114
Oravec, Christine, 230, 231, 255
O'Shields, Gloria Hartmann, 203
*Our Day: A Record and Review of
    Current Reform*, 177
Ovid, 75, 81

Paine, Thomas, 117
Papers in Rhetoric and Poetic (Bryant),
    294
Park, Maud Wood, 213, 221
Parmenides, 39
Parrington, Vernon L., 140
pathos, 251; Truth's use of, 233, 239
patriarchal dominance, 282–83
Paul, Alice, 205, 220, 221
Paul, Helen, 220
Peabody, Elizabeth Palmer, 147,
    163n2, 164nn6, 7
Peaden, Catherine, 6
pedagogy, 19, 147; dialogue in, 149; of
    Rosenblatt, 285–94, 298–99; *see
    also* education
Peloponnesian War, 13, 17, 26, 35
Pepwell, H., 75
Perelman, Chaim, 266, 278, 280–81
Pericles, 9, 10, 12–17, 19, 22, 27, 31,
    33, 259
Permanence and Change (Burke), 279
Perry, Frances, 186–87
Perry, Ruth, 93, 94
personality, style as expression of,
    191–95
perspicuity, 154
persuasion: by Astell, 98–103;
    Christine de Pisan on, 80, 81, 83–
    84, 87, 89; deceptive, critiques of,
    249; as dimension of literature,
    285, 286, 290, 294–97; feminist
    denunciation of, 138, 162; Fuller's
    rejection of, 156–59; as mutual
    inquiry, 268; by Wollstonecraft,
    118, 122, 129
Petroff, Elizabeth, 68n2
Phaedrus (Plato), 19, 29, 40, 249, 253

Phelan, James, 69n9
Phi Sigma literary society, 215
philosophy: Jackson's critique of, 258–59; of Langer, 265–75, 277; poststructuralist, 306; *see also specific philsophers*
Philosophy in a New Key (Langer), 265, 267–76, 278, 280–83
Philosophy of Rhetoric, A (Campbell), 5, 150
Philosophy of Style, The (Spencer), 187
Pi Kappa Delta, 217
Pierson, Elijah, 228
Pierson, Sarah, 228
piety: affective, discourse of, 54; of Astell, 94–97
Pillsbury, Parker, 229
Pizzano, Tomasso di Benvenuto, 76
Plater, Emily, 153, 157
Plato, 10, 14–22, 25, 27–42, 46–48, 81, 143, 147, 149, 209, 249–50, 255, 262nn5, 6, 297
Plutarch, 9, 10, 12, 14, 22n1, 32, 34
Poe, Edgar Allan, 141
Poetics (Aristotle), 209
poetry, 275–76; truth in, 248, 258
politics: feminist, *see* feminism; of Glorious Revolution, 104; Greek, 13, 14; Jackson's critique of, 257–58; medieval, 84; neutrality in, challenge to, 197; participation of women in, *see* woman suffrage movement
Polylogue (Kristeva), 307
Pomeroy, Sara, 22n5
Poovey, Mary, 117–18, 125–26, 128
Port Royalists, 106, 107, 108, 114
postmodern theory, 29
poststructuralism, 259, 306–10, 312
Powers of Horror, The (Kristeva), 308, 310–11, 313
Practical Criticism (Richards), 293
practical rhetoric, 185–91, 195
Praise of Folly (Erasmus), 331
Price, Dr., 119
pride, avoidance of, 114
Principes de la philosophie (Descartes), 108, 109
Principles of Psychology (James), 292
Progressive Education Association, 285
Progressive era, 199

Protagoras, 15, 27, 29, 43
psychoanalysis, 306–9, 311
public speaking: by African American women, 167–69, 171, 173, 227–43; Astell on, 109, 111; in Greece, 14–16; in nineteenth-century, 142, 146, 206–08, 217; *see also* debate; oratory
Punctuation Primer (Perry), 187
Purves, 300n4
Pythagoreans, 35

Quakers, 227, 231, 331
questions: of individuals, potential power of, 274; rhetorical, 87, 154, 178–79, 234
Quintilian, 111, 150, 209
Qui Vive Society, 216

Rabinowitz, Peter, 58–59, 69n5
Radcliffe College, 200n2, 209, 211–13, 218, 221, 222n2, 223nn9, 10, 266
Ramus, Peter, 107
Ratner, Sidney, 300
Reader (journal), 289
Reader in the Text, The (Suleiman), 288
Reader-Response Criticism (Tompkins), 288
reader-response theory, 288–89
Reader, the Text, the Poem, The (Rosenblatt), 287, 291–93, 295, 296, 300
reasonableness, ethos of, 84–86
recapitulation, 154
Red Record, A (Wells), 168
refutatio, 100
religion: and abolitionism, 228, 231–33; ancient Greek, 27, 39–46; Christian, *see* Christianity; Jackson's critique of, 257; of Transcendentalists, 139
Republic (Plato), 18
Republican Party, 239; National Committee of, 217–18
Restoration, 95, 104
Retrenchment Society, 228
Revolution in Poetic Language, The (Kristeva), 307
Rhetoric (Aristotle), 209, 278
Rhetorical Stance in Modern Fiction (Hunter), 294, 297

Rhetoric of Fiction, The (Booth), 287, 288, 294–96
Rhetoric of Motives, A (Burke), 280, 309
Rich, Adrienne, 70*n*17
Richards, I. A., 5, 277, 293
rights: expression of, in nineteenth century rhetoric, 229; natural, 119–20
Ripley, George, 141, 147
Ripley, Sophia Dana, 147, 148, 163*n*1
Road of Long Study (Christine de Pisan), 78
Robinson, David M., 140, 141
Romance of the Rose, The (Meun), 75, 80–82
Romantics, 143, 151; reinterpretation of Greek antiquity by, 10, 41
Room of One's Own, A (Woolf), 47
Roots for a New Rhetoric (Fogarty), 5
Rorty, Richard, 269, 274
Rosenblatt, Louise, 275, 285–301
Rosenfield, Lawrence, 255–56
Rosenthal, Bernard, 163*n*4
Rousseau, Jean-Jacques, 117, 120, 123, 135
Ruffin, Josephine St. Pierre, 182
Russell, Bertrand, 270

Sage: A Scholarly Journal on Black Women, 174
Said, Edward W., 21–22
Samourais, The (Kristeva), 308
Sancroft, William, 95–96, 98
Sangster, Margaret, 197
Sappho, 42
Sartre, Jean-Paul, 262*n*5
satire, 103–05, 210
Scarlet Letter, The (Hawthorne), 291
Scheick, William J., 141
Schiller, Friedrich von, 141
Schneir, Miriam, 240
scholasticism, 74
Schomberg, Lady, 97–98
Schreiner, Olive, 185, 200*n*1
Schuster, Charles, 305
science, 257
self-definition, 173, 178; through writing, 193
Semeiotike (Kristeva), 307
semiotics, 307, 308
Seneca, 74, 81

Seneca Falls convention (1848), 161
Serious Proposal to the Ladies, A (Astell), 98–103, 106–09, 113, 114
Seven Sisters colleges, 186–200, 203–24
Seven Types of Ambiguity (Empson), 248
sexism, culturally ingrained, 134–35
Shackford, Martha Hale, 200*n*6
Shakers, 331
Shaw, Ann Howard, 220
simile, 196
Sister Outsider (Lorde), 173
slang, 198
Smith, Adam, 292
Smith, Florence, 93
Smith, James McCune, 234
Smith, Paul, 313
Smith College, 186, 188, 190–93, 195–97, 199–200, 209, 212, 217–20, 223*n*9
Snyder, Alice, 219
Socrates, 10, 13–16, 19, 20, 22, 26, 27, 29–36, 38, 40, 41, 43–47, 253
Socratic method, 13, 15
solecisms, 189
Sollers, Philippe, 307
Solomon, 81, 86
Solomon, Barbara Miller, 213, 218
Solon, 14
Some Reflections on Marriage (Astell), 103–05, 107
sophists, 9, 14–17, 25, 26, 31, 47
Southern Horrors (Wells), 168
Southern Quarterly Review, 139
spelling, 110–11
Spencer, Herbert, 187–89, 191, 195
Springfield Republican, 194
Stael, Germaine de, 147
Stanton, Elizabeth Cady, 161, 205, 208, 220, 233–36, 239, 240
Stein, Gertrude, 248
Stevens, Clara, 213, 215, 223*n*9
Stewart, Maria, 182
Stone, Lucy, 205–07, 215, 222*n*5, 244*n*7
Story of an African Farm, The (Schreiner), 200*n*1
Story of the Woman's Party, The (Irwin), 220
Strangers to Ourselves (Kristeva), 308, 311
structuralism, 307, 313

Stuarts, 94
style, 185–201; as expression of
    personality, 191–95; metaphor in,
    195–96; suggestive, 155–56, 160; in
    practical versus belletristic
    rhetoric, 185–91
subtexts, 274, 275
suffrage, *see* woman suffrage
    movement
Suffragist, 220
suggestive style, 155–56, 160
Suleiman, Susan, 288
Sullivan, Dale, 262*n*8
Suppliants, The (Aeschylus), 39–40
Swift, Jonathan, 100
syllogisms, 209, 236
Symbolic Forms (Cassirer), 277
symbolic transformation, theory of,
    265–66, 268–72, 274, 275, 277–78
Symposium (Plato), 28, 30, 32, 34–42,
    44–47
syntax, Latinate, 78, 154
Szarmach, Paul, 69*n*4

Tales of Love (Kristeva), 308, 309
Talleyrand Périgord, Charles Maurice
    de, 117, 121
Tannen, Deborah, 309, 324
Tate, Allen, 248
Taylor (President of Vassar), 218
Tel Quel group, 307
Telling, The (Jackson), 247–62
Temple School (Boston), 143, 147, 149
Tennessee Supreme Court, 181
testimony, 152
Thales, 10
Thargelia, 12
Themis (Harrison), 39
thinking: collaborative, 48; Astell on
    method of, 108–10
Thomas, Martha Carey, 219, 221
Thompson, Mildred I., 169, 173, 182
Thoughts on the Education of Daughters
    (Wollstonecraft), 127, 128
Thucydides, 10, 16, 17, 34
Timandra, 32
Titus, Frances, 236–37
T&M Society, 216, 217, 219
Todd, Janet, 127
Tompkins, Jane, 288, 301*n*4
transactional communication
    techniques, 162

Transcendentalism, 138–41, 151, 156
transference, 309
Treasure of the City of Ladies, The
    (Christine de Pisan), 73–75, 78,
    80–91
Troy Female Seminary, 205
Truth, Sojourner, 183*n*5, 207, 227–44,
    320

Unitarians, 140, 143, 151
Urbanski, Marie, 141, 160, 164*n*8
"Uses of Rhetoric in Criticism"
    (Bryant), 295

Van Wagener, Isabella, *see* Truth,
    Sojourner
Vassar, Matthew, 207–09
Vassar College, 186, 188–90, 195, 197,
    199–200, 205, 207–12, 216–20,
    222*n*4, 223*nn*7, 9
vernacular: Christine de Pisan's use of,
    78, 87; Descartes as advocate of,
    106
Vindication of the Rights of Men, A
    (Wollstonecraft), 119, 128, 135
Vindication of the Rights of Woman, A
    (Wollstonecraft), 117–23, 128, 135,
    137
Virgil, 78, 81
Vision of Christine, The (Christine de
    Pisan), 76, 77

Waithe, Mary Ellen, 9–10, 16
Wallace, Janet, 191–92
Wealth of Nations, The (Smith), 292
Webster, Daniel, 186
Weissman, Hope Phyllis, 57
Wellesley College, 186–90, 192–93,
    199–200, 209, 211–15, 220, 223*n*9
Wells, Ida B., 3, 167–83, 322
Wendell, Barrett, 213, 223*n*10
Western Messenger (journal), 143
Wetzell, A., 185
Whately, Richard, 143–47, 149–60, 162,
    164*n*7, 209
"What Facts Does This Poem Teach
    You" (Rosenblatt), 291
Whigs, 146
Whipple, John, 146
Whitehead, Alfred North, 266, 277
Whiting, Mrs., 194
Wilkin, Rich, 96

Willard, Emma, 205
Willard, Frances E., 177
Wittgenstein, Ludwig, 269, 277
Wolf, Christa, 42
Wollstonecraft, Mary, 3, 117–37, 163*n*,
    321, 322, 330
Woman in the Nineteenth Century
    (Fuller), 137–43, 149–50, 152–61,
    163*nn*3, 4
woman suffrage movement, 197, 199,
    203–22, 227; Truth in, 229–31, 235,
    236–40
Woman Suffrage Party, 205
"Women as Reader-Response Critics"
    (Flynn), 288
Women's Christian Temperance
    Union, 177

Women's Party, 220
Women's Political Union, 220
Wood, Ellen Meiksins, 14, 18, 22*n*5
Wood, Frances, 208
Woolf, Virginia, 47–49, 321
Woolley, Mary, 219
World War I, 217
Writing a Woman's Life (Heilbrun), 54
"writing the body," 29
Wrongs of Woman: or, Maria, see
    Maria
Wylie, Laura, 190, 219

Xenophon, 15, 34

Yates, Josephine Silone, 182
Young Ladies Literary Society, 206,
    215

Notes on Contributors

Jamie Barlowe is Assistant Professor of English and Women's Studies at the University of Toledo. She has published essays on feminist theory and women writers. Her book, *Rereading Women*, is in progress.

Suzanne Clark teaches rhetoric, critical theory, women's writing, and modern studies at the University of Oregon. She has also published an interview with Julia Kristeva, a number of articles on rhetoric, feminism, and pedodgogy, and a book about women's writing: *Sentimental Modernism*. Currently, she is working on the rhetoric of difference and the discipline of writing.

Kathryn M. Conway has a special interest in women rhetoricians who taught at the Seven Sisters Colleges at the turn of the nineteenth century. She plans to complete her doctorate in communication and rhetoric before the end of the twentieth century. Conway is Research Assistant Professor of Architecture and head of the Technology Transfer Program, Lighting Research Center, Rensselaer Polytechnic Institute, Troy, New York.

Cheryl Glenn is Associate Professor of English at Oregon State University. She is coauthor of *The St. Martin's Guide to Teaching Writing* and has published articles on rhetoric, composition, literacy, and medieval literature. At present, she is completing *Rhetoric Retold: Regendering the Tradition from Antiquity through the Renaissance*.

Annika Hallin has published in *Rhetoric Review* and is working on the history of the relation between rhetoric and poetics in the American university during the nineteenth and twentieth centuries.

Susan C. Jarratt is Professor of English and Director of Women's Studies at Miami University. In addition to many essays on feminist writing pedagogies and on the history of rhetoric, she is the author of *Rereading the Sophists: Classical Rhetoric Refigured*.

351

Annette Kolodny's studies of the cultural mythology of the U.S. frontier, *The Lay of the Land: Metaphor as Experience and History in American Life and Letters* (1975) and *The Land Before Her: Fantasy and Experience of the American Frontiers, 1630–1860* (1984), have helped frame the developing inquiry of eco-feminism. Professor Kolodny has taught at Yale, the University of British Columbia, the University of New Hampshire, the University of Maryland, Rensselaer Polytechnic Institute. She is currently Professor of Comparative Cultural and Literary Studies at the University of Arizona, where she was Dean of the humanities faculty from 1988 to 1993.

Drema Lipscomb is Assistant Professor at the University of Rochester. Her research and teaching interests are rooted in nineteenth-century public discourse. She is particularly interested in reclaiming the rhetorical voices of African-American women who, despite the role of colonization and racial imperialism, played an active part in both the feminist and antislavery movements as they forged a language and a public speaking style that persuaded even white audiences. She lives in upstate New York with her husband, Norman Burnett, and their two feminist sons, Brian Brandon and Evan Anderson.

Andrea Lunsford is Distinguished Professor and Vice Chair of English at the Ohio State University. She has written or co-authored a number of articles and books on issues related to the theory and practices of writing. She continues to write with her friend and colleague Lisa Ede and to work toward making the academy a more open and inclusive place.

Arabella Lyon, Assistant Professor of English and Women's Studies at Temple University, has published articles on interdisciplinarity, pluralism, and the concept of community. Her current project examines the negotiation of meaning in disciplined reading and writing.

James Oldham works as a technical writer. His dissertation discusses the relation of rhetoric and poetics in Herman Melville's *Battle-Pieces and Aspects of War*, placing the text within the political debate over Reconstruction.

Rory Ong is Assistant Professor in the departments of English and Comparative American Cultures at Washington State University, where he teaches histories of rhetoric and Asian American Literature.

Jenny R. Redfern hopes this book will encourage women in both academic and nonacademic settings to claim their places as rhetors and rhetoricians. Redfern began her study of Christine de Pisan while pursuing doctoral studies in communication and rhetoric at Rensselaer Polytechnic Institute. She works at an International Business Machines software laboratory in San Jose, California.

Jacqueline Jones Royster is Associate Professor of English at the Ohio State University and formerly of Spelman College. She is also a member of the editorial collective of *Sage: A Scholarly Journal on Black Women* who, in addition to their semiannual journal, have published an anthology, *Double Stitch: Black Women Write About Mothers and Daughters* (1991). Royster, who has published articles on literacy studies and women's studies, is currently working on *Traces of a Stream: Literacy and Social Change Among African American Women.*

Christine Mason Sutherland is Associate Professor in the faculty of General Studies at the University of Calgary, where she teaches rhetoric in the Communications Program. Her publications include essays on the rhetoric of Saint Augustine and style in the seventeenth century. At present she is doing research for an essay on Margaret Cavendish. With Beverly Rasporich, she is coeditor of *Woman As Artist: Papers in Honour of Marsha Hanen* (1993).

C. Jan Swearingen is Professor of English at the University of Texas at Arlington, and she holds the 1994–95 Radford Chair of Rhetoric at Texas Christian University. She is author of *Rhetoric and Irony: Western Literacy and Western Lies* (1991). Recent articles and chapters focus on theories of narrative, dialogue, rhetoric, and interpretation in related fields; theorizing approaches to women and the feminine in classical literature; and ideologies affecting educated women and women's education from antiquity to the present. She is editor of *The Word: Studies in the Language of Religion and the Religious Meaning of Language* (in press), and is currently working on a book on classical rhetoric and multiculturalism.

Joanne Wagner, to whose memory this book is dedicated, was a doctoral student in Rensselaer Polytechnic Institute's Department of Language,

Literature and Communication from 1986 to 1991. An unusually promising scholar, she had published an essay in *Rhetoric Society Quarterly* and attended the Dartmouth School of Criticism and Theory. Most currently before her very untimely death, she was pursuing research on connections between rhetoric and postmodern fiction.

Pittsburgh Series in Composition, Literacy, and Culture

David Bartholomae and Jean Ferguson Carr, Editors

Academic Discourse and Critical Consciousness
Patricia Bizzell

Between Languages and Cultures: Translation and Cross-cultural Texts
Anuradha Dingwaney and Carol Maier, Editors

Eating on the Street: Teaching Literacy in a Multicultural Society
David Schaafsma

The Emperor's New Clothes: Literature, Literacy, and the Ideology of
Style
Kathryn T. Flannery

Feminine Principles and Women's Experience in American Composition
and Rhetoric
Louise Wetherbee Phelps and Janet Emig, Editors

Fragments of Rationality: Postmodernity and the Subject of Composition
Lester Faigley

The Insistence of the Letter: Literacy Studies and Curriculm Theories
Bill Green, Editor

Knowledge, Culture, and Power: International Perspectives on Literacy
as Policy and Practice
Peter Freebody and Anthony R. Welch, Editors

The Labyrinths of Literacy: Reflections on Literacy Past and Present
Harvey J. Graff

Literacy Online: The Promise (and Peril) of Reading and Writing with
Computers
Myron C. Tuman, Editor

The Origins of Composition Studies in the American College 1875–1925:
A Documentary History
John C. Brereton, Editor

The Powers of Literacy: A Genre Approach to Teaching Writing
Bill Cope and Mary Kalantzis, Editors

Pre/Text: The First Decade
Victor Vitanza, Editor

Reclaiming Rhetorica: Women in the Rhetorical Tradition
Andrea A. Lunsford, Editor

'Round My Way: Authority and Double-Consciousness in Three Urban
High School Writers
Eli C. Goldblatt

Word Perfect: Literacy in the Computer Age
Myron C. Tuman

Writing Science: Literacy and Discursive Power
M. A. K. Halliday and J. R. Martin